God—
in
fragments

Jacques Pohier

In 1979, Jacques Pohier was banned by the Vatican from preaching, teaching, and presiding at the Eucharist. The shock was profound. He had been a Dominican priest for twenty-five years, an internationally respected moral theologian, and a professor and then dean of the Dominican faculty of theology at Le Saulchoir. Previous troubles with the Vatican over the legalization of abortion and years spent in psychoanalysis had not prepared him for the wrenching dislocation that this disciplinary action would create. It caused him to look at himself, at the Dominican life and the religious life in general, and even at his relationship with God in a wholly new way. Through the pain of his personal crisis he was able to see more clearly the reasons for the widespread breakdown affecting not only religious life and the secular priesthood but the life of the Church as a whole. It is a breakdown that is at once individual and institutional but primarily

the literal sense of the word

cerned with our views of Go

ings, and the relationships b

The central chapters of *G*
ments set out to examine and

ditional links between God and death, God

(Continued on the black flap)

D1065127

GOD
– In Fragments

GOD
– In Fragments

Jacques Pohier

CROSSROAD · NEW YORK

1986

The Crossroad Publishing Company
370 Lexington Avenue, New York, N.Y. 10017

Translated by John Bowden from the French
Dieu fractures,
published 1985 by Editions du Seuil, Paris

Printed in the United States of America

Library of Congress Cataloging-in-Publication Data

Pohier, Jacques Marie.
God—in fragments.

Translation of: Dieu fractures.
Bibliography: p.
1. Theology, Doctrinal.   2. Death—Religious aspects—
Christianity.   3. Sex—Religious aspects—Christianity.
4. Guilt—Religious aspects—Christianity.   5. Catholic
Church—Controversial literature.   6. Pohier, Jacques Marie.
I. Title
BT78.P6413   1986   230'.2   85-25448
ISBN 0-8245-0744-4

To all those men and women
who have written to me in recent years
and to whom I have not had the strength to reply
despite the incomparable comfort
that their letters have brought
I dedicate this book
which is not enough to excuse my silence
but which will doubtless explain it
and in any case break it.

Contents

Note

Almost three years will have elapsed between the moment when I began work on this book and this moment when I am finishing it. So I ought to warn the reader that he or she will not find me occupying exactly the same positions at the end as I did at the beginning. This book is not the diary of a journey; it has neither the form nor the substance of that. Nevertheless, it is very dependent on inner events which have marked these three years. These events have changed me personally. They have also changed my positions on very important questions, both theoretical and practical. In some instances these changes are so great that I have been led to adopt positions which would seem to be diametrically opposed to those which I held to begin with.

Despite this, I have not felt it necessary to play down the apparent contradictions. In fact I feel that they are not so much contradictions as different and doubtless complementary points of view, like different views of a countryside, features of a face, forms of a body, which vary depending on one's standpoint and on the degree to which one changes position. Nor do I have the feeling that there has been a real break; rather, there has been a constant process of maturing, even if this process has involved wrenching myself away from what has gone before, sloughing it off; even if it leads to a fragmentation part of which originates from outside me and part form within (though can one really distinguish them ?).

One piece of fragmentation which originated outside me must be mentioned briefly in this note, because its internal effects were crucial for the present work. In 1977, Les Editions du Seuil published a book of mine entitled *Quand je dis Dieu*,'When I say God'. In spring 1979 the Vatican made public a doctrinal condemnation of this work, whcih in private was immediately coupled with disciplinary sanctions: a Friar Preacher, a priest and a theologian, I found myself forbidden to preach, to preside at the eucharist and to teach theology. These sanctions are still in force, and given the way in which the situation in the church is developing generally, and the treatment of my own case, everything compels me to regard them as final.

In this connection I must point out that in this book I do not claim

in any way to speak in the name of any institution whatsoever, nor
do I represent, nor am I backed by, any authority. I speak only in my
own name, represent only myself, and have only my own backing.
So you may feel as free in reading it as I have tried to be in writing it.

Since the lapse of time has an importance in this book to which I
have already drawn attention, I have felt that I should specify the
times at which its various parts were written. Rather than list here a
series of dates which the reader will have forgotten by the end, I
thought it more effective to indicate at the appropriate point the
period during which each section was written.

I end this present note in the middle of April 1984, pointing out
that since the notes are not so much footnotes or references as
digressions or comments, they have been collected at the end of the
book; you will see that the need for them disappeared as the work
went on. Here, as in other matters or greater importance, the writing
of this book has imposed a rhythm on me and has led me down paths
which I found quite unexpected. I dare to hope that, like me, you will
find it a good thing that I did not avoid this fragmentation.

I

Decomposition

The three chapters in this first part were written in July-August 1981 at Parc-Trihorn.

The emergence of a word

I disliked the word, and recoiled from it or avoided it. So for a long time a variety of factors joined forces in me and prevented me from accepting it even in my mind. It was like seeing those bubbles which sometimes break the surface of a pond and silently indicate that the depths conceal something unknown and vaguely disturbing.

But the word would not go away. Eventually it broke through by itself, infrequently to begin with, and then more often. Its repeated appearances did not produce bubbling on the surface of the water; one might say, rather, that the ephemeral point at which the first bubble had burst met up with increasingly distant points, as if what had emerged in this way could no longer be located at a specific spot but had extended so as to cover almost the whole surface of the pool.

Today I am defeated. I can no longer shield myself, as I have tried to do so far – calmly or desperately, depending on the day – by isolating myself in areas which have not yet been disturbed: there are none left.

Strictly speaking, I did not decide to write these pages: they are not the result of a desire to write. They are the traces of what is rising from the pool. They have overcome my last defences. They are invading me. Will I at least be able to read what is written in them? May they even make sense, contain a message, a call? I have no other way of deciphering these writings than to let them write themselves. However, regardless of whether or not they can be interpreted, I can no longer stop them writing themselves; I have been stripped of this last protection. Will I be submerged, drowned? Or will I feel that I have finally given birth, to a stillborn or a live child?

Decomposition. The more often the word has been borne in on me, the more impossible it has become for me to keep it to myself: I have been unable to keep it to myself, forced to try it out on those nearest to me. It has pained them and made them afraid. My own pain and fear have then been redoubled. As a protection, I took the precaution of making it quite specific: decomposition, not in the biological sense of rotting away, but as an indication of the way in which one has to dismantle the various elements of an inlaid surface in order to put them together again in a new order, since the old world has gone. It was a 'proper' process, marking the passage from one order to another, the interim disorder thus acquiring the double merit of both being provisional and preparing for the emergence of a new order. So there was no need to be afraid: I was still alive, I was not lost. Just astray.

It is a good thing that I took this precautions, for myself and for those close to me. Otherwise we would have been too afraid. We would have done everything possible to stifle what was expressing itself in me, in us, around us – the groans, the cries that indicated that this old order has become an order of death and that we have to die to it in order not to die from it. And no doubt, no matter what, we would have turned a blind eye to it and claimed that this decomposition was not decay.

Today I no longer have the strength to take the precaution, or rather, the strength that I exerted then is no longer enough. The other force is winning. I am condemned to look it in the face. Decomposition towards death or decomposition towards life? At the moment I do not know: all I know is that this force is stronger than I am.

It is so strong that today it is perhaps even my life. It is myself. I can no longer not say it, not write it. I have done everything possible not to be reduced to writing, to saying this. But today I am beaten. I must write this decomposition. To end a sorry existence if it leads to death. To stop living so badly if it contains life.

There. I've written it. Decomposition.

Decomposition 1

So I no longer had the right to preach, to preside publicly at the eucharist, or to teach anything about the faith. For more than a year I had fought, with others beside me, better than me, to avoid such an outcome. But in vain. The months which followed were taken up with my own agitation, and that of others, against and as a result of these measures. Some people protested and asked for them to be withdrawn or changed. But in vain. I began to learn to adopt a course marked out by other distinguished figures before me, some of whom were living with me; some of them – once my teachers – had become my companions and my friends, showing appreciation and giving me encouragement. It was a matter of holding on, waiting for the tide to ebb and for the submerged features to reappear with the shape that they had before being engulfed by the storm. One day I would again resume the preaching which I so loved and which others loved too; one day I would again preside publicly at the eucharist, as I so loved, and as others loved too; one day I would again teach... The way was difficult, but it had been traversed by others, and it was my good fortune that many people were ready to go along it with me and stand by me. There was no question of decomposition in all that: certainly there would be difficulties and sufferings, discouragement, diversions and setbacks. But nothing had to change; on the contrary, the important thing was that nothing should change.

I was surprised when things turned out differently, so differently that the surprise turned to anxiety, then to fear. What surprised me, then disquieted me and terrified me, was the suffering. Not its quantity, but its nature. To begin with, or in its most active stages, the suffering did not leave me any room to move, any possibility of self-examination: I suffered – and that was that. But on the one hand, bizarre though it might seem, one eventually got used to it; and on the other hand, there were remissions; finally – and why should I conceal the fact – some moderate happiness from elsewhere came my way. So sometimes I could achieve some detachment; and then this unexpected question popped up. Why was I suffering so much, or rather, why was I suffering in this particular way?

No longer being able to preach

For example, I would listen to sermons. If the sermon was bad, I was cross to think that I was being prevented from doing it better (and to judge from what others thought of my sermons, that was not always an illusion). If the sermon was good, if it did not, as so often, waste the word of God and the unsuspected capacity which people have for listening to it and finding happiness in it, then I certainly rejoiced at the word which I had received, at the goodness of the God who had spoken it to me, and at the happiness of the congregation celebrating it. But I felt mortally wounded at no longer being able to do the same thing myself. My community had an underground garage built immediately under the church: coming out of one Sunday mass, I fled into its darkness and isolation in order to weep, to cry out there, to shout, 'But why, why?... They're mad!'

The preacher that day had been someone who for long years had been my *père-maître* (the person responsible for the spiritual training of religious), then my spiritual adviser and then my friend. Some days before his sermon, this man – one of the two or three to whom I owe my best understanding of God and the gospel – had asked me for advice about it. 'What would you say?' He took notes, as I had done thirty years earlier during his lectures on spirituality: that in itself had shattered me, for this trust turned the world upside down, by reversing the master-pupil relationship. When the Sunday came, in his own inimitable fashion he gave a quite remarkable sermon. My ideas reappeared, transformed, alongside others; at one point he even said, 'A few days ago I was talking with a brother from this community and I pass on what he said to me all the more readily because he is no longer able to speak in public.' And while, as on every Sunday, after mass some regular members of the congregation were sharing their delight with the less shy among the religious (the preacher was certainly one of these), there I was in the garage, smelling the oil and the dust, and sobbing, 'But why? They're mad to stop me preaching. They ought at least to know that I would do no harm to God, that I would do no harm to believers. On the contrary, I would do them good, make them want to believe, make them have joy in believing, make them delight in God. They're mad, it's not possible.' And I shouted out 'It's not possible' at the top of my voice.

Perhaps there is something ridiculous or hysterical about this scene, but you can understand it. Others can understand it. I understood it myself, and at first sight there was nothing else to understand. However, it was on that occasion that I became detached enough for an unforeseen question to pop up. Not 'Why am I suffering so much?', but 'Why am I suffering in this way?' Something was wrong, less in the violence of this suffering than in its nature and the reasons for it. My 'vocation' as a 'Friar Preacher', my passion – there's no other word – for preaching, my genuine gift for it, were good reasons for this suffering, but they were too good not to be suspect.

The question which then emerged into consciousness was so unforeseen and affected me so radically that I quickly lost interest in the rearguard actions in which part of me was still with those of my brothers who persisted in a friendly way in their efforts to gain permission for me to preach again. Bizarre though it might seem – I had a more important and more urgent problem to settle. What was behind the nature of the suffering that I felt at no longer being able to preach? What had I invested in preaching, what had I made it into, that being deprived of it should wound me in this way? It was more important to answer this question than to be able to preach again as soon as possible. It was also necessary for me to see the question more clearly if I was to be able to answer it. The difficulty it had in making an appearance, its slow and laborious progress, was helped on by the way in which it served as a sounding board for the tribulations of another ban which was inflicted on me.

No longer being able to preside at the eucharist

I no longer had the right to preside publicly at the eucharist. After a great many hesitations, I had been allowed the right to participate in concelebrations when my presence among the concelebrants did not run the risk of shocking others, priests or laity, who were sharing in the celebration. I could celebrate 'in private' as often as I liked. Now I enjoyed presiding at the eucharist very much. As with preaching, I am constantly amazed at the capacity believers have for 'celebrating' and – if I may venture to put it this way – at the capacity God has for being celebrated, the capacity which Jesus has for what he has instituted in memory of him in which the Spirit makes him present to us. For me, presiding at a eucharist was always a festival concerned with sharing the pleasure that God has invited us to taste by sharing in it, a pleasure which does not hinder but, on the contrary, encourages a silent adoration and quest for that known-yet-unknown reality which is also the God who is shared here. '*Rühmen*', 'Celebrate': for forty years the echo of the first word of a sonnet by Rilke has never faded, even in my most sombre moments and in the least enthusiastic congregations. I have often had the good fortune and the happiness to see how I allowed others over the celebration of whose eucharist I had presided to find the same pleasure: pleasure in God and pleasure in one another.

I was also deprived of that. So I contented myself with sometimes taking part in concelebrations, with reservations the reasons for which I shall explain later because they are not relevant to what I want to mention next. There was no question of my celebrating a 'private' mass, though I had done so every day with happiness and profit during the first ten years of my priesthood. By then, the teachers who had shaped me and the liturgical renewal to which they had contributed had shifted the main accent of the eucharist, so that for me it could no longer be the personal devotion of the priest; it was the celebration of a community. So when I did not concelebrate, I went to mass as a layman, as one of the 'simple faithful'. Everyone knows that masses are sometimes boring, and that you have to have prayer coming out of your ears or to be really in a state of grave malnutrition to find any nourishment in them: you have to fight against the content and the form of the celebration, and sometimes the struggle is hopeless. There again, as with preaching, I was furious at being robbed of the power to do better (which, as I know after twenty-five years of celebrating mass, was not pure vanity on my part). There, too, when the celebration was a good and happy one, I was delighted, but could not stop saying to myself, 'Why not me?'

It was in this connection that one day a breach opened up in the monolith of my suffering, not so much to assuage it as to lead me to ask what lay behind it. I had been, in a 'lay capacity', to a mass which the celebrants, the priest-president and members of the congregation, had made into a modest yet genuine festival, for God and for us. It was a real 'Corpus Christi' (a description which I had used quite spontaneously one Maundy Thursday when I was presiding and preaching in front of a table strewn with flowers, with bread and wine, prepared by friends of our community). On the way out, when the inevitable 'why not me?' came back, I suddenly realized that, explicable or excusable though this question might be, it was in radical contradiction with the theology of the eucharist and of ministry that I had professed for several years.

I am not a specialist in these matters, but I have had the good fortune to live with such specialists, and above all I have been caught up in the current which has impelled so many Christian communities, formal or informal, to reappropriate the eucharist which is in fact theirs. So I have come to believe that the ministry of the priest in connection with the eucharist, while being irreplaceable, is very limited: in my view the priest is the one designated ('ordained', if you like) by the bishop, who is the principle and witness of the unity between the local church and the whole of the church, to demonstrate by being present and presiding that the eucharist celebrated by a community is celebrated in union with the whole church. In this way it can be recognized and authenticated by the whole communion of believers.[1] However, with the priest as president and in union with all that he is delegated to represent, it is the community which celebrates, and consequently consecrates (if we continue to restrict ourselves to this quite inadequate vocabulary). The ministry of the priest is his ministry of presiding over the eucharist and authenticating it by the link with the church which he represents, but it is the community which acts in the celebration.

What I was asking myself at that time was not whether this theology is sound (Rome detests it, although it is that of the primitive church and of many present-day theologians) but: given that I professed such a theology of the eucharist and of ministry, and that consequently when participating in a successful celebration in a 'lay capacity' I should have felt that I had the essentials and the fullness of the eucharist, why did I nevertheless continue to suffer because I was not presiding? What was my suffering about? The eucharist was there, in its fullness. Nothing was lacking: God, Christ made present in the Spirit, an ordained priest presiding over it, a community celebrating. No, nothing was lacking and I should have been completely happy. So what did I lack?

In contrast to what happened as a result of the prohibition against my preaching, the contradiction between my suffering at not being able to preside and my theology of the eucharist and of ministry made it easier for me to become detached from my suffering so that the real questions could emerge. Thanks to this contradiction, it became easier for me to push into the background not only my suffering but also the need to recover as quickly as possible the opportunity to celebrate. It became more important, and therefore more urgent, to understand what importance I attached to the fact of presiding, to understand why and how I had perverted the meaning that my theology made me attribute to the ministry of presiding at the eucharist.

Raising these questions made me understand immediately that it was not going to be easy to find a reply, and that the reply would take me a good deal of time and effort (at that time I was not yet speaking in terms of decomposition, far less of recomposition). The solution was certainly to be found first of all in the specific factors which had shaped my own personality and personal history, which had made me attach importance to the function of presiding, thus perverting it from what my theology said about it. However, the importance I attached to presiding and the way in which I perverted it were not there in a vacuum: they were amazingly like the manifest importance attached to the priestly ministry and the way in which it was perverted by the ecclesiastical system and the 'laity' whom this system had fashioned in its image, not without the complicity of their needs and desires. So I thought that I must have mixed motives, personal and ecclesial (not to say ecclesiastical), in attaching such importance to presiding and then perverting it. I may have had my own problem in this respect, but there must also have been 'a problem' quite independent of me (even if it must have infiltrated and contaminated me). So this problem became at the same time more difficult and more important than if it was solely my concern. In my own eyes, but *a fortiori* in the eyes of others, it called for more attention than if it were simply my own problem. Later, when I began to think in terms of decomposition, well before thinking of recomposition, the issue was not just the decomposition of the importance that I had attached to the function of presiding, but the decomposition of the importance which the Christian ecclesial system had attached to it. At all events, the question of knowing if and when I would be able to preside again was postponed *sine die*.

No longer being able to teach theology

The third measure which affected me, the prohibition against teaching, caused me much less suffering where it was a prohibition against official academic teaching. First, the faculty of theology at Le Saulchoir, where I had been a student, then a professor and then dean (its last dean), had had to close down five years earlier because there were not enough students. Secondly, it was now out of the question that the other French theological institutions whose offers of employment I had had to turn down while I had an obligation to Le Saulchoir would want my services, since I had displeased Rome (well before the prohibitions which I am talking about here) by my actions and my writings, particularly on the question of abortion. Finally – a more decisive factor – I had become increasingly allergic to the university style of teaching theology, academic and 'scientific'. I knew its merits, having received this kind of teaching and given it myself. I knew the long and complex labours it demanded, and I must not rule out the possibility that laziness was one of the causes of my allergy.

But academic theology is like the armour worn by the knights at the battle of Agincourt: it is so heavy that it overwhelms the majority of those who take it on, and only exceptionally strong men can stand upright and walk once they are in it. Moreover, the weight of academic theology and the objectives which it sets itself in order to prove that it *is* academic (though it alone in the intellectual world believes that this is the case) means that it talks a lot *about* God (or rather, about what others have said about God) but rarely *of* God. Now it seems to me that in every respect our age needs a confessing theology, a theology which is a confession of the faith by the very way in which it seeks to understand the faith.

Finally, the claim of academic theology to be systematic and exhaustive seems to me to be contrary to everything that the human spirit is seeking, undertaking and achieving towards the end of the twentieth century. Later, I shall have occasion to say why, in my view, all talk of God and about God, including theological talk, can only be fragmentary, not only because of the present state of the intellectual world, but more radically, to the degree that its subject matter is that God whom no theory or theology can circumscribe in a systematic way (even if the apparatus of the church seeks to circumscribe us by claiming to be the repository and the authorized guardians of such a word about God). For the moment, I shall do no more than mention this theme in passing, because it helps to explain what had already for some time alienated me from academic and scientific theology, and at the same time shows why I was less hurt by the prohibition against teaching.

However, this teaching was not the only thing to be forbidden me. From then on I could no longer hold classes, give lectures, and so on, in which I would be 'teaching' something in connection with the faith. This prohibition affected me much more. First, I am fond of teaching, if by that one means communicating one's ideas and fighting to have them shared. Furthermore, this concern to communicate, this conviction, had long been the best way I had found of developing and focussing my own ideas. I am not a born creator. Exceptional circumstances are required for something to emerge from me simply by the force of internal pressure; usually, invitations from others and meetings with them help me to develop my own thought. And lastly, when it is a question of God, Jesus Christ and their Spirit, here more than anywhere else it is the case that what we can know is sought, discovered and verified by a common quest among believers (and among non-believers too). This common quest may just as well involve silence, doubt or forgetting as celebration, the word, prayer, ideas... and theology. And by forbidding me even the non-academic forms of teaching, the authorities robbed me of the best way of keeping my own understanding of the faith alive and verifying it.

I suffered much more from this last prohibition that from not being able to accept a chair in theology. However, it did not break all my links with academic theology. For a long time I had been aware of the strengths of this theology and for a long time I had served its institutions, even helping with the more or less splendid resources with which it works; for me it may have been part of a bygone past, but the memory of it was still vivid, and even if I had had other reasons for not repudiating it,[2] I could not have gone back on what had been an important and happy period of my life. Moreover, above all I had practised other forms of teaching in a way which could not fail to be influenced by the 'magistral' position that I had occupied. That is why, as with presiding over the eucharist and even more with preaching, a contradiction emerged in connection with teaching which was easier to recognize because the suffering was less. I could no longer accept the different types of teaching position open to someone with experience in academic and scientific theology. But why was I suffering so much from no longer being able to practise the other forms of teaching, when these exceptional circumstances – harsh though they might be – gave me the opportunity to return to the ranks (as far as that is possible for anyone who has been outside the ranks for a long time)?

My theology made me profess a certain kind of relationship between ministry and community, my practice in presiding certainly presupposed quite a different one. My theology of the theological function made me profess a certain kind of relationship between theology and community, but what kind of relationship between theology and community did my practice really presuppose? Why did I persist in the suffering caused me by the loss of this relationship and the hope of being able to regain it, as if I was going to die from being deprived of it, rather than struggling to see whether such a practice was not perhaps fatal and that I had to die to this relationship? Perhaps now was a good time, though I did not know where or how it would happen, to allow the growth of new types of relationships which were suggested to me or imposed on me more from outside than by myself, and more by fairly informal groups and individuals than by academic or ecclesiastical institutions? Certainly, here too, there were more important and more urgent things to do than to recover what had been taken away from me. The question of knowing when and how to get it back in fact became meaning-less, in the strict sense. At all events it was secondary and to be postponed indefinitely, until I had a clearer understanding of these other questions which were obscured by the suffering of my present condition and the hope of returning to my former one (for there was no question of wanting to resolve them before they had had time to appear).

Towards a problem which is not peculiar to me

I already felt that these other questions were first of all about the kind of person that I was and the way in which my personality had been invested in the different functions of preaching, presiding and teaching. However, at the same time they were also about the various institutions which promote these functions or are promoted by them. So raising them could not just be a personal matter, depending solely on the successes and failures of my personal destiny. It also had to be a collective concern, in this case the concern of the church. Before coming to this institutional aspect, I must stress the individual aspect. I deliberately use the word individual rather than personal. In fact it seems to me that the majority of individuals who are personally involved in these functions of preaching, presiding and teaching share the kind of difficulties that I want to mention here, regardless of the considerable variables which the differences between their personalities can introduce.

It seems to me that all men of my age (fifty-five as I write these lines) who are involved in the priesthood or in religious life of an apostolic kind have committed themselves with an extraordinary degree of intensity which their juniors by only a few years find it difficult to understand and even feel to be somewhat excessive (that is not because their 'magnanimity' is any the less). Perhaps the reason is that we grew up during the Second World War, and that we were twenty years old at the time of the Liberation, at a time when an extraordinary vitality literally exploded in every dimension of life: the intellectual world, the arts, culture, politics, the trade unions, the church. I was not the only person of my age to be thoroughly committed to all that was offered by the renewals which burgeoned at this time. From 1949, in my case the renewal was that offered me by the Dominican life, which at that time was experiencing a period of extraordinary intensity and fruitfulness.

If one looks back, the traditional ways of training religious had an almost terrifying efficiency, so much did they instil in us the ideals and the motivations by which the group defined itself. Our personalities were so to speak refashioned. I shall have occasion to indicate the ways in which we sometimes helped this transformation on, and which of our most secret desires found fulfilment in it. For the moment, I want only to point out that the depth of this transformation meant that for the individuals of my generation or those whom we later trained in this tradition it is no easy matter to investigate the way in which we had been brought up in these ideals, motivations and functions: raising such questions is tantamount to asking what has become of one's very heart and soul. So powerful is the internalization, so evocative is the determination of personality by self and group along these lines of force, that one does not have the necessary detachment to judge them 'objectively'; and to put them at a distance would be to tear oneself apart.

For about fifteen or twenty years a number of us have been led to question the way in which we were moulded to this style of life, either because we have had good reasons to question the validity of the motives which led to such a commitment or because the transformations of these motives under pressure from changes in society and in the church have led us to repudiate the forms in which they were previously embodied. I know that very many priests of my generation or the subsequent one have left the priesthood or the religious life. I have followed many of my Dominican friends along the various stages of their departure, and some have become or remained close friends. For several of them, it was the very nature of their involvement in the religious life and its activities which thereafter made them impossible and insensitive. Others had convinced themselves, rightly or wrongly, that the rigidity of church organization and the inertia of the believing community made it very improbable that the new forms which they thought were needed to perform these functions would appear; so they withdrew, more or less dead inside, attached to what they should have been, but distressed because they were sure that they would never find fulfilment. For both sides, transformations of their existence and their personality were a profound upset which could not fail to leave scars, even if they freed energies which had become immobilized by commitments that now seemed to have neither outcome nor meaning.

If I sometimes feel nearer to some of those who have left than to some of those who have remained, it is because I myself have lived with both these types of questions. On the one hand I have had an analysis, and I would like to know, having heard my psychoanalyst friends talking now for almost twenty years, whether an analysis can go much deeper than mine; I did not fail to discover the nature of some of the motives which impelled me towards the religious life and the very deep desires they fulfilled in me: many are of doubtful value. Moreover, when a psychoanalyst friend, otherwise very respectful towards me, told me with a smile, 'You know very well that if you have a second analysis, you will leave all that behind', I was not sure whether I had much to say to him in reply. In addition, changes within the faith (the biblical, patristic, liturgical, pastoral, missionary, catechetical, conciliar 'renewals') have profoundly changed the view that I have of the religious life, to the point when it has sometimes come to be in radical contradiction to the one with which I had identified myself and my life at the time of my formation as a Dominican. For a long time I worked to reform the institutional life of the church and to change the attitudes of believers: I can see some positive results, but we are still so far short of the target that I no longer believe in reform; as it is even more difficult to believe in revolutions, or at any rate in effective revolutions, I too am not far from calling it a day, again more or less dead inside.

However, I am still here. First, because from a personal point of view there is no alternative. I am stuck to the spot, body and soul. My view of my position and what I do may have changed, and preaching, presiding at the eucharist and teaching may now play quite a different role in my life; indeed from now on my life itself may take on different contours and follow quite a different way. Nevertheless, I have the religious life stamped on my being. I do not know whether my motives are good or bad – doubtless there is something of each. But I shall soon be at retirement age, and I know that things will not change. I am the first to be amazed at this, and I understand that one could and should leave if things were different, but that is the way they are. Besides, I continue to think that the functions of preaching, presiding at the eucharist and teaching are indispensable to the life of the community of believers, and that they must be performed by some of its members, even if I am persuaded that the organs through which these functions are at present performed are incapable of generating new forms: thus their disappearance is the *sine qua non* for the appearance of these new forms. But I am still also keenly concerned for the appearance of these new forms in the life of the believing community, and I continue to be keenly concerned to put them into practice in my own individual life.

That having been said, the position I am in is not very comfortable. What is at issue disturbs the deepest levels and shifts the most crucial bearings not only of the personalities of the individuals concerned,

including myself, but also of the community of believers of which I
am a member. Even if such upheavals do not bring death in their
wake, or produce paralysis through anxiety and its defence mechanisms, they happen more than once and never according to a pre-
established plan. At one point one moves, sometimes without even
realizing it until afterwards; at another one gets stuck. At one point
one moves forward and a little light, happiness, pleasure appear; at
another one plods on or misses the way, one becomes discouraged
and wastes an energy which is not inexhaustible. Even though one is
well aware that the process will take several generations, it would be
good to see some dawn breaking before one's own death. Everyone
makes plans, becomes involved, arranges things, gets by or turns
aside less in accordance with his or her own merits than in accordance
with temperament and the more or less happy chances of environment
and history.

That was my position too when the prohibitions which I have
mentioned came to overturn what I would hardly dare to call an
equilibrium. To begin with, there was hardly any problem: first of
all there was the attempt to struggle against these measures, then
suffering, only suffering, when their victory was achieved and
complete. But after that, as I have said, things got complicated. And
again, but in a different situation and in a more pressing way, I began
to ask both about the nature of my involvement in these functions
and the nature of the functions themselves. In addition, I was deprived
of the essential forms of relationships between believers which would
have allowed me to join others in seeking and finding some elements
of a reply to this twofold question. There was no way out. Should I
slam the door and leave? That would not have been unreasonable.
But I couldn't do it. Why? That's how it was. I am just the same (even
if I see things quite differently). Should I stay and retract? The
condemnations of Modernism at the beginning of the century transformed the priests who remained – many of them left – into zombies
who devoted the rest of their lives to botany, stamp-collecting or
erudition. I could not do that either. Why? That's how things are.
Besides, many people kept asking me, begging me to do nothing of
the sort, as if something of their own hope, their own future was at
stake. It is true that others asked me to leave,to show that a word
about God, a word to God, a word of God could be free; and there
too, something of their own hope, their future, was at stake.

Blocked. I was blocked. No way out. No precedents. No directions.
No other prayer than to repeat, come what may, 'Your kingdom
come. Let me not be an obstacle to it, let me not be a scandal, let me

be useful, if that can still be the case.' But for all that, I did not see any more clearly, and when the word 'decomposition' appeared in my conversations with myself, at first I took no heed of it. When it began to force itself on me, I told myself that I would rot where I was. If I could not be cheerful, that was a natural consequence: since everything was blocked and yet I still kept on living, life was transformed into pus, into decomposition. Besides, that is what happens to life, whether animal, vegetable or spiritual, when its old forms are no longer possible and there are no new ones. That is what happened to me: I began to rot.

I was so tired that this discovery was almost a relief. At a pinch, I caused myself some amusement by recalling the dung-heaps on the farms of my childhood, and I told myself that this dung-heap might be of some use for a future of which I knew absolutely nothing, since dung is very useful for making things germinate and grow. I told myself that at my age many men and women are at the end of the most important stage of their lives, in their family, their job and their resources, and that many of them have not had the good fortune to succeed; I was fortunate enough to have had a good deal of success in my life. What more could I ask? Could I perhaps even go on to provide some dung for tomorrow's crops? The psalms had taught me something like this: some sow in tears and others reap in joy. It was my turn to weep. As I sowed?

Great suffering seldom produces much clarity. So I needed time to discover that not only was decomposition the only possible outcome, but it was the course I had to follow. Since I did not understand enough about what was composed within me around the functions of preaching, presiding at the eucharist, and teaching, it was necessary for it to decompose, for me to let it decompose. Since I did not understand enough about what was composed around functions elaborated by the apparatus of the church and the latent desires of those who were anxious to submit themselves to it, that had to decompose, in me and around me. Whether it was a matter of my person in my own specific relationship to these functions, or the social significance of these functions, since the forces involved were obscure and powerful, escaping as they did my consciousness and my power, I therefore had to allow these contradictory forces to come up against each other within me, beyond my consciousness and my power; I had to let these drifting continents clash and shatter. The old order had to decompose.

I felt that I was on the way. I felt that there was a way. I really believed it. But I was wrong about what would happen, though perhaps my inexperience might excuse the mistake. When I discovered that this decomposition was the only solution for dismantling the old order – both of my person and of its functions – I immediately thought that this was a 'proper' process, since it was an intermediate stage between two orders and the means by which a new world could arise from the ruins of the old. So I thought that things would happen properly.

I had still to discover that there is no decomposition without decay. One cannot control the decomposition, one cannot dictate its ways, which are unknown, and the phenomena which allow them to be identified afterwards are never very savoury nor reassuring. From then on it became vital to resist as little as possible. Not to be too afraid, not to be too disgusted, not to be too disturbed if others became too disturbed. Not to concede one thing in order to preserve something else better. Not to become attached to something, although it had always been the source of life. That was difficult, even impossible, beyond a certain limit: one fights against resistance, one forcibly tries to keep something, for oneself or for others. One wants to keep one's dignity, one cannot allow things to go so far. Be a man, have faith in God!

Now if decomposition was salvation, all that had to go. Particularly everything around which my personality as a Friar Preacher was organized, particularly that way I had of investing myself in preaching, in presiding at the eucharist, in teaching. That, myself in that form, I myself had to be decomposed. That was all I knew, except for having an almost suicidal conviction that life can sometimes win (not all moulds make penicillin, but in the end, sometimes...). I had a kind of almost suicidal conviction that God can raise up life from death. But that is deep down, vague, out there, almost beyond the borders of consciousness, will or desire. All the rest of the field is occupied by decomposition. As I write these pages, I wonder whether the fact of writing them is not itself a distraction, a resistance, a false diversion, a false respite; for writing, even on decomposition, is still composing. I just don't know. I can only say again the prayer that I have learned, for I have had to invent this version of 'Your kingdom come', which previously I would never have dreamed of: 'My God, my friends, if that is the way, help me not to shun decomposition, do not leave me to my resistances and my evasions. My God, help me to decompose myself: you see that otherwise we shall never get anywhere.'

Decomposition 2

Even if I found a good deal of pleasure in preaching, in presiding at the eucharist and in teaching, I had not invented these functions nor the ways in which they were practised for my own pleasure. Even if my personality had found the fulfilment of some of its deepest and least conscious desires in the Dominican 'vocation' and I had been only too happy to fall in with the system of training which had made its ideas more part of my being than my very self, I had not invented the Dominican 'Order' and the whole ecclesiastical system in which this Order had its place for my own personal needs. Now since I entered this Order some thirty or so years ago, and through it, this system, both have changed considerably. Many people – both believers and non-believers – see these changes as negative. So do I, but I do not see the term negative as having any pejorative connotations: on the contrary, I would see the term as having a positive sense (I shall explain that because it might seem too paradoxical). That is doubtless why I was able to use the word decomposition in connection with it much earlier and with less difficulty than in connection with my personal situation.

The situation of my Order in France in recent times

However, the use of this word did not come about either easily or rapidly. On the one hand – keeping to this thirty or so years – these institutions have long been vigorous and beneficial, even if a century hence historians will discover in them traces of the development which was to follow. On the other hand, I was too identified with these institutions not to be able initially to fight with all my strength against change in them and not to work vigorously for the 'reforms' which would allow them to take on new life. Finally, at the same time as it was affecting the institutions which were so dear to me, this development was also affecting individuals who were my brothers, my companions in prayer, in work, in life, in the struggle – and sometimes it wounded them deeply. It is impossible to talk of all that without raking over much suffering, intermixed with disillusionment, tension, accusations from others and self-accusation, the feeling of having been betrayed or swindled, rancour, confrontations and breaks between friends, and quite simply the dreams, the deceived dreams, so many deceived dreams, even when they were so very contradictory. But how could I avoid raking over these sufferings if I wanted to see a bit more clearly?

I am not a competent historian of institutions; and even if I were, I would not be far enough removed in time or emotionally detached enough to see clearly. Nor am I a social psychologist competent to analyse an institution; even if I were, I could not act as one, since I myself am a member of this institution. I do not intend to offer for general use a diagnosis of what has happened or a prognosis of what may happen next. My sole concern, primarily for my own use and benefit, is to understand how this decomposition which I must now talk about is connected to my own decomposition and to a decomposition I shall go on to discuss later which is even more radical, since it is concerned with God himself and the way in which we can represent him. These three decompositions are necessarily linked, for worse and for better, if there is a better. I am too involved to see very clearly and I am personally too affected by them to have a very coherent understanding. But I must try to understand, try to speak, try to give names, try to say things in order to learn their name. The hope of getting anywhere is slim, but what other hope is there?

When I arrived at Le Saulchoir, to join it, in 1950, fresh from my year's novitiate, I and the other Dominicans who were doing their seven years of philosophy and theology amounted to about a hundred men between twenty and thirty years of age who were preparing to go on to join the metropolitan communities or 'mission' houses which were then bringing together men in the prime of life and some old ones. When, twenty-five years later, those in charge of the theological faculty of Le Saulchoir – of which I was one – were led to suspend its activities, only fifteen Dominicans remained in training. An eighty-five per cent decrease in a quarter of a century! Today I am living in a major community of forty religious, the average age of whom is sixty-two, though this is one of the youngest Dominican communities in France: at fifty-five I am often treated as a young man, and sadly that is the case. Not only have really young men stopped joining us in significant numbers but, as I have said, many men of my generation and of subsequent generations have left us. In a quarter of a century the pyramid of ages has been completely reversed: it once had a broad base and a narrow apex; now it is broad at the top and stands on a point. The communities are emptying and their inhabitants are growing old (mine is becoming an old people's home, perhaps even a geriatric institution); posts are closed, activities fade out and soon die because no new personnel are being appointed.

Now these were groups and activities which had quite remarkable successes in their active period; and the quality of these successes should have guaranteed their permanence and attracted new and energetic people. I had the good fortune to live in the Order at a time when our elders were embarking on and completing works which will remain their glory and which are definitive achievements: from the worker priests to the Jerusalem Bible and the Ecumenical Translation of the Bible, via the Centre of Pastoral Liturgy, the Pastoral Mission in France, ecumenism, implantation in other cultures and civilizations, the publication of Sources Chrétiennes, religious broadcasts on television and radio, the Rosary (which involves people whom our other activities neglect almost completely) and so on. Let me leave it at that, since I have no intention of being exhaustive. Certainly the Dominicans were not the only ones to work at these and succeed: we did so with other Orders and with the secular clergy. However, the point is that this sort of thing was going on everywhere, with a dynamism which overthrew or at any rate lowered the traditional barriers between the various ecclesiastical bodies. And just as one could have begun to see the signs of inadequacy or breathlessness, there was the Council, with its formidable breath of fresh air and the almost crazy hope of renewal which it produced. We were right inside it; the older ones among us who had been got at and ignominiously ridiculed by Rome had been made experts and were working there like beavers; at some stages of the Council around a dozen professors or former professors of Le Saulchoir (out of a mere twenty) were experts.

Fifteen years later, the situation is such that while there may be arguments over my diagnosis, it is not improbable, even if it is too sombre to be admitted by many; we survive in a state of advanced coma. Some organs still function, others have not yet completely stopped, individuals do more than survive and still produce things (as also do the cells and organs when the patient is in a state of coma), but the organism as such can be considered dead. Time, the simple lapse of time, is enough to make survival machines useless. So what has happened? We are all too involved in the situation to see clearly. Men so seriously wounded in the activities that make up their lives cannot help sketching out explanations – above all when many of them are intellectuals and all of them reflect; they suffer too much not to have the reflexes which suffering triggers off in every sphere of life.

Whose fault?

The first course into which both explanations and reflections rush headlong is that of accusation, self-accusation, as is fitting for good religious. 'We have been unfaithful, we have not been holy enough, we have betrayed the spirit of our blessed father St Dominic, we have not been open to the inspiration of the Spirit. Let us get a grip of ourselves, let us be more faithful, let us return to our origins, and life will revive.' Certainly one is never faithful enough nor holy enough, and one can hardly be wrong in accusing oneself of that. However, since a similar decomposition is affecting many other religious Orders with an 'apostolic' life and also the secular clergy (I shall return to the exceptions provided by the real vitality of certain contemplative Orders, the success of certain integralist groups and the strength of the East European church), that means that we must suppose that all at once, and for a mysterious reason, all the religious of these different Orders and all the priests in a variety of countries have become so unholy and so unfaithful that such a collapse has inevitably followed. Moreover, one would have to deny the facts; I have known these men, I have lived with them. They were not all saints, but their average talent and that of the groups that they formed was remarkable – hence the quality of their enterprises and their successes. More significantly still, they were not so inferior to their predecessors as to explain how they could have failed to develop the vitality of the Order where their predecessors had succeeded. It always hurts me to see these men, who for the most part were men of quality, accusing themselves in this way and making themselves responsible for a decomposition for which they were hardly to blame. Certainly I know the benefit of this self-accusation; I shall come back to it, since it is fallacious and detracts from the truth. But it is already quite enough that these men should have to spend their old age watching the decomposition of an institution that they loved so much; at least they should be able to grow old and die enjoying the well-deserved satisfaction of having done good service.[3]

Self-accusation might seem necessary, but for all that it does not stop us perhaps having to accuse others. Those responsible are easy to find. Since their function gives them responsibility, this group is that of superiors of all kinds. For us the process of accusing superiors – which in itself is very simple – is complicated by the fact that all our superiors, no matter at what level of the hierarchy, are chosen by us, at first or second hand depending on the case. Our superiors are our delegates, and reflect us, since we chose them. Hence it becomes difficult for us to blame them without blaming ourselves. However, since we chose them, we have a real responsibility for them: besides, our institutions – which are a model of democracy, recognized and studied as such by historians of constitutional law – provide for a periodic check on the activity of superiors during their mandate by those who have chosen them. We therefore have the duty of checking and correcting our superiors, which provides an ideal base and cover for anyone who wants to consider them the prime culprits of the evils under which we are suffering. Thus some of our number – many of them eminent – regularly blame superiors or teachers, using failings in their administration or their training to explain the decline which is affecting us.

Certainly the superiors and the teachers between 1950 and 1968, and also in the years which followed, had their faults: they certainly made mistakes. However, the mechanism of accusing superiors must provide considerable benefits for those who resort to it for them to do so without being able to observe what all the world around them perceives. First, this accusation loses all value (but reveals its nature) by being stereotyped: I heard well-known Dominicans thirty years ago make exactly the same accusations against superiors whose politics, qualities and failings were diametrically opposed to those of today; the only difference in their accusations was the proper name of the accused. Someone who was vilified when he was a superior often becomes a worthwhile person in their eyes when he ceases to hold that office. The person whom they called on with their good wishes and their votes to replace the unworthy superior in turn becomes unworthy soon after he begins to exercise the charge for which they have elected him. Furthermore, how can we explain why suddenly, between 1950 and 1968, the majority of superiors and teachers in all the apostolic Orders and in all or almost all the dioceses in the West became bad superiors? And above all, how can we explain why *en masse* they should have been so inferior to their predecessors, the quality of these predecessors explaining why the Order went so well in the happy period when these accusers were young religious, whereas their own faults explain why the Order has begun to fare so badly now that these same accusers have become confirmed adults? The mechanism in question, which prevents eminent figures from seeing the infantile nature of all this, is too bound up with the suffering that they experience and too useful to spare them even greater suffering for one to be so cruel as to want to deprive them of it: let each one suffer as he can. But for all that, the mechanism does not explain anything. One could wish that the people who did so much so well for the life of the Order might be spared this useless suffering, growing old and dying with the satisfaction of having done all their duties well. Similarly, one could wish that the superiors and authorities of yesterday and today would not see their tasks, and the numerous trials and tribulations which go with them, aggravated by accusations whose violence is sadly in inverse proportion to their value as explanations: the superiors and other authorities should also have the right to grow old and die in peace, with the satisfaction of having done all their duties well. It is already hard enough for them to see what they had worked so hard over crumbling away.

If it is not enough to accuse oneself or to accuse superiors, one has to accuse individuals, groups or forces outside the Order. One can blame the church and those who govern it: I know several crypto-St Bernards of Clairvaux or Savonarolas who have not dared to address to the popes, as these did, the philippics (again stereotyped) which they circulated in the little groups where they brooded by themselves. One can also blame the youth of the day, or the 'world'; some texts from the Gospel of John interpreted wrongly or in a contrary sense can be very useful here. One can blame secularization, the consumer society, the influx of eroticism or politics, the loss of a sense of obedience, a sense of transcendence, a sense of God, or more recently lack of courage in the face of the radical demands of the gospel. One can add all this together and say that our contemporaries and the rising generation are going to the dogs, and withdraw into the cult of a golden, inevitably bygone age, which one hopes will return in the more or less short term and the least sign of whose coming one avidly laps up.

How can people so obstinately fail to recognize that nothing is more stereotyped than this process of blaming modern civilization, of praising yesterday's civilization and boldly projecting it on that of tomorrow? The writings of religious or lay moralists, pagans or Christians, of realists, sceptics, cynics or satirists, the exhortations of preachers, have for the last two thousand five hundred years been filled with accusations which are demonstrably identical down the centuries, whether the guilty party is today's youth, eroticism, being ensnared by material goods, the loss of a sense of generosity, of obedience, of transcendence, and so on. There is no denying that all this can play a major part at all times. But for that very reason this part is almost the same in every age: and when a given age – ours or any other – uses it to explain some specific difference from what went before or what will come afterwards, it necessarily loses its force. French society was neither better nor worse between 1950 and 1968 than it was between 1940 and 1950 or 1920 and 1930 (to compare it to two periods when the Dominican Order attracted a great many vocations).

It is true that at that time this society saw the beginnings of considerable changes, the first outlines of which were already appearing, even if they only became evident afterwards in the later convergence of forces which hitherto had been separated. To note the distinctive features in the development of society (in contrast to previous developments, since society has always evolved) would allow us to understand better the decline of which I am speaking here. But what is in question is whether this development is specifically new, not whether society is better or worse. Here again, if they could see what was happening people could grow old and die more happily, without getting at odds with their world (or what ought to be their world); that does not meant wholesale approval of its major faults or complicity in them, but it does make it possible to live in the preent rather than shutting oneself up in the reconstruction of a mythical past or imagining a future which is the projection of disappointed dreams or former successes. To be faithful to ourselves, are we obliged to be at odds with what has changed from yesterday to today? My old brothers have done themselves an injustice and deprived themselves of the possibility of being so much better by shutting themselves up in what was the best of their past.

What protection is there from so severe a wound?

If accusing oneself, one's superiors or the present-day world is a procedure which has so much success among such intelligent people, though it makes them suffer so much while providing such feeble explanations, it must be because this procedure has an advantage great enough to transcend all the inconveniences and compel quite strong personalities to subscribe to it blindly. Wounding though it may be, it provides protection from an even more serious wound which everything seems to indicate should be avoided at any price. Even if awareness of this is the fruit of a slow and distressing process, the truth which inflicts this much more serious wound is simple to formulate: the religious life in general and the Dominican life in particular, as we have known it, were based on a certain conception of God, a certain conception of humanity and a certain conception of the relation between them. Now these three groups of conceptions have perished, are dead, even if one or another element still survives. As a result, the form of religious life – and Dominican life – which was based on them has perished; it is dead, even if one or other element of it still survives.

It is all the more dead and gone since it was so well fitted to these conceptions. I doubt whether it could have survived had it been less well fitted, so great has been the transformation of the conceptions on which it was based. There are limits to the adaptability of a living organism, however great that adaptability may be, and here it is restricted by the weight of institutions and of past successes. If the Dominican life is decomposing, it is not because its ideal was false or illusory: it was remarkable, and St Dominic was not only a great saint but a brilliant founder, in inspiration as well as in what he instituted. If the Dominican life is decomposing, that is not because its followers have practised their ideal too badly and have corrupted it: to keep to the twentieth century and to France, the Dominicans – ordinary men that they were – realized their ideal in a remarkable way. If the Dominican life is decomposing, it is because the view of God, of man and his world, and of their relationships with God on which this life was founded and to which in turn it sought to provide a basis, are also decomposing.

It is that which could prove more deadly to men who have identified themselves with the ideals of the group to the point of defining themselves by the group and its values. The remarkable effectiveness of their training here rebounds on those who have been trained in this tradition, since it does not leave any possibility of survival for the values which were so radically inculcated in them. That is why the majority of these people are ready for any procedure, even the most infantile and the most desperate – like the accusations I have mentioned – which will save them having to acknowledge the death of that with which they had identified their life.

The decomposition of the Dominican life proves to be only a particular case of a much wider process. For those who are not Dominicans, this decomposition of Dominican life is of interest only to the degree that it is a specific case of a phenomenon which affects every man and every woman in our Western world, believers or unbelievers, since it concerns the conception that we can have today of God, humanity and the relationships between them.

Bizarre though it might seem, can there be anything here on which one might base a hope? If a certain conception of religious life is dead because it was based on a certain conception of God, humanity and the relationship between them, who among us can know what will grow or not grow from a new conception of God, a new conception of humanity and a new conception of the relationships between them? It would seem that these new conceptions have still to emerge. That is because we are not yet there; it is because we are between this death which does not finish dying and this life which has not yet begun to emerge that we are in this time of decomposition.

In search of the specific features of religious life

One of the points from which this intermediate situation can be best seen is the way in which over the last fifteen years attempts have been made to identify the specific character of religious life over against lay life. At the same time it would seem that this situation does not just concern religious, men and women; it concerns everyone, since how the lay life should be lived out is equally in question. Over the centuries, there has been no difficulty in defining the specific nature of the religious life: it was the most perfect of the states of life. Such a conviction of its particular value goes back a very long way: St Augustine had to devote the whole of the second part of his treatise on consecrated virginity to warning these 'virgins' against the principal danger which affected them. In his view, this danger is not impurity or unchastity – as it would be for a theologian or a bishop in later times – but pride. Reading the extravagant eulogies of this state of life which he produces in the first part of his treatise, one can understand why he thought he should struggle vigorously against the vanity and pride which were almost inevitably aroused by such admiration. This conviction of living out the most perfect state of life is expressed in two affirmations which are linked together: on the one hand religious life is that which most pleases God and which allows God to be honoured, loved and served to the best of his deserts; on the other hand, and as a result, religious life is that which is most fitted to human nature and which permits the noblest energies of human beings to deploy their richest potential. So the religious life lays claim to being the most perfect not only in relation to God but also from a strictly anthropological standpoint.

In essentials, this twofold conviction did not vary over the centuries, but took on different colouring and was expressed in different ways depending on the period. The men and women of my day, in the free colleges or movements of Catholic Action in which they were involved between 1935 and 1945, were told that the religious life or the priesthood were the highest form of service, and that it was best to consecrate oneself to this when one had had the good fortune to receive from God qualities which might be wasted in another form of life. When I was barely sixteen and was thinking of being trained for a job in public service which was very badly paid but seemed to me to be a real *service* to society and humanity generally, a priest played a by no means negligible role – to keep to the conscious level – in the first glimmerings of my later vocation by saying, 'So you want to spend your life earning money?' This anecdote would hardly be very important had not this priest been a most intelligent and even 'advanced' man.

This period between 1935 and 1945 was also the time when, especially as a result of Catholic Action, lay people began to acquire a certain status in the church. This status was still quite modest and they had only very limited functions and powers. However, as a Cardinal Archbishop of Paris before the Second World War had predicted, without any regret, once this movement began, there would be no way of stopping it. Now once lay people were given a certain status, lay life was also given a certain value. That began to set in motion a process which is still going on: the more Christian practice and reflection attach value to the 'lay life', to 'earthly realities', and so on, the more difficult it becomes for the religious life to be defined as the most perfect state of life and to reserve for it a monopoly of Christian perfection.

People rediscovered – for it was an ancient but neglected conception – that it was baptism which consecrated the Christian to what was still called Christian perfection, and not the choice of one form of life or another. There was a rediscovery – here again an ancient but neglected conception – that it was the living out of life in Jesus Christ inaugurated by baptism, that is to say the practice of faith, hope and charity, which realized the perfection of Christian life, and not the choice of one form of life or another. The best thing about Catholic Action was that it showed to lay people (for they still needed the clergy to show it to them) that their professional, cultural, political, trade-union, family, emotional life could be the sphere for this practice of faith, hope and charity and therefore of their Christian perfection, so that this perfection could be full and attain to what was called holiness.

Any idea that the religious life might have of itself would never have suffered from such a development had it not carried within itself the more or less explicit conviction that it had a monopoly of perfection, or at least the conviction of an indisputable superiority in respect both of God and of human vocation. As it happens, any idea the religious life might have of itself has suffered a great deal from this development, and that confirms the place held in it by the awareness of this monopoly or this superiority. For more than twenty years the theology (and the practice?) of the religious life has been entangled in this dilemma: how can one stop claiming that the religious life is the best state of life, most in conformity to the gospel and its teachings, most in harmony with the eschatological future of humanity (for to do so would be to pour scorn on the 'lay' vocation), while continuing to preserve for the religious life a specific character which cannot be made more precise without the reappearance by one device or another of an idea of superiority? The text of the Second Vatican Council on the religious life, promulgated in 1965, is beyond question the best, and in any case the most official, example of this embarrassment. It is the result of a compromise between two opposed currents: the traditional one, which sought to define the superiority of the religious life in classic fashion, and the other current, which sought to replace the religious life in the wider framework of the baptismal vocation to Christian life and the practice of the teaching of the gospel. When one reads the literature devoted to the specific question of religious life over the past twenty years one gets the impression of a series of enthusiasms for courses each of which always proves to be false. All possible patterns of relationships between the religious life and the lay life have been explored. Each time people have thought that they have at last found an approach that respected the specific character of the two states, and each time one of the two states concerned found itself wronged in the affair. People ended up by saying that each state has a kind of perfection of its own, irreplacable by the other and inaccessible to the other, each realizing the different perfections of humanity and the gospel that the other cannot.

For the moment this pattern of 'complementarity' is in favour; it seems to satisfy most people, or at least give them some relief. However, for some time there has been an awareness of the snags in the pattern of complementarity in other spheres where there are now similar attempts to redefine status: above all in connection with the discussion of the respective status of men and women. We are indebted to the feminist movements for having shown once and for all how deceitful the pattern of complementarity is, and how much it reduces the differences. And this reduction always works in the same way: as if by chance, it is always the party that enjoyed the privileged status which works out the scheme of complementarity by which the status of the other party is defined.

While those at the head of the religious Orders, male or female, and the theologians or bishops concerned work like fury to define the specific quality of the religious life, the rank-and-file men and women (and sometimes even some of those who hold higher office) are taking their leave: on tiptoe or with a fanfare. The young no longer come forward, or leave; the houses become empty or turn into old people's homes. There has never been so finely balanced a theology of the religious life, but there have never been so few men or women religious (once again, I exclude the very different cases of certain contemplative Orders and certain integralist groups, to which I shall return). Do we have to conclude from this that what was most effective both socially and for individuals was the sense that the religious life was superior, because it was the sole place, or at any rate the first-fruits, of perfection? Do we have to draw the conclusion that once this scheme has been abandoned, rightly or wrongly, the religious life necessarily disappears because it loses its main interest, whether that is explicit or not? I all but believe that, but it seems to me not to be the most important aspect of the problem.

For if we keep to this aspect, we reduce the crisis of the religious life to a crisis of identity, a crisis, moreover, that would affect those seeking to define it more than those living it out. And that is in fact what one reads and hears everywhere, from the Vatican to the smallest religious group. In my view the crisis in question is much deeper than a crisis of identity, and it primarily affects those who live the religious life. It is not a matter of knowing how to define oneself in relation to points of reference which remain completely unchanged or have been superficially renovated in the style of the day. What we have is the transformation of the landmarks themselves, a transformation so radical that they no longer serve as landmarks or mark out quite a different route – that is, when they do not seem to bar the way altogether or lead one to wander around in circles. The crisis is not over the identity of the religious life but over the representation of God, of humanity, and the relationship between them. The question of the religious life as a state can only be raised again (at this point I am not talking about what individuals or small groups can undertake according to their needs and their pleasure, though this is the most interesting and most important thing!) when we have new views of God, humanity and their relationship. While we are waiting for those, it is natural that the type of religious life which was so radically attached to conceptions and experiences in these three areas which have come to grief should suffer decomposition. Furthermore, I personally am convinced that, whether intentionally or not, the structure of the traditional religious life was too much bound up with the conviction that it had a monopoly – or at any rate a primacy – of Christian perfection, for it to be able to survive with ease the least challenge to this monopoly or this primacy. Now as well as being an incontestable fact, this challenge is an indispensable task: the honour of God and the honour of humanity are at stake.

What can the vows 'signify'?

The fact that some of the laurels of traditional religious life are in question clearly does not mean that in its spirit, its institutions and its practices, it has brought disgrace on God and on humanity. On the contrary, it does great honour to both, and its individual and collective successes have been innumerable, even if its failures have been as numerous as is usual in human enterprises. However, the transformation of views of God and man means that these very institutions and practices of traditional religious life, instead of signifying (in the strong sense of being a sign of) God and the human condition in a way which used to do them honour, now prove to trivialize or ridicule the God and the human condition to which they point, or to be radically unsuitable for signifying God and the human condition as they now appear to us. The consequence of this is that these institutions and practices represent quite the opposite to that of which for a long time they have nevertheless been remarkably adequate signs, and risk distorting the face of this God and this human condition to which they have sought to bear witness.[4] I deliberately use the word 'signify' because it has been used for a long time, and even more these last years, to denote the function of the religious life, which is thought to be to manifest and to realize in a particularly 'significant' way the essential realities of the Christian life. Traditionally the three vows are the most specific signs of this function of the religious life. Now the transformation of the realities with which each of these three vows is concerned makes it very problematical whether they are still capable of signifying *à propos* of God and human beings what they formely sought to and were able to signify.

I have no intention of becoming involved at this point in a criticism of the essence of the religious vows, whether constructive or destructive, nor do I mean to demonstrate whether or not they were capable of signifying what they sought to signify. I have practised them with great conviction, if not with great perfection. Nor do I intend to assess the way in which they have been practised; after thirty years of confidences and responsibilities, I know something about this, but how does one judge, and why? All I want to say is this: the significance of sexuality and human love, of possessing goods and of autonomy, have changed so much over the last century or so that the meaning and purport of the vows which were connected with the former significance of these anthropological realities have been profoundly changed. Here again, it was to the degree that they were remarkably adapted to this former significance that the vows of chastity, poverty and obedience could claim to be meaningful. This remarkable degree of adequacy is the very fact which from now on condemns them to lesser significance, not to say insignificance, in a different anthropological context.

What relationship is there between the significance of the possession of goods in feudal or post-feudal society and possession of them in the urban industrial society of the West at the end of the twentieth century? Whether at the bottom of the scale it is a matter of the spread of wage-earning and social welfare or, at the top of the scale, of international ownership of the means of production, instruments of credit, raw materials and capital, the possession of goods and the use of money has such a different significance that to deprive oneself of possessions or money must inevitably have a totally different significance also.

Things are hardly different in matters of sexuality and human love. Over almost two hundred years, our biological, psychological, ethnological and historical knowledge of sexuality has considerably changed any ideas we might have had of it. Love between man and woman, between parents and children, has changed just as much. Moreover, love and sexuality have seen profound changes in those relationships and institutions which are their privileged setting: the family, the married couple, the respective status of men and women have changed in demographic, economic, emotional and institutional terms. The historians of the family, of the married couple, of love or sexuality give us insights into the twelfth, sixteenth or eighteenth century which, though fragmentary, are enough to prove to us that our loves and our relationships are played out on a different planet from that on which our ancestors evolved. As for sexuality itself, it has become impossible for us to believe that it is only concerned with sexual relationships in the strictest sense of the word: we know that it is at work – and not in a pathological way (though that can be the case) but structurally – not only in all 'affective' relationships, including that with God, but in all human activities, including those of the faith. I shall return at greater length in another part of this book to the problem posed to Christianity by this new significance of love and sexuality, since the vow of chastity must necessarily be put in this wider context. For the moment, since we are concerned here with the transformation of the conditions in which the religious vows can have the value of a sign, I shall content myself with stressing that depriving oneself of what is represented by human love and sexuality at the end of the twentieth century cannot have the same significance as depriving oneself of what they represented in the thirteenth century, and such a course of action runs a serious risk of making quite different statements about God and the human condition from what one would want to signify or believe that one was signifying, in such a renunciation.

It might seem that such profound transformations have not affected the vow of obedience by which one renounces personal freedom for an organization of one's life, through the intermediary of superiors, which puts it at the disposition of an 'Order'. However, I believe that transformations in this sphere have at least as important consequences, even if they are not so obvious. Their effects are all the more profound since, from an anthropological perspective, freedom and autonomy, and also dependence and subjection, are at least as important as love and sexuality or the possession of goods and use of money, if not more so. This anthropological importance has its equivalent in the primacy which the Christian tradition has long accorded to the vow of obedience over the two other vows, considering that to sacrifice one's liberty was to sacrifice the greatest good, that to devote one's freedom to God was to devote to him one's most precious possession, and consequently to give the most useful support to the coming of his kingdom.

However personalist one might want to be, one is obliged to consider that freedom and servitude, independence and dependence, autonomy and subjection are not realities which are defined and elaborated uniquely within and as a function of our individual natures. They are realities which are closely bound up with the social structures into which we are inserted and by which our individual characters are actually formed. These realities are themselves exposed to the interplay of economic, political and cultural forces in such a way that our individualities are determined (if not in the sense of determinism, though that could be the case, at least in the sense of the determination which shapes the contour and moulds the form) by the whole of our society, but in such a way that we are in a living and operative relationship to this society (even when we are unaware of the fact). To have stressed this social dimension of freedom, independence and autonomy dispenses me from having to stress at length that, even if words do not change, the collective and individual reality that these words denote differs considerably depending on whether one thinks of them in the third and fourth centuries (the time of the origin of the religious life), the sixth century, the twelfth and thirteenth centuries, or the nineteenth century (the periods of some of its renaissances). To deprive oneself at the end of the twentieth century of what is signified by freedom, independence and autonomy to say something about God and the human condition cannot therefore have the same significance as to deprive oneself of them in the thirteenth century, and those who do so run the grave risk of saying something quite different about God and the human condition from what they would want to signify by such a renunciation.

So we would seem to have the same situation with each of the three vows. The problem is not to know whether or not they were to no purpose; as I have already said, I myself practised them with great conviction, if not with great perfection. Nor is the problem to know whether religious have lived out their vows so badly that they have corrupted and ruined their aim: I personally think that that is not the case. The problem is what the vows can possibly signify when the anthropological reality with which they are concerned and which they seek to signify is changing so radically and when perhaps – and I shall come to this in a moment – the God with whom they are concerned and whom they seek to signify has also been transformed. Now any possible new significance cannot be purely and simply deduced or transposed from the ancient significance of these vows. On the contrary, it will have to be reinvented inductively by generations to come, starting with the significance which has been acquired in their culture by the possession of goods and the use of money, sexuality and love, freedom and autonomy, and starting with what these new generations want to say and signify about all these matters and about God. I have no doubt that these new generations, too, will be able to locate their new ideals in the tradition of what Christians of previous generations sought to realize, but after they have worked them out, and only then. For the moment, such new significance has not yet appeared: people are looking for it in a tentative way, and sometimes its emergence is hampered – or even unconsciously distorted – by the weight and resistance of ancient significance which is not yet completely dead. So we are in an intermediate stage; the ancient meanings of the vows are now so devalued that they are no longer operational (except among minorities which are too small and heterogeneous to be representative) and new meanings have not yet appeared clearly enough to serve as points of reference for projects which are equally indefinite.

While we wait, things go on, willy-nilly, in a compromise between the old which is not yet dead and the new which is not yet born. To keep to the community in which I live, which is no worse nor better than the next, we are about forty men, three-quarters of whom are more than fifty-five, and I know very well that among us we represent the whole spectrum of possible attitudes and forms of behaviour in relation to poverty, chastity and obedience, leaving aside the extremes of the sublime and the ignoble. Anyone who knew our lives in detail in all these three spheres would doubtless feel a mixture of respect and disquiet about us – if he were well-disposed; he would feel that mixture of admiration and slight hesitation which is aroused by a deeper knowledge of the real life of human beings. He would note a real love of God, real service of the gospel and our neighbours; he would doubtless note the mixture of harmonious and radiant equilibria, of false equilibria based on the annihilation of all or part of the personality; neuroses well compensated for and neuroses badly compensated for, neither more nor less than elsewhere, even if the distinctive living conditions give a certain specific character to the local pattern of symptoms. In short, he would find something to love, something to be grateful for, something to pity, something to forgive, and also something to grieve over with impotent rage at the sheer waste in some cases. Yes, one could feel all that in coming to know us; we feel all that: I feel all that. But to whom would it occur that the specific form of our way of life is especially a sign of the nature of God and the human condition? To whom would it occur that this form of life expresses, *signifies*, the nature of the possession of goods and the use of money in the light of the gospel; human love and sexuality in the light of the gospel; freedom, independence and autonomy in the light of the gospel? But surely that is what the vows claim to be expressing. To whom would it occur that all this expresses, *signifies* the God of Jesus Christ in the light of the gospel? But surely that is what the vows claim to be expressing? The facts prove that these ideas no longer occur to people since no one, or hardly anyone, joins us any more. And I must stress yet again that this has nothing to do with our present or past weakness or with the folly of the ancient plan.

Having spent thirty or so years of my life in the Dominican Order, having received so much from it and wanting so much to serve it and make it fruitful, having lived with people and remarkable groups which have brought me to life, with all that in my bones so that it has become an intrinsic part of my identity, I still find that it costs me great effort and tears, bravery in the face of panic, passion which is nevertheless coupled with hesitation and evasion, to dare to say of this institutional decomposition what I dared to say about the decomposition of my personal identity as one who preached, presided at the eucharist and taught theology: 'My God, my friends, if that is the way, help us not to shun decomposition, do not leave us to our resistances and our evasions. My God, may your kingdom come. Help us to experience our own decomposition; you can see that otherwise we and you will never get anywhere.'

Decomposition 3

Preaching, presiding at the eucharist, teaching theology, is always, in one way or another, a matter of saying God. Being a Dominican, living the religious life, organizing one's life in accordance with the vows, is again, in one way or another, a matter of saying God. I chose the title *When I say God* for my earlier book, published four years ago from the moment when I write these lines, the one which caused me the troubles I have mentioned, because I recalled a phrase from Meister Eckhart: 'God becomes God when the creatures say God.' It was bad enough to have to allow the decomposition of all that was organized in me and in the apparatus of the church around the functions of preaching, presiding and teaching; to allow the decomposition of all that was organized in me and in my 'Order' around the aims of the religious life; it was almost more than a human being could bear. But hope and faith extended to the point of making me believe that it would be possible, and perhaps even desirable, in so far as it was a matter of allowing ways of saying God to decompose because they proved less capable of saying God than they had once been. And there was the uncertain certainty that this decomposition would allow a recomposition by means of which it would prove possible to say God in a better way, or rather, by means of which God would be able to express himself better through the better things that men and women tried to say of him. Though I myself might be no longer young enough to hope to see this recomposition flourishing in my lifetime, at least it might flourish later, whether or not my decomposition had proved useful in preparing the means, perhaps by clearing the ground and destroying what might hinder new growth, even if formerly that had been the heart of the house. I did not know if I would have the strength, if I would hold out. But if I collapsed at the side of the road, it would only prove that I could do no more, not that the road was the wrong one: others would go further, whether or not they remembered the one who had not been able to go right to the end.

However, I had to discover that my road was not the right one. Or rather, that something else had to happen before I found a road:

not another preliminary step but rather another standstill, another immobilization, another shaking of the most solid ground. Another decomposition. It was that of the very fact of saying God. That of the very fact of being able to say God. Not of the fact of wanting to say him. But of the fact that one could say God. It was the decomposition of God in so far as he could be said. If, according to Eckhart, God becomes God when the creatures say God, then in one sense this would indeed be the decomposition of God.

So that would never end. I had to postpone indefinitely the question of knowing if and when I could recover what I had been deprived of, because it would prove more urgent and more important to know what was happening here. I had to postpone indefinitely the question of knowing if and when I – and several others with me – could rediscover (here or elsewhere) the vitality of an Order which had been our way of life and our reason for living, because it would prove more urgent and important to know whether it was possible to say God at all. It was not just a matter of the theological games that I had known and practised, which consist in beginning by proclaiming that we cannot say what God is but that we can only say what he is not, and then go on to the writing of enormous *Summa Theologiae*s or twenty-volume dogmatics (dying before finishing them) in which one says in a singularly precise way who God is. No, it seemed to be a matter of asking myself what I was doing when I was saying God, what sense it made to say God, what it might mean, much less in respect of me than in respect of God. Can one say God?

Many people will doubtless think me very stupid not to have begun there. Some people may even think that I should have begun there thirty or so years ago. I know that in fact this is a classic question: it is even an examination question. I was taught it, and I studied it in all the relevant disciplines. Philosophers raise it, and I studied some of them, even if I did not have much of a head for philosophy. Theologians raise it: I studied many of them for a long time, and I do have something of a head for theology. Mystics raise it, and I had often meditated on it, assiduously, even if I have no head for mysticism at all. Non-believers raise it, and I spent a good deal of time with many of them, who paid me the compliment of being interested in what was happening to me because they knew that I was a believer and just how much I was a believer, for I have a very good head for believing. In short, it is a question that everyone asks; and everyone knows that it is an important question. So I asked it of myself, since I am no more stupid than the next man, and I asked it – or I thought I was asking it – as a prelude... or almost a prelude, since even in

Thomas Aquinas it is only the thirteenth question of the first part of his *Summa Theologiae* (to my dying day I shall be able to give the reference in a hundredth of a second).

However, had I known that the decompositions I have mentioned were going to end up with the decomposition of the possibility of saying God, had I only foreseen what this decomposition was going to be, I am certain that I would have turned right round and run away as fast as my legs could carry me. Or rather, I would have remained transfixed on the spot, finding whatever means I could (and I can see plenty of them around) of stopping my ears, of no longer letting myself be disturbed, of barricading the doors and windows and shutting myself up with some supplies to survive on – well aware that although they were relatively worthless, it would not prove disturbing to have them. I had the good fortune or the misfortune not to understand immediately what was happening, and even of not suspecting it at all. I already had a good deal on my hands anyway. And then, was not God my rock? That at least was certain, and it was the smallest matter for him if it was true that I had to let myself be undone, dismembered, decomposed. For even if I did not have the choice, even if I was also doing it for myself, in order to be myself, nevertheless I was also doing it a bit for him. For him to be himself. I even dreamed that if I rediscovered the energy to write a new book I would call it 'Let God be God'. So come what might I attended to the various decompositions which I have just mentioned. And most fortunately, slowly, very slowly, almost imperceptibly, their internal logic introduced this new decomposition. Most fortunately, it began to appear to me in its most logical, most reasonable, most 'proper' aspects. This made it easier to accept. And I accepted it. Here is how.

Saying God?

I have said that on the occasion of the measures which prohibited me from exercising various functions, a breach progressively opened up in the suffering which I felt, a breach into which questions were introduced about what these functions represented, for me personally and for the community of believers or its ecclesiastical apparatus. These two points of view, moreover, were inextricably mixed. Now a third kind of question came to be added to these other two: I began to ask myself about the significance, in respect of God himself, of the conviction common to these three functions, namely that, if I might venture to put it in that way, they provided a hold on God. Of course, if someone had asked me before I preached or presided at a eucharist whether what I was going to do did not presuppose that in one way or another I had a hold on God, in all good faith I would have claimed the opposite, and I would have replied with a good deal of admiration for God that it was he who was stooping towards us and not we who were managing to raise ourselves up towards him.

None of that is false, but it is no more false for a preacher, someone presiding at the eucharist, a professor of theology, to think that he can nevertheless say something of God and even make him really present. I did not doubt that; for me, Christianity makes no sense if God cannot make himself present to human beings; really present, since it is in reality that God wants to be present to them. Besides, I had devoted the first quarter of the book about God which caused me all the problems to saying what this presence of God might be, resorting in it to the Jewish figure of the Shekinah. That is one of the parts of that book on which I have no reason to go back: for me, and for others who have been kind enough to say as much (which was a great help to me) this still remains an achievement.

What I was progressively led to put in question was not the possibility of God being present to humans and of humans being present to God; it was rather the way in which, as a preacher, as a president at the eucharist, as a professor of theology, I virtually took this presence for granted, as being almost there for the asking. I began to be amazed that for so long I had found it quite natural that one could preach, preside and teach theology. Let's be clear about this: in one way I was well aware that all this was impossible without action from God, without a gift of his Spirit. At the beginning of my career as a professor of theology, religious discipline required the professor to recite in Latin at the beginning of the course a prayer to the Holy Spirit: and I suppose that none of my students ever realized that I always, every time, said this prayer from the bottom of my heart. Before saying mass, alone or publicly, I had a gesture which my friends knew well: I would stand up straight and draw my hands slowly over my face as if to compose myself and efface myself so that God could do what he had to do. In the hours and the days which preceded a sermon, even if the slightly hysterical side of my personality rather came to the fore, I would try to be as open as possible to variations of inspiration and therefore – if I may dare put it that way – to the Spirit: that is one of the reasons why, unlike the majority of my fellow preachers, I was absolutely incapable of putting down in writing, even an hour beforehand, let alone days or weeks earlier, what I was going to say. I have begun a celebration by imploring the Spirit, 'Grant that in five minutes I shall make the right choice from the two or three completely different themes that I have prepared and between which I am hesitating. Inspire me; after all, that is your job.' So I was utterly convinced of the role of God and his Spirit in all that.

But the question which was struggling to take shape in me was different: I did not doubt that God would and could play his part in all that, but I began to find it curious that the rest of us, preachers, presidents at the eucharist, theologians, found it so natural, so normal, almost automatic to devote ourselves to these actions and actually live out the type of relationship to God that they presuppose. I felt the need to set up some distance between these activities and the God who was at the same time their source and their object, not by devaluing the activites but rather by revaluing God, and by revaluing him not because I knew him better, but on the contrary because I was better aware of the fashion in which he is deeper than, higher than, beyond all these activities. I began by having the need not so much to preach, to preside, to teach, as to set up this distance between God and theology, to let God stand back, to allow him free play. It is not that God interests me less and that I want to stand back from him; on the contrary, I want him to be able to be what he is, to be able to be more truly what he is. I increasingly felt, while apprehending him less and less, as though I were being taken beyond all the words, celebrations and theories with which we mark out the ways of his coming.

For all that, I was not against sermons, celebrations or theologies, whether in connection with myself personally or in connection with communities of believers. However, I did feel the need for them to become more modest – I might venture to say, more restrained – more fragmentary, more aware that they can only be fragments in relation to their object, and not the grandiose theological, cultural or oratorical syntheses which no longer seem to doubt their capacity to do justice to the totality of the mystery of God. I personally needed to find it less natural, less immediate, less self-evident, that one should preach, celebrate, theologize. I also needed the believing community to find it less natural, less immediate for the church as an institution, less self-evident for the Christian faith to speak, to celebrate, to theologize. Not – will I manage to explain this adequately? – by a devaluation of these functions, but by a revaluation of their object. I needed to spend some time asking myself whether it was possible to say God, without forcing myself to give a reply, and accepting that if I had to die before being able to give an answer, I could be convinced that even here, this silent quest could at least be as useful to others as my presiding at the celebration, my preaching and my theological activity had been – for sometimes they *were* useful.

1. Saying Jesus Christ?

And Jesus Christ? In him, at least, it was possible to say God. In him, at least, God had spoken: 'The Word was made flesh and dwelt among us'; 'God, in these last days, has spoken to us by the Son.' And this word has not passed away like the flowers of the field or the days of man: twenty centuries afterwards, the Spirit still makes it just as alive. I have never ceased to believe that, even if people have maliciously suggested the opposite. So in Jesus Christ at least it proved possible to say God. However, the various developments of which I have spoken so far contributed towards giving a new direction to a reflection begun earlier, one which was not peculiar to me, but which from then on came to insert itself into the complex of preoccupations which arose out of the new situation which had been created for me.

Like many Catholic men and women of my generation, for a long time I lived in a situation of complete immediacy with the person of Jesus Christ. Of course I was far from always being in contact with him, but that was my fault; it was because of my human weakness, the mediocre quality of my prayer life, my sin. Had I been able to overcome all that, as I tried to without great success, I would have been able to profit from the immediacy of this presence. And that was the essential thing; the feeling was that this presence could be a matter of immediate experience, at least ideally. We had the eucharist: Jesus Christ was there, immediately present. We had scripture: the Word was there. We had the church, its bishops and its pope: they were the infallible guarantee of the presence of the Spirit of God and of Jesus Christ. We had prayer, collective or individual: he was there. We had the common life, we had caritative love: where two or three are gathered in his name, he is there. Where one gives food to the hungry, where one suffers persecution for justice, he is there. We had history: he was there because he is the meaning of history, the alpha and the omega.

A great many Catholic men and women of my generation have rejected the immediacy of this presence: others have rejected the thought that for them Jesus Christ could be the sign that God can be said and the reality in which he is expressed. However, the immediacy of this presence holds such a place in the way in which Catholics understand that Jesus Christ is the Word made flesh that to question whether the presence is immediate is confused with questioning whether Jesus Christ is the Word of God, and people react as though to question the former put the latter in doubt. In fact, once they have begun to ask these questions many believers have been led to doubt; but the false association and its terrible consequences must be seen essentially as a direct result of the failure of the Catholic system itself to make an adequate distinction between this total immediacy and the fact that Jesus Christ is the Word of God, and of its claim to base the truth of this fact on such a total immediacy. So I must explain how I came to have to distinguish the two. Many different approaches are possible, depending on the individual's personal history, each of which presents the discovery in a different light. For me, everything combined for this discovery again to find its context in the establishment of a distance between Jesus Christ and the way in which the believing community could claim to know him, grasp him and possess him.

Do the Gospels say Jesus Christ or talk about him?

My way was chiefly that traced by reading the gospel, meditating on it in prayer, proclaiming it in liturgy and preaching, and seeking to understand it in theology. After all, that was a very ordinary way for a Dominican. I had studied theology between 1952 and 1956, at a time when the biblical renewal was beginning to bear fruit in Catholic exegesis. However, it had yet to reach the holy of holies, which at that time was dogmatic theology. For us, dogmatic theology was for ninety and sometimes even a hundred per cent of the time a commentary on the *Summa Theologiae* of Thomas Aquinas. Even in our courses on Sacred Scripture (the term used at the time), the renewal remained very modest and was limited to our acquiring the least hazardous elements of the historical-critical method as it had been courageously practised at the École biblique in Jerusalem since the beginning of the century. Nothing in the teaching that I received could allow me to guess that exegetes like von Rad, Jeremias or Bultmann had already reached an advanced age by then and had a good deal of work to their credit.

So it was much later, and virtually by teaching myself, that I came to discover their works, in the little oases of time and energy which were left me by the very different work demanded by my teaching and my researches (I was a moral theologian, and tried to get some familiarity with psychoanalysis), not to mention numerous duties in

my community and in the academic world. My theology, and also –
I would stress – my prayer, my celebration and my preaching, and
therefore in a sense almost my personality, all arose, came into being,
were formed and structured before and independently of questions
arising from a modern reading of the gospel. So I would suppose that
in my own way I am fairly representative of the shock which this way
of reading the Gospels caused among the Catholics of my generation,
even the youngest of them, and the developments which followed.
(Perhaps I should have said, the developments which would have
folowed had not the communication of them been restrained by the
church apparatus which is afraid of losing some of the foundations
of its power and therefore makes sure that the doses which it gives
are small ones; it is also restrained by the fear of some believers that
they might lose what they believe to be the essential foundations of
their faith.)

So I learned that the Gospels were not stenographic reports of the
words and actions of Jesus. I learned that they represented the last
stage of very complex redactional processes for which we do not at
the moment have any generally satisfying theory, even if some
elements in it seem settled: very diverse communities, sometimes very
divided, had celebrated and preached this Jesus of Nazareth and their
experience of his resurrection and his Lordship as Christ, each in its
own way. The process which had led to the regrouping of these
different elements was so complex that in the smallest parable one
could discover two or three different and successive stages of the
story, corresponding to the different situations and intentions in the
communities in which each of these stages had come into being. Of
course the first reaction was to want to decipher this riddle, to clear
the rubble in this veritable archaeological site in order to get back to
the real Jesus, his real words in their original state, the original
contours of his real actions. How could it be otherwise? The need
for an immediate relationship to Jesus Christ was so deeply rooted
in the majority of forms of Christianity that Bultmann could not
avoid some exaggeration when in the 1940s he asserted that the
Christ of faith, the Christ constructed by the faith of the first
Christians, did not have a great deal to do with the Jesus of history,
and that besides, not only was it impossible to know the latter, it was
not really of very much interest to faith. After some decades of
upheaval, the problem of the relationship between the Jesus of history
and the Christ of faith has been clarified and eased to some extent;
relations between the two are better, if I might put it that way; the
Jesus of history has become more important for the Christ of faith

and the faith of Christians. However, the important thing is that for over a decade the main problem for faith has been rather different. Faith no longer looks for its truth and its foundation in the discovery of the very words of Jesus, his very actions (the *ipsissima verba*), though it is nevertheless thought very important that what is said of Christ should have its roots in the history of Jesus. Faith seeks its truth and its basis in the process of anamnesis and the construction of the written Gospels, which are the work of the believing community inspired by the Spirit of the Risen Lord. Faith has renounced the impossible immediacy of the historical presence of Jesus Christ, not because it has renounced the historicity of Jesus but because it has understood that its truth and its foundation go back to the construction of a memoir beginning with fundamental events rooted in a word which was recognized, whether immediately or afterwards, as being original in the strict sense of the term.

From then on, what initially seemed a peril for faith, namely the fragmentation in this immediacy of the life and words of Jesus Christ, proved rather to be a better understanding of the process of faith, and also a better understanding of the way in which God might express himself to human beings. People abandoned the thought of having one theology of the New Testament which could be any more unified than the way in which the Word – the unique Word – had been made flesh – uniquely – in Jesus Christ. With Käsemann, they discovered that the plurality of Gospels, the plurality of confessions of faith, the plurality of communities and their theologies was, rather, the *conditio sine qua non* for God truly to be at work and for Jesus Christ to be able to be considered the Word made flesh, since no confession of faith, no community, no theology, no gospel can circumscribe the mystery of God and that of Jesus Christ. Again, it is essential that this plurality should be a real plurality, with the irreducible differences that that implies, and not a plurality of façades the features of which could easily be brought together in a synthesizing generalization which one power could control and guarantee. It is precisely because he is the Word made flesh that Jesus Christ escapes the kind of immediacy in which I had been trained and which I believed, with almost all the Catholic system, to be the indispensable sign and necessary consequence of the fact that Jesus is the Christ. It is precisely the fact that he is the Christ that introduces a distance between him and every word, every gospel, every confession of faith about him; and if that distance were abolished. far from preserving his unique originality as the Word made flesh, he would be reduced to being just one human being among others.

I ought to expand on the nature of the road which led me to
question the immediacy which Catholicism too often attaches to its
relationship with Christ, for if this question starts from the essentials,
namely scripture and tradition, it runs headlong into the central
aspects of Catholicism as it is specifically lived. A whole series of
facets of the immediacy of the presence of Jesus Christ, the immediacy
of his presence in scripture, in the eucharist, in the church, in
individual or collective prayer, in the common life and in charity, in
history and in action, all these facets of the immediacy of the presence
of Jesus Christ, are modified. What is modified is not the reality of
his presence but the immediacy of this presence. Just as I was
feeling the need to establish a certain distance between preaching,
celebration, theology and the God who is their object, because it
seemed to me that such a distance had been neglected too much (it
devalued God and over-valued these functions), it was therefore
natural for me to set up a certain distance between Jesus Christ and
everything in the Catholic system which functions as if we had a
direct and immediate hold on him. There again I felt a certain need
to breathe, to be silent, to leave the field open to the Spirit of Jesus
Christ. This was not primarily – would I come to understand this
properly? – to devalue scripture, the eucharist, the church, prayer,
or the liberation of the poor and the oppressed, but to permit a re-
evaluation of Jesus Christ who, if he is the Word made flesh, cannot
be reduced to any of that or even to the sum of all that. For me it was
not a matter of being silent about the fact that Jesus Christ is the
Word made flesh and that God has spoken in him, but of being silent
so that the question of knowing how Jesus Christ himself may be
said could be felt to the full.

The contingency of the historical forms of Jesus Christ

If I had had any doubts that the way in which we can now read the
Gospels forced this new development on me, it would have come
home to me from the way in which Christianity has represented Jesus
Christ over the twenty centuries of its history. There have been
histories of christology or histories of religious feeling: we have no
history of the way in which Christianity has represented Jesus Christ.
We have some ingredients for it, and we can see clearly that for
example the Christianity of the fourteenth century did not represent
Jesus Christ in the same way as that of the twelfth or the thirteenth.
The changes to be seen in statues, in stained-glass windows, in the
liturgy, in popular or educated forms of piety, attest it even better

than that of theology. The Christ of Jansenism, of the missionaries of the French Restoration or of Thérèse of the Infant Jesus at the beginning or the end of the nineteenth century, the Christ the King of Pius XI (1925), the Christ of Catholic Action and the Christ of liberation theology, while being in each case quite close together in time, are nevertheless so different that if one loves the one, one hardly loves the other. At the same period of history, ours for example, the Christ of half of Latin America, that of the doctrine of National Security, and the Christ of the other half, that of the liberation of the poor, are so different that people sometimes fight, even to the death, depending on whether they relate to the one or the other. The Christ of the Polish church, the Christ of an African church and the Christ of one or other nuance of American or French Catholicism are again very different. Sceptics could find something here to make them doubt; cynics (who are not necessarily wrong) could see here a proof of the formidable capacity of Christianity and its ruling powers to adapt, and the worried might ask whether there is not here the dangerous source of an unacceptable dogmatic relativism.

I personally have often succumbed to the temptation to sweep away one or another Jesus Christ, that of Vincent Ferrier or of Bossuet, or the Christ the King of Pius XI, because they seemed to me to be so little in keeping with the Gospels (as I read them, without being too aware of the presuppositions of my reading) and dangerous because of the way in which they prompted human beings to look at their condition. Since then I have understood better that (leaving aside the most aberrant of these forms) each age and each version of Christianity has constructed its Jesus Christ depending on its own authentic spiritual experience and basic anthropological and social situation. In order to formulate its understanding of Jesus Christ and his salvation, each age had to break with the form of Jesus Christ that had earlier been elaborated as a result of just as authentic a spiritual experience, albeit different, in an anthropological and social situation which was also basic, but different. Of course in turn this new image perished when a new spiritual experience and a new anthropological and social situation called for yet another new one. It is only afterwards that we see the continuity; at a particular moment it is the discontinuity that comes to the fore. However, this continuity must not lead us to relativize these different images as if they did not have value in themselves, or to relativize the differences between them, which correspond to profound changes in society and spiritual experience. When one approaches in this way each of these contingent historical forms elaborated by Christianity over twenty centuries, one almost always comes to understand the experience of faith in Jesus Christ and the anthropological and social situations which have given rise to the form in question. And one has to admire each of these forms, since believers, men and women, have committed themselves to Jesus Christ with all their faith, and in his light have tried make sense of their anthropological and social situation.

This plurality of the forms of Jesus Christ through Christian time and space is always simply the transposition over twenty centuries of history of the plurality to be found at the birth of faith in Jesus Christ, at the dawn of the New Testament. There is the same radical necessity for it, if it is true that in Jesus Christ the Word is made flesh. It does not in any way question the truth of each of these images, for their truth does not depend on a similarity between them or a similarity to what is supposed to be a unique primitive model (which does not exist even in the New Testament); it depends on the fact that the reality of Christ is represented there in a way which, in a particular experience of faith and a particular anthropological and social situation, plays a role *analogous* to the role which was proclaimed as that of Jesus Christ by believers who founded our faith in their own particular anthropological and social situation.[5] If it fulfils this condition (and it is a vital condition) – and not because it resembles one or other form of Jesus Christ – any contingent historical form of Jesus Christ is true, and we must rejoice that through twenty centuries of Christianity the faith of believers, inspired by the Spirit, has proved capable of developing such diverse representations of the mystery of Christ.

However, for better or for worse, each age or each current of Christianity has to recognize the contingent character of its own form of Christ. Here again, the need for immediacy, the fear of losing control, a mistaken belief that the truth of our faith is related to the permanence of its forms, its dogmas and its institutions, rather than trust in the fidelity of God towards humanity, all comes together to make each contingent historical form of Jesus Christ equivalent to the totality of the mystery of Christ. Many forces came together to oblige me to introduce a distance between preaching, celebration, theology and the God who is their source and object, so as to open the field much more widely for God. A modern reading of scripture taught me to introduce an analogous distance between what we say (and what scripture says) of Jesus Christ and Jesus Christ himself, in order to open things up more to the Spirit of Jesus Christ. So it was inevitable that the discovery of the necessarily historical and contingent character of the forms of Jesus Christ over twenty centuries of Christianity should also have impelled me to introduce the same distance between what the spiritual experience and the anthropological and social situation which have fashioned me said about Jesus Christ and Jesus Christ himself. Having spent so many years preaching, celebrating and theologizing Jesus Christ, and acting almost as if it went without saying that one could speak of him, it was inevitable that I should take a break and allow the question of knowing how it was possible to say Jesus Christ himself to assume its full breadth. But in that case, how could I go on living and not decompose, when to say Jesus Christ had been what made up my life?

The resurrection of Christ makes him pass into the transcendence of God

I was also led to ask myself this question about the distance that needs to be put between Jesus Christ and what can be said of him by a really surprising development in the upheavals which the situation in which I had been placed had triggered off in me. Among the points which had been given me as reasons for the condemnation of my book there were two which in fact raised questions: about death and what various forms of Christianity had thought about life after death, in connection both with Jesus Christ and with human beings. In due course I shall return at more length to the way in which Christianity today must confront the reality of death, and to the effect that the anthropological significance of death in our present-day Western civilization can have on Christian faith in the resurrection. For the moment it is enough to point out that in the book which was condemned I had allowed myself to be carried away by a struggle, which I still thought necessary, against the fallacious ways of denying death which seem to me to play a very great role in Christian faith in the resurrection. At the time this role seemed to me so great that I had become unable to find any way of believing in the resurrection which avoided it. So it is understandable that Christians were disturbed. Even the reaction of the authorities was understandable, and I myself never protested against the principle of such an intervention, even if I said to everyone concerned (but never in public) what I thought of the iniquitous, lying, underhand and stupid way in which it was made. That having been said, the condemnations were no help with the problem, above all when the judges and the censors were more interested in condemning and affirming their power than in raising the question that the accused was attempting to raise and setting out to provide a better answer to it. The problem was still the same: are there ways of believing in the resurrection of Jesus Christ and in that of human beings which are other than the products – in a more or less subtle form – of the fear of death and denial of that fear?

In the course of numerous meetings and discussion which arose as a result of this book, I found that the factors in the problem had gradually shifted, at least as far as I was concerned. After two or three years, it seemed to me that the question of Jesus Christ had to be raised in a different way from that in which I had raised it. People persisted in arguing against me that for the first Christians, the resurrection of Jesus Christ had been the proof that he really was the Messiah, the one sent by God; and it had been the act by which God had made him Lord in their eyes. Obviously I accepted that, since it is a historical fact which anyone can establish, believer or not; and that is certainly the way in which Christian faith was born. But I persisted in thinking that after twenty centuries of Christianity and experience in the Spirit of the vitality of Jesus, and in view of the new anthropological significance of death, we cannot purely and simply repeat the primitive faith without evacuating it of meaning. People told me that the whole of Christianity would collapse if I challenged the resurrection of Christ, which was its foundation and the evidence for it. I would retort that for us modern men and women the question can only be raised in quite the opposite terms: it is because we believe that Jesus Christ is the one sent by God that we believe that he is still alive. His resurrection is an effect of his status as Word made flesh, and not the source and the proof of this status.

For the moment the important thing is not to know whether I was right or wrong, but to stress that such a way of looking at things obliged me to restore a degree of reality to the resurrection of Jesus Christ. For – again despite the false accusations made against me – I believe that Jesus Christ is the Word of God made flesh. I believe that he was a man whose relation to God and God's relation to him make him a being above the level of common humanity. As a result I was led to believe – and for the moment it does not matter much whether I was right or wrong – that death cannot have the same type of hold over him as over us simple mortals, and that if he dies, his future cannot be identical to ours, to the degree that he is something of God that we are not. In contrast to the book that was condemned, that was a notable development. But while it seemed to me to approach the classical affirmations of the faith, which I do not reject in any way, it proved to have quite unforeseen consequences which in a strange way came to emphasize the need to insert the distance that I have mentioned between Jesus Christ and what one says of him.

In fact, if Jesus Christ is risen, that is to say, if death does not have the same type of effect on him as it has on us, his resurrection tips him – if I may dare put it that way – over into the transcendence of God, leaving our historical and empirical world. It is the very premise of his resurrection, namely that he is something of God that we are not, and that God, after raising him, frees him from our historical and empirical world. I had long interpreted the resurrection rather along these lines, as inaugurating the absence of Jesus Christ from our empirical world, while at Pentecost the Spirit inaugurates his presence in a way quite different from the presence of a risen form which can can be discovered historically and empirically in our world, or from any traces of it. However, the more I discovered a possible meaning for the resurrection of Jesus Christ, the more, paradoxically, this resurrection set up a distance between Christ and us which is just as great, since it is the same, as that between God and us, by tipping Jesus over into the transcendence of God.[6] So the two questions had to be raised in the same terms: can one say God, and can one say Jesus Christ?

It was enough for me to return to the earlier stages of my personal faith, or to the way in which Christian faith in the resurrection is lived out, to see that very often the various forms of Christianity understood it in a totally different way. Instead of seeing the resurrection of Christ, as I do, as something which opens up greatly the distance between what Jesus Christ is and what one can say about him, because in the resurrection God makes him Lord, these seem to see it, rather, as the most direct guarantee possible for their scriptures, their sacraments, their institutions and their powers. And so we arrive at the staggering paradox that an authority can itself declare its actions infallible in a historical, empirical and contingent world, taking as its authority the fact that it is a direct successor to the witnesses of this resurrection which has in fact been transformed into the empirical basis of an absolute empirical immediacy. What opens up a distance becomes that which abolishes it. Everything goes on as if the most important thing about the resurrection of Christ were that it gave us a direct and adequate hold over God, in other words, as though it tipped the Risen One down into our world, rather than tipping him up into the transcendence of God. So I personally suddenly found myself in a truly strange situation: the closer I came to the Christian belief in the resurrection of Jesus Christ, the more the very factor which brought me closer to it led me to ask questions about the perversion which so completely overturns the meaning of the resurrection of Christ in this way, and thus to distance myself from all that seemed to me to use such a perversion for its profit. I was not led to distance myself from scripture, the sacraments, the institutions and so on, but from those authorities which are made the instruments of an immediate possession of Jesus Christ as a result of a certain conception of his resurrection.

This new reason for asking about what one can say of Jesus Christ and about the distance which has to be put between him and what one can say of him, coming on top of what had gone before, put me in a situation that seems to be forced on all Christians in the present conditions of our culture, whether they hide from it or not. This situation was no less difficult for not being an original one, not only because it disturbed aspects hitherto essential to my faith, but also because it confronted me with problems which could only be seen properly and solved by the collective labours of several generations of believers. So it was far beyond the limits of my strength and my lifetime. However, that did not prevent it from bearing down on me with all its weight and dispossessing me of something that was as deeply rooted in my individuality as in the institutions which had fashioned me and for which I had worked. So I had the feeling of finding myself naked and powerless, simply by virtue of the questions that I was persuaded my survival and the survival of faith required me to raise. But I was equally persuaded that it would have been even more fatal – although less tiring – to return to the former state of affairs.

2. How does God express himself in Jesus Christ?

Just as real decomposition does not content itself with affecting just one organ or another but ends by extending to all parts of the organism, so the decomposition which affected various ways of saying who Jesus Christ was extended to other questions about him. There again, even if I could only feel them as the somewhat terrifying symptoms of a real decomposition, these were essential questions about the whole of the believing community in its relationship to Jesus Christ, the content of which was such that it was impossible solely to impute them to the changes in my personality or the recent circumstances of my individual history. Their common feature was that in the end they raised not only the question of the distance which separated Jesus Christ from all that one can say of him but also that of the distance that it might perhaps be fitting to put between Jesus Christ himself and God. If it had been immediately apparent to me that this was what was at stake, I would certainly have done everything possible to prevent these questions being raised, since this time, being the Christian that I am, I seemed to feel the ground giving way under my feet. I had already had to accept a number of disturbances so that a distance could be opened up for me between Jesus Christ and what one could say of him, and I would have been very happy for things to remain there. Moreover, these questions initially posed themselves to me in their least disconcerting form; so I thought that I could accept them, all the more since they arose out of questions that were more or less disparate and scattered around in my experience. After that it was too late: this least disconcerting form, like a Trojan horse, brought in less reassuring forms which themselves came to resonate with a question which I shall mention in a moment, ending up with the frightening feeling that it might be necessary to introduce a distance between Jesus Christ and God himself; or, to be more precise (though this precision only appeared later; to begin with, the idea appeared in its brutal and unacceptable form), a distance between Jesus Christ and the absolute and divine image that has been made of him because of the manifestation of God in him and his unity with God.

What Lordship for Christ?

For the Christians of my generation, and beyond question especially for priests and religious, one theme related to Christ has been very important in our prayer, our spirituality and our apostolic life: the perfection of Jesus Christ, the way in which all the potentialities of the encounter between God and human beings are recapitulated in him, the way in which he possesses to the full all the perfections of the Christian life, not only because he was God in person but because with all his potentialities as true man he had committed himself to the realization of the plans of his Father. So Jesus Christ was both perfect man and the perfect form of encounter between human beings and God. I had long lived on the basis of that conviction, and I had seen many people around me doing the same thing; it was an important thing which led to other important things. Moreover, it was only in a very fragmentary and spasmodic way that I could entertain a question which, put more brutally, would have seemed to me to be too blasphemous to accept.

I understood very well, for example, why Paul (or the author of the captivity letters, if Paul did not write them) had felt the need to formulate the Lordship of Christ in the grandiose terms of recapitulation and plenitude which had so helped me to adore Christ as I used the christological hymns included in these letters. However, I came to ask myself how the great figure set up in certain writings of the New Testament and later orchestrated in Christian liturgy and art (as, for example, with the theme of the Pantocrator) fitted with what one could detect of the historical Jesus, particularly through the Synoptic Gospels. Faith in the lordship of Jesus Christ and his resurrection called for such a transformation of the assassinated Galilean prophet, who seemed to have renounced this type of power, not out of modesty, but to bear witness that this was not the kind of divine power that he came to manifest. Did Easter make what Jesus had refused in his lifetime, not only for himself but also for the God whose emissary he was, the best way of saying who Jesus Christ was and who was the God who had been manifest in him? I already had plenty of reasons for asking myself about the kind of megalomania which can be at work in the setting up of such figures, and later I shall say why I find it necessary to reject totalizing, generalizing and synthesizing representations, even – above all – where God is concerned. To this first question a second more radical one, more in keeping with the gospel, came to be added: I asked myself what Jesus of Nazareth would have thought of a certain kind of exaltation of himself and his God, since the three Synoptic Gospels told me through the temptation story that this is what he had refused for himself and for his God. Did the fact that he was raised from a death which was the most extraordinary sign of his rejection of this type of power for God and for his envoy authorize the restoration of this kind of power, as if the post-Easter conditions of the faith abolished what seemed to have been a key point in the life of Jesus and his manifestation of God? In that case, what was the significance of this exaltation of the omnipotence of Christ and of his utter perfection?

Does Jesus Christ recapitulate all human and Christian perfection?

The same question was bolstered by another reflection. The perfection of Christ was presented to us as the full realization of all that could and should happen between God and human beings: our own sanctity, our modest personal perfections were only a participation in what had been accomplished once and for all in Jesus Christ and would continue to the end of time as the total consummation that we would adore for ever. I began to feel some difficulties with this way of looking at things, all the more so since rightly or wrongly I rediscovered in it a conception of God that I had thought it necessary to give up and fight against: that of a God in whom the humanity of man and the worldliness of the world were finally to be absorbed so that he could be truly God and perfectly accomplish his plan. I had devoted the second quarter of the book which was condemned to the theme of God the creator. It seemed to me that for God to be creator did not mean that God should produce creatures whose supreme destiny would be to return to him in order to be absorbed in him as the river is dissolved in the sea. To be creator seemed to me to consist in producing creatures both different and like, creation being all the more perfect – as Thomas Aquinas had taught me – the more the creature had an intrinsic consistency and a vocation to be itself. This certainly implies a relationship with the creator but not dilution in its origin.

One way of conceiving Jesus as perfect man also seemed to me to dilute and absorb the specific character and consistency of human life in what Jesus Christ was thought to be fully, once for all. Because he was the Word made flesh, did Jesus Christ realize the potentialities of Christian perfection as they were realized, for example, by Thomas Aquinas, Thomas More or Teresa of Avila? Indeed he was the Word made flesh, but he was made flesh as a Galilean, and not as a Greek, a Roman, a Frenchman or a Chinese; he was only a prophet and not the father of a family, a peasant, an intellectual, a politician, a monk or a bishop; he was a man and not a woman. I reminded myself of something very obvious which one may nevertheless have powerful reasons for hiding from oneself or reducing to trivial banality. Jesus Christ had not by himself been all the perfection of human life: he had had the perfections corresponding to his individual condition and his vocation, and not others. His own perfection did not devalue the others any more than it replaced them, but for all that it did not find itself devalued. For his perfection did not consist in having all perfections, nor was his mission not to accomplish everything. What was true of his human perfection was equally so – if one can speak of Jesus Christ in this way – of his Christian perfections. Jesus devoted himself wholly to the realization of his vocation and his mission, and for him that was to bear the name which is above every name and before which every knee bows. But he is the firstborn of a multitude of brothers and sisters and not an all-embracing totality of which each of these brothers and sisters would only be a part, destined to be absorbed into the whole. Jesus did not have all the Christian perfections, but this does not devalue the other Chirstian perfections which were not his. It is even necesary to reject the view, however widespread, that the perfections which he did not have are only the development of the potentialities that one could find in those which he did have: this would be to make the same mistake as over God the creator. Jesus Christ is the principle and the initiator of the Christian life; he is not its totality.

Someone might tell me that all this is trivial stuff. I would reply that these trivialities are almost blasphemous in the context of a view of Jesus Christ which has been so evocative over so mnay centuries, and that these trivialities decompose the view in question. When I had to express them for the first time I had an inner compulsion to use the device of a kind of *Charlie-Hebdo* style, a style which I had never used before. Nor did I usc it again. Nevertheless it forced itself on me: a certain kind of satirical comic is a way of looking askew at what it would be impossible to look at directly. This foray should not be imputed to the vagaries of my personality, since certain of my fellow theologians who are generally well disposed towards me thought that my text was literally blasphemous. So we have to accept the power of the mechanism which impels us to attribute to Jesus Christ perfections which were not his and a type of plenitude which is not his. People carry on as if to deny him these perfections amounted to denying the perfections and the plenitude which are his. So are we condemned to the 'all or nothing' attitude to Jesus Christ on the grounds that he was the Word made flesh? One certainly cannot find the basis of the widespread terrorism which cries out 'Jesus Christ or nothing!' in what can be discerned of the historical Jesus. What kind of omnipotence or panic does such terrorism produce? If it is so strong, think of the decomposition needed to put an end of it and to introduce the distance which allows one to say that Jesus is not the whole of Christian life, even if he is the Word made flesh!

Does Jesus Christ recapitulate all revelation of God?

To tell the truth, perhaps this last question only takes on its full force when it is joined by another question which Christians of today cannot escape having to ask themselves. What distance should be established, not just between Jesus Christ and the totality of Christian life, but in a certain sense between Jesus Christ and God? Some integralist circles showed evidence of very clear thinking when, in the course of the Second Vatican Council, they fought in a particularly obstinate way against the conciliar text on religious freedom. This text recognized that forms of Christianity other than Roman Catholicism had a real and authentically Christian value; it also recognized that other monotheistic religions (Judaism and Islam) had a real religious value, and it even went so far as to recognize that all religions could have a certain religious value. Of course the authors of this text did not in any way renounce their conviction that Roman Catholicism was the most perfect form of religion, but they did not present the other religions as void or non-existent, or as degenerate forms or pale foreshadowings of the true Roman Catholic religion. In so doing, they confirmed a conviction acquired at great cost (sometimes even against the Roman Catholic church) in the course of the last two centuries, by the most high-minded of thinkers. But they confronted the Catholic mentality with a difficult situation, which the integralists saw could well be formidable.

In fact, once one attaches a real value to other religions while seeking to preserve the superiority of Catholicism, the first thought is that the authentic elements in the other religions derive from their more or less conscious participation in the qualities of the Catholic religion. Now this problem is directly related to one's conception of Jesus Christ and the way in which he is the Word made flesh. If Jesus Christ is, according to certain traditional dogmatic formulations, the Son of God made man, he has a monopoly – if I might put it that way – in the encounter between God and human beings. Any other encounter between God and humanity to which one would want to accord some truth must have the capacity in one way or another to be associated with the full and unique encounter that is Jesus Christ. Indeed that was claimed by the Fathers of the church from the first centuries of the Christian era, whether with regard to Judaism and the Old Testament, or the Greek philosophers, for example Plato: with more conviction than historic sense, they did not hesitate to show that all religious achievements before Christ had been announcements and anticipations of Christ.

In theory the method remains the same today. However, a number of factors have made it harder to apply. On the one hand, unlike the fathers of the church, we are no longer just confronted with religions which preceded Christianity and have existed in the same cultural sphere. We are confronted with religions existing in completely different cultural spheres from that in which Christianity was born, or with later religions which were sometimes formed to counter it, not to mention those which have arisen out of its own inner divisions. On the other hand, we have a completely different sense of history from that of the men of antiquity or the Middle Ages. We are certainly aware of a degree of continuity between Judaism and Christianity, since Christianity is a Jewish heresy which has succeeded; however, even if Judaism no longer existed today, it would be impossible to reduce its essence to being an announcement of Christianity. As for seeing Buddhism, Hinduism, or African or Amero-Indian religions as announcements of Chrsitianity, that would be utterly ridiculous.

But how does one recognize the religious value of the other religions without devaluing the unique role of Jesus Christ in the encounter between God and human beings? How does one stress the unique role of Jesus Christ in this encounter without devaluing the real religious worth of the other religions? I myself think that the Christian mentality is not yet equipped to overcome this dilemma, and that we shall doubtless have to wait for several generations before we can tackle it. At present, in fact, Christianity formulates and proclaims the absolutely unique role of Jesus Christ in the revelation of God by means of categories which it has inherited from former centuries; however, these categories were not developed in connection with this problem and do not allow it to be resolved. According to them, to affirm the specific role of Jesus Christ necessarily implied attributing to Jesus Christ the value of all other religions; that is certainly why the integralists protested so violently against the Council's affirmation of a religious freedom which recognized a specific value in other religions. However, the majority of us find it impossible to conceive of the truth of these religions in this way. I am not a great expert on such matters, but one of the rare services that I still perform for an academic institute of theology is to make extracts for review purposes from a review of the history of religions and an archive of the sociology of religion. Once one has the occasion, however limited, to enter the universe of other religions, one is compelled to acknowledge that there are other quests of God which pass by other ways than Jesus Christ. One even has to ask whether there are not other revelations of God which pass by other ways than by Jesus Christ. The question is not purely academic: an older Dominican whom I knew, an eminent specilaist in Iranian and related religions, said as a joke that to his knowledge he was the only priest of his generation specializing in the history of religions who 'had not been defrocked' (*sic!*). That is an indication of how true it is that once one discovers the authenticity of the other religions one comes to put in question the status of Jesus Christ as the revealer of God.

Are we here once again condemned to 'all or nothing'? Must we practise the terrorism which consists in refusing all religious value to other religions (except in so far as they anticipate or participate in

Christianity) in order to preserve the originality of the role of Jesus Christ as the revelation of God? Or are we condemned to reducing Jesus Christ to the level of being no more than a great religious genius of humanity in order to respect the religious value of these other religions? In the present state of our thinking this dilemma would seem to be inescapable. But the absurdity of the dilemma shows that our way of thinking must change, even if we do not yet know how, even if we perhaps have the feeling that beyond the hyperbolic exaltation of Jesus Christ that we find in Christianity we have to rediscover that the assassinated Galilean prophet in whom the Word of God was made flesh was perhaps less pretentious than these hyperboles (while being more convinced and more committed to his God than any integralist or progressive group). In other words, is it not in Jesus Christ himself that we shall find the most effective pointers towards establishing a distance between Jesus Christ and an inadequate absolutization of Jesus Christ? Is it not in Jesus Christ himself that we shall find a possible principle of coexistence between two groups which seem contradictory to our present way of thinking: on the one hand the proclamation by faith of the radical and plenary decision of Jesus Christ for God and of the radical and plenary commitment of God in his revelation in Jesus Christ, and on the other hand respect for radical and plenary decisions of another kind for God, and for the radical commitment of God in these other revelations which are realized in these other decisions? Can Christianity perhaps find its truth and that of Jesus Christ otherwise than by arrogating a more or less explicit monopoly of divine revelation? I do not know the answer, and as I have already said, we shall probably need several generations to find it. While we are waiting, I should point out that such a question, inevitable though it may be, is often dismissed because it would seem to erode the role of Jesus Christ as the Word of God made flesh, Lord and Saviour. Because Christianity hitherto has usually thought of this role in terms of a monopoly which excludes or swallows up the other religions, putting the question correctly necessarily involves the decomposition of the Catholic system at an absolutely essential point, namely that of the relationship between Jesus Christ and God. The idea that perhaps there should be some distance between the one and the other can only appear to Catholicism as a decomposition of that on which it is based and which it seeks to announce (not to mention the universal power which it claims in the name of this foundation and this mission). Since I have been trained and formed by this system, such an idea inevitably presented itself to me as a decomposition of my being as a Catholic and even of my being as a Christian.

3. How does one bring a word about God to birth?

Metamorphoses in the decomposition of communication

The theological character of the different questions that I have just raised about Jesus Christ should not give the impression that the process of decomposition that they provoke is purely intellectual. If that were the case, it would not amount to much: ideas aren't a great deal. But that is not the case, since I do not study the theology of Christianity as a scholar at Paris, Oxford or Harvard might study the theology of very ancient religions which do not have an immediate influence on his or her personal way of existing, because he or she is not a believing adherent of such religions. I believe in the God of Jesus Christ, and even if my way of believing has changed a great deal since I was a child, the fact of believing is much more important to me today than when I was a child. Moreover, I have been a Dominican for more than thirty years, so I am devoted to speaking of God and Jesus Christ; for twenty-five years I have been in the front line of this vocation to theology. Even when this vocation to speak of God and Jesus Christ, to pray to them and celebrate them, began to occupy a different place in my existence, it still continued to play just as basic and irreplacable a role in my life, and doubtless it will continue to do so until my death, whatever may be the changes in my mode of life which are forced on me or which I decide to adopt.

It is not only my person which is steeped in and structured by the importance of the fact of saying God and Jesus Christ: so too are the institutions to which I have chosen to belong and which have so profoundly shaped me by the importance which they attach to 'praising, blessing, preaching' (this is one of the mottoes of the Dominican Order) that I am no longer very sure what in me is of their making rather than of my own. The decomposition of the idea of God and the idea of Jesus Christ, or rather – if one can put it this way – the decomposition of the God and the Christ who once were mine, is something other than a purely intellectual process: it touches me at my innermost core, dismembering me and weakening me. I began here by speaking of my decomposition as preacher, president at the eucharist and theologian; I went on to speak of the decomposition of the 'apostolic' religious life, and I am ending by speaking of the decomposition of the God and the Jesus Christ who for so long were mine. However, to tell the truth, any distinction between these three decompositions is somewhat artificial, so closely are they entangled. Without doubt they were already more or less at work during the period when I was writing the book that was condemned, but its very title, *When I say God*, and its content prove that I was not yet raising the questions that I am raising here. The circumstances which resulted in its condemnation without doubt accelerated the process, while bringing to the forefront of my preoccupations matters more directly related to the functions which were forbidden me.

Ultimately, however, these prohibitions have only a secondary importance in that the processes of decomposition in question do not depend on them and do not even depend on me; they depend on a situation which is both internal and external to Western Catholicism, a situation which many men and women of my generation, younger and indeed older people, may have experienced. How many of us do not ask what they can still say about God and Jesus Christ, how many of us do not ask whether we do not need a pause so that we can see how God and Jesus Christ can be said? Some people, of course, feel precisely the opposite: that they need to go back to rediscover the ancient certainties; others feel the symmetrical need to leap over the gulf and rapidly rediscover the ancient certainties dressed up in new finery. Yet others more or less provisionally shut up shop in order to take stock and occupy themselves with other things, including 'religion' (because it is very easy to get caught up in 'religion' and hardly ask about God at all). However, a great many men and women have taken upon themselves the hard task of the alchemy which will allow the decomposition of the old and the appearance of the new. To judge from my own case, this is not so much as a virtue or by a personal decision as by the force of circumstances and a sense that it is impossible to do otherwise; to be oneself, one must be caught up in this process the consequences of which one does not know; one only knows, at least in the rare moments when one can look oneself in the face, that things would be far worse otherwise.

My past and my choices mean that I enjoy conditions that I have to regard as being very favourable; I have no family or professional responsibilities, and I have hardly any problems over money and lodging. In a sense, to decompose is all I have to do (though might that be a disadvantage?). At all events, I can devote more time and energy than the majority of my lay friends, men and women, and even than the majority of my religious friends, monks, nuns and priests, since technically I have been made redundant. So I have more opportunity to devote myself to this decomposition, which seems to me to be indispensable. Perhaps the measures taken against me even create even more favourable circumstances, to the degree that – as one learns in physics and chemistry – particular conditions of pressure and temperature allow one to achieve processes that are impossible in usual conditions – provided that the safety valve does not blow. However, over the days, the weeks, the months, indeed over the years – since this has now been going on for several years – I have had the painful feeling that these more favourable conditions of availability, pressure and temperature have their other side. I am more deeply affected, more thoroughly taken over, more completely decomposed than if I had something else to do; if I had work which was interesting enough, useful enough, dynamic and companionable enough to keep me going, or quite simply work which helped me by its immediacy, everyday nature or even triviality. It would also be less hard if the temperature and pressure were lower. But I have no choice. Besides, how many men and women of my age still have a choice, and over what? I must try not to fail over the last stages, and since the present stage takes this form I must try not to spoil my decomposition by interrupting it or slowing it down, putting limits on it, tracing its ways. I must simply try to hold on, if that does not go against the very process of decomposition...

The mystical way?

But how does one hold on? I have never claimed to have a head for mysticism; in these circumstances I found it difficult not to dream of what all the mystics say about the trials which they experienced in their quest for God, the long nights which have come down on them without any gleam of light appearing to help them to believe again in the day. Perhaps their experience could be of some help to me? Was this at last a precedent? Had I companions at last? But that could not be the case, for several reasons (I firmly leave on one side the difference between these geniuses and me as human beings and as believers). The first reason is that the mystics almost always present the trials that they encounter as stages marking their successive progress along the route that they are following. These trials seem to be both the consequence of their earlier advances and a preparation for later progress. Beginners do not experience them, since the first trials are a sign that they must go beyond the naivety of the first stage; similarly, those who are more advanced know that the most painful trials follow the most sublime joys. So these trials are proportional to the quality of the subject who undergoes them and to the degree of his or her previous attainments: they are both a sign of advanced perfection and a way towards an even greater perfection.

It is impossible for me to give such an interpretation of my own situation. The categories of perfection and imperfection or of progress and setback seem to me to be unsuitable as a guide to what is happening to me. Certainly faith is branded on me, body and soul, and I have the feeling of having made progress. At least I feel that I have developed in a positive direction, even if this development has often opened up a gulf separating me from traditional conceptions of God and attitudes towards him, in a way which might seem to others to be more of a setback. But how could I experience that in terms of the increasing perfection of my faith, when I am not even sure that I am right in believing, and when I am quite sure that many of my reasons for believing are not of the best kind?

Besides, the mystics experienced their trials in great affective solitude and often in the face of the marked hostility of those around them. Now I am not in a great affective solitude – that is the least that one could say. While the supreme authorities of the organized Roman Catholic church may have maltreated me to some degree, that part of the church which is my prime authority, namely my local church, has done more than just support me, even if it does not approve of all my ideas and all my behaviour; in the Dominican Order, my local and national superiors and their governing councils have fought vigorously on my behalf and even now continue to be a precious support to me; in my community there is certainly a small minority of religious who will look on my departure with relief, and one eminent and venerable Dominican who lives on my floor has long muttered a litany of, 'Villain, villain, villain...' whenever he meets me; however, the majority treat me in a brotherly manner, and some have a way, as they pass me in the corridor, of saying, 'Hello Jacques, how are things?' which on some days introduces a little breath of air without which I sometimes wonder how I would find the courage to go on. So even if I am the only one who can follow my particular course, I am not in the situation of solitude and hostility described by the mystics. That is all the more the case since to the various kinds of support which I have just mentioned must be added countless friends, men and women, believers and non-believers, individuals and groups. I have had the good fortune to share in the quest for, the sharing of God which inspires a number of informal groups of which I am a member; I have had the good fortune that my personal quest for God has proved important to a certain number of men and women, and even to unbelievers whose esteem and friendship are as precious to me as those of believers. So I belong to a kind of local church which matters a lot to me, even if it does not always cast light on what my route should be.

There is yet another reason why I cannot draw inspiration from the experience of the mystics in facing the various decompositions that I have to undergo. Their experience is in fact essentially an individual experience, while mine relates to reasons which have very little to do with the vicissitudes of my personal career. In saying that the experience of the mystics is essentially individual, obviously I do not want to say that they live in a vacuum; when one knows the lives of Teresa of Avila, John of the Cross or Catherine of Siena, it would be wrong to present them as living out their mystical experience in a vacuum. Nevertheless, the vicissitudes of their mystical journey are directly bound up with their personal relationship with God, and we watch them in wonder pursuing their hard road as one admires Alpine climbers making solo climbs of exceptional difficulty. The fact that their exploits can later have consequences for so many Christian men and women in search of God does not detract at all from the primarily and predominantly personal character of their ventures. This character is confirmed by the way in which people have then gone on to designate by their first name or their surname a kind of sanctity, a method of praying, a family of experiences: the mystics leave a name, not only because of their exceptional individual worth but also because of the personal character of their venture.

It is quite different in my case. Certainly I am good for something in what is happening to me, I am its agent and its subject, for better or for worse. My faith – in the sense of the virtue of faith – is there for some reason; it may also be that the experience of psychoanalysis has taught me not to shunt my fear and anguish into a siding and let them build up in me without resorting too much to the protection of different defence mechanisms; it could equally be that the various confidences that people have placed in me allow me to venture into areas inaccessible to anyone who did not enjoy such help. But while all that is certainly important, it is little to set beside the collective character of the factors in the decompositions in question here. Whether it is a matter of preaching, presiding at the eucharist or teaching, of the forms of apostolic religious life, or of the distance to be put between God or Jesus Christ and what we say of them, the factors in question are in no way specific to me and concern the whole

Western Catholic system. Numerous Christian men and women have to cope with them as I do.

My way of doing things is certainly personal, and I have been fortunate enough to gather evidence that others could use to their advantage; so it is not strictly individual. But the essential thing is that what we have is a decomposition of systems: systems of religious activities, systems of religious ways of life, systems for representing God and Christ. And even if one has to gather all one's strength and commit oneself individually with all one's strength, to a degree that I could never have imagined, the processes in question are above all social processes, in which the mutations and decompositions endemic in present-day Western society and the mutations and decompositions which confront the Roman Catholic system come together and multiply. From this perspective, what is happening here is rather different from journeys in which nights of meaning and the spirit alternate with the ecstasies in the life of mystics in a way which is essentially personal to them and is not directly related, as in my case, to social structures and what is happening to them. There were days when I regretted this, because had mine been an essentially personal journey I might perhaps have been able to entertain the hope of coming out of it, even if I do not feel very well endowed for that kind of venture. But once the causes and solutions of problems, and even a proper perception of them, are related to social structures which at every point extend beyond my personal case, it becomes almost impossible to see a solution in the medium term (since I am no longer young enough to wait for the long term). But in some ways misfortune is a good thing: the collective character of the problems in question allows me to have some companionship with other men and other women, which was not the experience of the great mystics, since their elevation gave them disciples or detractors rather than companions.

The last reason which prevents me from looking for support to the example of the great mystics is more decisive, since it involves God and the image one has of him. I shall not speak here so much of the actual letter of the texts that these great mystics have left us or of their personal experience as deciphered by their interpreters in all the meanderings which are accessible to us, since I do not feel that I have the competence for either of those studies. I shall content myself with the use that we make of these texts and experiences at a less elevated but more common level, and of the role that we make them play in the conception that we have of the knowledge of God and of the more perfect forms that it can take. What dissuades me from this use of the great mystics is the dialectic of 'all or nothing' in which it imprisons us, as though this dialectic were that of God himself. Everything seems to happen as if for God to be God, the creature has to become nothing and to consider itself as being nothing; once it accepts this annihilation, it can hope to receive everything from God and be almost identical to God, through being united with him and submerged in him: the strength of this 'mystical union' and this fusion are proportionate to the magnitude of the annihilation which has made them possible and prepared them. The 'Nothing, nothing, nothing' of John of the Cross is highly praised, but people are more discreet about its exact counterpart, his otherwise very beautiful poem which says, 'All is mine, the sky is mine, the world is mine, God is mine...' People stress the *little* way of Thérèse of the Infant Jesus and cannot find adjectives delicate enough to say how humble and discreet is the littleness of her way, but the exact counterpart of this littleness is less well known: *little* Thérèse is the one who said, 'I just want to be a queen.' People praise the phrase heard by Catherine of Siena when Christ appeared to her and said, 'I am He who is Everything and you are she who is nothing', and do not see the link between this annihilation and the omnipotence which allows her to put herself above the laws of nature (she is said to have lived for a long time eating only one eucharistic host a day), to lead popes by the nose and to guide those men and women whom she directed along the ways of salvation with an iron fist which made the most intrepid tremble.

I already have good psychological reasons for mistrusting the strategies and stratagems of this 'all or nothing' dialectic; I know something of the significance for the unconscious of the profound conviction that this man or woman who has nothing also has nothing to lose, and can, by the same token, be everything: the first assurance is no less powerful – and no less fallacious – than the second. Moreover, I have found reasons, which I believe to be important both for Christianity and for theology, for thinking that this dialectic of 'all or nothing' is not the right dialectic for the relationship between God and human beings. God does not want to be Everything to the human being and his name is not Everything: his name is God, and it is God that he wants to be for human beings. He is not God because human beings reduce themselves to nothing in order to make him Everything (and to make certain that they, poor mortals, can unite themselves and fuse themselves with nothing less than Everything). God is creator: as I stressed so strongly in the part of *When I say God* which I devoted to this, the creation, far from finding its fulfilment in the annihilation of the creature, finds it in the establishment of the creature in its difference. The fact that God is creator signifies both that he does not want to be Everything and that he does not want humans to be nothing.

However, at the same time – and this is where the shoe pinches – the creature can no longer hope, in annihilating itself before the one who is Everything, to shelter from the risk of losing nothing and to guarantee that it can be everything. So I think that we do double injury to God if we impute this dialectic of 'all or nothing' to him, since we deform what he wants to be as God the creator and we also deform what he wants for his creature, thus doing damage both to human beings and their world, and to God. Such a way of conceiving God is definitely ruled out for me, and even if certain assertions or certain hypotheses in *When I say God* now seem to me mistakes or dead ends, I remain proud that a Swiss Protestant psychoanalyst said to me that a good sub-title for this book would have been, 'or the victory of faith over all or nothing'. I said there, and I say it again: I do not claim that the letter and the spirit of the great mystics or their personal experience, carefully deciphered, allow one to reduce their message to this dialectic of 'all or nothing'. I simply claim – and there is abundant proof of this – that that is the way in which they are used. And I was not concerned specifically with them, though I have read them and meditated on them, but with the role which Catholic spirituality and mysticism have made them play by popularizing them. And I learned that that was fatal: the massacre of human beings and their world, but also the massacre of the Creator God and his creation. So the mystical way was closed to me, not only because of my scant aptitude for it, but also because it so often seemed to me to be a dead end.

Easter 1981

But in that case, if even that way was closed to me, what could I do? I did not see any other course, and in a sense I still do not see any other course than to let decomposition do its work: all the decompositions that I have mentioned, and others which will doubtless only reveal themselves later. I must let them do their work, not disturb them, let this fermentation, this alchemy, this obscure geology take place. I must not hold back the continents. I must not break the moorings which prevent them from clashing, and I must not be too disturbed (for I am only human: I cannot but be disturbed a little, indeed a lot), I must not be too disturbed by smells, fermentation, decay. I once read Aristotle on corruption and generation. I found a

comfort which some people may perhaps find surprising in what
Prigogine said about the unstable systems of non-linear thermodyn-
amics and the role played there by 'dissipative structures' (an apparently contradictory expression, but one which was enough for him
to have won the Nobel prize): I was caught up in an unstable linear
thermodynamic system and I had not to stabilize it too soon; above
all I had not to try to replace the dissipative structures with fixed or
fixative structures. In a sense that is where I still am. I know nothing
of the future. I believe – why do I believe it, and how? – I believe that
God is faithful. I believe that he does not do things wrong. But how
is he faithful, and to what? I do not want to force myself to reply too
quickly, to be too quick to give a content to this fidelity. Not because
there is none, but because of the distance that needs to be introduced
between this fidelity and the content that I have given it.

However, a strange light appeared in this gloom some months ago.
It is still shining faintly. It was Easter, this year. On Maundy Thursday
I had gone – in a lay capacity – to a celebration in a provincial
cathedral where the chances of liturgical arrangement had put me
behind the bishop. He shook my hand in all innocence and with great
affability when he gave the peace: the poor dear man who more than
ten years ago had done me a real service with great kindness evidently
had not recognized me! I had not been too unhappy at this celebration
and I had thought more of Jesus Christ than of the celebrations and
sermons of which I had been in charge on earlier Maundy Thursdays
– and that was rather a good sign. On Good Friday, in the quiet of a
friendly house where the lady of the house and I were the only
believers, in my room we read the text of the passion of Jesus Christ
according to John and then we prayed Psalm 22: ' My God, my God,
why have you forsaken me?' I was in the state of malaise which
almost always comes over me as I remember Maundy Thursdays
twenty or thirty years ago at Le Saulchoir: parts of the night spent in
adoration before the blessed sacrament, the almost complete fast
throughout the whole of this long day, the total silence (even the
clocks were stopped), the black scapular that we kept on even at
table over our white robes, and the offices, the splendid offices of
Tenebrae and above all the Adoration of the Cross, which I knew by
heart, having participated in it as cantor over the years. I had
experienced all that and loved it, and ⁊ do not regret it. Since then I
have experienced and organized other celebrations, and I have
preached on other Good Fridays: 'It is good that a man should die
for God; it is good that a God should die for man...' I do not regret
that at all. I know that nowadays we should do something different,

something that we have not yet invented. Meanwhile, I was there, between two worlds, between two ages, I still had this text and this psalm, this celebration *à deux* reduced to a bare minimum, with this inner feeling of decomposition and incorrigible nostalgia. A strange Good Friday. The Saturday was even harder: nothing. No celebration, many memories, especially of a somewhat fantastic episode helping my brother Cardonnel to celebrate a paschal mass at Plogoff in a country setting with the background of the nuclear power station, and deep down this certainty that it was wrong to go back, impossible to go forward, and unbearable to stay still. I went for a walk, at least content that nature had made me in such a way that I did not inflict the burdens which sometimes overwhelmed me on those around me – except for very, very intimate friends.

And then, all at once, something made itself felt: gently, almost crudely. Inconvenient, unacceptable, revolting a minute later, and suddenly there, tranquil and soothing in spite of its content. I had just understood something. I had to renounce God. Renounce God... Incredible! All the more incredible since it was not a matter of no longer believing in God, no longer bothering myself with him, for the moment or once and for all. What I had to do was to renounce the God on whom I thought I had a hold, of whom I thought I could speak, whom I thought I could celebrate, to whom I was dedicated. I had to let God go, liberate him, break the ties by which I wanted to hold him because I was too afraid. I had to let him be himself, let him go, so that he would return as he wanted, when he wanted, in the way he wanted. I had to renounce God. If someone had told me this some moments earlier, I would not even have understood. Some moments later it was clear, simple, evident. It was also tranquil and soothing. Decomposition had to go to the point of renouncing God. I knew all at once that it really had been Easter. I don't know very clearly what death and resurrection are. But I do know that it was a good Easter. A transition. A deliverance. It called on me to renounce God.

I shall try.

II

On the Other Side

Interlude

Six months have elapsed since I wrote the previous pages. Six months of a long silence. True, they were broken up into weeks by the various courses I had to go on in the provinces in order to earn my living in part-time 'secular' work (all that is now possible for me if I do not want to sponge off my community). And I spent many hours with groups, some of which met regularly and some of which did not, with friends or strangers, groups often formed to seek God and share him. But the length of my silence is due above all to my having in some way to catch up with what I had written.

The first weeks which followed my writing had been peaceful and surprisingly happy: I returned to it just after shaking off the decomposition that was disturbing me, and while I was not suprised that this release had exhausted me, I was astonished that it left me not so much empty as alive, indeed almost mobile. As the weeks passed, I was to discover that I had projected these pages before me, as part of me which had ventured out beyond the advance posts. The bulk of the troops found it difficult to keep up. The decomposition had been enough to show breaches in my defences which allowed me to worm my way out, but it had not yet sufficiently eroded the bulk of the fortress.

With a weariness combined with a degree of repugnance, I had again to let decomposition dominate the days and weeks and occupy them, the latter word having more the military sense of occupation than that of purposeful activity. Those days were long. And empty. In comparison with earlier periods, I still had the slight advantage of having written the preceding pages:the hope of being able to emerge again had its fragile basis in this viaticum. But this hope and faith are also 'the substance of things that one does not possess'. And the emptiness, the unknown, the virtual certainty of not being able to emerge from the decomposition made my few pages, which were all too likely to remain incomplete, seem somewhat derisory. I was sometimes frightened to feel the force of the resistance which had been set up in me to the victory that I had achieved this summer by having sufficient of an inkling to be able to write. This force was all the more discouraging since I had not succeeded in identifying what lay behind it. I simply noted, with a helplessness that was sometimes sad and sometimes angry, that I had not succeeded in detaching myself from what had seemed to me to be the kingdom of death.

In a bizarre way, I knew that there was no need to despair when I saw that decomposition was attacking a region which hitherto had been relatively stable, despite the upheavals that I have already described. I was clearly subject to a strange liturgical cycle: at Easter, it had become evident that I had to renounce God; the following Christmas, it seemed to me that I had to accept another renunciation, which I shall mention again in due course. However, I would not have believed that there might have to be yet another renunciation: had I not tried to let go of the essentials? Obviously not. This is something to which I shall return. But the fact that part of me could again worm its way through the defences that I had erected in order to venture into new regions at least indicated that the defences had been shifted.

Without doubt I would have preferred to be able to breathe a little, to nurse some wounds, enjoy a convalescence, regain health. But I had begun to learn that one does not dictate the ways and rhythms of decomposition, even if one resists them. This summer's writing had certainly been made possible only because part of me had already managed to rejoin that other part of me which had ventured into the regions that only that writing had allowed me really to discover, even if it had then taken weeks and months for another part to come after it. I have still not caught up with this more recent movement which was set off by my discovery at Christmas. Only the scouts have crossed over the wall, and if I forced myself to describe the way they have struggled through, I would be anticipating what might be achieved by the consolidation of a more important part of my forces which at this stage is impossible. Certainly, writing makes one aware of what one has written, but before that a more or less unconscious alchemy has had to allow what is about to be written to feed on a more substantial part of oneself. I think that the moment has not yet come: it will doubtless have to wait for the end of this book. If I were to anticipate it, I would be making a mistake similar to the one which compromised the last part of my earlier book (*When I say God*), the part about death and resurrection. I think in fact that if this last part is unsatisfactory, it is because I was too eager to put into writing what were still only tentative experiments, byways and obscure tracks in a region which was still almost virgin. So I must wait.

This need to wait has produced a favourable opportunity for another piece of writing which is a necessary sequel to what I have already written, and prepares the way for what comes next. I do not yet know what the last part will be called. I gave the first one a name: decomposition. I am calling this section 'On the Other Side'. I want to venture on this other side that we have not yet explored enough. It is where faith must spend time if it is to have the power to speak of God again. It is the side that believers have to reach, since that is where life now goes on, rather than where we were. That is where we must go, leaving Ur and our native land. Those who are alive are over there. And at least I know that God is the God of the living and not of the dead. If he comes today, if he comes tomorrow, he will come there.

To tell the truth, what I shall be writing about is not so much a side of which we can have an overall view as regions the precise relationship between which cannot yet be described, even if it is already quite clear that they are very dependent on one another. Not only do we not know what ties unite them; we cannot draw their exact contours, take stock of what lies within them. Each of these regions is still unfamiliar to us; we must stay there, live there, steep ourselves in them before we can say any more about them. It will already be something if I manage to give some impression of the air that one breathes there, the energies one needs, the way in which they conflict, counteract one another, combine. We are at a stage of human experience, a period of the spirit in which there must be no rush to reduce the many to one, to organize diversity, to derive the plural from the universal. We must know how to postpone the syntheses in order not to distort what we are just beginning to glimpse.

That will be very difficult, since we shall be dealing with the oldest and commonest phenomena. How can one make their newness pierce through all previous experiences, words, theories? It will be very difficult, since we shall be dealing with the most fascinating and the most disturbing realities in the human world. They are so powerful and so dangerous that people feel the need to rush to master them, out of a need to eradicate them, or conversely to allow themselves to be carried away with them without taking the time to decipher their appearance somewhat.

We shall in fact be dealing with death, with sexuality and with guilt. Perhaps we shall be dealing with other things, too, but as yet I do not know whether there will be anything to write about them. Nevertheless, I know just how much they exert pressure on our life. These are such matters as work, money, power, the relationship between the rich and the poor. People have talked a great deal about them and keep on talking. However, they do so in a way which is often strangely dumb. As a 'moral' theologian familiar with psychoanalysis, I have myself written a great deal about all these things, in works which since then have come to seem to be written almost in a foreign language. Today, while I would not claim, far less be able, to forget all my previous knowledge and experience, in trying to escape the need for system and synthesis where we are impelled less by our intellectual twitches than by the disturbing power of those forces which we must control at any price, I want to compel myself to feel, to sense what is new in our experience of death, sexuality and guilt. I want to allow the new relationship that we have with these things to burst through the surface of the never-ending talk and gigantic institutions that we have built to make ourselves masters of what escapes us, while still controlling us.

My reason for speaking of these things is connected with God: how we can view him, talk about him and seek him. Faith has always been partly bound up with death, sexuality and guilt and has run into trouble with them. God is a God who comes, and who comes from elsewhere than man: he comes from God. But he comes among us, in us, and in what we experience of him; what we say of him is taken, fashioned, conformed, deformed, annexed, humiliated, subjugated, served, exalted, magnified by all that takes place in us and among us under the signs of death, sexuality, guilt, power and the power-relationships between rich and poor. However, it seems to me that our experience of death, sexuality and guilt in the West at the end of the twentieth century is in process of changing. It no longer happens at the same place, and what happens is no longer the same thing. So we must go to the other side, and let this other experience break through. The old alliances and the way in which the old experiences embodied God must decompose so that new alliances become possible, until they themselves have to disappear in another century.

I make no claim to be able to give a good description of these new experiences. Who could, since they have only been with us since yesterday and have hardly begun to express themselves today? Moreover, I am no longer particularly young, and a good deal of me belongs in the old world. Finally, much that I have chosen and much that I have done over the years has perhaps made me more remote than other human beings from areas and ways of living where what we are looking for might appear. But I am sufficiently aware of the fact to be obliged to say that these old alliances are now fatal, and we must break them. Not primarily because they have been pernicious and false in themselves – I no longer have the taste nor the strength for such diagnoses – but because the old world is passing. And we must allow the decomposition of the way in which that world took advantage of God, the way in which faith took advantage of him, if we want God to be able to be God as he means to, that is to say, the same and the other, the eternal and the new in a world which is new because it has changed. And after almost thirty years of work, I think that that is something I can talk about.

Because I had the good fortune – yes, it really is good fortune, provided that one does not die of it – to experience the decomposition of these old alliances between God and death, between God and sexuality, between God and guilt, I want to indicate here how they take God prisoner and alienate human beings, distort faith in God, turn God from human beings, put human beings off God, themselves and one another. I want to destroy these figures which become idols of God and humanity, which transform God and human beings into idols. Destroy them for what God? I do not know. For what human beings? I do not know. For what new alliances? I do not know. But we have to begin by leaving the kingdom of death. And to do that we have to try to identify the faces of the idols, call them by their names. So that we can go over to the other side. So that human beings are not held back from going to stay there, since that is now where their life lies. So that God can come, if there is a God and if he is a God who comes. To establish whatever new alliance there may be, if there is one.

I

Death*

An original experience of death

What do I know of death, personally and in not too indirect a way? Virtually nothing. During the 1939-1945 war I only spent a few days clearing up (ruins and corpses) after bombardments which I had not even experienced. Some years later, a road accident almost cost me my life and that of my passengers; however, at the time, since I was driving, I was too busy trying to get my vehicle under control to think of death, and immediately afterwards, since my injury proved slight, I was much more preoccupied with the others in the accident who were more seriously injured, since the whole thing was my fault. I have never had a serious illness which made me fear death. As for a certain spirituality of death which was once much prized, according to which death is the key moment of our destiny, the one in which we can again become aware of the whole course of our life, it has never had much appeal. I have never been tempted to resort to it in order to think of my own death and to integrate this thought into the awareness of my life: the little that I know of life and death persuades me that death most often presents itself as a decomposition of life and particularly of consciousness, and that therefore it cannot be its climax.

It is true that what we know of death is inspired less by our own death than by that of others, particularly those close to us. Even if I have found myself very closely involved in the death of one friend or another, the little of the ministry of the classical type that I have been able to perform has hardly brought me to the bedsides of the sick or the dying. As for the death of those closest to me, certainly I have often found myself alongside friends, men and women, who have just lost a child or a partner. It was difficult to know what to say if

---

* This chapter on death was written in February 1982 in Paris and in July-August 1982 at Parc-Trihorn.

they remarked that it was hardly something that I, a celibate priest, could understand. Be this as it may, even if I was able at a very late stage to begin to feel what such a break could mean, is it pain that allows us to understand pain? Just think how much better we would understand one another were that the case. I have not yet had what is said to be another crucial experience, that of the death of my parents. I saw mine yesterday; they are eighty-five and eighty-four years old, sound in wind and limb, as loving as they have been for more than sixty years, and were cleaning out their old house from top to bottom... No, I certainly have not had much experience of the event of death, either in myself or around me.

And yet I think that I have something to say about death. On the one hand because, like anyone who is involved in psychoanalysis, I have had to confront the way in which death is woven into my unconscious as into the unconscious of all those born of a man and a woman; and that is no small thing. On the other hand, as a theologian working in Western Catholicism in the second half of the twentieth century, I have had to reflect with others on what the significance of death may be in the future, and I have had to involve myself in the study of – and to take sides over – questions like abortion, euthanasia, the death penalty and suicide (problems that I have tried to work with as closely as possible: perhaps rather too closely for some people's liking).

But my main claim to being able to speak about death is what seems to me to be a rather rare kind of encounter with it; I have not yet completely come to terms with it, but I would like to try to decipher the traces of it here. To put it in a phrase: I have been on the receiving end – as one is on the receiving end of a ceiling falling on one's head – of the fear that death inspires in some Christians and the way in which they use their faith in the resurrection to deny death and domesticate the fear that it provokes. For more than four years, since I wrote the pages in which I expressed my difficulties with the resurrection, I was on the receiving end of this fear of death in full force, in full flood, to the point of being swallowed up, suffocated, submerged by it. It could take the most diverse forms, even amounting to hatred. But none of these forms was lukewarm or slight; each struck me firmly, wherever it chose to, and with all the force that it claimed for life against death. The flood has now abated; not because it has dried up, but because it has gone past me, swept over me, leaving me far behind like a piece of flotsam. I have escaped the flood, I am revived, and of death there is one thing I can say for having seen it face to face and undergone its furies: I know the fear that it inspires in some believers and the way it has of distorting their faith in the resurrection, and more radically their faith in God.

In fact I found myself in a quite special situation. It was not the common one of the man or woman who, having measured the role played by the fear of death in any religious faith, has chosen to stop believing or to cope with the disturbances that this fear inescapably arouses in any human being in another way. I too had measured this role and I too had chosen to cope with these disturbances in another way; but for all that, I had not become an unbeliever. However, belief in the resurrection seemed to me to have been so affected by this fear that after an intermediate stage (which I described under the revealing title 'A Case of post-Freudian Faith in the Resurrection?', *Concilium*, 105, 1975; it was in the period when *Concilium* did not always appear in English and so was never translated), I came to a more radical position in *When I say God*: I no longer believed in the resurrection, I no longer believed in eternal life. There was certainly nothing original about that; my originality lay in the fact that rightly or wrongly, for good or ill, I continued to believe in the God of Jesus Christ and in this Jesus Christ himself, as in a certain number of less important things which are not without importance. Scripture, the eucharist, the church remained vital for me and I was involved in them happily and with conviction, if not always – it would seem – in an orthodox way. In short, I believed in all the 'essential truths of the Christian faith' except the resurrection.

As I have already said, a later development led me to rediscover meaning in the resurrection of Jesus Christ, even if this meaning is probably rather different from that which is most often given to it by Christianity. It is worth noting that this development, which I felt to be crucial, was dismissed completely by my censors, who even thought it out of place that I should have made it public by writing and on television. To begin with, I was stupefied by their reaction. What! Did the fact that I said that the resurrection of Jesus Christ again made sense for me not change anything? One always takes a long time to track down one's own naiveties: I took a long time to understand that in essentials that did not change anything and that they were right, since what I thought of Christ and his resurrection did not matter much; what mattered was what I thought of the resurrection of human beings, of the death of human beings. The resurrection of Christ does not matter much, because what matters is our own; or rather, the resurrection of Christ matters enormously, but in respect of ours, of which it is the guarantee, the foretaste and the anticipated realization (for good measure we should add the glorious assumption of the body of his Mother, since in the last resort it is on the mother's side that we need to be reasssured). What I believed about God and Christ did not matter very much: what mattered was what I said about death. This is how one arrives at a complete reversal of perspective, which some people have been right to diagnose in Christianity (after which they immediately cease to be Christians), but which those who hold the most senior positions of authority in the hierarchy proclaim with great vigour and equally great unawareness: human death and the fear which it inspires are the centre of gravity in the system and not God or Jesus Christ. Galileo was indeed wrong and had to be condemned because the heavens, their angels and their deities revolve round man, his life and his death, and man is the centre of gravity. You can believe in God and Jesus Christ as much as you like: if you have the least doubts in the world about the resurrection of man all that counts for nothing; indeed you are putting everything in danger because you are weakening the centre of gravity.

It was because I affirmed my faith in God and Jesus Christ while expressing my difficulty – indeed the impossibility I found – of believing in human resurrection that I found myself in such a rare situation (leave aside for the moment the question whether it was valid or coherent) over against various kinds of believers and unbelievers. My position allowed me to encounter – almost face to face – the fear which death inspires and the way in which it weighs down on Christian faith. The violence of the attacks, the rigour of the condemnations, the depths of the dissent of which I was the object could not lay claim to either faith in God or faith in Jesus Christ as their pretext or their motive: their only possible cause was the fear of death. I experienced it, I saw it almost naked; it is terrifying. I do not know how terrifying death is, but I do not know whether it can be more terrifying than the fear which it inspires.

I took a long time to understand why, in connection with other 'dogmas', I had been accused of 'errors' of every kind which were the direct opposite of what I had written in this book. I ended up by coming to realize that since it would have been indecent for the fear of death to press crudity to the point of claiming to be the only important thing, it had to exert sufficient pressure to relate everything to itself and to affirm that there were mistakes in everything else since its own claims had been demolished. I took a long time to understand why some friends or readers – for the most part scholars of either sex – who had expressed what was sometimes an enthusiastic agreement with the essential points of my thinking about God and Jesus

Christ along with strong disagreement over what I said about the resurrection, became progressively more silent about what they had approved and banished me from the Catholic theological community even more surely than any condemnation from Rome. Had I been at least a Protestant, an extremely strict Jew or a Moslem, had the heresy had been connected with God or Jesus Christ, or at worst with papal infallibility, I would have still been able to be a member of the republic of theology, and would have been quoted in articles or lectures. However, my heresy was connected with the resurrection of human beings; so nothing could be done and it was impossible even to use what had been good in other respects, as happens with other heretics.

I think that I have had occasion (should I say the good fortune) to observe from quite a unique position the weight that bears down on Christianity from the fear of death. I would not have dared to believe what I saw had I not had the good fortune also to encounter Christians for whom the question of eternal life was secondary to the question of 'knowing God and him whom he sent: Jesus Christ' and also the good fortune to meet Christians who, while having a great fear of death (like them, I too have a great fear) were not ready to let their fear make them say just anything about God and man; finally, I had the good fortune to meet unbelievers who were interested in what I said about God and Jesus Christ because, if it all proved to be rather more than a shoddy way of coping with the fear of death, then perhaps it was worth spending time on, without at the same time losing one's human dignity. I must try to say something to all these people. I would even be so bold as to say that I owe it to God, I would not go so far as to say that it will be easy.

Without doubt, the least difficult course will be to begin with a theme which kept recurring in all the more or less formal meetings to which I was invited after the appearance of my book and which was always expressed with the same simplicity. 'If there is no eternal life, nothing makes sense; life is not worth the trouble, and faith is not worth the trouble. God is no use.' Despite the great simplicity in this reaction, we must distinguish two elements in it which are not identical: that relating to human life and that relating to God and faith. If we look at the former we shall find that light will be shed on the latter.

1. 'Without resurrection, life makes no sense'

The acquisition of unbelief

For almost twenty years now I have lived and worked more with non-believers than with believers. These twenty years would not have been too long to discover within myself a conviction which was both radical and spontaneous and which I found to be just as radical and spontaneous among some of the believers with whom I talked: if there is no eternal life, life and death make no sense and everything becomes absurd. It is both indisputable and amazing that we believers could continue to have such a deep conviction when everyday life sees to it that we have evidence to the contrary. Like the great majority of lay Christians (I shall not talk too much in this connection about the clergy, above all those who only live with believers, still less those who live with other clergy), I am surrounded by people who do not believe in eternal life and for whom things make some sense: loving, hating, being born, dying, working, struggling, seeking, making mistakes, beginning again, finding, taking and giving pleasure, truth, justice, goodness, beauty. It is certainly not necessary to believe in eternal life to believe that all this makes some sense, and some of those who see birth and death as the limits of human life work with even more conviction than those for whom human life extends beyond death. True, the meaning that they see in life is always limited, not to say indecipherable, but it exists independendently of faith and an eternal life.

Confronted with its limited character and its often radical absence, believers rush forward, crowding on all apologetic sails, to cry out: 'So you see, without eternal life nothing makes sense.' For example, there has been much talk recently of the return of the religious, and people have thought that they could demonstrate the need for faith – in particular faith in eternal life – by diagnosing that our Western civilization, having exhausted any significance that it might want to give itself outside God or outside an eternal life, will turn towards God and towards faith in the resurrection. Man will discover that history escapes him while being too narrow for him, that his world is too limited, that he aspires to transcend it. So he will discover the need for God and his own vocation to eternity.

Quite a different diagnosis is possible, even if it satisfies the desires of the apologists less. If our Western society is disenchanted with the significance that it had attached to life and death, it is perhaps because it had transposed to them this unhealthy infinite inherited from a certain form of Christian faith. In that case the solution will not be found in a return towards this unhealthy infinite, but rather in the discovery beyond, or rather this side of this unhealthy infinite which had contaminated them, of the real value of those meanings which human beings have been able to perceive, or in the elaboration of new meanings. However – and this is where there is a big difference from those who want to take their stand on the vocation to an eternal life – none of these meanings will be total nor exhaustive, nor will the sum of the various meanings: man is a being of limited significance – and with limited responsibility. Our civilization is not yet post-Christian enough to be sufficiently aware of this; it is post-Christian enough to find – and rightly so – a certain form of belief in eternal life to be alienating, humiliating and totalitarian when it claims that without it nothing makes sense.

'All right,' someone might say to me, 'suppose we accept that faith in eternal life is not necessary for giving meaning to human life; in that case what do you have against the fact that it would give it an additional and – you have to confess – superior meaning?' Certainly I have nothing against that *a priori*, provided that it does not happen at any price. I have allowed myself for too long to be exploited over the price to be paid and I can see too many other people allowing themselves to be exploited for me to be able to accept the suggestion readily from now on. However, it seems all the more difficult to take refuge there when one associates this additional meaning which eternity gives with the need for the infinite which for so long has been made the essential privilege of the human condition. People very often argued against me, using as an example human love, of which I was thought to have no experience. 'So don't you see,' someone said to me, 'how such love bears within itself the desire for eternity.' I had every conceivable difficulty in trying to point out that while the desire for eternity in human love may be incontestable, that does not amount to saying that human love only makes sense if it is eternal by right and in fact. It is wrong to move from the observation of a desire to the conviction that this desire has a foundation as if there were no difference between the two. This illegitimate shift is what vitiates the affirmation that nothing makes sense without eternal life.

In fact I would claim that it is an alienation and perversion of the human condition to demand that our various human enterprises should last for ever, since otherwise they would make no sense. Is it loving to find meaning in the fact of loving a man and woman only if the love lasts for ever? On the contrary, that is a perversion of love, it estranges the lover and the beloved by producing a relationship which hinders each from being present to the other and accepting him or her to the limited but real degree which love between human beings allows. As St Augustine said, that is loving love rather than the other; it is loving love so much that one finds that it makes less sense to love the other in a limited fashion, in time, than to love eternally. Whether one is thinking of relationships between human beings, scientific or artistic creation, technical or commercial enterprise, work, or any human activity, to claim that it would not make sense unless it lasted for ever is to prevent oneself from giving and receiving the meaning that it can have in the space and time which are those of humans, namely finite space and time.

Desire for the infinite, longing for eternity and contempt for the finite

That is the point at which an appeal is made to this desire for the infinite which is meant to be the greatness of man even more than his wretchedness. It is also the point where, in *When I say God*, I very clumsily complicated things by casting too many aspersions on this desire of the infinite which I reduced to the pernicious forms of it which I knew all too well. The deciphering of the unconscious by psychoanalysis shows the ravages made in the life of men and women by the conviction that an object exists which would fulfil their every desire. My personal history probably explains why I had been so assiduous in positing such an object and why I was so sensitive to such a deciphering. It is even more probable that the way in which I was involved in the functions of a preacher, celebrant and theologian had reinforced everything which impels Christianity so strongly to present God as fulfilling every human desire: I shall devote the last part of this book to showing how that is a fundamental error about God and how this error is as catastrophic for God as it is for human beings. At all events, I had to undergo many vicissitudes to discover that God was not this object that our desire forges to convince itself that it could be entirely fulfilled by a single object; I also had to undergo many trials and tribulations to identify in myself and around me (as far as I was able) all that deforms and perverts God in Christianity – as in all religions – so that he is made to play this role of the total fulfilment of desire, and many trials and tribulations to abandon the practices and ideas which are inspired by such a conviction and which end up with this same perversion. All these long and laborious trials suggest that in such a course we are involved not only in changing all or part of an intellectual theological system of representations of God, but also in reshaping the way in which our desire relates to God, ourselves or any other of its objects in the depths of our personality.

The length of this journey and the severity of the internal and external conflicts which it involved ended up by giving me some kind of myopia: through fighting against these unhealthy infinites in myself and around me, I had come to the stage of no longer being able to see beyond them. It is hardly paradoxical that this myopia was revealed to me less by the objections of certain believers than by the remarks of psychoanalyst friends, almost all of them non-believers. During a seminar that they devoted to the study of my book they pointed out that my legitimate denunciation of the setting up of an object fulfilling all desire – even though it was God – took me too far afield and put me off course since I had almost come to suspect as pathological the presence in a human being of any desire for the infinite whatsoever. Coming from them, such a remark did not produce the reflex action which would have almost inevitably followed had it come to me from Christians, so great would have been my fear (not without good reasons, as experience has shown me) that in that case it would have served to reintroduce by the back door the figure of the God who fulfils all desire.

So I came progressively to discover that I had misunderstood a basic anthropological reality, namely that there is no human being without a desire for the infinite, that every human enterprise, from the humblest to the most grandiose, is supported and driven on by a desire for the infinite, just as in turn it supports the infinite and urges it on. I had proved a master in the denunciation of the way in which Christianity exploited God and man by announcing that God would fulfil every human desire, and I was very good at diagnosing the numerous forms of this perversion of God and humanity. However, at the same time I myself had perverted the human condition – and perhaps God – by failing to recognize that this desire for the infinite – pernicious as it may be when it projects the existence of an object which can provide infinite fulfilment – is a basic factor of human existence and that it is even more the source of our greatness and our vitality than of our illusions and our failings.

Faced with the authority which had so often been opposed to me and which stressed the fact that every human enterprise is a vehicle for the infinite and moved by a desire for the infinite, I was therefore more suspicious than I had been for a long time. But I was all the better placed to grasp the difference which separates the recognition of such a desire from the affirmation that it can be fulfilled by projecting it on eternity. Here again, the majority of believers find it impossible to understand the way in which non-believers actually live. For there are plenty of non-believers who stress this almost transcendent dimension of man in relationship to himself without believing in an eternal life. The fact that they distinguish the desire for the infinite from beliefs in eternal life obviously does not prove of itself that they are right, but it does prove (in a way which is reinforced by the witness that they give to this quasi-transcendence in their own life) that this desire and this belief cannot be reduced to one and the same thing, as believers are so ready to do. It is not the dimension of the infinite in human enterprises that proves that they are by nature capable of being eternal. Now that I was less hesitant to recognize this dimension in the human condition, I was even better placed to ask myself what impelled believers so strongly to see it as a proof of the vocation of human beings to eternity, while non-believers do not read it in anything like the same way.

Someone once said to me that it was faith that made the difference to this reading. That reply is too easy. And above all, the way in which it is habitually given contains an unacceptable element, the pernicious character of which calls in question the whole of this response. Among believers, moving so easily from the recognition of this dimension of the infinite to the affirmation of eternal life in fact very often goes with a kind of deprecation of the human condition as it can already be experienced – as non-believers experience it – within the limits of time and space marked out by the birth and death of human beings. One would not have to reject such a argument for eternal life so strongly if it presented itself only as an argument for something over and above a human life the humblest potential of which one cultivated with as much enthusiasm as humility, and the grandeurs and miseries of which one respected for what they are with wonder and pity.

Unfortunately, one could fill whole libraries (as historians have begun to) with the innumerable discussions of theologians, preachers, moralists and bishops who cannot find any better way of speaking of the benefits of heaven than to speak of the ills of earth, and to make us desire the one by making us scorn the other. When the flood of these discussions dies down and begins to ebb a little, it gives even more prominence to the rock of the innumerable practices, liturgies and prayers of all kinds which resort to the same strategy. The facts are there to prove that most often the Christian case for eternal life thinks that it can derive strength and support from a denunciation of the mediocrity of human life and even of its infinite dimension if it is not referred to eternity. It is all as if the Christian case for eternal life needed to overwhelm human beings with the weight of the negative aspects of their finitude, claiming that it alone is able to rescue the positive aspects by tapping them in to this same promise of eternal life.

It is unacceptable that a human life which is not related to God and eternity should be devalued. It is unacceptable to human beings who have the least sense of their dignity; though it may be true that we are most often weighed down by the burden of the negative aspects of our finitude, it is an unworthy piece of blackmail only to use this oppression as an apologetic means for presenting eternal life as the only outcome worthy of consideration, devaluing in passing what we succeed in making of the positive aspects of our finitude despite everything. This procedure is not only ignoble but false: it is not true that human enterprises have no value when they are not related to God or to man's vocation to eternity. Once again, the life of non-believers is an irrefutable testimony. We must reject any presentation of eternal life which accommodates itself to such a devaluation. Unfortunately we know that even when they are not directly set up on such a basis, such presentations can accommodate themselves very well. The reason is simple.

If so many Christians slide so easily from noting that all human enterprises are prompted by a desire for the infinite to the affirmation that these enterprises only find their true meaning by being raised up into an eternal life, it is that this mode of affirmation and this slide are a powerful and effective way of negotiating the fear of death by going so far as to deny it or simply to make it the passage from a devalued form of human life to a full form. For death is not just death: it recapitulates and symbolizes all our experience of the negative side of our finitude as human beings and the finitude of our world. That is why the fear which it inspires in us is bound up with all the sufferings, all the wounds, all the vicissitudes that we have experienced in the various dimensions of our human condition. The fear of death comes in some degree to orchestrate all these experiences by providing them with a unifying theme. That is why, in pressing its claims, the case for an eternal life which would relegate death to being perhaps an important but by no means a decisive episode must both stress the negative side of human experience and present itself as being able to change this negative into a positive, or as being able to deliver us from what would be too negative to merit such transformation (sexuality, for example, of which I shall speak later). That is also why the case for an eternal life, addressing all the sufferings of human beings, can mobilize them with such power that one has every interest in sliding without pausing over the observation that a desire for the infinite is constitutive of human beings to the proposition that the positive aspect of human beings cannot be conquered by death.

A guarantee against the precariousness of the present

Obviously there is no question of our reproaching other human beings for having a fear of death and wanting not to be overwhelmed by the negative aspects of our finitude, or even of being afraid to the point of denying death and this finitude of which it is the symbol. On this point too, I clumsily clouded the issue in *When I Say God*, sometimes reacting as if the fear of death or of our finitude was almost pathological in itself. There again, it was above all my non-believing psychoanalyst friends who helped me to discover this trap. The fear of death and the rejection of our finitude are also part and parcel of being human, and yet also as 'healthy' and 'normal' (if we keep strictly to this terminology) as the desire for the infinite. If there is anything to be held against the current Christian argument for eternal life it is clearly not that it is prompted by the fear of death and the denial of our finitude. It is that this argument is presented by them in such a way that it comes to devalue the reality of the human condition, even if does so in order to revalue it. If one has to make some criticism of this most current form of the argument for eternal life in Christianity, it is not that it beats to the rhythm of our fear of death but that it allows itself to be led on by that fear to the point of our being deceived about the way in which life beats in us, sometimes to the point of our crushing this life under the weight of the restoration that it promises. I shall also go on to show in a moment how this way of being afraid of death must also be rejected because of the mistakes it causes us to make about God and the life which he makes us live. First of all, however, I must note a consequence of what I have just described: we Christians must put ourselves on this other side of the experience that we have of death and our finitude; we must negotiate another kind of relationship with our human condition of being mortal and finite from that in which we are swallowed up by the fear of death played on by this account of eternal life.

What in fact was striking in the way in which someone told me that without eternal life nothing in human life would make sense was that what was to be made sense of in this way seemed either to make no sense or to have too fragile or remote a meaning. Militant

Christians said to me: our fight for justice does not make sense if there is no eternal life. Parents said to me: why have children and bring them up only to give them over to death? Men and women said to me: our love makes no sense unless it is going to last for ever. Their claim to an eternal life had been swollen by all the forces which are involved in our various human enterprises, and what struck me with full force was that they were not so much a direct expression of the fear of death (in fact many people said that they did not fear it) as an expression of the mixture of hopes and doubts, strengths and weaknesses, confidences and terrors which are the flesh and blood of our lives.

It appeared equally clearly that faith in the resurrection and the desire for an eternal life were not so much the desire to live fully in the presence of God, which would be enough to fulfil all human desire for ever, as a way of coping with the changes and chances of present-day life. If the comparison were not too frivolous to use in connection with the matter in question, one might use as an illustration the game of billiards, where the cushions are a decisive element in the game to the degree that one uses them for ricochets in order to get at the ball aimed at. Often faith in the resurrection would seem to be less a mystical aspiration to live eternally with God than something off which to ricochet in order to attain the goal a person seeks in his or her present historical existence; that the fight for justice sees itself assured of success with no possibility of failure, that love, work, every human enterprise thus finds itself grounded in an unshakable way.

Going over to the other side

This is the way of coping with the experience of our condition that we must leave in order to go over to the other side. Not so much primarily in order to deny or affirm a faith in eternal life and the resurrection as to abandon an experience of our condition which now proves to be fallacious. Proceeding from the better known to the less well known, when we ask questions about the resurrection and eternal life, we must begin not from what proves false in the realm of what we know least badly, namely our human condition, but from what proves least false. This is an indispensable precaution if we want to open up a way towards what we know even less well, namely eternal life and resurrection. Again, if we are to begin from what is least false, we have to have lived with it, to have stayed with it. However, I do not think that this is what the majority of believers, myself included, have done. We have to familiarize ourselves with a way of living which is very unfamiliar to us, to discover what intrinsic meaning our condition has without reference to God, what intrinsic meaning our temporality has without direct reference to eternal life. We have to discover a purely human relationship to our world, to ourselves, to others, to all the dimensions of our life. We must become human beings instead of sometimes wanting to be angels and sometimes being reduced to the level of beasts. Before introducing the type of meaning that can be given to our life by the fact that God is God and wants to be a God with us, we must have the courage to abandon the meaning that we have come to give to the human condition by using as a pretext the claim that this is the life that God wants to give. That is false. We must patiently – and even humbly, since beyond question we have been too pretentious – rediscover at the human level the nature of our human condition, rediscover a human relationship with our human condition.

I know that I am proposing an approach which believers find unfamiliar and which seems so contrary to the usual approach of faith that people will not hesitate to attribute to me intentions radically opposed to my own. I do not claim (I must repeat this, even if experience has taught me that such repetitions are rarely effective), I do not claim that the fact that God is God and that he wants to be a God-with-us does not confer an extra meaning on our human life: I believe (*credo*), I hope, I love to exactly the opposite effect. Nor do I claim that if we keep making the experience of our condition more profound we shall be led to discover God and the meaning that we can be given by the fact that he is God and that he wants to be God with us. God is not born of human flesh and blood; he is born from elsewhere and he comes from elsewhere: from God. I only claim – but in this 'only' I now believe that all my life as a human being and a believer is at stake – that in order to be better at receiving what comes from elsewhere, in order to be where God can come, we must exist humanly in our condition, discover the significance of our human existence independently of any reference to God, since it makes sense without reference to God. That is the whole achievement of the modern experience of unbelief. To be where we are, in our space and time, we must first explore them, inhabit them, independently of any reference to what would abolish this space and time.

It seems to me unacceptable to define unbelief as the view that the human condition and our universe have a meaning independent of any reference to God, since I consider that believers must have that view also. But if someone were to force me to accept such a definition of unbelief, I would say that in fact we other believers must go to the other side, that we must become non-believers (in the unsatisfactory sense of the word I have mentioned above) before being able to become believers, and in order to become non-believers if it proved God's pleasure and our own that this is what we should be. Our stay on the other side will be all the longer, the more our way of staying on this side has made it too impossible for us to live our lives as men and women in a human way. We must not be afraid of the inhabitants of this other side: if we do not go up to them and tell them that their life does not make sense and that we are giving it sense *par excellence*, they will receive us well: I have done this and have experience of it. They are more accustomed than we are to seek without always finding, and they do not need to found a secretariat for believers in order to welcome us. Let us begin by discovering our earth, our humanity, with them. It is the same as theirs, and it is there that God comes, if he comes to human beings.

2. 'Without resurrection, God and faith make no sense'

'If there is no eternal life, nothing makes sense, human life makes no sense, faith no longer makes sense, God makes no sense and is no use to anyone.' I have pointed out that in this way in which people often reacted to me, two elements were closely connected which should nevertheless be distinguished: so far I have kept to the first, which concerns human life. Now I come to the second, which concerns God and faith.

I do not think that I could have had a more devastating or disturbing experience than to be able to hear myself saying right through these last years that in the end God and faith did not make sense if one did not believe in eternal life. I prayed: in one sense more than ever, since more than ever I needed not to lose contact with God. I sought him more than ever, because more than ever I needed not to lose my way. I shared him, and others shared him with me, no longer because I preached, presided publicly at the eucharist or taught theology (I did not once contravene the prohibitions made by Rome in any substantial way), but because believers, men and women, had invited me to share in their quest, their prayer, their eucharists – and did so more than ever because of the questions asked in the book which had been condemned and the echoes that they aroused. Not a day went past without my asking myself whether it would not have been better to let everything drop or without my feeling obliged – by whom?, I wonder – to start again. In what direction? And did that make no sense because I did not believe in the resurrection of human beings?

Were the happiness, the pleasure, the wonder I felt at the God whom Jesus Christ has shown us rather than the God constructed by our social, psychological and religious mechanisms for making gods meaningless because I did not believe in the resurrection of human beings? Were my wonder, my pleasure, my happiness at what the Spirit could raise up and bear witness to among us down to the end of time, at what for two thousand years men and women had shown by their faith to be alive among us, meaningless because I did not believe in the resurrection of human beings? Were the happiness and joy, but also the toil and the pain, that my quest for God had cost me, whether alone or with a community, worth nothing, simply by virtue of the fact that I did not believe in the resurrection of human beings? So people wanted to leave me nothing, to reduce me to nothing! For this time it was not just the Roman authorities: it was either close friends, lifetime companions, who said that I was not a Christian, less publicly but more radically than any straightforward prohibitions could do, or unknown people whom I might encounter during a meeting and who were eager to ruin what my faith might be because it seemed to them that their faith had been ruined by my lack of belief in the resurrection of human beings.

Moreover, not only did they seek to annihilate my faith; they also accused me, very violently, of what they saw as contempt in my way of looking at things. I was told that if I did not believe in the resurrection of human beings it was because I had too much contempt for their suffering and their wretchedness, for which one day they deserved to be able to enjoy eternal happiness; I was also told that I had contempt for their successes and their happinesses which deserved to be extended into an endless fulfilment. People would add that this contempt went with a contempt for God and his justice; for how could God still be God if he did not do justice to human beings by giving them the blessedness which their misfortune and their happiness also deserved? As one of my Dominican brothers once remarked to me in passing (we were, in fact, collecting correspondence from the pigeon holes at the community): 'Your God is a God for the rich and the happy: I would be ashamed to present him to people who were suffering and desperate.' This man – who in fact did spend a good deal of his time with people who were suffering and desperate, in a way which makes me admire him and which lends weight to his words – will never know how much his words still dog me and afflict me with a terrifying sadness. But what did people want of me? What had I done?

Still, one voice stood out from the rest in the midst of the outcry. It was that of Nadille, Nadille who was dying of cancer and whose marvellous blonde hair had already fallen out. Nadille said to me, 'Jacques, I do not understand how someone who speaks so well of God cannot believe in the resurrection: you must be wrong somewhere, but I'm blowed if you are wrong about God, and it is with your God that I want to die.' Yes, someone who knew the death that awaited her, someone whose death was going to be a terrible waste even more for those close to her than for herself, someone who believed in the resurrection and who knew that I did not, said to me at the doors of death, 'Jacques, it is with your God that I want to die.'

I have spend months, years, being tossed around by these accusations and expressions of approval, telling myself that the God by whom I wanted to live and bring life made sense, that Christ and the Spirit in whom I believed made sense, asking myself if I truly had contempt for human unhappiness, if I was spoiling human happiness, if I was insulting divine Justice. I have come as close as I could to some quite terrifying forms of unhappiness, at the risk of being scarred by them, in order to test myself and to see if it was really true that I scorned them, so that the excess of their suffering might burn away the contempt for them that there had been in my faith. I have also come as close as I could to happiness, at the risk of scarring it if there had been anything in my faith which might have endangered it. I have come as close as I could to God, asked him to come close to me; I have asked believers, men and women, to bring me to God, to apply their faith to mine so that any contempt there might be in it for the justice of God could be burned away – as by the coal on Isaiah's lips.

Have I done well or badly? I have got no further over the resurrection of human beings. But I have learned something about suffering, about happiness, about God. And above all, I have learned more about the way in which faith in the resurrection of human beings, in its most current form, organizes relationships between God and the happiness or misfortune of human beings. For we are talking about an organization, a system. Some of its features have made it impracticable for me from now on and suggest to me that we must look for another.

Ambiguities in the almost self-evident character of the resurrection

The first of these elements is the way in which the resurrection of human beings is thought to be both an irrefutable and an unassailable fact. Certainly no one would dare to claim that this resurrection is self-evident without taking precautions. If one were obliged to take precautions, one would have to acknowledge that the resurrection is an article of faith the content of which is no more evident than the three persons of the Trinity, the divinity of Jesus Christ or the real presence in the eucharist. But in fact people do not feel the need to take many precautions in connection with the resurrection: it is always as though belief in the resurrection of human beings was based on a more profound, more powerful, almost more instinctive sense than on the deepest and most powerful faith. The rejections of which I became the object seemed to me to be quite different in kind from those that I could observe among Christians in connection with the questioning of other dogmas of the Christian faith.

A number of my Dominican colleagues and friends work in a remarkable way at 'dialogue' with members of other Christian confessions or of other religions which reject one or other essential dogma of the Catholic faith as it is now defined: in the case of Protestants or Orthodox these may relate to the church and the sacraments; in the case of Moslems or Jews and even more of representatives of Far Eastern or African religions, they may relate to God and Jesus Christ. I have observed that these ecumenical theologians, while firmly confessing their own view of the faith, accept that others can think and believe differently, and that is what enables them to begin this dialogue. While they believe that there are three persons in the Trinity and that Jesus Christ is the Son of God, they do not regard this belief as a kind of proof outside which nothing, certainly not God, would make sense.

I noted to my cost that things were very different when it was a matter of the resurrection of human beings. I was told that to believe in God and Jesus Christ as I believed in them did not make sense unless I also believed in the resurrection of the dead. The type and the degree of the demands which were made on believing here proved to be of a different order from those which would lead one to believe in the Trinity or the divinity of Christ. In a sense, it was the order of things which required one to believe, it was the reality of human misfortune and happiness which called for a resurrection of the dead, and without it not only the life of human beings but even God and

Jesus Christ themselves would no longer make sense. The way in which I was required to believe proved by its force and its exclusiveness to be of quite a different order from the way in which it was hoped that Jews or Moslems might recognize the Trinity or the divinity of Christ, or Protestants and Orthodox might think of the church and the sacraments as Roman Catholics do. Furthermore, the faith of all these believers was thought to have some meaning and value: it was not supposed that their refusal to believe in what they did not believe deprived the rest of their faith of its value. So what was so special about the resurrection of human beings, that whether or not one believed in it had such different consequences and rescued or ruined the fact that one believed in all the rest?

In any case, it is true that one form of Catholic faith considers the resurrection of the dead as being of a different order from the other truths of faith. The First Vatican Council (1870) ratified as an article of faith the whole theological and philosophical movement (dating from before Christianity) which affirmed that the immortality of the soul could be demonstrated by the unaided power of reason and that it was therefore a truth which, while not evident, was demonstrable – a great deal of comfort if one notes the gaps in the evidence and its varied quality! Granted, the question here was that of the immortality of the soul and not of the resurrection of the body, but once the former is demonstrated it must be relatively easy to guarantee the latter. In fact, if the immortality of the soul is a feature of human nature, and if the presence of this soul in a body is equally a part of it, it is enough to find an explanation of this provisional difference in the relative destinies of the soul and the body and a final resolution of it. Catholic doctrine has no difficulty in providing these: original sin has vitiated human nature and made it lose not only the immortality of the soul – which is part of its nature – but the immortality of the body which God graciously ('preternaturally' is the term used by the theologians) bestowed on it when creating it in a state of grace. The victory of Christ over sin and death and the consummation of this victory after death in anyone who has believed in Christ will allow the human being to regain whatever of the eternal destiny of the body it has been deprived of through sin. In such a view, belief in the resurrection is from now on concerned only with the resurrection of the body, since the immortality of the soul has in any case been achieved and even safeguarded against the ravages of sin. Nothing similar can be invoked in connection with belief in the Trinity or in the divinity of Christ, so it is true that for one form of Catholic faith the resurrection of human beings is of a different order from the other orders of faith and that it is guaranteed in a different way from them (if not a better one).

In *When I say God* I explained at length that such a view of looking at things raises difficulties which in my view are insoluble, and does so as much from the perspective of reason as from that of faith. Because of that I shall not return to them, although these difficulties still seem to be insuperable. What I have been led to discover since then seems to me to be instructive. The theologians and believers around me think, like the very eminent and very cautious Protestant theologian Oscar Cullmann, that such a conception of the immortality of the soul is strictly in conflict with New Testament faith in the resurrection and that one cannot profess both at the same time. Besides, like many of our contemporaries, these theologians and believers would find this anthropological dichotomy between soul and body meaningless. It was neither this doctrine (declared *de fide* by Vatican I) nor this anthropology (still officially in force in the Catholic church) that they defended when denouncing my way of believing in God and in Jesus Christ without believing in the resurrection of human beings.

The difference between their attitude to the other 'heretics' or 'schismatics' and their attitude to me, the different kind of certainty that they invoked over the resurrection of human beings, the different way in which they argued that not to believe in the resurrection had a detrimental effect on other aspects of faith, were all factors which indicated that what was involved here was something other than the action of faith in connection with the Trinity, Jesus Christ and other aspects of belief. An elementary procedure from logic, that of controlling the variables, showed that variables other than faith had come into play. I had nothing against this in principle, but I felt it vital to note the fact.

It is somewhat paradoxical to see theologians and believers reject the Vatican I affirmation about the possibility of rational proof of the immortality of the soul in connection with the resurrection of the dead while still appealing to 'evidence', an 'order of things' and a 'need for meaning' in human existence, a 'requirement and a necessary consequence of divine justice'. These are all elements to which they give an analogous role (though in the end it is less critical, if not more affirmative) to that attributed to the demonstrative power of reason by the members of this same Vatican I, good rationalists that they were—like all the eminent figures of the end of the nineteenth century. If in the eyes of these theologians and believers not to believe in the resurrection made it foolish to believe in God and Jesus Christ and

still attach some importance to human existence, the reason was not
something related to faith itself, without which not to believe in some
other truth of faith (the Trinity, the divinity of Christ) would have
the same consequences. However, these theologians and believers do
not have anything like the same views about these other truths of
faith when they are talking with Moslems or Jews, Protestants or
Orthodox. If not to believe in the resurrection of the dead has the
effect that I have had to experience, it is because this non-belief
murders a certainty, a kind of proof about death. It is this proof, this
certainty which people defend, not only in the name of faith, but also
over and above that. Once again, I have no objection in principle.
But at least they should acknowledge the fact, recognize that this is
the case. For the refusal to recognize this, or, more deeply still,
the very impossibility of becoming aware of it, are incontestable
indications that there is something here that this kind of faith cannot
accept and appropriate without believing that it has been ruined and
deprived of its own foundations.

Is the essential task of Christianity to solve the problem of death?

Another difficulty that I feel over the way in which faith in the
resurrection of the dead is connected with relationships between God
and human happiness or unhappiness relates to its tendency to make
this resurrection the centre of the whole system, or in any case the
element on which the system depends to such a degree that to remove
it, as I did, risks making the whole edifice collapse or become
absurd. That is the basis of the accusation against me. The social
psychologists, and in particular the social psychologists of religion,
have shown how a social and intellectual system in which orthodoxy
plays a constitutive role in the identity and the life of the group and
the interplay of powers exercised within it functions within a closed
circuit. Such a role is considerable in Roman Catholicism, and no
one will be surprised if the effects identified by social psychologists
are powerfully at work in it. However, no matter how great this
aptitude or this need to think in a closed circuit may be, it cannot go
so far as completely to prevent an understanding of the diagnosis of
the function of religion that is presented from all sides. The various
disciplines in the human sciences and, more simply and more sweep-
ingly, the man in the street (quite independently of these disciplines
and even of their diffusion by the media) would consider that the
essential function of religion is to help to resolve the problem of

death. Death is the centre around which every religious system revolves, the axis around which it is completely organized. I personally have been helped by psychoanalysis – more by the experience of personal analysis than by psychoanalytical theory – to see how well-founded this diagnosis is. In a certain sense, though, this particular personal approach is not in itself significant, since all possible approaches to the matter converge: death and the attempt to resolve the radical question that it poses indeed lie at the heart of religion and are almost certainly its source, and indeed its goal and expected consequence. As the mother of one of my friends, herself a non-believer, said of my theological views, 'Honestly, what's the point of being a believer if you don't think that there is anything after death?'

Such an analysis is in any case not necessarily pejorative; in itself, it is neither ridiculous nor wrong to help people to raise the question of death and in any case to confront the fact of death. No matter what point of view one takes, death is so radically bound up with all dimensions of life, so radically bound up with our own identity and that of our fellows, that it would be naive or sadistic to criticize a human enterprise – in this case religion – for devoting itself to the fact of death and furthering life, since we have to live with death while we are living with life. So I have no objection in principle to a religion being preoccupied with death and being orientated on it, though I do have objections to the way in which the majority of religions do this by diminishing life, and sometimes even by obliterating one or another essential dimension. I have explained many times, in *When I say God* and elsewhere, what bothers me about this point of view in some very widespread forms of the Catholic fatih. Here I would like to stress a point that the situation in which I find myself helps me to see better.

About thirty years ago, French Catholic theologians made great use of the distinction between faith and religion, which they had taken over from German Protestant theology. They used it to concede to modern 'critics' of the phenomenon of religion all that these critics denounced, but were anxious to point out that the criticisms related only to religion and not to faith. Faith could benefit from being scrubbed clean of religion; in essentials it escaped this type of criticism, because it was of quite a different order from religion. A short time afterwards I was one of the first theologians to object to such a clear-cut division, on the one hand because the questions raised by the modern critics of the phenomenon of religion seemed to me to be as much concerned with faith as with religion, and on the other hand because it did not seem to me to be an unworthy thing that faith should fulfil certain functions of religion. So I did not disguise the fact that the Catholic faith also fulfils certain functions of religion, including its essential function, that which concerns death.

That having been said, I think that what Jesus Christ has made possible by what he has revealed to us about God and man, and what the Spirit of God can raise up, since Jesus Christ, among believers, cannot be exactly defined by the particular functions of religion. Certainly, over the centuries, Christianity has tended all too much to be reduced to one religion. But I believe that more than religion is at stake in Jesus Christ and in the Spirit who bears witness among believers that he is alive, more at any rate than what a religion is about. In this respect I would gladly take over Origen's proud replies to the philosopher Celsus, who demonstrated that Christianity has none of the essential attributes of a religion. Since Celsus listed altars, statues and temples among the essential characteristics of a religion in his criticism of Christianity, Origen explained proudly why 'we avoid building altars, statues and temples' (*Against Celsus*, 8.20; cf. also 7.64). The subsequent course of events has shown that Christianity was all too eager to fulfil the programme that Celsus had assigned it – and more!

Reading and re-reading, studying and doing theology, praying and praying again, sharing and passing on what Jesus Christ has shown of God, I have come to the conclusion that one can transpose what Origen said of other essential attributes of religion and state: 'No, we are not a religion, our essential problem is not that of death and our essential task is not to resolve the question of death.' In fact it seems to me that this is not the essential axis of what has been manifested in Jesus Christ and revealed by him. Now the charges that were made against me show very crudely that death and the resurrection of the dead have such an essential place in Catholicism – which I was accused of ruining – that to touch them brings the whole edifice down. So it would seem that the question of death occupies a different place in Catholicism from that which it occupies in what has been manifested in Jesus Christ. Therefore there is a problem.

It would be ridiculous to deny that Jesus, his disciples and the first Christians believed in eternal life and the resurrection of the dead, though two comments need to be made on this topic. On the one hand, this belief was not specific to them and did not derive from the original features in their new way of conceiving of God, but came to them from the Judaism from which they had emerged. On the other hand, their eschatological and apocalyptic expectations gave this belief quite a different colouring from modern Catholic belief in eternal life, since eschatology and apocalyptic are related to this world and consist in an expectation that it will be transformed by a being or a power which comes from elsewhere in this world; they are not concerned with another world, nor do they look for a transition from this world to another world, as is the case with modern forms of Catholic belief in the resurrection of the dead. That having been said, it is still true that Jesus of Nazareth, who evidently believed in this resurrection of the dead, did not make life in another world the centre nor even the essential consequence of his teaching, his behaviour and his own life. The good news that he announced was not: the kingdom is near because you will soon pass on to another world, but: the kingdom of God, i.e. God, is here because God is coming to this world. The Beatitudes and the Sermon on the Mount are not the map of a life in another world but the map of another life in this world.

Jesus Christ did not primarily come to resolve the question of death; he came to inaugurate a new type of relationship, in this world, between God and human beings, and as a result a new type of relationship between human beings. The touchstone, the sign of the reality of this coming of the kingdom, is not a victory over death, which would be a stunning demonstration that the question of death had been resolved, but the specific and immediate behaviour, first of Jesus and then, following him, of his disciples. This behaviour bears witness that in fact a new type of relationship with God and among human beings has been inaugurated; Jesus himself and then his disciples were ready to die, if necessary, for the realization of these relationships and not to prove by their bravery that death had been conquered.

If the problem or the fact of death had been the centre of what was shown forth and begun in Jesus, the three miracles of resurrection that the Gospels attribute to him (Jairus's daughter, the son of the widow of Nain and his friend Lazarus) would have been enough for the evangelists to say what had to be said. Now not only are they not content with these, but they did not even give them a superior status to that of the other miracles of Jesus: the multiplication of the bread and fish, the healing of the blind, the deaf, the lepers, the paralysed and so on. However, no one supposes that Jesus came to solve the problem of under-nourishment or those of blindness, deafness, leprosy or paralysis (if they did – as Augustine already pointed out – what a failure Jesus would prove!). The new type of relationship with God and among human beings in which the work and witness of

Jesus consists and which he 'founded' (to the degree to which he 'founded' anything) certainly affects all these problems, as it affects the problem of death. But that is not the essential thing, nor even the essential significance of the person and work of Jesus.

The decisive significance which Christianity rightly attaches to the death of Jesus and his resurrection can blur the issues here. The death of Jesus of Nazareth is not primarily proof that his life was dedicated to resolving the problem of death, and his resurrection as Christ is not primarily proof that he victoriously resolved this problem. His death and resurrection, like his life, are essentially a manifestation of God and a realization of what from now on can be the relationship between God and men. His death is the proof that Jesus was wholly committed, that he devoted himself, offered himself, consecrated himself to the God whom he had come to manifest and to the people to whom he wanted to manifest him. At the same time it is the proof that this God and this new relationship with him and between human beings are literally intolerable to the religious, social and psychological mechanisms which construct gods: so this man had to die. Similarly, his resurrection by God is the attestation by God that God is indeed as Jesus manifested him, that Jesus was indeed the one who manifested him as he willed, and that his spirit can win out over all the death-dealing forces which are opposed to this manifestation and this attestation.

Had the object of the resurrection of Jesus Christ been to prove that death was the essential question and that victory over it was the essential task and the essential glory of Jesus Christ, the ultimate destiny of Jesus would have had to be that of someone empirically present among us, risen, whose presence was such that it showed in an irrefutable way that death had been conquered, and that this was the essential thing because death was the essential thing. As I have shown in *When I say God*, some forms of Christianity do in fact seek to reduce the presence of Jesus Christ among us to this sort of presence: they transform the testimony to the resurrection, the apostolic succession, the church, scripture, the eucharist into guarantees of this sort of presence of the risen Christ, a transformation which in part derives from a reduction of the message and the testimony of Jesus to the question of death and its solution. But that was not the subsequent destiny of Jesus Christ; his resurrection (since I believe in that) tipped him over into the transcendence of God (or, if you prefer to put it that way, made him sit as Lord at the right hand of the Father). The only presence of his which is possible for us is that inaugurated by Pentecost which the Spirit brings about among believers, men and women, who, following Jesus Christ, seek by him, with him and in him to initiate the type of relationship to God and among human beings which was manifested and inaugurated by Jesus. The work of the Spirit is not primarily to prepare the disciples of Christ to pass into another world by virtue of the victory of Jesus over death; the work of the Spirit is primarily to inspire the disciples to change this world by fighting against whatever is opposed to this transformation, a fight which the resurrection of Jesus Christ shows us that it is possible to win.

That is without doubt what most distinguishes the function of Christianity from what is in effect the essential function of religions, namely a resolution of the problem of death. In Christianity the question of death comes second; it is completely secondary. That does not mean that anthropologically the question of death does not remain a radical question, one of the basic questions. Rather, it indicates that the essential function of Christianity is perhaps not primarily and above all to solve the great anthropological questions (perhaps human beings are called to raise them and live with them rather than solve them). There is a problem here to which I must return at greater length and depth in the last part of this book, in which I shall try to show that God is not Everything; I shall show that *a fortiori* Christianity is not everything and cannot solve everything. Certainly, Christianity is necessarily involved with the essential human questions. But it does not so much produce decisive answers as inaugurate a new type of relationship between human beings and God and between human beings. Christianity transforms the way in which we raise these questions rather than solves them.

As for death, Christianity does not primarily raise and answer the question that it poses to us; rather, the new type of relationship with God and among human beings which is its specific concern transforms the way in which we can raise the question of death without answering it. We must dare to say that the resurrection of Jesus Christ does not answer the question raised by the death of Jesus, the question which his death posed to Jesus as an individual ('My God, my God, why have you forsaken me?'), the question which his death posed to his first disciples on the Emmaus road and the question that his death will pose to his disciples to the end. The resurrection of Jesus Christ does not answer the question raised by the death of Jesus; it is an event which is added to the fact of his death, a revelation of God and about God which is added to this other revelation given by his death; it is a summons which is added to the other summons expressed in his death. We must also say that it is a question which is added to this other question posed by his death, and that neither of these two questions can provide an answer to the other, can settle it, seal it. If the question raised by the resurrection is not annulled by the fact of death, the question raised by death is not annulled by the event of the resurrection.

Do not the other realities of faith have an intrinsic value?

One last difficulty rules out, as far as I am concerned, the way in which some forms of Catholic belief in the resurrection of the dead organize the relationship between God and human happiness or unhappiness: the way in which it centres them excessively on the problem of death and its resolution has the compensating effect of more or less devaluing the realities of the life of faith, however essential. I was amazed to see how at one point or another many Christians were so much under the shadow of the question of death and resurrection that they said to me, 'If there is no resurrection of the dead, what is the point of faith, of knowing God, of Jesus Christ? What is the point of his Spirit making him alive among us? What is the point of praying, of celebrating, of wanting to construct a better world? If there is no eternal life, what is the point of all that?' I found myself facing the same disturbing gut reaction that I mentioned earlier, the one which makes believers say that human realities do not make sense if there is no eternal life. This reaction was more disconcerting still when it was applied to the realities of the faith to such a degree that their intrinsic value – quite independently of any extension into eternity – was supposed to be even clearer to believers than the intrinsic value of human realities.

So does praying to God not have enough intrinsic value, does it not have enough substance, does it not produce enough happiness, pleasure, wonder, does it not demand enough labour, attention, silence, renunciation, to be worth something in its own right? Is there no intrinsic value in celebrating, preaching, doing theology (could I ever give that up?)? And if there was nothing after death, would it not already be something to have led a good life, to have had the exceptional good fortune to have been able to spend some time doing that? Is there no intrinsic value in being able to know something about God, to be delivered from the oppression of the gods constructed by our social, psychological and religious mechanisms, to be liberated from the powers which thrive on the building and the cult of these idols, to be able even to recall Jesus Christ who, by his death and resurrection, has delivered us from these idols and these powers? Is there no intrinsic value in being able to enjoy the good fortune that the Spirit wants to raise him up alive among believers, to enjoy our good fortune that down the centuries men and women have made it possible to realize – even if only very partially – the type of relationship to God and among human beings that was inaugurated by Jesus Christ, to have the good fortune today and tomorrow of being able to share with other believers in building up this kind of relationship, though in a very partial way? Is there no intrinsic value in working for the publicans and prostitutes, the sinners, the blind, the crippled in mind and body, the Samaritans and the Gentiles of all races, the poor, the outcast, the rejected, the persecuted, so that they rediscover their rightful place in the community of believers through God and through Jesus Christ; in working so that fear, anguish, guilt, shame, hate, domination, tawdry riches, devalued pleasure, perverted power no longer enslave human beings and lead to their destruction; in working at this because one has had the good fortune to see in Jesus Christ that God was not afraid of fear, of sin, of shame, of hate, and that pleasure, power, well-being can represent happiness and worth to human beings? And would not all this be worth something in its own right, in itself even if there were nothing after death?

The most disconcerting thing for me about the accusations hurled at me (and they were often violent) that I was ruining the value of the realities of faith because I was casting doubt on the resurrection of the dead was that my own experience from enduring these radical and often hurtful accusations was precisely the opposite. It was as though, once I had stopped attaching value to the realities of the life of faith by believing that they lasted for ever, I discovered more of their value and their depth here and now. Far from losing their savour, the various aspects of the life made possible with God by Jesus Christ in the Spirit took on both a stronger and a sweeter taste. Not because from now on I had to hasten to live a life which would not last for ever, but because, like the bread and wine already given, the love already shared, something of God, of Jesus Christ, of the Spirit, something of the community of believers, something of faith, hope and love was there, already given, already shared. And it had to be taken up. Or perhaps it was because nothing, or too little of that, was there, and one had to work, struggle, endure, die, to make it come tomorrow, the day after tomorrow, God knows when... For while there may not be eternal life, there is certainly a future – however limited. There is a history. Even if there may not perhaps be a stunning and complete victory over death and life for ever, there is certainly the difficult, long, interminable work needed to introduce even the slightest breath of life and happiness, which is also required to introduce even an atom of faith and the presence of the Spirit. The world is terrible enough and people are unhappy enough, believers are bad enough at believing, for there to be an urgent need for our involvement, however feeble the resources that we can contribute. And would all that really make no sense if there were no eternal life? Would all that really be so meaningless in its own right that it would be not worth bothering about – as people have said a hundred, a thousand times – if there is no eternal life for human beings? Is the fear of death so strong and the need to be reassured about it so demanding that it is impossible to notice the perversions it involves us in, when we come no longer to be able to grasp the value of what is possible for us and the taste of what is offered us, except under the auspices of a pledge of eternity?

Going over to the other side

I have almost come to think that believers should, at least for the moment, put their belief in the resurrection of the dead in parentheses and cope in a different way with the kind of fear of death which corrupts this faith, so that they rediscover the savour of the realities of their faith here and now – because this savour is an intrinsic one. I think that at least for the moment they should put in parentheses their belief in another world in order to discover the savour that God can have in this world, and also to discover that it is a far more urgent matter to transform this world than to prepare to live in the other. I think that this bracketting off of belief in the resurrection should last all the longer since the weight of death has pressed down so heavily on the Christian vision, and the witness and the message of Jesus Christ have been shifted off centre by such an excessive concentration on the problem of death and its solution. I know that I am thus suggesting to believers a very different course from the one usually suggested to them and which tends to lead them astray; I am in fact suggesting that their faith in the resurrection of the dead should be put in parentheses so that there can be a revival among them of the savour that God can have through Jesus Christ in the Spirit and the kind of human relationships that this makes possible for us. Believers have often been told the opposite – just as I have myself been told, a hundred times, that it is belief in the resurrection of the dead that gives grounds for, and at all events guarantees, the savour that can be found in God and the life that he makes possible. But at the end of the day, what is the centre of gravity in the system? The way in which we can use God to resolve the question of death, or what God is in himself, and what he wants to be for us?

Besides, the different way of appreciating the savour that God and the things of faith can have is relevant to our way of appreciating what are 'simply' termed human realities, and even more the relationship between God and these realities. We already appreciate the latter in a different way when we see that they make sense – albeit limited sense – by themselves, without being related to an eternal life which would guarantee some and abolish others. But the way in which we appreciate human realities changes even more when the weight of death no longer presses down in the same way on the conception that we have of God and the realities of faith. To the degree that a certain way of coping with the question of death no longer shifts the balance of Christian life by organizing it around another world, the presence of God in this world does not imply this more or less explicit abolition of the realities of this world.

These realities have no longer to be experienced under the shadow of their future abolition, a shadow which is imposed by the need above all else to resolve the question of death and by the type of belief in the resurrection which this need arouses. That does not do away with their contingent character; that is inevitable. Nor does it do away with what is sometimes the very limited character of their worth and their significance, or even their sometimes heavily negative character, not to mention their non-sense and their absurdity. But it is not necessary for the significance and the value that they can have to be putatively immolated in God or absorbed into him. Besides, it is not in God but in death that they are immolated, to the degree that this immolation seems demanded by the victory of the resurrection over death, in the terms in which the victory is so often conceived. In *When I say God*, I stressed what seemed to me to be the absurdity and incredibility (in the sense of being opposed to the creed) of the conviction that the destiny of the creature was to disappear or be abolished in a return to his creator so that God could bring to his perfection that mode of being present to human beings which was thought to be his aim. I failed to understand at the time the role played by death and the fears that it inspires in us in such a conception of the consummation of life through a return to its origin. The long familiarity with these fears, and through them with death, which has been forced on me since, has allowed me to discover that this return to origins was doubly the work of death: it absorbs created reality into its origins instead of furthering its existence, but above all it is the fruit of a way of wanting to conquer death of which some ritual and pathological murders are no more than a slightly exaggerated form, since at that time to kill a human being was the only way to make him immortal or to guarantee to those who sacrificed him a possible victory over their own death. A return to origins makes the creature disappear and kills it, but it makes it participate in the immortality of its divine origin.

If I suggest to believers that they should go over to the other side, it is because the way of looking at things that I have described seems to me to represent a perversion of the God whom Jesus Christ has shown to us and of the life that God wishes for us. On this other side it is not primarily and above all else a matter of settling the question of death; it is a matter of discovering the intrinsic meaning of the realities of our human condition independently of their possible extension into eternity or their possible suppression in favour of eternal life. It is a matter of discovering the meaning and the savour of God and the realities of faith independently of the value that they may have for raising the dead. It is a matter of discovering that God is not the enemy of human realities and that these are not contrary to him. It is a matter of realizing here and now what can be realized of the alliance between God and us, between God and our world.

On this other side we shall have to defer a reply to the question of death all the longer, the more this question and the reply given to it emerged too quickly and conditioned all our thoughts about God, about our lives and about the relationship between human beings and God. The important thing will be not so much not to be afraid of death (who can manage that?) but to cope in another way with the fear that it inspires in us. The important thing will be not so much to deny death (who can do that?) as to cope with this denial in another way. Beyond question – and this will be the most difficult thing of all – we shall have to learn to cope with the meaninglessness, the absurdity, the failure, the unhappiness, the suffering which are so often the human lot, not by leaping immediately (or hopefully) through the looking glass into a world where all that is done away with, but by working to banish all these things as far as possible from this world and looking with compassion in this world on what cannot be abolished.

Above all, we shall have to discover that we shall only be able to look at the question of death and the resurrection of the dead in a better way if we first begin to seek and experience the meaning and the substance of our mortal realities, the savour that God can have in this world. That will doubtless happen much later, too late for my life to be affected by it. I cannot foresee what changes moving to the other side will bring; we shall only know when we get there. I can only foresee that this change will be considerable, since the way in which we conceive of human life and the Christian faith and live them out is deeply stamped by this primacy of death. While we wait, we must learn to live. And to die. While we wait, perhaps even as we exclaim, 'Death, where is thy victory?', we shall have to discover the price, the weight and the truth of this first victory over death. And that is that we should not make it the first question, to which everything else must be subordinate.

3. Our experience of death is changing

In this way we may break the bonds in which one way of raising the question of death holds captive our conception of God, the Christian life and human reality. However, that clearly will not stop the question of death continuing to arise in a radical form. Nevertheless, the breaking of these bonds will produce cracks in this monolithic system through which we may be able to glimpse changes in death and its significance which the extreme urgency of the question and the tyrannical primacy accorded to it may have prevented us from seeing. For death is in process of changing, and if we want to cope differently with the radical question that it poses for us and the inescapable fears that it inspires in us, we will be well advised not to misunderstand it. Now it transpires that these changes have important consequences for the way in which Christian faith can raise the question of death. How is it possible that there can be a change in death, given that it is the only event that we can be sure will happen and that it seems to be identical everywhere, simply because it happens to everyone?

The increase in longevity

The first and perhaps the most considerable of these changes has come without our seeking it, as a secondary and unforeseen effect of a change which of itself owes nothing to philosophical, religious or ideological factors: it is quite simply the change in longevity in the countries of the northern hemisphere. Demographers distinguish three types of equilibrium between fertility and mortality. Humanity lived everywhere for millennia in accordance with the first of these types, where high fertility and high mortality balance each other. For example, in the time of Jesus the life-expectation at birth was about

twenty-five years. However, this was an average which concealed
very great differences in longevity, depending upon age-group. It has
been calculated that during the centuries when this type of equilibrium
prevailed, half the children who were born did not reach the age of
fifteen, and the majority of them died in infancy or as very young
children. Half of those who reached the age of fifteen did not pass
the age of thirty-five. Among the quarter who did, there was always
a more or less variable percentage of old and even very old people,
but these were the exception.

Longevity has increased very slowly since the late Middle Ages: by
the middle of the nineteenth century in France, say, less than one
hundred and fifty years ago (the days of my great-great-grand-
parents), life-expectancy at birth was still only forty. In 1900 in
France a manual worker aged twenty (i.e. the majority of the active
population) had a life expectancy of twenty more years, and on
average died at forty. In 1977 the life-expectation at birth was almost
seventy for men and eighty for women, and it was people aged sixty
(and no longer those aged twenty, as at the beginning of the century)
who had on average another twenty years to live.

How does this staggering modification of longevity change our
experience of death? In an almost imperceptible but decisive way:
over the millennia death has been the prerogative of small babies,
infants, children, adolescents and what we now call young adults;
when high fertility and high mortality were in equilibrium, of every
one hundred dead, fifty were less than fifteen years old (the majority
of them were very young), twenty-five were between fifteen and
thirty-five years old, and only twenty-five were more than thirty-five
years old, a very small number of them (the strongest, as the psalm
puts it) reaching the age of eighty. Because it primarily affected
children and young adults, death necessarily seemed to be an accident,
a brutal, unjust and unnatural break with life (even if it was very
frequent). To reach thirty-five was already an achievement.[7] Just as
death appeared to be an accident and a set-back to life, so the
prolongation of life appeared to be a chance and fragile victory of
life over death, the checkmating of death by a force too often
conquered by it, which nevertheless could sometimes win. So death
appeared as the implacable enemy of life, and life appeared as a
miraculous force which was often more fortuitous and menacing:
the respect once paid to old people also owed something to the fact
that they were the rare and valiant incarnations of this chance victory
of life over death. The drastic reduction in child mortality, the
spectacular progress of medicine, the improvements in diet, hygiene,

work and life explain how today longevity has increased considerably, and how sexagenarians can look forward to a longer period of life than the total average life-span enjoyed by half of humanity over the millennia. The number of very old people is also increasing in a spectacular way, and for the same reasons: there were more than 200,000 people over eighty-five years of age in France in 1950; they will total 800,000 by the year 2000, a fourfold multiplication in fifty years.[8]

The result is that we are the first human beings since humanity began to have a completely different experience of the relationship between life and death: certainly the death of children and young people always seems to us to be an accident and a setback to life, but because it is increasingly rare thanks to our intervention, this setback no longer seems to us to be an inevitable act of fate but the result of a human error that could have been corrected and for which we blame ourselves. It arose from neglect by parents, friends or the nursing staff, mistakes in medicine, the injustice of the social and economic structures governing the distribution of money and goods, and so on. So the death of children and young people seems to us to be both an even more intolerable scandal and an evil which can be remedied: its causes lie in our hands and control of them is therefore within our reach. On the other hand, since the majority of us will reach old age, we shall be the first human beings in the long history of our species to note in ourselves and around us, in a massive way, that death is natural. We shall see, as we already see among millions of human beings, how life decreases and the senses atrophy (sight, hearing, taste, smell, touch); the bodily frame shrinks and the muscular mass diminishes; the sphere of physical, intellectual, emotional, and relational activity contracts; memory and the consciousness grow dimmer. Since for the first time in the history of humanity death has become the prerogative of old people (of every hundred who die, half will be more than seventy-five years old), we note empirically that it is natural for life to fade away and then be extinguished, and that even if this process is sometimes accelerated by illness, it is essentially a vital process (if one can put it that way), as much inscribed in our genes as embryonic development and the transition from childhood to adolescence and then to adulthood. So we are the first human beings to be able to note empirically that death is not essentially a setback to life, an accident coming to life from outside it, but is part of life, natural to life, a stage of life which is not contrary to it nor its enemy.

This is a formidable development, the effects of which on our conception of the relationships between death and life are further accentuated by another consequence of the increase in longevity. The greater the number of individuals who live to a very advanced age, the greater will be the number of individuals who will have to experience a stage of life marked by all the effects of senescence, the most serious of which cannot be fought by medicine, since they are not connected with illness but with a normal and natural biological development. If it is possible to alleviate them slightly, medicine runs the other risk of multiplying the extension and duration of a senile life by curing sicknesses which formerly cut off or nullified this phase of life.

From now on death will appear to be not only natural but even desirable: desirable to the individuals concerned if they are still in a state of having desires and expressing them, desirable to those who love them (if they are still around), for no filial piety can lead one to wish others to live for a long time a life which is too marked by senility. So people come to want to fight against the effects of this process of degeneration or to want to avoid it. This is not a case of racism directed against the aged or euthanasia of the very old. It is a phenomenon well known to those whose family situations or professions lead them to share the calvary of the senile degeneration of those[9] whom they love. Gerontologists and representatives of all disciplines concerned with old age, and even more those directly involved in it, have changed their aims. It is no longer a matter, as it was for millennia, of adding years to life; it is a matter of adding life to years. However, the inevitable biological character of the progressive extinction of life means that beyond a certain threshold, depending on the individual, it becomes impossible to add life to years: these are the years which take something out of life until there is nothing left worth living. So we see a multiplication of reflections on euthanasia and suicide; we are beginning to see associations appearing in various countries in the northern hemisphere which claim the right of those with the great incurable illnesses and the very old to die with dignity, and which defend this not only as a right for those involved but as the duty of society and those near to such people. While it is all too evident that such claims can be contaminated by motives of varying degrees of respectability, they nevertheless have the merit and the courage to confront a problem which is disguised not least because it puts us in the presence of a completely new type of relationship between life and death: not only will death be natural to life, but it will not be its enemy, since it is one of its phases; and for life itself it could be a deliverance and a blessing.

So it is no exaggeration to say that the amazing increase in longevity entails a considerable revolution in our experience of the relationships between life and death and that this revolution is not the result of philosophical, political or religious options which could be open to discussion and which by their nature would be the preserve of a small number of those discussing 'major problems'. It is the result of transformations which concern everyone and of which everyone can be aware, since we all have, or will have, experience of them in and around ourselves. So this revolution has had its effect by the least perceptible yet most effective way: by the banal, everyday experience of each and every one of us. And it is about nothing less than the relationships between life and death, death being only rarely an accident and a setback to life (all the more scandalous because of its rarity and because its causes seem to be capable of being under our control), and appearing to us above all as part of life, as being a natural stage in it, no longer being the enemy or the curse of life, but as sometimes even deliverance and blessing. How many habits of millennia will have to be changed: individual and collective reflexes coming to us down the ages, mind-sets, philosophies, rites! And, it must be added, how many religions! We must ask how such a radical and recent transformation of the relationships between life and death can be integrated into Christianity, which seems to find it so essential to consider death as the enemy of life, as an accident which should not happen to life (and would not happen to it had there not been sin). We must ask how it can be integrated into this Christianity which seems to find it so essential to announce a definitive victory of life over death. Before raising this question, however, it is worth bringing out other aspects of the current transformation of our experience of death and its relationship with life, other aspects which also enlarge and reinforce those which I have just mentioned.

The acquisition of a medical mastery over sickness and death

The increase in longevity is very closely related to the increasing possibilities that medicine has of combatting not only infant mortality but also sickness at all stages of human existence (to the point of prolonging the phase of senility more or less deliberately). At least in the West, we are now so used to resorting to medicine and relying on its effectiveness that we can no longer imagine how over the millennia and until almost a century ago human beings had no knowledge and no power over sickness and death. Both were facts of everyday life, evident yet completely mysterious: they were well known from constant experience; they were the malevolent, familiar companions of existence, but people knew nothing of them.

It is not surprising that human beings should have sought their causes in the superior and hidden world of spirits: angels or demons, saints or devils, God himself or Satan. However, while resorting to such causes might possibly furnish explanations with which people had to be satisfied, it was not so helpful in providing remedies, all the more since to respect the power of these authorities was not enough. It was necessary to know how to secure the support of friendly powers and protect oneself against evil powers; that was inevitably problematical and there were always explanations of why such powers did not intervene which did not in fact cast doubt on belief in their efficacy. The gravity of death required it to be seen as deriving not from inferior powers but from God himself, or from an evil spirit with a power approaching that of God. So death was spontaneously experienced as a personal intervention of God in the destiny of a human being; God determined the hour of a person's death and it was to God that he or she had to pray – directly or through the mediation of the saints – in order to persuade him to defer the moment. Whatever happened, the death of a human being was an expression of the will of God, of his 'good pleasure' (in the Louis XIV sense of the words), as is still evidenced today by the phrase that one can read in the announcements of deaths in French newspapers: 'It has pleased God to call to himself'.

I have studied elsewhere the factors in this conviction that our death, like our conception, is the result of a personal intervention of God, and the view of ourselves for which it seeks to provide a basis. For the moment I want to stress the effect that the habitual and common use we make of medicine has on such a view of death. For if this use of medicine transforms the view that we have of relationships between life and death it is not because medicine attacks head on and in a theoretical way the idea that death is the result of a personal intervention by God, who fixes its hour. In a less ostentatious but more effective way, medicine itself changes the hour of this death in a way which is now so common and everyday that we come to be scandalized when medicine fails, and we are ready to drag doctors to court because they seem to us to be necessarily at fault for not being able to change the hour. The list of fatal illnesses which medicine can cure constantly increases; that of new techniques which allow interventions hitherto thought to be impossible, even inconceivable, is also lengthening, and what even yesterday was laboratory research or the latest technology, not to say futurology, becomes current practice.

This changes our views of death in two ways: on the one hand, as I have said, the greater the success of action against sickness, the more it can be shown that death is not intrinsically the result of sickness or accident, but is natural to the living organism, and that in the end one dies, not through illness, but by virtue of the simple fact of being human (as cynics put it, the only incurable mortal illness). On the other hand, in the same way, the more successful action against sickness proves to be, the more death becomes an empirical reality over which we have knowledge and power. Each time a new fatal illness is conquered it is because first of all people have understood the mechanism which allowed it to imperil life, and then they have developed the different techniques of intervention which allow the correction or abolition of the action of this mechanism. If researchers do not succeed in conquering a fatal illness, it is either because they have not yet discovered the mechanism at work in it, or because they have not yet discovered techniques which allow intervention in this mechanism. These diseases and deaths may still remain inexplicable, but it does not occur to us to say that they are mysterious, in the sense that over the millennia human beings have experienced sickness and death as mysterious realities related to powers which, because they were not human, were hidden from them.

One can understand that after so many millennia of ignorance and anxiety over what was nevertheless the daily bread of existence, human beings were caught up in an excessive hope, convinced that medicine would conquer all disease and even death. This megalomania is neither less, nor less explicable, than that which attributes the conception and death of a human being to a personal and special intervention of the Trinity itself. So one can also understand that what is called medical power – and which is often criticized advisedly – is less connected with the ambition of doctors and the desire of their associations for power than with the formidable force of the demand presented to them by the need of human beings to live and their fear of suffering and dying.

It is necessary to stress the transformation made in our view of death by the fact that from now on we know its mechanisms and can already very often control them, provided that we are dealing with illnesses and not with the degeneration and death natural to living beings. Death is no longer the act of God, still less of good or evil spirits; it no longer involves mysterious powers whom one must try to conciliate and who one can believe ultimately to be able to deliver us from death because they are its masters. Death is the action of biological, physico-chemical, socio-economic mechanisms, and the like, which are of the same nature as the mechanisms which govern other phases of life (including conception); without doubt we shall never know the whole story, and *a fortiori* we shall never achieve complete mastery over death. But the fact that something will always escape us is a result of the limitation to our powers and our knowledge, which will never be completely adequate to the complexity of living reality (though that is also limited), and is no way connected with the fact that death (and conception), unlike the other phases of life, are mysterious phenomena whose essential nature is solely connected with the power and knowledge of God. That does not mean that the fact of death will no longer be an issue for humanity, made up as it is of thinking individuals, even if we succeed one day in coming to understand the mechanisms of life (and therefore of death) which are accessible to our intelligence. But that means that this question, not to mention this mystery, of death cannot be raised and experienced as it was before by human beings who from now on have the everyday and collective experience of a knowledge and a power which are effective over death.

It is still too early to guess what will be the essential impact of this transformation: here again, habits of millennia, reflexes which come to us from down the ages, tutelary mentalities and rituals are in question. And they are in question in the context of nothing less than one of the most powerful and most obscure dimensions of our individual and collective life: our relationship as living beings to death. However, it is certainly too soon to be able to see how deeply the Christian view of relationships between life and death and the Christian view of death as following from a direct and immediate intervention of God in the life of a human being will be modified by it. And if it is the case, as I tried to show above, that the Christian view of God, of Jesus Christ and of the life of faith was often too indebted to a certain view of death and its relations with life, we must be aware that a modification of this view of death will have vital consequences for the Christian view of God, of Jesus Christ and of the life of faith.

Biologically, life needs death

The consequences of medical practice for our views and experience of death lead us as a matter of course to discuss the natural consequences of the account of life and death with which modern biology and the natural sciences have made us increasingly familiar for our thinking on the same issues. It would seem to us, more clearly than to earlier centuries, that just as the universe and matter have a history, which means that they did not always exist and one day will quite naturally disappear, so life is an episode which is both very ancient and recent in the history of the universe and of matter. It is natural for it to appear and then disappear; this happens by the very nature of the physico-chemical and biological processes which are at work in it. The death of individual living beings, including those of individuals belonging to the human race, has already been put in a quite different context, from which it takes on another significance.

Biology notes *ad nauseam* that the death of individuals is one of the most remarkable inventions of the process of evolution, as beneficial to life as the concomitant invention of sexuality. We shall have to return to this link between death and sexuality as the two complementary aspects of the same progress in life when, in connection with the Christian views of sexuality, we consider why Christianity makes the abolition of sexuality one of the conditions and one of the consequences of the abolition of death and the advent of eternal life or its anticipation in this world. For the moment, I want to stress how our representation of death is changed by the biological observation that the death of living organisms and also their reproduction through sexuality represents a considerable step forward in the development of life.

Here we must look at the remarkable explanations given by the best of contemporary biologists. Without sexual reproduction, life is condemned to repetition of the same thing; the combination of the characteristics of two different parents allows the differentiation of individuals and the development of life as a result of the combination, the encouragement or the elimination of these differences. But that presupposes and calls for the death of the individuals of the preceding generation: if the earlier forms of what they embody did not disappear, the interplay of the combinations of new forms resulting from their sexual reproductive activity could not come about, and life would be condemned to the infinite repetition or persistency of the same thing, modified only by the much less rich and varied processes of transformation like those which prevailed before the appearance of death and sexuality.

So it proves that human death is the daughter of life to the degree that life invented death, and that, far from being life's opposite and its enemy, death is a condition for its progress: without doubt this is the most remarkable step forward in the history of evolution. It also proves that the death of individuals is in a way the mother of life, to the degree that this death makes possible the development of life: far from being a curse on life, death is a blessing for life itself and for the living individuals of later generations. This is an extraordinary transformation of our usual conception of relationships between death and life, and in any case an extraordinary reversal of the antinomian relationships between death and life which seem so much part of Christianity that Christians feel their faith about to collapse once questions are asked about them. Have we to ask whether Christianity can integrate another conception of these relationships into its thinking, or must we suppose that it is irremediably bound up with what from now on is an untenable conception of the relationships between life and death?

People will doubtless be led to retort that the question should not be put like this, for what biology tells us is true only of living matter and not of thinking beings, men and women, and that the extraordinary superiority of thinking life over non-thinking life means that the question of the relationship between life and death is put quite differently where human beings are involved.[10]

Biology would be the last scientific discipline to want to deny the extraordinary difference between human life, with all that makes thought possible, and the infra-human forms of life. Biologists recognize that this appearance of humanity and thought are as decisive a threshold in the history of life as the appearance of sexuality and death; so great is its originality that from that point on we cannot conceive of the future of evolution in the same categories and in accordance with the same laws as those which have gone before. But for all that, they do not think that the appearance of thought alters the fact that sexual reproduction and death are necessary and favourable conditions of life, including the life of human beings. And they would go on thinking this unless proof to the contrary were produced by discipines concerned with the specific nature of human beings (and that has not happened).

The historical forms of the human condition are mortal

Here in fact the historical disciplines take over from biology to show that in the context of the supreme achievements of the human spirit and its most noble activities, death is not the opposite of life but – as in the case of biological life – an essential condition which favours it. How is that? First of all, we have leaʳned that civilizations are mortal. They die not only because they are annihilated by other civilizations or because they ruin themselves by their own mistakes (though both these things happen) but because, as with the solar system, the planet earth and living species, it is as natural for them to disappear as to grow. What are interpreted as errors leading to their decadence are sometimes equivalent to the signs of senile degeneration among individuals. We are now almost as familiar with the historical sciences as with the use of medicine. So for good or ill we have to take account of the radical new development in which the historical sciences make it possible for us to see how over the last five millennia (the human species left no traces during the longer period prior to history) being human took many different forms, with very different conceptions of the gods, human beings, life and death.

This plurality through time and space already introduces us to the contingency of the historical forms of civilization; however, along with their contingency we are led to discover not only their tendency to fall but also the natural character of this downfall. Languages are born and die, arts are born and die, institutions are born and die; certain fashions of loving and hating, certain ways in which human beings gather together, moralities, philosophies, are born and die. Religions are born and die. Certainly, history allows something of all that to survive. But on the one hand it gives life to the historical reconstruction that we make at a given moment (every century has its Middle Ages or its Athens) rather than ensuring the survival of what really existed; on the other hand, while history allows us to know about, for example, the existence of the Latin language and to understand Latin inscriptions, it does not make people love, hate, trade, think, talk in Latin. The same is true of institutions, the arts or philosophy: one can read Plato or Thomas Aquinas, one can, if need be, seek to be a Platonist or a Thomist (experience shows, by the extreme diversity of the different forms these attempts have taken that the aim is in fact impossible), but one does not think by oneself and in oneself as did Plato or Thomas Aquinas; there is no perennial philosophy.[11]

This is one of the factors which have led Western thought to discover the radically historical character of the human condition. That means not only (as certain Christian thinkers seeking to introduce history into Christian thought have believed) that the human being and its institutions are subject to chronology, to development, to genealogy and to diversity in time and space, but also that it is intrinsic to human beings only to realize themselves in the contingent, historical and transitory figures of their condition. The greatness of humanity is not that we escape this contingency in order to exist outside or above it, but that we create the historical form of our condition. The transitoriness of these historical forms can be expressed by sayig that they are mortal and that their mortality does not relate to their possible imperfections but to the fact that they are part of the human condition.

All this has become evident to a number of our contemporaries. But one only has to go back to earlier centuries to understand at what point this sense of the historicity of the forms of the human condition was alien to them (this is a very different matter from the relativism, scepticism or cynicism inspired by the vanity of human affairs). I have already had occasion, in the first part of this book, to stress how it proved difficult for believers to accept this historicity in connection with the historical forms of their faith in God or in Jesus Christ, or in connection with the institutions which Christian life has produced (like the forms of religious life) and how at some point there needs to be a real decomposition of what might claim to be able to exist outside or alongside this historicity, in order to make possible the resurgence of what can be achieved in the specific historical conditions of generations to come; our own generations will doubtless have to accept the role of devoting themselves to the less exalting but indispensable decomposition which is called for.

It is inevitable that the transformation of our conceptions of the natural character of the death of civilizations and of all the works of the human spirit will produce a transformation of the way in which we represent the character of the death of human beings, whether natural or not. But as with what we have learned from biology, there is more, and its consequences are extremely important. The death of artistic and intellectual works is as beneficial to the life of the spirit as that of living individuals is to the life of the species to which they belong. To be convinced of this one only has to visit one of the neo-Gothic churches with which the Catholic restoration covered France between 1830 and 1930. People wanted to ignore the fact that Gothic art was dead; they thought it a good thing to resurrect it, or rather, revive it, since it was not dead. The result is a series of edifices from which all beauty has been banished: indeed, beauty was impossible there, because it was stillborn. And all the time that people were producing these horrors, they were preventing another art from appearing and living, making its own form of beauty. The same thing is true of the other constructions – this time intellectual – that this restoration sought to set up: neo-Scholasticism and neo-Thomism were not only doomed from birth because of what inspired them (the belief that a philosophy or a theology could be perennial); they were also an obstacle to and a damper on theologies which could have emerged from communities of believers to which such communities could have resorted in order to understand their faith.

The death of specific historical forms of art and thought is the beneficial *sine qua non* of the life of the spirit. Romanesque art was a great enterprise, and those who love it today can still enjoy it, even if many later centuries have scorned it and other centuries to come will doubtless scorn it or admire it again (until every trace of stone or paper has disappeared). But one day human beings no longer saw themselves in it and invented Gothic art, not through versatility, through fashion, through rivalry or through a failure to understand it, but in order to be themselves. Romanesque art was dead as a living art. And that was a good thing. It is good for civilizations to die, whether Egyptian, Greek, Roman or Mediaeval. Twentieth-century Western civilization will also die. And that will be a good thing. If civilizations do not die, civilization will die. If languages do not die, language will die. In the first part of this book I mentioned the most important decompositions in the historical forms through which Christian faith has been achieved and said how burdensome they were, decompositions which are all the more necessary and trying because these historical forms are claimed to be intangible, infallible and definitive. Unless these historical forms die, faith will die. Here again, death is not the opposite of life, but both its daughter and its mother; perhaps it is even its twin sister, and neither gets in the way of the other, as is shown by the way in which the aspirations of the unconscious are expressed.

It is not easy to experience what is not only the natural and inexorable but also the necessary and beneficial character of the death of the historical forms of art, of thought, of civilization and even of Christian faith. Even if someone partly accepts and understands it, because such an experience promotes something of life and sets it free, he feels as though he is resisting from the depths of his being. This new conception of the relationships between life and death provokes a particularly strong resistance in Christianity, because the experience from which it emerges has disturbing consequences for the conceptions of death and life that Christianity feels to be part and parcel of itself. In fact the death of human beings is affected in a series of different ways by all the deaths which might be said to provide its context.

Is death the enemy of the life that God wants to give us?

The increase in longevity shows us the natural character of the death
of individuals; medical practice makes us feel death no longer to be
a mystery directly connected with a personal action of God but an
empirical event about which we have knowledge and over which we
have power, and a phase of life deriving from the same processes as
all the other phases of life. Biology teaches us that death is one of the
greatest and most effective inventions of life and that the death of
individuals is beneficial to the life of the species; history teaches us
that the death of specific forms in which civilization, art, language,
thought and religion are embodied is an essential condition which
favours one of the most noble features of human life. So are we not
imperceptibly but inescapably drawn towards venturing to say that
the death of individuals is not only inescapable and natural, but
beneficial for life and also beneficial for the life of other individuals?
Since one cannot indefinitely get round the obstacle by using the
euphemism 'the death of individuals', will we not be led to say that
our own deaths, the deaths of those whom we love, however cruel
and devastating they may be when they are accidental, are not
only inevitable and natural, but could be a beneficial and essential
condition, if not of our own life or of theirs, at any rate of the life of
other men and women whom we love, of life, and quite simply of the
life that we love?

For those among us who are believers, how can our faith react to
the evocation of such a conception of death? What becomes of our
God, what becomes of our saviour Jesus Christ, if death is no longer
significant in such a way that the salvation which comes to us from
God and by which Jesus Christ is defined no longer has the essential
function of delivering us from it? Have we also to say that death is
not the enemy of life that God wants to give us, just as it is not the
enemy of any other form of life? Have we to say that God saves us
not from death but from what imperils the life which he wants to
give us (what we call sin), just as all human enterprises — medical,
biological, cultural, not to mention religious — are not aimed at
delivering us from death, since it is natural to our life, but at delivering
us from all that could endanger the quality of this life as long as it is
possible?

I have no answer to these questions, to this radical questioning.
Moreover, I refuse to have any, and I am postponing all tentative
answers as firmly as I can. Not because I think *a priori* that the
question cannot be answered (perhaps it can), but because I think

that I am not yet in a position to answer it because I have hardly begun to raise it. Yet again, this is not peculiar to me, nor does it have anything to do with the characteristics of my personality or with the ups and downs of my personal career. It has to do with the general situation of Christians in the West. First of all we must spend time on the other side. At present, not only have we failed to spend long enough there, but we only have inklings of what it is like, rather than personal experience. Even the most adventurous of us have hardly begun to see its contours; we have hardly begun to feel that the air is not the same, the atmosphere is different, the colours and forms differ, and there is another relationship between life and death.

If we try to reply too quickly to this question which obviously presses in on us, we risk taking with us to the other side answers and even ways of raising questions which were true on the side we came from, the side of our tradition and our past, but can no longer be true in the same way on the side which I have just shown, though in a fragmentary and superficial way, to be different in certain points. We shall not be colonizing this other side with our old conceptions. We shall not be evangelizing it, if by that one understands (as was once the case) importing a different culture with a particular historical and contingent form of Christianity, adequate though it may have been for the culture which produced it. If we do that, we shall either break on this otherness what we thought we could impose on it, or we shall break the otherness by imposing on it something which does not fit, preventing the growth of life on this other side in the new form which it must have. We are only at the dawning of this different world, and I do not necessarily claim that it will be better than the previous one, only that it will be other. Perhaps we are not yet even at the dawning of this new world, but only at the twilight of the world which was ours.

We too are afraid of the night, we too want to go back in time. The most aged among us – and I am not far from being one of them – turn back to the still perceptible glow of their past. The youngest among us are in the night, between two worlds, between two lives. Both of us must at least try to have some of the typical experiences of this new world. We must patiently let ourselves be steeped in what already exists of it, savour the scents of it that the wind has already brought us from the other side. We need time, plenty of time. The night will be long and the journey may well seem to us to be interminable. It will be all the harder, the more deeply we are marked by this old world of which we were the subjects, sometimes the workers, and sometimes even the princes or priest.

That is why I refuse to give any hasty answer to the question of death. That is why I think it my duty – and my honour – as a human being and a believer to hold to this certainty which is mine. In the long run, to keep to the old and safe conception of the antinomian relationship between life and death, even if it is canonized by the most familiar forms of Christianity, can only kill both life and faith instead of making them alive. I must also hold to what is not certainty but faith: that God is alive, that he is for us, through Jesus Christ and in the Spirit, the source of life. And I must wait, making what contribution I can, so that the generations to come can construct the historical form of this God who will speak to the civilization that will be theirs. On this other side. Confident – and I am confident – that at the end of my days I shall be able to put my life in God's hands and that in any case he will take it back if I no longer have the strength and the consciousness to give it back to him. Not that I believe that he will transmute it into eternal life; once again, I do not believe that. I shall do it just as I shall hand it over to those men and women who love me, if there are still some around me and I still have any awareness of them. My life was myself; so it is all that I shall be able to give them, since it is all that I can give them today. I think that they will remember me a little. And then one day this memory will die with them. My fate will be that of all living beings: to disappear into the flux of the life and death from which they gave me being, in which they bore me.

I believe that God's memory is eternal, as he is. The memory that he has of me – as of all living beings, as of all the works of his hands – will not die. I do not see any form of survival for myself. But I do see a form of this fidelity of God to himself and the human creatures he has made in his image, and by whom he wants to make himself known. It is improbable, unbelievable enough that God should remember me as he remembers all his works. It is improbable enough that a creature should leave this trace on what he believes to be immutable and intangible. As the painter Turner said, looking at a canvas that he had just painted, at this trace that he had just left of himself, it is a great mystery. Can you understand that the little whose echo I know and welcome speaks to me more of God and his fidelity than of my resurrection and that of human beings? Can you understand that the noise made by a certain passion for life over the resurrection prevents me from hearing the echo that comes to me from God, 'the still small voice', as when the Lord passed by Elijah leaving a trace of himself? Can you understand that it seems to me more urgent, more vital, to perceive this small voice, to perceive what can help life to go to the other side, what life can understand of death on the other side? And that it would be important for me, if I were young, less marked by the old world, less petrified, less paralysed by anxiety, to leave all that behind, to leave Ur and the city of my fathers, to go to this other side? At least I might be able to breathe the air a little, to sense the colour. Is life anything other than this love of life? Are we living beings no more than that?

Human suffering and divine justice?

'But what about the dead?', someone will say to me. 'What about the agony of death, and the tears, and the blood, and the laments, and the devastated lives? Does your good news amount to no more than the still small voice, the Stoic expectation, distinguished yet nebulous, of a possible difference in the relationship between life and death? How can you say that to those who suffer? How can you give hope to those whom death and suffering have annihilated? How does that balance out the thought of those thousands, millions of human beings whose life has been nothing but misery or who have hardly had time to live, just time to suffer and die? It is no compensation whatsoever. I can say nothing about unhappiness, suffering, uselessness, the scandal of what so many lives consisted of in the past and so many lives will continue to consist of in the future, except that they are indeed an intolerable misery, scandalous suffering, absurd uselessness. I can only struggle with all my feeble strength; we can only struggle with all our might – which may not prove so feeble – against whatever there may be of this today and whatever there may be of it tomorrow. But I am well aware that the success will only be partial and that failure will remain failure.

How can one dare to say, write, think that? How can one say it and still think that one is a believer? Please believe me when I say that my reasons are strong ones. Had they not been, they would not have been able to overcome everything in me which was so vigorously opposed to my thinking in this way, far less could they have proved stronger than all the furore directed against me because I had come to think in this way. As I have already said, the attitude of non-believers faced with life and death has taught me a good deal about life and death and also a good deal about God. Believers tell me that my attitude towards death and suffering is unacceptable because it is a mixture of levity and desolation, disrespectful and scornful of the sufferings of the past, debilitating and demoralizing about the sufferings of the present and the future. But how can the believers who reproach me in this way fail to see that they are surrounded by non-believers who have precisely the same views as mine about the relationship between life and death and that the life of many of these non-believers, their struggles and their efforts, their dignity and their hope, their successes and their rebellions, give ample proof that they are not scornful or frivolous about the sufferings of the past and are not idly resigned over the sufferings that will come? How can these believers fail to see that there are other ways than theirs of respecting failure, suffering and death, other ways than theirs of being wounded in soul and body by misfortune, other ways than theirs of hoping that everything is not in vain in the fight for happiness and life? How can they not see that there are other ways of experiencing death and loving life than believing in the resurrection?

Granted, the fact that there are other ways does not discredit theirs. Or rather, it does so only to the degree that it lays claim to be the only way, claims to have the most respect for suffering and offer the most hope. However, after all the years during which I have suffered so many accusations from them, I owe it to the truth to bear witness that the intensity – and sometimes the fury – of the reproaches which such people have directed towards me proves that for a number of believers, belief in the resurrection of the dead is not only the best but the only way of respecting the suffering of those who suffer and offering hope to the living. Who would deny that their faith is a form of this? But who can accept that it is the only one? How many times, though, have I been told over these past years that I was scornful of the suffering of those who suffer? How many times have I had suffering and death thrown in my face and been told that I minimized them, failed to recognize them or despised them since I did not believe in the resurrection of the dead? How many times have I been told in these terms or others, 'Either you believe in the resurrection of the dead or you are an insensitive scoundrel for being so contemptuous of sorrow and misery'?

As I have said, my own experience as a result of my opinions about death and what it inspires is doubtless quite original. It authorizes me from now on to regard it as certain that those who believe in the resurrection of the dead are discrediting the possible validity of their belief by affirming with such fervent terrorism that this belief is the only way of respecting suffering and death. Even had I doubted it up to that point, their attitude would have been enough to convince me that it is my duty – and my honour – as a human being and a believer to reject the dilemma in which they want to trap me. As a human being I do not have the right to insult like this the way in which so many of those who do not believe in the resurrection of the dead also respect suffering, pain and death and suffer failure and absurdity. As a believer I do not have the right to accept such a way of assuring the truth of faith. For not only does it spoil that to which it claims to give grounds by lending it an exclusiveness that in fact it does not have, but it ends up with a conception of God and his relationship to human suffering which is no more satisfying – far from it – than that which is held against me.

I am accused of not treating the justice of God adequately by not believing in the resurrection of the dead. People accept that if God raises the dead, it is not to honour an immortality which is part of human nature and to achieve some kind of restoration *ad integra*. But they assure me that if God brings about this radical reversal which makes mortal beings eternal, it is to abide by his own justice, in faithfulness to himself, since he could not be faithful to himself if he left so many sorrows unconsoled, so many failures unremedied, and so much suffering and so many tears unrelieved. So it is to be truly God, to honour what he must be, that God must raise them from the dead – far more for his own sake than for that of human beings. It is this God, even more than human beings, whom I would misunderstand and despise if I did not believe. It is the rather desolate friendship with which some believers have spoken to me rather than the dogmatism and the fury with which others have hurled this accusation against me that have made reflect on this question: I was all the more aware of the pain of parting company with them on this essential point. But how does one accept the kind of God and the relationship of God to suffering to which their way of looking at things condemns them – whether they like it to or not? I cannot fail to find this way even less acceptable than mine, since mine has the added advantage over theirs that it does not claim to be a response to the question of evil, nor does it seek to make this question soluble or this evil bearable, since neither of those things is possible.

For if what God's justice inspires in him is that every tear, every suffering, every failure, every absurdity, every death in this world should be effaced and compensated for in a different world, a world in accordance with his plans, how can we explain how this selfsame divine justice can tolerate the formidable weight of suffering in this world? There are not unlimited answers, and my friends are less logical on this point than my detractors or my censors: the only possible reply is that the justice of God cannot tolerate this, but finds itself checkmated by the sin of human beings. Sin which is the cause of death and suffering: once divine justice triumphs over sin in Jesus

Christ, as we all say we believe (since I say that I believe this too), both death and suffering will be conquered.

I spent too much time in *When I say God* on the unacceptable features of this link between sin and contingency to want to return to the question again here. So I will content myself with again stressing two features of the present matter which seem to me to be decisive. First of all, it is impossible to attribute purely and simply to human sin the fact, for example, that for hundreds and hundreds of thousands of years out of the numerous millennia during which our species has been evolving, groping towards its most recent forms, there has been an almost sub-human level of life. Similarly, it is impossible for us to attribute to sin the fact that millions and millions of people lived a hardly more satisfying life before the most recent form of the human species had achieved some of its most important conquests: fire, then agriculture and stockbreeding, then writing, and so on. It is impossible to attribute to sin the fact that, as I recalled earlier, for millennia half the children who were born did not reach the age of fifteen, and half of those who passed it did not reach the age of thirty-five. It is impossible, at least in specific terms, to confuse sin and contingency, to attribute to sin the fact that the human being is a historical and contingent creature and that it is inevitable and natural that the human species should have taken millennia to emerge from its origins. That does not reduce by one iota the weight of suffering, unhappiness or sheer inhumanity, the non-humanity represented by so many human lives past or, alas, still to come. But it does rule out the 'explanation' given of them by the most current forms of Christianity, which resort here to sin. Now if sin is no longer the explanation for this setback to the justice of God and therefore there is no longer hope that the victory of God over sin will ultimately provide compensation, how can one accept that the justice of God should accommodate itself to this suffering and this misfortune since, to stress the fact once again, sin can no longer be considered a satisfactory explanation?

This is the second unacceptable element in such a conception, and it is even more unacceptable than the first to the degree that it affects the portrayal of the God who is involved in all this. We already need to ask questions about the portrayal of God which is being presented when sin is invoked as an interpretation of the existence of evil as a setback to the divine justice. Who is this God whose justice is of such a kind that human sin is enough to produce the terrifying procession of sufferings and death? The classical doctrine replies that the infinite greatness of the God who has been wronged is an explanation and justification for this infinite series. What splendid homage is paid to divine justice, what splendid homage this infinite justice pays to itself, what a splendid God! I prefer my lesson in despising divine justice – since it would appear that I do despise it: in the end it does not end up by turning God into such a monstrous Baal!

I have to recognize that a number of those who contradict me do not resort to such an argument, and like me they find pleasure in the fact that Jesus has shown us that God is not like this, that this is not his attitude to sin, but rather that his attitude is one of infinite mercy. However, the picture of God in which that results poses just as many problems, even if it is less barbarous. If sin is not the principal and essential cause of human unhappiness (for there is clearly no question of denying that it can be a major cause), how and why does the justice of God accommodate itself to the suffering and all the forms of death that human beings know in this world? Suppose we take ourselves back in time to one of the 'hospitals' in London or Paris where in the eighteenth century people collected abandoned children: fifty per cent of the children born in these cities were abandoned at birth, and more than eighty per cent of those who were brought into these hospitals died before the age of one. I am told that I despise the justice of God by thinking that God need not resurrect these millions of sucklings and the millions like them over the centuries. All right. But I do not see how the justice of God can accept the fearful waste represented in the here and now of our world by these thousands, these milions of dead infants, on the grounds that one day God will raise them up again. On the contrary, I find that such justice, if its aim was to give eternal life to these millions of infants, was very unjust towards them (and towards their parents, whose misery was their main reason for abandoning them) in the first place. And one certainly has no concern for the burden of such terrible waste if one simply thinks in the same way that, sad though it may be, it is not as bad as all that, because everyone will be raised again. What kind of justice is that? What kind of God? What respect for suffering and death is there here? I cannot see anything here that entitles us to give lessons on human suffering and divine justice to anyone who does not believe in the resurrection of the dead.

To tell the truth, the only possible logic of such a conception of the justice of God is the one that resorts to human sin and explains human misery in terms of human sin and its punishment, while at the same time explaining the abolition of this unhappiness by the redemption of sin. I shall therefore have to return to this important point when we discuss guilt, later in this book, and consider the other side to which more recent ideas of guilt are leading us, and the consequences that these more recent ideas can have for Christianity. Here I must note that, whether or not we resort to sin, the ideas of evil and suffering called for by a divine justice which compensates for them through the resurrection of the dead in fact represent a human attempt to achieve control over suffering and death. In other words it is an attempt to master human destiny. Precisely because it is most difficult of all to master suffering and death in life, these are the factors that must be mastered at all costs. Even if it means going through a divine intermediary (since one might not perhaps dare to claim such a mastery directly), one way of believing in the resurrection allows people to be assured, at least in a vicarious way, of a degree of mastery over their destiny. What I personally learned from psychoanalysis is that whether or not one is a believer, one has to learn to divest oneself of such mastery in order to become more human – and a better believer, if one is a believer.

The denial of death and the desire to master it in the unconscious

So far I have not said much about psychoanalysis. The reason for this is that I have often been told that my positions owe too much to psychoanalysis. So I did not want to bring it into any of the previous discussion, in order for it to be clear that there are plenty of other reasons for going over to the other side which have nothing to do with it, and there are plenty of other experiences which change our views of the relationships between life and death. There are also plenty of other reasons for rejecting the frequent assertion of believers that life and death would not make sense if the dead were not raised. That having been said, I owe it to myself to introduce psychoanalysis now. On the one hand, this is because it has in fact played a major role in my personal history. Without it, perhaps I would not have been able to see all the reasons, the experiences, the themes I have mentioned so far. They have nothing to do with it, and can be seen apart from it, but my own personal way of living and believing might perhaps have prevented me from seeing them, for personal reasons which still remain more or less unconscious. On the other hand, regardless of whatever part it may have played in my personal history, psychoanalysis is indisputably one of the experiences and theories which have most profoundly transformed our views of the relationship between life and death; consequently it is one of the most typical 'regions' on this other side to which we have to go and live, one of the 'regions' where we find in the crudest and most disconcerting way what makes this new side radically different from that on which we have lived, and where so many of us still live.

However, I shall not say much about that here. Not in order to avoid triggering off the resistance that the mention of psychoanalysis, however slight, may bring, since it is too late for that. I know by experience that one only needs an element of psychoanalysis to be involved – even quite implicitly – in a form of behaviour or a remark for it to trigger off this kind of resistance. There has for too long been a degree of psychoanalysis in what I have done and said for me to be able to avoid provoking this resistance. If I say only a little about it, it will be for two related reasons, one concerned with the nature of the object of psychoanalysis and the other with my situation in regard to it. To the degree to which the unconscious is the specific object of psychoanalysis (the analytic situation sets up an original space in which the unconscious can take shape and be manifested), I do not find it very easy, not being a practitioner, to set out and explain something of which I have some experience and indeed some theoretical knowledge. The unconscious would not be the unconscious if its processes and what it produces could be explained and passed on in the same way as the process and products of our conscious mind. So I can only try, come what may, to describe in a random way some of the changes which psychoanalysis seems to me to produce in our views about the relationship between death and life.

People are often amazed at the dual theory which Freud developed in the last part of his life about the instincts of life and the instincts of death, Eros and Thanatos, for this theory in fact is not entirely satisfactory. But they often fail to note that the reason why Freud nevertheless maintained the theory, though he reformulated it, since he himself did not find it entirely satisfying, was that his practice of psychoanalysis forced him to note the constant interplay of the two great forces of life and death which makes up a human being. Freud could have changed the theory (he often changed his mind on essential points), but he could not keep faith with what his practice taught him of the unconscious if he ignored this inextricable interlacing of death and life, forces more complementary than opposed, just as love and hate are more complementary than opposed. Better still, perhaps it should be said that love and hate are only two aspects of the same force which does not exist outside their duality, and that death and life are two aspects of the same force which does not exist outside their duality.

The comparison with love and hate is not arbitrary, since it proves that the death wish is one of the most powerful – and the most natural and normal – forces in the life of the psyche. A minimum of familiarity with our unconscious makes us cease to feel the death-wish as a pathological feature of the life of the psyche or a force contrary to it: rather, in it we have the repression and denial of those desires – however inescapable they may be – which are harmful to the life of the psyche: not only the psyche of the one who has the desires but also the psyches of those who are its object, for these are affected all the more, the more deeply this desire is repressed or denied. One could say that it is not the death wish which kills or does damage but rather its denial or repression. And to experience that almost daily in one's own life, whether one knows the theory or not, is not the least of the changes in our experience of the relationships between death and life that psychoanalysis brings.

Another of these changes is related to the experience that it allows us of the need to deny death, which seems necessary to the very constitution of the human being *qua* subject. Everything suggests that the human subject could only exist thanks to the active exercise of this denial of death and its own mortality, and as if the processes and behaviour thus set in motion nevertheless threatened the human psyche with further obstacles, if not paralysis or even annihilation. As I have already said, in *When I say God* I was too sensitive to the second aspect, in a way which concealed the first from me. I mentioned that it was psychoanalyst friends in particular who commented that my concern to dismantle the traps in which our need to deny death ensnares us made me fail to understand the basic and radical nature of this need. Just as it is not the death wish that kills the life of the psyche but rather the repression and denial of it, so possibly the processes and behaviour inspired by the desire to be immortal are what destroys the life of the psyche, rather than this desire itself, which on the contrary is an intrinsic part of the subject. That is why, contrary to what is sometimes imagined, the aim of psychoanalysis is not to rid the human being of this desire but to decipher the way in which it is organized and the forms which it takes, and allow them to be identified. A well-analysed patient (a myth which is unfortunately as reified by some psychoanalysts as it is in its popular form by the general public) will not be someone who no longer has a need to deny death, but someone in whom this need is less hidden and less pernicious both for himself or herself and others. Here again, to have almost daily experience of the way in which this wish is part of our human human make-up and of the disastrous effect that it can have on us and others inevitably introduces profound changes into our experience of the relationship between life and death.

That is all the more true since one of the most powerful effects of this denial in fact consists of dreaming of making ourselves master of our origin and our death, in short of the origin and goal of our destiny. In his book *L'Enfant Imaginaire*, published in Paris in 1971, Conrad Stein has clearly shown the role played in the make-up of the human being as subject by the way in which we imagine ourselves being present at our own origin. I watched him writing this book and saw what it cost him to bring to light and to formulate the most deeply-rooted processes of the unconscious. My inexperience of the analytic situation from the analyst's perspective prevents my going that far, but at least I have been able to see something of what is involved. One can guess why coinciding with one's own origin would also be the only way of escaping death, since by being both our own origin and our own work, and therefore no longer dependent on being engendered by two mortal parents of different sexes, such a coincidence would make us beings with an independent existence and thus immortal gods on whom death would have no hold. Once our existence no longer depends on ourselves but on two mortal parents (here we find again the link between death and the difference in the sexes which has already been brought to light by biology), we in turn become mortal subjects and are marked by the difference of the sexes. We are no longer the masters of our destiny; our origin and our end are no longer the result of our own actions; and we have only the limited control of our life characteristic of contingent beings between this origin and this end.

I have shown elsewhere how a certain type of religious faith could serve to bring imaginary relief to this incurable narcissistic wound. True, this belief does not allow the believer to put himself directly at his own origin and end, or to confer on himself a total mastery over life. On the contrary, it obliges him to transfer this mastery to God and to represent his origin and his end as being immediately and radically dependent on God. But the type of relationship that this kind of religious faith affirms, established by God between himself and human beings, allows the believer to regain real and complete mastery over his destiny, albeit in a vicarious way. To believe that the evil and suffering of the world are the result of human sin is to make man the cause and source of his destiny, since even divine justice suffers a setback when God is forcibly caught up in the destiny for which he is responsible as the result of human error. To believe that evil and suffering will be abolished when redemption proves victorious over sin is indeed to make human destiny dependent on Jesus Christ (again, it must be made quite clear that he is *truly* man), but it also makes it dependent on human beings themselves, since some will rise to eternal happiness and others to eternal misery, depending on the value of their achievements.

People sometimes go even further in extending human control over our destiny. In the New Testament there are two conceptions of resurrection: the one which I have just recalled, for which some are raised for heaven and some for hell, and another, which holds that only the just will be raised, and that the rest will be condemned to annihilation by their sin, their death returning to the nothingness whence they came. In a conversation about my views on the resurrection, a very eminent theologian – with whom I had the good fortune and the honour to live – told me that his position was a variant of this second view: only the just who believe in the resurrection will be raised and not the others, because they will not be interested. Hardly had I left his room than I told myself, being one of the latter, that he had just gently condemned me to annihilation, not because of my sin (as in the second view to be found in the New Testament conception), but simply because I did not believe in the resurrection of the dead, which is a further step. Some moments later I told myself more appropriately that I should have detected in his affirmation a trace of this aspiration to the total control by human beings of their destiny (many different forms of which I knew so well).

True, this kind of religious faith affirms very strongly that our origin and our end are directly the result of a personal intervention of God: 'It has pleased God to call...', people say of death. But on the one hand, immediate dependence on such an eminent power is most honourable and is no small consolation for the incurable narcissitic wound inflicted by the need to depend on the chance encounter of two parents of different sexes and the fact that death is a quite natural consequence of the kind of life initiated by such procreation; on the other hand, the believer is not without ways of influencing the decisions of God in questions of procreation and death, so that in this way he becomes an agent ('I know from God that...', 'God wanted us to understand and see to it that...'); finally and above all there is the fact that at every moment of his life, and even more at the supreme moment of his death, the destiny of the believer depends on the way in which he lives and responds to the God whom he makes the master of his destiny, since everything depends on his sin or virtue.[12]

This is the type of omnipotence that a certain experience of the unconscious, however limited, makes it impossible to take literally. Not that it delivers the human subject from the unconscious desire to be present at his own origin, to be his own creation and have control over his destiny. What is true of the death wish or the denial of death is also true of this desire: like them it is part of the make-up of the subject, and the aim of analysis is not to deliver the human being from it but rather to decipher the way in which it is organized and the forms it takes, and allow them to be identified. On the other hand, some of the ways in which it is organized and the forms that it takes are all the more noxious since they are based on the denial of their actual origin and content. Just as it is not the existence of the death wish that threatens the life of the psyche but rather the repression and denial of it, so it is not the existence of a desire for such omnipotence and such mastery that threatens the life of the psyche but rather the repression and denial of it. In so far as certain forms of Christian faith promise the believer such control over his destiny, the experience of what these wishes inspire cannot fail to change profoudly the Christian experience of our relationship to our destiny and the way in which it is expressed.

I will not say any more about psychoanalysis and the way it has of changing our ideas of the relations between life and death. However, two complementary remarks seem to be to be called for. The first is that I have not felt the need here to take stock of what is usually called the psychological criticism of religion. That is not because I think this criticism uninteresting; on the contrary, I find it very interesting, from the perspective of both psychoanalysis and faith. I also believe that it is often relevant, and essentially right. But it seems to me that the essential contribution of psychoanalysis, even in connection with faith and religion, does not lie in such criticism but in elucidating its proper object, namely the kind of experience of the unconscious that it makes possible. The most important thing is not to read the works of Freud or some other psychoanalyst on religion and then discuss them in order to reject this and keep that; here again, the most important thing is to go over to the other side and feel the effects of the experience of the unconscious allowed by psycho-analysis on ways of living and dying, on one's ideas about life and death. The effects on faith of this experience count more than a psychoanalytic criticism of religion conceived as one theory or one psychoanalytical application among others, or one criticism of religion among others. That is why I thought it more necessary – though more difficult – to try to indicate some of them.

The second thing that I want to say is that these consequences are both more difficult and more substantial than those which follow from a critical reading of psychoanalytical works devoted to religion.

It took many years after I stopped going to a psychoanalyst for the first effects of the analytic process which had started then to begin to flower. All kinds of resistances joined forces, and will always join forces, in one way or another to prevent the appearance of these effects or to combat their result. It took me many years for my faith to be affected by what grew out of this experience, and I can see around me that most often believers reject this and prefer not to expose themselves to it, or find their faith as it were paralysed, sometimes killed by it when they turn in its direction. For me, the result was not to be what I and so many others tried to believe would be what we called a 'salutary purification' by psychoanalysis of a faith which needed no more than that, but a radical transformation of the Christian view of relationships between life and death.

Listening to the ebb and flow of life and death

This transformation – like all those which seem to me to be implied by the increase of longevity, medical practice, biology and the historical disciplines – will seem to many people so radical as to be impossible. Non-believers will see it as yet another reason for considering Christianity to be out of date and religion a pernicious illusion. Some believers will see it as an argument for going backwards and getting rid of the changes. This strategy is now very much in vogue among leading groups in the Catholic church; in France, such circles call it 'the reaffirmation of Christian identity', since it would seem that the time of questions has passed and it is necessary to move on to answers and to a witness to the Christian faith that is sociologically effective.

This is certainly the case for the steadily diminishing flock of those who are obliged to form the rearguard in the churches and other institutions which they are the only ones still to frequent. At all events the calculations of their leaders make sense: ten per cent of the fifty-three million people in France, the great majority of whom are theoretically Catholic, that is, the proportion of more or less regular, practising members produces a group of about five million self-confident Catholics. This number is sufficiently large to allow the group to achieve internal consistency and exercise on the outside world a social power which is all the more real because it can appeal to the glorious past of the Church of France.

But what about the other side? What about all the women and all the men who already live on the other side? What about all the men and women who, sometimes without even being aware of it, are slipping over to this other side so slowly and gently that we do not even see them leave? And, since I am one of them, what about me? Do I not have the right to be a Christian? Is the God of Jesus Christ not for us? Is Jesus Christ not for us? Is he the high priest and chief of your tribe, and not the first born, the friend, the assassinated prophet, the master, the Lord, the mystery, absent from yet present in our world?

To tell the truth, while I am morally sure that the church is commiting suicide and killing the faith by staying on the side where it was so well established and has left its mark so deeply, I have no other certainty than the hope that Christian life will be possible on this other side. Still less have I very precise ideas or practices which enable me already to sketch out its features. We must begin by leaving the old side, by breaking one by one the thousands of ties which weave us into its web, or even begin by discovering one by one the existence of these ties. We must begin by already living out in a fragmentary way some of the experiences that are characteristic of the other side, without being able to see what might one day bring them together in what could be called a culture, a civilization.

And since we have been discussing death, we must begin by seeing in a fragmentary way towards what ideas and what ways of living and dying the various experiences of which we are not yet aware will lead us. All we know is that they will be very different from the ideas and practices which have presided over our lives and our deaths. Doubtless we have still to discover all these experiences. I have indicated just some of them here; I know that there are many others and that my account is partial. I am not very bothered; I would no longer claim to be able to present the whole of a subject – though presenting the whole of a subject was something that was instilled in me by a certain ecclesiastical conception of the role of the theologian and a certain academic heritage. That is all the more the case when one is talking about death; death is not a subject that one dominates. There are certainly many other decisive experiences of the way in which death has changed that I have not mentioned here because I am not even aware of them or am not in a position, personally or socially, to experience them. Let those men and women who can have such experiences because they differ from me do so, and then describe them.

I personally am concerned with something that is part of my own world. Those close to me know that the increase in longevity, the discoveries of biology, medical attitudes to death, the death of civilizations are some of the topics I keep harping on, in a way which half amuses and half horrifies them. Before they learned about it at school, the children of my best friends knew about the phytoplancton because they had heard me say a hundred times that 'for people who come from plancton, we are not too bad, but obviously it is rather foolish to regard ourselves as God.' And as for psychoanalysis – I had better keep quiet about that. All that is part of my world, forms the universe in which I try to be a Christian, in which I try to understand the God of Jesus Christ, to leave room for his Spirit; in which I try to decompose what needs to be decomposed in order to provide room for things that are in process of growing. This is where I try to understand death, to hear the sound of the ebb and flow that it sets up. Where I try not to let myself be driven by this fear into various kinds of impasse.

While I was writing these lines, a woman friend of about my own age arrived in the house whose kind owner welcomes me to work there. Her partner had just died of cancer after a two-year illness. She is a psychoanalyst and I know that she was profoundly and mystically a believer; I know that she is no longer a believer and I know that she is interested in my quest for God and my way of believing. She is a big blonde woman, beautiful, healthy, and alive. She is alive, yet mortally wounded: calm and collected though you can see the distress in the set of her lips, the tips of her fingers, in the shape of her eyes, feel that it is there in the depths of her heart, in the pit of her stomach. I admire her. I respect her. I am rather afraid of her. She knows that I spend most of my days writing: I do not dare tell her that it is about death, far less pass on these pages to her. Who am I to speak to her of death? I try to be beside her, to be there without being there, to be silent, to be near and listen until she no longer needs to talk if she does not want to nor have to ask herself whether I am listening or not when she is talking to me in the presence of other friends. I try not to seek to dominate death; I try to be silent, to listen to her, to respect her.

In this same house, six years ago, at the very time when I was writing the pages on the resurrection in *When I say God* which were the origin of all this, a woman of ninety-one died. She had become progressively blind, then deaf, then bed-ridden and incontinent, in the course of a year. Every evening, I said to her in a loud and solemn voice the Our Father which she had been accustomed to recite every day. One evening a light passed over her face, and she tried to articulate some words to join me in this prayer which was so rooted in the depths of her long memory; she only managed to utter some incoherent sounds and then stopped, as if that facility too had just gone. Afterwards there was nothing but the hand seeking to grasp another hand and closing on it, the mouth opening to try to dispose of the accumulated saliva. Some days later she died, like a candle going out. We celebrated mass and then we buried her in the smart long black cape which she had worn when she walked, holding her crucifix, among the roses in the garden. Three years later, it was Nadille in this same house with her husband, taking advantage of a remission in the cancer which she and we knew was incurable. She was still so beautiful, so tanned, so alive: 'It's the first time for months that I've woken up without immediately telling myself that I've got cancer.' With death in her, with the death that she wore, the little bonnet of white wool which she had worn on her head since it had been shorn of her marvellous blonde hair. Nadille, who said to me, 'It's with your God that I want to die', who knew that I did not believe in her resurrection. And who three months later died with my God...

...Do not say that I do not respect either death or God because I do not believe in the resurrection of the dead. Rather, help me to hear death, to hear the ebb and flow that it sets in motion. Do not make so much noise with your accusations, your objurgations, your arguments. Nothing is important except the power to hear and understand. Help me to go to the other side. If you cannot help me or go with me there, do not forget me. If you do forget me, remember that there are living beings on the other side. That they are human beings, living and mortal. Some of them want to live from God by Jesus Christ in his Spirit and be in communion with one another. Do not pursue us, do not reject us. Do not kill us, since death will kill you as it will kill us. In the name of God, do not disdain to give us life and happiness, even if we are mortals as you are.

II

Sexuality*

New interlude

Four months have elapsed since I wrote the preceding pages on death. First of all I had some real holiday after the months of constant work. I was a bit disappointed not to have been able to touch on other themes, as I had planned, since I had not expected to devote so many pages and so many weeks to death; but the book required this part, and I had to wait a while before going on to what came next, especially since, as I have already observed, I always need some time to catch up with what I have written. It is as if the writing were the work of part of me which projected itself beyond me in a forward direction, and it took weeks and months for the rest of me to catch up with and accustom itself to what initially could prove surprising and even terrifying. Then came weeks when I never had more than two or three days free in a row, and that made it impossible for me to take up writing again. That is no longer the case at the end of this year: now I have several fairly free weeks ahead. So I must write. Come what may. Regardless of cost. Where will this writing take me next?

Having felt for several weeks that this moment was approaching, I asked myself whether I should follow my plan and continue to explore some of these other aspects of the side on which it seemed to me that we others, believers, should spend time in order to be able to liberate God, to set him free, for him again to be able to introduce what he and a new humanity could achieve. But I hesitated to follow this plan. Doubtless because it meant that having discussed death I would have to go on to discuss sexuality, and the one topic is just as dangerous as the other. Besides, while in more recent years I had had to cope within myself and outside with a kind of link between faith and death which now seemed to me to be unacceptable, for a great

* This chapter on sexuality was written between December 1982 and January 1983 at Parc-Trihorn and in July 1983 at Parc-Trihorn and Pontaillac.

many years previously I had had to cope within myself and outside with a kind of link between faith and sexuality which also seemed to me now to be unacceptable. Over these years I worked long, hard and patiently to change the nature of these links. I fought with the weapons available to me at that time by virtue of the fact that I was professor and then dean of a not unimportant faculty of theology. I wrote several 'theoretical' studies which, whatever else, were important for me and for what was happening to me. I also fought a number of battles, often long and difficult ones, on grounds which present conditions impose on moral theologians like myself: contraception, abortion, sterilization, artificial insemination, the status of remarried divorced people in the church, the celibacy of priests, the hypertrophy of a particular kind of theology of the married couple, of love, of fatherhood, of motherhood, of the child, of the sexuality of adolescents or young adults, and so on.

These are battles into which one does enter lightly or with impunity, since one wages them with the whole of one's being that is involved, in faith as in sexuality. I fought all these battles. And I lost them all, if winning them should have meant that the official hierarchy of the Roman Catholic church changed its doctrine and its way of talking. Between 1960 and 1970 many of us could hope for such a change; after all, at that time certain bishops had the same hopes and were hard at work to achieve them. At the very end of 1982, when I am writing these lines, we know what happened: nothing. If one takes as a measure of success a criterion other than a shift of position in the hierarchy, for example not only the private practice of the majority of Catholic men and women of which they may be ashamed, but their considered public position, or even the way in which certain minority Christian groups have found it impossible, in the name of what they call Christianity, to prevent the social and legislative developments which many people would feel to be necessary, then these battles certainly have not been lost; indeed they have even been won. But I am worn out with them, and I have suffered many blows. I certainly would not have been condemned so severely over *When I say God* had I not had such a brush with the Holy Office over all the points on which I had been led to affirm as Christian positions which were contrary to its own. The Holy Office was prompted to open my dossier in 1962 by an article, in fact quite a mild one, on the celibacy of priests, and the most difficult moment had been that of my support of the Veil law on abortion in 1974 (in spite of its faults); the political situation had made it impossible for the Holy Office to condemn me or declare me excommunicated (though this came up several times), despite the public and official character of my interventions as high up as the deputies and the government, or my militancy on the side of doctors, lawyers and social workers who had decided to practise abortions illegally and make their action public in order to put pressure on the powers that be. Inevitably I had to pay a high price for the way in which the Roman authorities found it impossible to condemn me: I did not believe that I would pay so dearly, but I had underestimated them. People will doubtless understand my hesitation, above all at a time when the official statements of the papal hierarchy are more rigid than ever, to raise the question of sexuality once again and to try once again to unravel the way in which Christian faith and sexuality seem to me to be so bound up that each does damage to the other. I hesitate all the more since I am anxious to get to the last part of this book; anxious also, perhaps, to put in order what I think that I shall have to write: so it might be better to leave the theme of sexuality aside.

However, I cannot do that. About a month ago, when I was troubled by these hesitations, I was at a monthly meeting of one of the various groups in which I am involved where we try to talk a bit about the God whom we seek. I no longer remember how we came to talk about contraception and the Catholic church: these were not our usual topics. I was struck by the vigour, not to mention the violence, with which a number of women of about fifty years of age expressed their regret at having allowed themselves to be exploited by the Catholic hierarchy's teaching on contraception that they had been given – and at that time had accepted. They had all had three, four or five children, but what struck me was not so much their regret at having had more children than they would have wished as their regret at having had imposed on them a view of sexuality and pleasure which they now rejected with all their might, as women and as believers. I sensed the pain, the bitterness, almost the shame they felt at having been swindled in this way, I guessed at the hard course that they had had to follow, I hardly dared listen to what they thought (perhaps without being able to express it), not only because it was too late for them to have fewer children but because it was too late for them to experience the sexuality that had been stolen from them in the name of what was called the faith. That evening, I promised myself that I would take up the theme of sexuality again. I felt that I owed them at least that, not because I would be capable of miraculously repairing the damage, but out of respect for them and for all their kin. It would be a bit like paying them homage. I also promised myself this out of respect for God, as homage to God, since the idol to whom his priests and his devotees have sought to sacrifice the sexual life of these women must be destroyed.

Other reasons for not leaving this theme on one side are less clear to me, but I can feel that they are no less powerful. I feel myself incapable – who would be capable? – of giving a good definition of the relationships between death and seuxality, but these relationships are so numerous and so strong that I could be certain of having spoken badly about death earlier were I not to speak now, however imperfectly, about sexuality. I could be certain of having spoken badly about the way in which death and Christian life are bound up together if I did not now try to speak of the way in which Christian faith and sexuality are connected. Similarly, I have recently found my conviction confirmed that anthropologically speaking it is almost certain that we distort, pervert or truncate the human condition if we avoid the question of sexuality and particularly that of the difference between the sexes. So theologically we run the risk of distorting or perverting what we call God if we distort or pervert what we call sexuality. Finally, since in this part of the book I want to explore features of that other side on which we other believers now have to spend time because it is there that human beings seek a new understanding and a new situation for themselves, is not sexuality one of the aspects of this human condition in which what is involved – practices, views and institutions – has changed a great deal over the last hundred or hundred and fifty years? If a particular view of God and a particular way of organizing Christian faith were inextricably mixed up with an earlier form of sexuality, must not we other believers explore, live with and help to build up this new side of sexuality in order to be able to liberate God, to set him free from the place where we have chained him to an obsolete form so that he can again be the 'God-with-humanity' of this new humanity?

So I cannot escape the theme of sexuality. However, I feel much less certain than I was when I began on it ten or twenty years ago. At the beginning of the first part, on death, I said that I had not had much experience of death. Evidently I cannot say the same thing of sexuality. Not only have I a sexual character, that of being a male, which has been mine from the second when I was born, but I also have a sexuality which has functioned more or less consciously all my life and will function until my death, or at any rate until the time when my various faculties begin to diminish and thus extinguish it. Besides, I have 'studied' sexuality a good deal: in theology, psychology, psychoanalysis, anthropology, the history of cultures, of ideas, of institutions. The strange thing is that the more I discover sexuality in and around myself and the more I study it, the less I feel capable of talking about it, as I once tried to, in a systematic and theoretical way, or even simply of describing it. So I do not see any other way of describing it here than by reflecting on the way in which I came to discover and then explore the relationship between a certain view of God and the Christian faith and a certain view of sexuality (and vice versa).

1. On the usefulness of study

Thomas Aquinas, Summa Theologiae *Ia IIae, qq.49-70*

Without doubt I shall cause a good deal of surprise by saying that to do this I have to transport myself back thirty years to the enormous monastery of Le Saulchoir, where about a hundred Dominicans aged between twenty and thirty were studying philosophy and theology. They spent their time there, without leaving it, in the tranquillity of the countryside. Their study of theology made them virtually live in the thirteenth century, since it essentially consisted in scrutinizing the *Summa Theologiae* of St Thomas Aquinas, which served as a manual for both teacher and students. The first four years of my training had given me no occasion to study sexuality: as to its practice, I shall come back to the way in which the vow of chastity was considered so self-evident that it was hardly worth talking about, and to the collective silence (in contrast to the individual anxieties which I must also go on to mention) about the slight failings in this vow which might be expected among men between twenty and thirty. This double silence is quite amazing, and no less instructive than the excesses of traditional Catholic doctrines and practices and their obsession with the 'sin of the flesh'. For the moment I shall keep to what in fact occupied us most, the study of the *Summa Theologiae* of St Thomas Aquinas (which – do I have to spell this out? – I had never heard mentioned during my four years of foundation studies and philosophy at the Sorbonne. Nor did I hear mention of sexuality, for that matter.)

In the first year of moral theology we studied the first half of the second part of the *Summa*, where Thomas Aquinas, having shown that happiness is the goal of life and morality (which was not already evident to the kind of Christianity in which I had been trained) considers what today would be called human action and its freedom, then the passions (a fascinating treatise which is also quite remote from the traditional Catholic way of raising problems) and then the *habitus*, that is to say the way in which the various faculties of the psyche are structured by their action. After that he touches on the two great families of structures of this kind which relate to morality: the virtues and the vices. It was in studying the treatise on the *habitus* and the virtues that I was almost thunderstruck, in a way to which I must now return; the first effect of this was that during my last two years of theology I devoted the 'thesis' that some of us had to produce at the end of our studies, in order to qualify and eventually to become teachers of theology, to this subject.

What did it comprise? The whole Christian tradition that I had come to know, first in the family and then as a religious, automatically made me think of virtue as a mastery of the will over the passions, and specifically over those two great families which, following Aristotle, St Thomas called the concupiscible and the irascible (one does not go very far wrong in approximating these to what modern psychology, if not psychoanalysis, calls sexuality and aggression). Virtue was necessarily the result of the mastery of the will over the passions, sexuality and aggression, and vice was necessarily the result of the mastery of the passions over the will. However – and this was the thunderbolt – St Thomas rejected this conception, though it was dominant in his time, as indeed throughout Christian tradition. He claimed that this sort of virtue was not the act of the will or its triumph but that it was the expression of the passions themselves, and that it did not consist in seeing that they were controlled by the will; the important thing was that the passion concerned should be expressed and possess its object in conformity with the order of the spirit. So virtue in the matter of sexuality was not a matter of the will dominating or obliterating sexuality in a more or less Stoic way; the important thing was that the concupiscible should experience its object, namely pleasure, in conformity to the order of reason, and find there its own good, namely pleasure. So if I may dare to put it that way – as St Thomas did – the passions have their own consistency and personality in relation to the will and the intellect. Their vocation is not to disappear in favour of the latter; rather – in the case of the concupiscible – it is pleasure, and virtue does not consist in diminishing pleasure or evacuating it but in promoting a life in conformity with the human vocation.

In spite of the commotion produced at that time by positions so alien to what was almost the unanimous Christian tradition, Thomas Aquinas, with characteristic calm and boldness, drew several conclusions for which the Christian tradition was hardly prepared and which it has never truly appropriated, despite the quasi-canoniz-ation of other aspects of his thought. He argued that continence is a sorry virtue since in it the will exercises external constraint over the passions; it certainly succeeds in throttling them, but this violence is also contrary to the true nature of the will – which is not tyrannical – and to the true nature of the passions – which is not to be slaves. Moreover, and above all, the passions do not achieve their end, which is pleasure, and if continence has at least the merit of averting moral evil, for Thomas it has the great failing (as the other Thomas would have said) that it 'gets in the way of the music', that is, pleasure. Here was something to make the faces of continent men and women of every order fall (I was one of them), and they are not always very happy to begin with.

There was another no less logical consequence: gently taking the opposite view to the whole of Christian tradition without stressing it too much, Thomas Aquinas affirmed that sexual pleasure would have been even stronger and more marvellous between Adam and Eve in paradise before the primal sin than it has been since (which is saying a great deal). In fact, original sin diminished all the values of the human condition to a greater or lesser degree; since sexual pleasure is one of these values, it was clear that it too had been diminished by original sin and therefore must have been even greater and better before sin: something to make Origen, Augustine and other real but deplorable sources of Catholic sexual morality turn in their graves, since they thought more or less explicitly that there had been no sexual life in Paradise and that the mere existence of sexuality – at all events of its practice – was both the specific sign and the context of human sin.[13]

The sight of a young Dominican aged twenty-six, not too abnormal in temperament, clothed in shining probity and a white robe, discovering through writings more than seven centuries old the vast domain of sexuality and pleasure, might be an amusing one. Obviously I am not going to claim that I had not had any experience of sexuality before: I had been very loving, even if it was in an almost completely platonic way, as was often the case at that time for young people in their twenties in my surroundings. Besides, I had no more attained perfection in the practice of my vow of chastity than in that of my other vows. But my practice of sexuality, whether virtuous or sinful, had never led me to reflect on the views of sexuality and pleasure which my Christian training had instilled in me and which governed my personal conduct. If I now have to go back to my first contact with these theories of St Thomas, it is because that was the time when I did first begin to reflect, in a way which was all the more decisive since the questioning which followed from it was not provoked from outside the Christian faith by a more or less anti-religious theory or a more or less deviant practice, but by the thought of a theologian, a genius and a saint in whose intellectual company I had had the good fortune to spend a good deal of time. In many other spheres of theology, people had shown me the radically new options that St Thomas had taken; they demonstrated how the Christian tradition had been enriched by adopting them and impoverished by rejecting them. However, in the sphere in question people hardly stressed what had been so radical and so revolutionary in this option; there it stayed, in the text, certainly not left out or crossed out, but not brought to light or exploited. I was the only one to be enthusiastic about it; I wrote my thesis about it and was received with an almost universal indifference which cannot be explained only by the limitations of my personal work. I foresaw vital consequences for Catholic sexual morality, but hardly anyone paid attention, and some years later, I taught this part of the *Summa Theologiae* with an enthusiasm which nothing ever indicated to me to have been communicated.

Nowadays I am not very surprised at the naivety in my amazement at that time, having learned since then the cost of going down certain roads. I shall come back to the reasons why the factors most often involved in the choice and practice of a certain form of religious life in 'chastity' are precisely the ones that prevent people from taking in such texts even if they read them, study them, scrutinize them or edit them. The fact remains that almost exactly thirty years ago, in the decisive years of my intellectual life (because at that stage the intelligence is approaching maturity), St Thomas Aquinas taught me that sexual pleasure was a positive value of the human and Christian condition and that the moral and Christian virtue of chastity was to promote it. Certainly it had to govern it, but by serving it rather than subjugating it, and by serving men, women and God through not subjugating them. You may smile at the course of such a discovery; I smile at it myself. But anyone who is inclined to smile should consider its consequences: instead of opening my dossier in 1962 in connection with an article on the celibacy of priests which was thought to be dangerous, the Holy Office should have opened it in 1952, since that was the time when I read – and understood something of – the treatises on *habitus* and the virtues in the *Summa Theologiae* of St Thomas Aquinas.

Psycho-physiology

Though other appointments were envisaged for me when I had finished my theological studies, the story I have just told indicates that it was almost inevitable that I was destined to become a professor of moral theology. After some deliberations, it was decided that I should prepare myself for that by completing my training with the study of modern psychology. At that time (1956) people did not yet talk of 'human sciences' or the pernicious influence they might have on faith. Nevertheless, my superiors showed real courage and firm optimism in encouraging me to begin not by studying the dangerous disciplines in which one had to acquire competence in order to be able to refute them, but disciplines the acquisition of which could not fail to be beneficial to a better understanding of human conduct through moral theology. I had the good fortune to spend three years studying at Montreal. One substantial advantage this had, among others, was that it removed me from what was still rather a tense and dogmatic climate of controversy in Europe involving theologians, the faithful and the *magisterium*, and put me in a cultural milieu where American and English, not to mention Swiss and German, works were more important than French. It also acquainted me more closely with one of the most astounding forms that Catholic sexual morality was ever to take, namely that which had dominated the training of the unfortunate men and women of Quebec up to about 1950-1960. However, I must limit myself here to the consequences of my study.

For the first three years I studied neurophysiology, of both the higher mammals and of man, and psychology, animal and human, both taught in a remarkable way. I discovered and learned once for all that the higher one goes in the scale of living beings, the less sexual activity is unambiguously centred on reproduction and dependent on neuro-hormonal mechanisms, and the more it comes to depend on the central nervous system and the functions which are peculiar to man: language, symbolization and so on. Reproduction certainly remains an essential function of human sexuality, but it is only one of its functions and in any case cannot serve to define it, since it is incapable of defining the other psychological functions of sexuality. Three years were not too much to introduce me to the numerous physiological and psychological proofs of this fact, since it not only went against a permanent dimension of the Christian tradition about the matter and against the constant and vigorous teaching of the pope of the time (Pius XII), but it even went against a by no means negligible part of the moral theology of my dear Thomas Aquinas.

In fact, while Thomas Aquinas wrote a treatise on virtues in general which contains the original and audacious points of view that I have recalled, a very few years later he also wrote a treatise on the particular virtue of temperance. While parts of this are new and brilliant, in the part on sexuality he seems to have completely forgotten what he had argued so audaciously, and keeps to a very narrow point of view: the essential criterion for moralizing that he maintains is that reproduction is the essential objective of sexuality. He stresses this so much that when he asks whether adultery is a sin, he neglects all the traditional arguments, including those contained in the Gospels, and keeps only one: adultery is a sin because it could bring to birth children who would have no family to bring them up, or it could harm the well-being of legitimate children. I am indebted to the serious study of neurophysiology and psychophysiology that I made at that time – against all the weight of all tradition (one need only remember the famous dispute over the two aims of marriage) – that it was scientifically wrong to make reproduction the first goal of sexuality or even to make it such an important secondary goal that any other goal envisaged for sexuality should not contradict it. Here again you may perhaps be amused at what led to such certainty. But it is worth remembering my starting point, which is still, a quarter of a century later, that of official statements of the Catholic hierarchy. That may take the smile off your face! And you will smile even less if you note the public silence to which so many theologians, priests and bishops feel themselves to be committed when in their inner faith, their private advice and the exercise of their ministry they think and do exactly the opposite to the statements of the official hierarchy.

Ethnology

I did not just study neurophysiology and psychophysiology: I was initiated more briefly into what was sometimes called ethnology and sometimes anthropology. To say it again, this was in 1956-59, and I had heard very little talk about it in philosophy, whether at the Sorbonne or among the Dominicans, or in theology. I then learned enough about it, thanks above all to the English and American schools (the first works of Lévi-Strauss were still quite recent), to discover that over the centuries and the continents societies had thought of, expressed and organized sexuality in just as varied and different ways as all the other dimensions of the human condition, and that here too, while reproduction had always been an essential element, it had never been the unique or even the principal factor of the social and individual functions which impel societies to organize and control the sexual life of their members. Steeped as I was in my Western Christian culture, I discovered with astonishment that the way in which these societies had experienced and conceived of sexuality was not to be explained merely by their 'savagery' or by their ignorance of the Christian faith but also by values unknown or inaccessible to my culture and my religion. Since biological reproduction depended, if not on the same views, at least on the same mechanisms, the other aspects of sexuality would seem to prove susceptible to being experienced, organized and institutionalized in just as varying ways in different cultures as the other dimensions of the human condition. While some of these ways could without doubt be dismissed as inferior or immoral, particularly when judged by the criteria of Catholic sexual morality, several had known or been able to express aspects of sexuality which had escaped my culture and my religion yet which could not be accused of being deviant or immoral.

So that was the end for me of a feature which had hitherto been implicit but essential in my practice and in my faith, and which was perfectly explicit in the official statements of Catholic morality, the notion that the Catholic view of sexuality was necessarily the most perfect and anthropologically the most valuable one, self-evident because it was as well founded on the natural law as on the gospel. At a later stage I came to learn the history of Catholic moral theology and pastoral practice over twenty centuries, how in the twentieth century sexuality is experienced and conceived in very different ways by the Catholics of Latin America, by those of Africa and Europe, or even within all the variants of contemporary French Catholicism. I then came to discover – no doubt thanks to what had inclined me towards this first contact with cultural anthropology – that the Catholic conception and practice of sexuality were not themselves unique but pluriform in space as through time, and this discovery was reinforced by my reading of the historians of institutions, customs and mentalities.

Here again, people may well smile at what was still the very bookish character of my voyages of discovery (at any rate those to which I am limiting myself here). But they will smile less if they remember how the the *magisterium* presented – and still presents – the Catholic conception of sexuality as a monolith extending over and tran- scending cultures. And they will not smile at all if they note the ravages produced in the non-European churches by the imposition of a Western model of the social institutions of sexuality (itself reduced to uniformity) and the way in which this model has been canonized in the name of the gospel. Here again, one of the ways in which Christian faith and sexuality are combined unravelled itself all the more effectively, as did others of which I have spoken previously, since it did not derive from an anti-religious theory or a deviant practice, but from observing the way in which the various human societies represented sexuality.

The psychology of child development

Over these years of very intensive study I also made the acquaintance of the psychology of child development and psychoanalysis. For the moment I am lumping them together because it was the two of them together which taught me about the existence of sexuality in the child. This was Freud's most scandalous discovery: I should have mistrusted the ease with which I subscribed to it, not because it now seems to me to be wrong (it is one of the numerous points on which one has first to catch up with Freud before overtaking him), but because I discovered later that to subscribe to it called for something other than the almost purely rational approach which I then had. At the same time as they introduced me to infantile sexuality, the psychology of child development and psychoanalysis – again a combination of the two – made me realize me that all the dimensions that go to make up personality are present and operative in all the important human conditions. There is no intellectual activity or even perception without affectivity (I am glad to have learned the theory and practice of projective tests); no intellectual or affective behaviour which does not involve motor functions (Aristotle had already said this, but we can see it and observe it better). At the same time I learned that there is no human behaviour in which sexuality is not operative, not only in a pathological way (though that can be the case) but as a necessary and determinative ingredient. Of course, here again I should have mistrusted the readiness with which I subscribed to all this. But after all, one has to begin in one way or another: besides, people made the transition (just as much as the resistances) easier for me by going all round the houses, since we professors were far from all being of the same school and even fought vigorously. In the end some spoke of libido, others of sexuality, others of 'affective investment', others of 'dynamic psychology', and so on. In short, people took precautions, which the enormity of the matter justified. However, ultimately they were forced to admit that there is sexuality everywhere, and not by way of 'pansexualism', just as one admits that there is intelligence everywhere, and not by way of 'panintellectualism'.

This was again a challenge to one of the most characteristic ways in which Christian belief and sexuality are often bound up, even if at first sight it seems less obvious than in the case of the other ways I have discussed so far. Catholic morality has never neglected sexuality; indeed it has sometimes been obsessed by it. But it has put it in a well-defined context and has tried to focus it on reproduction. Those who wanted to bring it into the open performed the same holding operation by restricting it to what they called the 'genital', thus making nonsense of the significance attached to this word in psychology, and particularly in psychoanalysis (where it does not denote the sphere of sexuality but one of its modes). Outside this realm, sexuality has no place other than that of a pathology the curing of which would presuppose a return to normality, that is to say that sexuality goes home and stays there. Catholic moral theology resolutely waits for it there: that is what is called 'the sixth commandment'. However, once it is accepted that sexuality is coextensive with the whole duration of human life from birth to death, and is not just limited to periods of so-called 'genital' activity, and above all once sexuality is seen to be essentially present and operative in every human activity, whether it is sexual or not, traditional Catholic morality finds its object slipping away and is left with the impossible task of finding something to say about a reality of the psyche which proves to be of quite a different type from that to which it sought to confine it.

The problem is not purely a theoretical one: plenty of clergy or groups of clergy are eager to reduce sexuality to reproduction or to the 'genital', thus condemning their own sexuality to an inadequate fixation on the exercise of power or submission; the prestige of theology and erudition or the humiliation of the intellect; or on their mother, their father, the church, the pope or the Blessed Virgin. It would be better on the one hand to be less reductionist over sexuality in its own sphere and on the other hand to cope better with the ways in which it is quite normally at work in the 'non-sexual' activities of the human being. While I had to follow quite a different route to get there, it was nevertheless during those years of contact with the psychology of child development and psychoanalysis that a discovery took shape that I was to venture to propose ten years later to a very close group of Dominican theological friends and colleagues. The first question to raise about the sexuality of priests is not that of their celibacy, its obligatory nature and the practice of it. We need to ask how their sexuality is involved in the actions specific to their state: celebration of the mass, eucharistic action, forgiveness of sins, ministry of the word, and so on. That caused quite a stir; had I not myself been submerged deep and long in such turmoil before being able to speak about it? Anyway, if it was sexuality that led me to discover the psychology of child development and psychoanalysis, here again one of the most characteristic ways in which Catholic faith and sexuality are linked came to be severed.

Psychoanalysis

Even if I have just described one aspect of psychoanalysis, it is difficult for me, twenty years later, to reconstruct the impact that my first contact with it had on me. In fact, since then I have, as they say, 'had an analysis', and even if one day one stops lying on a couch, the process thus begun does not stop completely. I even think that in my case the main effects only appeared later and very progressively. Besides, for twenty years now I have been spending a good deal of time with psychoanalyst friends, men and women, listening to them talking about their practice, their theories, their institutions, and so on. I have never personally taken up the practice of psychoanalysis or even that of psychotherapy, but these twenty years of familiarity with psychoanalysis make it almost impossible for me to go back in time to reconstruct my first impressions.

Keeping to sexuality, it nevertheless seems to me to be possible to establish several points. On the one hand I learned that sexuality, on the confines of biology and physics, was the result of a history: the history of the relationship of the subject to himself which he fabricates from the relationships which are woven between himself and his milieu, a history which begins at birth and evolves in accordance with the transformations in his own life and also those in the desires of which he is the recipient or the prompter (despite the inevitably male language, this is also, of course the case with women). Far from being a biological mechanism or a purely instinctive game, sexuality thus proves human in three ways: first of all in the sense that it is strictly personal to each individual, depending on even more individuated symbolic configuration than the most individuated features of our biological make-up; secondly, in that it is a result of our relationships, our being modelled by the desire of others, and finally in that it is historical.

In addition, though this might seem to contradict what I have just said, psychoanalysis taught me that sexuality, like all dimensions of the life of the human psyche, is experienced less consciously than unconsciously. One of the most radical misunderstandings of psychoanalysis, which at the same provokes the most radical resistance to it, is to see the unconscious as a pathological aspect of conscious psychological life and not as one of the basic authorities in the human psyche. The unconscious is not an illness which needs to be cured by being transformed into the conscious. The vicissitudes of the drives, to use Freud's term, and thus of sexuality, are more unconscious than conscious in their effects and their processes. There is nothing here to contract the threefold human character of sexuality which psychoanalysis otherwise taught me, apart from seeing the unconscious as infra-human. But the unconscious is specifically human: animals do not have it. There again, it took me time to become less unfamiliar with the specific nature of the unconscious and what makes it distinctively human while at the same time it also contributes to characterize what is specifically human. However, it seems to me that on my first contact with psychoanalysis – and I owe a debt to those who introduced me to it – I saw in connection with sexuality something of what I have just described here, though I cannot escape the different perspective of a reconstruction.

I would not pretend to limit what psychoanalysis has taught me about sexuality to what I have just said: still less do I claim that this is all that it teaches us. I am happy simply to stress the points which could not fail from then on to make profound changes in the way in which I understood the relationship between Christian faith and sexuality, a relationship which hitherto I had viewed in the same way as the Catholic culture of the period. Several features of the relationship between the two were directly open to question. On the one hand there was the irrepressible tendency of Catholic morality to reduce sexuality to the least human aspect of the human being: the physical and chemical mechanism of reproduction and the supposedly animal character of instinct. There is no point on spending time on the massive evidence of this tendency; as I have said, there were terrifying examples of it before my eyes in the Quebec of the 1950s. But I had read Origen, Augustine, and many other church fathers; I had read the mediaeval theologians; I had read the manuals of moral theology and moral practice; I had been trained to make my own confession and then to hear confessions. As Augustine had said: sexuality was the beast in us, sadly necessary, though – as everyone was agreed – we should be rid of it in the glory of heaven. With a naivety encouraged by misunderstandings which I shall mention again, I was amazed that Christians did not give a warmer welcome to a conception of sexuality which made it a distinctively human adventure because it was personal to each individual, the result of the relationships that have formed us, and essentially historical. That seemed to me closer to an anthropology that believers would profess with enthusiasm if it had to do with anything but sexuality. But I had to recognize that since it was a matter of sexuality, most of them would favour a biological, instinctual, not to say animal (in the sense of the higher mammal) model. It seems to me that one of the greatest difficulties in a certain Christian conception of humanity is the acceptance that *human* sexuality is quite radically human and as worthy of humanity (and of God) as intelligence, love or faith. I have been making this point for twenty-five years, and I cannot go back on it now; so it is easy to see how I could not fail to have problems in feeling at home in contemporary Catholic moral theology, or that its guardians should have found some difficulty in giving me a place there.

Another aspect I can remember of the impact that psychoanalysis made at that time on the Christian view of sexuality in which I had been trained might seem paradoxical, compared with what I have just said. I have said that sexuality is normally unconscious, and thus for the most part escapes our conscious processes, not by pathological or pathogenic repression but by the very nature of the make-up of the psyche. Now Catholic tradition sets against the tendency which I have just indicated – to reduce sexuality to the biological, the instinctual and the animal – a tendency to seek to scrutinize, understand, control and judge the least meanderings of this same sexuality and its expressions. That is less an anthropological or philosophical tendency than a moralistic and practical one. The forms of this that can most easily be caricatured are the detailed lists for examining the conscience with a view to confession, in which so many adolescents – and even adults – have made ravishing or horrified discoveries about the innumerable possible modes of sexual behaviour. One would be wrong to fail to see that this caricature is simply the distortion of a concern for both moral awareness and self-control, apprenticeship in which is pursued from the first years of puberty and even before. The point that I want to stress here is not whether psychoanalysis would lead one to judge this concern for awareness and control to be bad or not; it is a more radical matter than that. Such a concern is impossible, precisely because of what is normally the unconscious element in sexuality. Freud was right in sensing that human beings would find it difficult to forgive him for the narcissistic wound which he inflicted on them by showing them the place of the unconscious in the life of the psyche. The damage is even greater to a concern for awareness and control of the manifestations of sexuality as it has been brought to a climax at certain periods and by certain forms of Catholicism (I refer the learned to the interminable discusssions of the Scholastics on the morality of the first beginnings of sensation).

What is in question here is not so much a theoretical conception as a practice. The questioning of it is perhaps even more radical, above all when we know the importance attached to this practice by certain forms of Catholicism. By nature, sexuality to a large extent evades such a possibility of control and awareness, and does so even when psychology has taught us to appreciate it as being more human, more consonant with the specific character of man than the animal and biological instinct to which it has been – and still is – so often reduced by Catholicism. By humanizing sexuality and showing it to be historical, symbolic, relational, and distinctive, psychoanalysis dissolves one of the major elements in it as presented by Christianity. But by humanizing it, too – for it still has to be humanized – and showing the place that the unconscious has in sexuality, psychoanalysis dissolves yet another of these major elements.

Boldness equal to anything

The assessment which I have just made of the impact my contacts with various psychological disciplines had on the traditional views which I shared has inevitably been reconstructed in the light of the twenty years which followed. However, that fact does not prevent me from making some comments on the points which still amaze me. I remember very well, for example, that these different challenges to the traditional Catholic conception of sexuality which I shared did not pose any problem, bring about any crisis in intellect or faith. Is that because this conception had already begun to weaken or collapse for me without my being aware of it? I doubt it, since in my personal life it was always the dominant one, the one by which I gauged the successes, the ups and downs or the failures of the vow of chastity that, like all religious, I had made several years earlier. Was it perhaps due to the fact of a dissociation between intellectual life and the life of the drives, a dissociation which I then learned to be a 'defence mechanism' of which adolescence – a period when it is strongly at work – does not have the advantage. Whatever it was, not only did I feel no anxiety at seeing the questions raised, but I was very optimistic that Catholic sexual morality and through it Christian views of humanity and God could benefit from them. Had I not been taught that in many areas, and particularly in moral theology, the perception and the progress of Thomas Aquinas (though sadly he had little lasting success) were due to the fact that he had not hesitated to introduce Aristotelian anthropology into Christian morality, though in his day this was thought to be wicked and a danger to the faith, and had got him into trouble with various ecclesiastical and theological authorities? When I asked my superiors for an extra year of study in psychology – which I was granted – I argued my case by referring humbly to this illustrious example: I did not doubt that the introduction of certain anthropological findings from modern psychology would raise questions for some people, but it did not raise any for me, and I found great intellectual satisfaction in them as much from an anthropological point of view as from that of faith.

Furthermore, even if my views about my own conduct in this sphere continued to be governed by the traditional conception, I had no difficulty in using different conceptions in my 'priestly ministry' (by then I had been a priest for a while). My rather advanced age (thirty) put me half-way between my fellow students, men and women, who were rather younger than I was, and my professors, who were not much older. I made friends in both groups: some were married or engaged, others already had two, three or four childen. I was asked all the more questions since, as I have said, in the Quebec of 1950-1960 Catholic moral theology had taken on an unbelievable form of rigorism and stupidity. The majority of my friends belonged to the group of those men and women who were beginning to ask questions. I had no difficulty in giving them a different answer from their teachers or their acquaintances in the church and I did not give it – or so it seems to me – with an anti-establishment irresponsibility or by separating the sphere of sexuality completely from that of faith. On the contrary, I tried – as I always have done – to show that the new Catholic morality of sexuality which was emerging was not only more respectful of sexuality but more in keeping with the God of Jesus Christ.

As I look back on it, another point seems to me quite amazing: the different disciplines in which I was becoming involved were not esoteric disciplines, nor did they call for a personal process of initiation (I leave aside here the problem raised by considering psychoanalysis a branch of psychology). To this degree their results, their hypotheses and their methods were public and accessible to a wide audience: in fact many people studied them and practised them. At that time the problem of their relationship to the Christian faith

did not seem to me to be an individual matter depending for example
on the vagaries of my own personality (and therefore on my faith
and my sexuality); rather, it was a collective enterprise which I put
at a certain level of rationality, though I did not totally fail to
recognize its irrational, individual or social aspects. Certainly I was
not unaware that the majority of the founders, practitioners and
theoreticians of these disciplines were areligious, not to say anti-
religious, or had become so. Nor was I unaware of the reticence on
the part of most believers and their pastors towards these disciplines;
finally, I was well aware that it was over sexuality that the conflict
seemed likely to be most lively. But I attributed all that essentially to
a misunderstanding arising out of both the legacy of the past and
mutual ignorance. After all, certain aspects of traditional Catholic
sexual morality and the arguments and practices associated with
them deserved the scorn, not to say the wrath, of pioneers in all
disciplines, or quite simply that of men and women trying to express
their sexuality in a human way. I did not doubt that, in the end, the
majority of opposing individuals, authorities or groups would accept
the evidence that it was possible to establish an authentically Christian
sexual morality which integrated the new awareness and the new
experience of sexuality that were beginning to emerge.

I stress these attitudes. not to be ironical twenty years later about
their naivety, but because this naivety – which was far from being
limited to me personally – cloaks and disguises an essential aspect of
the way in which faith and sexuality were intertwined in traditional
Catholic sexual morality; I only became aware of it later, by other
ways. Moreover, this naivety, or more exactly the misunderstanding
that it cloaked, largely explains the failure experienced by all believers,
men and women, all theologians, all pastors, priests and bishops who
between 1960 and 1970 hoped that a profound change would appear
in the statements and practice of the Roman authorities in the matter
of sexuality. For from this point of view the failure is total; since
1983 the statements have been firmer, more rigid and more repetitive
than ever; to explain this in terms of personal psychology or the
nationality of a pope or his advisers shows the same naivety and
cloaks the same misunderstanding. But I am anticipating, or rather,
this quite naturally introduces the next stage of my journey.

After these three years of psychology I returned to Le Saulchoir to
teach theology in the way that we did it at that time, that is to say,
by commenting on the text of the *Summa Theologiae* of Thomas
Aquinas which teachers and students brought to each course. So I
commented first on the treatise on the *habitus* and the virtues, which

had so won me over eight years earlier, and then further treatises year by year. Those who have practised this kind of teaching know the enormous work it requires to begin with: nevertheless, I kept an eye on the various branches of psychology, while editing numerous review bulletins on the bibliography of psychology. It increasingly seemed to me that of all the disciplines with which I had made contact, psychoanalysis was the most important for the practice of moral theology. I also asked for and obtained from my superiors permission to have an analysis, since for all that I had not taken my resistance to the point of thinking that one could take psychoanalysis seriously without having had an analysis. That having been said, one should not be too severe on these resistances: one of them was very useful to me. I made up my mind, asked for and obtained permission to have this analysis for a reason very similar to the reason why I had studied psychology: for the greater good of moral theology, and therefore for the greater good of God, humanity and the relationship between them; my own well-being hardly came into the affair. With the same mixture of optimism and naivety my superiors had the courage to give approval and support – including financial support – to the enterprise, which was no mean thing in 1962. I stress that all the more readily since one of the superiors who were so courageous at that time was to be one of those more recently in Rome who pressed the Holy Office most vigorously to have my book condemned and to have me deprived of all my functions. So it is important to stress that, at least on the conscious level, I did not have an analysis because of the personal problems posed to me by the clash between faith and psychoanalysis, or even because of the problems that the clash between them was beginning to raise for the community of believers, still less to 'resolve' my own personal psychological problems. For me, having an analysis was what studying Aristotle had been for St Thomas. I was sensible enough to give other more 'personal' reasons to the psychoanalysts whom I had contacted: there were in fact some. Even more sensibly, they understood better than I did that such fine motivation was worth looking at. And that is what happened.

There is no question here of my presenting a kind of psychoanalytic autobiography, which is something of which I would in any case be incapable. Far less is there any question of trying at this remove to discover the impact of psychoanalysis on my attitude to my own sexuality: I would be equally incapable of that. But I could not pass over in silence the fact that from then on (at last!) the changes in my views on sexuality and my questioning of the way in which

Christianity and sexuality were intertwined in traditional Catholic morality were no longer just the result of intellectual studies or participation in the currents of thought within or outside the churches, but also the result of my own analysis. I am incapable of assessing the relative importance of each of these factors, and in any case have little inclination to do so. So I must simply stress that while as far as I was concerned the role of analysis was crucial, its effects were not dissimilar to – and sometimes coincided with – the impact that experiences or reflections completely removed from psychoanalysis had on other believers.

2. The exceptional status of sexuality in the Catholic moral tradition

The climate of the 1960s

Many people do not know, and many others have forgotten, what the period between 1959 and 1968 meant to a number of French Catholics. This was essentially the period of the Second Vatican Council (1962-1965), its preparation and its immediate conse-quences. As I have already said, many of our best theologians from Le Saulchoir, including those who had been condemned by Rome ten or twenty years earlier, worked there, along with several other French theologians. They had hoped against all hope; against all hope they were in process of winning. I shared the enthusiasm, the disquiet, the consoling, but from some distance. The first years of teaching are demanding, above all when new material is added each year. Moreover, I had started on my analysis. In addition, I was performing various functions in the monastery, either all together or one after the other (librarian, cantor, and so on), and some of them were very heavy; so I progressively abandoned the reviewing of psychological works. And why mention all that here? Because the publication by Pope Paul VI in 1968 of the encyclical *Humanae Vitae*, on contraception, may well be regarded as the brutal end to this period. To understand why this text marks such a brutal end, it is necessary to recall what had happened in the previous decade.

From the beginning of the 1960s, a number of Christian men and women, and a number of theologians, priests and bishops, were persuaded that Catholic moral theology could very well consider so-called 'artificial' contraceptive methods (the pill, and so on) as well as the 'natural' methods (Ogino method, temperature method –

or abstention) to be legitimate. Similarly, an important minority considered that questions could be asked about the obligatory character of celibacy for Catholic priests of the Latin rite (and at that time this was not bound up with the decrease in vocations). A by no means negligible minority also thought that in dealing with the status of divorced people remarried in church and in particular their access to the sacraments, the Roman church might well be inspired by the broader practices of the Orthodox and Protestant churches. The conditions and the demands of studies at Le Saulchoir and Canada had kept me relatively outside all these movements, but everything that I have said will indicate that from the beginning of my career as a moral theologian, I had no difficulty in joining company with those who had gone before me in such quests and struggles. Since I was often invited to speak on these questions in working parties, including groups of bishops, I can bear witness that between 1960 and 1965 the front line of French Catholicism was expecting developments in these various spheres which seemed to them better and more plausible than the sometimes unexpected changes that the Council produced in various other areas. The battle, as they said, had been 'won', and the bishops of an apostolic region of France told me expressly what many others repeated: 'Wait for the death of John XXIII (or that of Paul VI); their personality prevents them, for all their good qualities, from embarking on changes in the sphere of sexuality, but their successor...'

This conviction was so deeply rooted in the active minority of several north-European churches (a minority which became the nucleus of a new majority at the Council) that no one was secretive about writing or teaching it, and there was no question of their receiving a note from the Holy Office (which is what happened to me in connection with the celibacy of priests). At that time the Holy Office was considered to be an outdated organ, which had become peripheral as a result of the intransigence of its head and embodiment, Cardinal Ottaviani. It is worth noting that those who worked in other sectors and were not particularly preoccupied with sexual morality tended to consider these questions both relatively secondary and in practice already settled; they felt that the obstacles to be overcome in their own sector were much more considerable. Besides, there had been so much to do to promote, explain and apply the various reforms or new perspectives indicated by the Council that people hardly noted that nothing had been done in this sphere; however, nobody worried about this much, since the question was thought to be virtually settled. Consequently, the appearance in 1968 of the encyclical in which Paul VI condemned the use of 'artificial' contraceptive techniques, caused real consternation to many people. Several groups of bishops (the French, for example) were so disconcerted that they took several months to produce documents in which the approval of the encyclical was so confused and embarrassed, not to say reticent, that the Vatican was very discontented. So what had happened?

The exceptional behaviour of the church authorities

The disarray and bitterness were so great among many people that they were led to be content with superficial explanations: the tormented and scrupulous personality of Paul VI, the return to power of Vatican factions which the Council had neutralized, and so on. With the passage of time, and above all with a little less naivety in these areas, I am persuaded that the cause does not lie there but in the fact that sexuality was involved: people had forgotten too easily what it was, what they were unleashing, and the conflicting character of the relationships that a certain view of Christian faith has with it. In the enthusiasm of the first phases of the Council, people did not realize that of the hundreds of subject proposed by the bishops as a possible agenda, three had been discretely but firmly withdrawn from free discussion by the fathers at the Council. These were in fact three subjects which were particularly connected with sexuality, all of which were known to cause problems and to figure often in the demands made by the bishops: contraception, the celibacy of priests and the status of divorced people who remarried. The behaviour of the bishops was no less exceptional here than that of the pope, in the event especially Paul VI. In fact, right from the beginning of the Council the bishops showed considerable independence over against the services of the Holy See and even a degree of freedom of mind over against the popes themselves. They did not hesitate to change the suggested procedures or reject texts presented to them. The two popes concerned, John XXIII and Paul VI, were arbitrators over these conflicts or took initiatives which showed their concern to respect the freedom of the Council. However, when it came to sexuality, the bishops curiously and rapidly fell in with the wish, expressed clearly (whether directly or indirectly) by John XXIII or Paul VI, that the Council should abstain from discussing the questions of contraception or the status of divorced persons who remarried. There were certainly some questions from the floor on these subjects, but everything came to a halt once the pope's veto was confirmed. In fact the pope's attitude was no less exceptional on this question than that of the bishops and was symmetrical to it, in so far as the veto contrasts with the concern of Paul VI in all other spheres to ensure that the Council operated freely.

The conditions in which the encyclical *Humanae Vitae* was prepared must be seen in the light of this strange exception. There are excellent books on the subject.[14] The only point that matters here is that John XXIII, who himself was also concerned to reserve the question of contraception to another authority than that of the Council, had set up a commission of experts in April 1963. Over the months and years, Paul VI was to enlarge this commission by adding members all of whom were chosen by him. However, the more this group increased and worked, the more the dyamics in the opinions represented moved away from favouring the pope's personal position. To begin with, the majority was against allowing so-called 'artificial' means of contraception; however, as the work continued with the help of new members, even though they had been chosen by the Holy See, the majority emerged in favour of so-called 'artificial' means. After three years of work, at the end of June 1966, a majority took this line in a final report. Paul VI had the final report sent to him, but with it also a minority report.[15] He went to work with the aid of his confidential experts. In summer 1968, *Humanae Vitae* appeared: the pope had adopted the minority view. The point that I want to stress here is not whether or not such a procedure is illegitimate: in present Catholic ecclesiology the pope is in no way obliged to endorse a majority view (whether one likes that or not). What must be stressed is that from the beginning of Paul VI's pontificate, *Humanae Vitae* was the one and only occasion when he behaved in this way. So sexuality seems to trigger off behaviour which nothing else does, as in the case of the veto against conciliar discussion of the three points put forward. In fact, throughout the second part of the Council, Paul VI could be seen to be extremely concerned to obtain as large a majority as possible for each text under discussion, doing everything possible to gain quasi-unanimity, pruning, not to say emasculating some texts of their essential points, to the great annoyance of their authors and the vast majority of those who already supported them, in order to bring in some hesitant votes. Why did this very honourable concern for as large a majority as possible disappear so suddenly, and why did the minority win in the one and only case of sexuality?

A similar thing happened somewhat later, in 1971, not only at a papal level but also at that of the episcopate, in the synod devoted to the priesthood. The obligation of celibacy for priests had been one of the three points withdrawn from free discussion at the Council: nevertheless, like contraception, it had to be discussed; it was included in the whole series of questions prepared for the synod of bishops meeting with the pope. Several synods of bishops in a variety of countries had spent a long time preparing for it. The American bishops had even carried out a very serious sociological enquiry among priests: a large majority were against the continuation of this obligation; as to the problems and practices of the African and Latin American clergy, they were so notorious that no enquiry was necessary. The synod nevertheless reaffirmed without any qualifications the need to maintain this obligation, and the American bishops fully endorsed the doctrine that Paul VI wanted to uphold.[16] Here again, in present-day Catholic ecclesiology – rightly or wrongly – there is nothing against the bishops and the pope adopting a point of view diametrically opposed to that of the majority of their clergy; the point to be stressed is that we do not find an attitude of this kind in any other sphere than that of sexuality.

It is worth stressing that exactly the same thing happened more recently in connection with another synod, this time centred on John-Paul II. The subject of the synod, held in 1981, was the family, and sexual problems were inevitably raised in it. Several European councils of bishops (including the French), and several councils of African and Latin American bishops had presented preliminary reports explaining the problems posed to them by some aspects of traditional Catholic doctrine on the family and sexuality. To their great surprise, virtually nothing about this found its way into the final report, but they nevertheless approved it. The burying of their questions by the authorities of the Holy See and the papal entourage was nevertheless sufficiently cavalier to raise some protests, but after the event and in a discrete and dispersed way. One rising young star in the French episcopate, who had won his spurs as a future bishop by being the only professor of moral theology in France to accept the encyclical *Humanae Vitae* and to comment favourably upon it in 1968, has perhaps compromised his spurs as a future cardinal by speaking out on this subject, even if since then he has regained ground by some particularly trenchant and rigid declarations, again on matters relating to sexuality.

The exceptional adage of the moral theologians

It is an elementary clinical rule that, if an individual or a group of individuals behave in a completely different way in one sphere from the way in which they behave in all others, this exception indicates that the individual or group has a problem in that particular sphere. It would be a bad mistake to raise this question only in connection with popes, bishops, councils or synods. The popes and bishops did not invent the traditional adage in moral theology according to which every sin in matters of sexual behaviour must be considered grave. It is important to note that traditional Catholic morality uses three criteria to assess the gravity of a sin: the objective gravity of the matter, full knowledge and full consent. Each of these criteria clearly has degrees, and confessors were trained to help their penitents to appreciate the gravity of their sins by using them. In all the other spheres than that of sexuality, it is also possible to judge the degree of gravity of the substance of the sin; it is taken as self-evident that in matters of charity, faith, hope or any other virtue there can be failings which are 'light' in substance. In matters of sexuality – and nowhere else – the Catholic moral tradition has considered for centuries that every fault is a mortal sin *ex toto genere suo*, though its gravity can indeed be lessened if the two other factors (full knowledge and full consent) are absent. But the substance of the sin is always considered to be mortal: for example, in 1666 the Holy Office condemned the opinion that the carnal and sensual pleasure to be found in a kiss was only a venial sin if the couple took great care that things did not go too far. No, even in this case, it was utterly a mortal sin *ex sese*: this decree of the Holy Office was countersigned by Pope Alexander VII, who at the same time was also fighting a most rigorous battle against Jansenism. I shall have to return later to the reasons why sexuality is a privileged theatre of guilt whether or not one is a Christian. The point that I want to stress here is again that matters to do with sex have been put in a special category. The theologians who have developed this adage and the clergy and faithful who have for long ensured its success are in fact the first to say that charity, hope, faith, justice and so on are higher virtues than chastity and that consequently faults against charity and justice are in themselves more serious than those against chastity. However, it is only in the sphere of failings against the virtue of chastity that they have felt the need to state specifically that the matter is so serious that no failing is intrinsically slight, not even that of a gentle kiss with no further consequences.

The exceptional behaviour of well-trained religious

The factors that lead to sexuality being given such an exceptional status that people do not hesitate to contradict themselves and to behave in quite a different way from that in which they behave in any other sector are no more peculiar to theologians than they were to popes or bishops in the examples I gave above. My experience of confession, as penitent and confessor, shows the universality of the exceptional treatment prompted by sexuality. I have had the good fortune to spend my years as a Dominican in a very open atmosphere, with men who showed great evidence of their intelligence and their true freedom of spirit (in such a way that one can spell this word with or without a capital). In numerous spheres they had proved capable of innovating, provoking and transforming, when the need arose. In the sphere of sexuality they were certainly more open than the majority of Christian circles at that time, lay or religious. Moreover, like our master, Thomas Aquinas, they acknowledged that sins against the virtue of chastity are in themselves the least serious of sins (though that clearly does not prevent them from perhaps being very serious), since the other virtues – faith, hope, charity, prudence, justice, fortitude – are more eminent than the virtue of chastity. Chastity indeed relates to an important matter, pleasure, but that is considered less noble than what is associated with the other virtues. So sins against faith, hope, charity are intrinsically more serious than those against chastity. All my brothers, students or professors, agreed on this doctrine, though it was far from being unanimously accepted in Catholicism, where one is often led to consider the faults against chastity more or less explicitly as being the most serious ones.

Nevertheless, when these colleagues and friends asked my advice, they often said to me, *à propos* specific problems of chastity that they themselves judged to be relatively minor: 'I would like to get this problem settled once and for all.' It took time, patience and confidence to lead them to discover how they were making sexuality an exception here. For there was no other matter on which they would have expected to be able to 'settle the matter once and for all'. None of them expected to be perfect in questions of charity, faith, justice and so on, and if they expected that they might be able to settle one or other problem in these various spheres they were well aware that there would always be some 'imperfection' or some 'sin'; they would have been horrified to catch themselves thinking that they could become perfect and impeccable. Nevertheless, they found it quite normal, healthy and holy to want to 'settle the problem once and for all' in matters of chastity, giving their imperfection in this sphere a status which was quite different from that which they accorded to it in their theological reflection inspired by St Thomas. Similarly, without betraying any secret of the confessional, I can say that when people asked me to hear confessions urgently before the community mass which was celebrated at half past seven in the morning, they were never concerned about a serious fault against charity, hope or justice. When it was possible to take things up again at more leisure, we almost always agreed that the fault that had had to be confessed so urgently could not have been the major event nor the most serious fault of the week (since at that time we made our confessions every week).

The exceptional character of sex education

I have no hesitation in adding another example of this type of exception which sexuality triggers off in the Catholic mentality, since it is the done thing to suppose that this example does not fall into that category, or that it does not matter very much if it does. In fact this exception plays a far from negligible role in traditional Catholic mentality and is at work there in a whole variety of forms. When in France, in 1973, the Minister of National Education decided to make sex education compulsory in all teaching establishments, the authorities who controlled free education in France set up crash courses so that men and women working in free schools – many of whom were religious, both men and women – could cope with this new task. An important Catholic academic institution in Paris invited me to collaborate in a session of this kind. It took the form usual in such exercises: first of all a biologist was invited to talk about sex, then a doctor, then a psychologist, then a sociologist, then a philosopher, and so on and so on, and to end with, a theologian, representing the 'queen of the sciences'. At that time I was still regarded as a theologian of this particular institution (which is now no longer the case) and I took part as a theologian. I told these men and women, who in many cases had spent long years teaching effectively a subject that they certainly knew and practised better than I did, the two necessary principles of all teaching (though obviously more is needed!): to teach something well it is necessary first to love the subject oneself and secondly to want those whom one is teaching to begin to love it also. As a professor and teacher myself, I was well aware that this is not always the case, and that sometimes people detest what they are teaching and those they have to teach.

But I also knew that one is not just a professor or teacher during the days, the minutes and the seconds when one loves what one is teaching, and I have every reason to suppose that my audience of teachers and instructors had the same experience.

So I asked myself in their presence whether or not these two fundamental principles of teaching applied to sex education or not, and whether the two prior conditions for all sex education were not that those teaching in it should on the one hand themselves love sexuality and on the other hand want to make their pupils love it. Since I was there as a theologian, I went on to ask whether there was anything in the Christian revelation and tradition that was opposed to one's applying these two prior conditions for all teaching to sex education. I had no difficulty in pointing out that in the traditional Catholic mentality there were many features which seemed to suggest that once again sexuality was made an exception to what was considered normal and even indispensable in all the other spheres. And I tried to show that if from a theological perspective sexuality was a creation of God, a gift and a divine blessing for men and women, Christian teachers, men and women, should have another reason for loving sexuality and wanting to make it loved. Even more than any other teachers, they should have a theory of sex eduction based on the same principle as the theory of their teaching on all other matters: to love what one teaches and to want to have it loved. I was never invited back, either by the organization in question or by the very honourable Catholic institute which had allowed the use of its premises, and my post brought me a good crop of insults. I am not so naive as to be amazed at that. But as well as being a very good illustration of the special mechanisms that sexuality often triggers off in Catholic circles, the episode has the advantage that in matters of sexuality, it is pleasure itself which causes problems for Catholicism.

A theological meeting on abortion

This difficulty was to emerge in an even more controversial and more dramatic way in connection with abortion. Since 1969, along with two or three other Catholic theologians, I had been a member of a group of doctors, lawyers, social workers and various other figures (including an eminent Protestant moral theologian) who were studying the different aspects of the problem of abortion. After some years of work it became obvious to all of us that the French laws on the matter had to be changed, and that not only should abortion not be made a crime but that it should be made medically, legally, socially and financially possible. We were certainly the least radical of the groups which had come to the same conclusion, and none of us had come to it lightly: our training and our medical, legal, ethical or religious traditions had predisposed us to approach the problem from a much more traditional perspective. Years of work and contact with the daily reality of abortion had progressively shown us that it was our moral duty to fight for a new state of things, and even to take action and make public statements, if that was the only way of moving the authorities, on whom none of our earlier approaches had had any effect. There were two Dominicans, in the group and in declared solidarity with it, a philosopher colleague and friend and myself, a theologian. We had told our local superiors what we were doing; before it became public knowledge and got to the ears of the Roman authorities, it provoked different reactions in our Dominican circles. I want to mention one of them, since it seems to me to embody attitudes that I want to bring out in this chapter.

My colleague and I were invited to a working group on abortion in a distinguished Dominican house in Paris: there were about fifteen Dominicans there of very high repute, nationally and internationally celebrated for their activity in theology, in writing, in preaching, on radio and television, or teaching in the most illustrious chairs in France or elsewhere. Passionate and impassioned, the meeting was at a very high level. My colleague and I began by explaining the reasons why we had moved in this direction and what we were doing. I had chosen to use some very striking specific cases as starting points, and in connection with each I raised two questions: what is the view of life that obliges us to think that this pregnancy must be brought to term at all costs and despite everything? What is the view of God that makes us believe that God wants this pregnancy to be brought to term at all costs and despite everything? To my intense stupefaction I met with virtually no resistance: that hardly seemed to be the problem. I sensed very soon that the problem lay elsewhere. Several people in fact quickly said to me, 'That's all obvious... each of us has met that sort of case in his ministry... we have even given moral, not to say financial, support to couples or women facing this situation... But these are the exceptions; and they must remain exceptions and therefore not form the basis for a broader permissive law.' In short, some cases of abortion could be legitimate, but they had to remain behind the closed doors of ecclesiatical or medical casuistry; otherwise, abortion had to be forbidden loudly and clearly.

I found it very difficult to get people to pause for a moment before passing on to other considerations and to reflect a little on the internal logic of what had just been said. On the one hand it seemed to me indispensable that questions should be asked about the significance of the fact that the privileged ones who had had the good fortune to know the very famous Father X or Y could be advised – not to say be given financial help – by Fathers X or Y, while others – that is to say, the vast majority – did not have this good fortune, and would be in even worse state if Fathers X and Y refrained from all public pronouncements on the subject and contributed by their prestigious silence to strengthening the brick wall encountered by all the men and women who did not have their ear. I asked those present to reflect on the conceptions of ethics, of priestly ministry and of pastoral help implied by such a way of going about things. The Dominicans who had met together there were of such stature that I had no difficulty in making them aware that in all other spheres of their ministry they would recoil in horror at such an attitude; besides, it would not even have occurred to them, and a number of them had shown with much courage and determination that their conception of ethics, priestly ministry and pastoral help were quite different.

A second point seemed to me to need discussion before going further. I was in effect being told that some cases of abortion could be tolerated, not to say accepted as being the lesser evil, but that since in all other cases they could not be, it was vital to observe the civil and religious laws which condemned abortion without any possible exception. The intellectual honesty of those involved in the discussion was such that I could easily draw their attention to the fact that one never usually argued in this way on moral questions, lay or religious. Moralists or legislators never forbade a practice on the grounds that although it could be legitimate in some cases, it could not be so in others. Far less did they forbid such a practice to those for whom they considered it legitimate on the grounds that others could exploit it in an illegitimate way. On the contrary, moralists and legislators always defined the conditions of legitimacy and illegitimacy, when they considered that a practice might be legitimate in some cases and illegitimate in others: they would permit, approve, not to say facilitate the practice in question in some cases, and prohibit, not to say punish, it in others. One does not prohibit people from using motor vehicles on the grounds that some individuals drive too fast, or when they are drunk, or keep the vehicle in order to steal, murder or commit adultery more easily; but one does prohibit driving above a certain speed and with more than a certain level of alcohol in the blood. I took other examples, as simple, or more subtle, to try to show how extraordinary and contrary to usual principles and practice was the position on abortion opposed to mine, one which distinguished figures of the time took to be self evident: it was wrong to allow abortion when it was legitimate because there were more cases when it was not.

Stressing the two points that I have just mentioned and trying to disentangle their logic – or their basic illogicality – had taken up almost all the time set apart for the meeting, but in the end my colleague and I were very satisfied. Not because we had won the others over to our views, though given their combined influence, it was a pity that we did not. But we had the feeling that they were going to go on asking themselves questions about the anomaly we had succeeded in showing them, how over abortion they behaved *qua* priest or reasoned *qua* theologian in a way which was radically opposed to their practice and their reasoning in other spheres, in which by contrast they had often fought against practices and arguments analogous to those which seemed to them to be self-evident on the question of abortion. We knew those with whom we were discussing well enough to expect that they would not fail to reflect on this anomaly, and we knew their influence well enough to suppose that their reflections would bear fruit. The meeting had been heated and sometimes tense; moreover, we were two unknown young men face to face with established experts. But we were happy; we felt that some of them had been moved.

One of them was sufficiently stirred up to make some closing comments in the final minutes which ruined almost all our efforts and identified the cause of the exceptions of which we had made people aware. So it is worth my relating the episode here. This member of the group, having had to retreat step by step, having first been compelled to recognize that in his own priestly ministry he tolerated or admitted certain borderline cases of abortion, having then had to recognize that it is contrary to ethical theory and practice to forbid behaviour when it is legitimate on the grounds that there are cases when it is not, suddenly launched into an impetuous speech. I must stress that this was one of the most committed, the most audacious, the most avant-garde theologians of the time, a priest of incredible pastoral zeal, who had truly brought strength, light, the gospel, to an amazing number of men and women, and particularly to non-believers; he was one of the few French theologians to have been very quick to take up a resolutely brave position during the Algerian war, and not just over the question of torture. This man, yes, this man said (and I must quote him word for word, since this was language that he hardly ever used, so that his use of it here is as revealing as what he said): 'All right, but in that case what is one going to do with all those little bitches who fuck around here, there and everywhere?' It was both disconcerting and too good to be true. It was disconcerting because once again (and we were now in the final minutes) we had to go right back to square one. Even if the problem of abortion came up in connection with these 'little bitches who fuck around here, there and everywhere' – and that is completely untrue – it is ethically illegitimate to forbid a practice to women for whom it would be legitimate on the grounds that it could also be resorted to by 'little bitches' to 'fuck around here, there and everywhere'. It was also disturbing to see that the birth and life of a child was being used as a deterrent to prevent these 'little bitches' from 'fucking around here, there and everywhere'. But it was also almost too good to be true: in front of such an Areopagus, after three hours of good, heated discussion, a man – and what a man! – handed us on a plate proof that in these matters, in the last resort the problem is posed by pleasure. I owe it to the truth – and to the memory of this man – to add that he then changed his mind on what should be the Catholic attitude over abortion, and in his usual way had the courage to say so, and to restate his view publicly. This involved him in a new and serious conflict with Rome: he had had many others, but this one caused him especial suffering (not least because of his deep devotion to the church).

A fight on two fronts

More than twenty years separate the literary discovery that I made in studying the treatise by St Thomas Aquinas on the virtues, namely that sexual pleasure was a value which the virtue of chastity did not have to repress or suppress but to change and promote, from the discussion on abortion that I have just described in which it became crystal clear that pleasure poses a particular problem to Catholicism, and that it leads Catholics to behave and to argue in a way which is quite different from the way in which they behave and argue in other spheres, and indeed contradicts it. In my personal development over these twenty years in connection with Catholic views about sexuality and the links between these views and a certain view of God, it is very difficult to differentiate between what emerged from intellectual discoveries, of which I have given some examples in connection with my first contacts with psychological disciplines, what emerged from practical contact with and theoretical reflection on the various problems which contemporary theology and pastoral work brought home to me (contraception, abortion, sterilization, artificial insemination, the status in the church of divorced persons who have remarried, the theology of the married couple and the family, fatherhood and motherhood, the celibacy of priests, the significance of the vow of chastity and so on), and finally those arising out of my own way of experiencing my sexuality. My analysis clearly must have played an important role in my development, and must at the least be said to have influenced all the other factors, if the scholastic maxim is true that *quidquid recipitur ad modum recipientis recipitur* ('whatever is received is received in accordance with the character of the recipient'). But if this personal aspect is decisive, for all that, it does not obliterate those features that my own career has in common with the careers of so many other men and women; so there is no need for me to say more about it here.

As these twenty years went by, I found myself in an increasingly paradoxical situation. I was dealing with non-believers or believers who were all disposed to attribute all the ills of the world, and particularly those of sexuality, to the Catholic view of sexuality. Accordingly, all that might seem to be needed to put things right, was to get rid of Catholicism, or at any rate its sexual morality. Slight though my knowledge of psychoanalysis was, I knew enough to be aware that the radically conflictual character of sexuality does not have a great deal to do with authorities like religions, except to produce them or feed on them. I noted that one of the most pernicious misunderstandings of psychoanalysis lay in denying that the various consequences of the drives were internal, personal matters and attributing them to external authorities: a bad mother, a bad church, the devil or God, and so on. So almost against the world I was forced to argue that the problem posed to Catholicism by sexuality is only a variant of the wider and more radical problem posed by sexuality to the human condition, and that non-believers and believers alike would be even more wrong about Christianity than over sexuality if they thought that they could settle the problem by getting rid of its Catholic variant, even if I was the first to stress that this variant had a disturbing originality and rigour.

However, I also had to fight on another front, against believers, men and women who minimized the importance that this view of sexuality had at the very heart of Catholicism: not just a practical importance, since it governed the behaviour of so many people, but also and perhaps above all a structural and even dogmatic importance. This traditional Catholic view of sexuality is not a superficial detail that one could change without affecting the rest: it is bound up with a certain view of God and it governs – and at the same time derives from – a certain view of God, a certain view of Christ, of the church, of salvation, of sin, and so on. It cannot be changed, if it needs to be changed, without changing all the rest. Now if on the one hand people failed to recognize that the Catholic view of sexuality was only a more radical variant of the anthropological problem raised by human sexuality, on the other hand they would fail to recognize the strength and depth of the link between this view and views of all the other essential elements of Christianity. In this respect the 'integralists' saw more clearly than the 'reformers' or the 'progressives': they were very well aware that altering one thing meant altering all the others. By contrast, the 'reformers' and 'progressives' thought it possible to alter some features of Catholic sexual morality without too much difficulty. Had not the Council changed so many other things which had been thought to be more unchangeable, and were not the majority of laity and clergy virtually in agreement over contraception, the status of divorced persons and the celibacy of priests? Because the 'progressives' and 'reformers' had failed to recognize the strength of the bond between the Catholic view of sexuality and its view of certain essential features of the Christian faith, when they saw their failure with the Roman hierarchy, they found consolation in attributing this failure to the personality of one pope or the nationality of another, or again to the obstinacy and inertia of the Roman curia. Certainly all these factors could have played some part, but they are secondary: the essential cause of this failure does not lie there but in the fact that the men and women who wanted to promote these reforms had not come to terms with the idea – far less begun to put it into practice – that a substantial change in the Catholic view of sexuality required them to be ready to reconsider their views of God, the resurrection, and so on.

I also found it very difficult to make myself understood on this point when I had to explain to others (and even to the same people) that the problem posed to Christianity by pleasure is only a variant of the more general problem posed by pleasure. Moral theology has never had a very high reputation: at present, the most respected disciplines in theology are dogmatics, fundamental theology, ecclesiology, exegesis, ecumenics, or, in another dimension, hermeneutics, semiotics and so on. I tried to explain to my colleagues in dogmatics and ecclesiology how a reconsideration of Catholic views of sexuality would affect the structure of dogmatics and how the reforms in Catholic sexual morality (which they themselves most often wanted and which they left to their colleagues in moral theology to bring about) implied such changes. But all in vain. As I write these lines I can see that this failure clearly made a substantial contribution to my decision to jump in at the deep end by saying, after these twenty years, how I thought of God. It was in fact in 1973-74, when the battle over legislation on abortion was in its last stages, that I decided to say who my God was. In the faculty of theology where I taught, I obtained permission to give a course on 'dogmatics' (the programme had been developed in discussions on equal terms between teachers and students), which I entitled 'And they say to me, Where is your God?' That was the course out of which the book *When I say God* appeared. I have pointed out that in it I was led to reconsider Christian views of death and resurrection. I had forgotten that, in 1968, I concluded a report on the foundations of Christian sexual morality for a French episcopal commission (following the flurries produced in Rome by the lukewarm response of the French bishops to Paul VI's encyclical *Humanae Vitae*, on the pill) by using views about the resurrection as one example of what Catholics would be led to reconsider if they thought they had to reconsider their views of sexuality.

What reason did I have for fighting like this on two fronts, a combination which made me even more isolated than I had already been on either of them? One reason relates to what I believe to be the better side of my life as a human being and a believer. In fact many believers, for want of having discovered the link between a certain Catholic view of sexuality and a certain view of God and the faith, and rightly realizing that this view was now unacceptable, rejected it and with it any thing to do with God and the faith, since they believed the latter to be vitiated by this view of sexuality. God was spoiled, faith was spoiled. But others, equally for want of having discovered this link, refused to reconsider views of sexuality as they should have done because it seemed to them that such a course would necessarily damage the faith; yet others compromised the prospects of any reconsideration of views on sexuality for want of tackling the various questions which it involved; others again compromised what we must dare to call God's opportunities by not delivering him from views in which he was imprisoned by a conception of sexuality which had become outmoded. So God was spoilt and faith was spoilt. But so too was sex, the sexual life of men and women, and if one is a believer that meant that God, his creation and his blessings were spoilt. Could I keep even a little of my dignity as a human being and a believer without fighting on these two fronts?

So I fought. I made a stand, always after first having spent several years 'on the ground', in close contact with the men and women who were directly confronted with the various problems involved and those whose calling or vocation it was to help them. In the majority of cases, and in a by no means systematic and general way, but step by step, problem by problem, I was led to adopt positions contrary to those held by the Roman Catholic authorities. I never did this without engaging in theological reflection. In other words I was not content to dismiss without further ado an official position whose inadequacy I had noted on the ground; on the contrary, I kept trying to find a theological basis for my position. I tried to demonstrate those features of the God of Jesus Christ and the Christian tradition which could authorize my views and even find themselves enhanced by them; I also tried to demonstrate those features of the God of Jesus Christ and the Christian tradition which on the contrary were hidden or contradicted by the traditional position through the development of conditions beyond those in which this traditional position had taken shape. I was always concerned to show how in one case both God and sexuality could be spoilt, and how in the other there could be both blessings for sexuality and blessings for God. I always held myself back from taking action until I had reflected in this way for a long period. Then I did take action: articles, books, interviews, lectures, meetings, militant action on the ground, various interventions – public or more discreet – with the civil and religious authorities. In parallel I continued more abstract reflection, combining a theoretical theological approach and a theoretical psychoanalytical approach, on the reasons why pleasure poses a problem to human beings and on the reasons (the basic reasons rather than particular circumstances) why Catholicism presents a very original variant of this problem.

I am the worst placed to appreciate the worth of this action, which was an essential part of my activity as a theologian and my witness to God between 1965 and 1975. Its effectiveness has been nil, as I have already noted, if the criterion is the effect that it has had on the affirmations of the central authorities of Roman Catholicism. However, I am not concerned here to assess the worth and effectiveness of this action, since other things are happening elsewhere, in a different way, which are far more important for what I want to talk about, namely going over to the other side. From the beginning of the second part of this book I have been trying to show that in order to say God, to live him out and share him in a way which means something to the men and women of today and tomorrow, believers must go over to the other side and live out the major experiences of the human condition in the new way which they are laboriously sketching out today, so that it will become clearer tomorrow or the day after. I have been trying to show that some views of God and some practices of faith are so inextricably bound up with views – for example – of death and life, sexuality (and I shall be coming to guilt soon) that we must let God go, free him from the net in which the mesh of these now obsolete views holds him, so that he can become the 'God with us' of men and women who – with him and thanks to him – will have to represent him and do his work in the world of ideas and the behaviour that will be theirs. This operation of liberating God thus requires (of course, among other things) believers, men and women, to pass over to 'the other side', abandoning their old homes and the views of their forbears, and move to this new ground.

3. Believers begin to change sides

It seems that in matters of sexuality, something of this kind is in process of happening, and it is much more important from now on to bring that to light than to present the findings of any personal theological research. It would seem that in sexual matters, a by no means negligible (to judge by both their number and their stature) number of believers, men and women, are in process of going over 'to the other side'. The paradox is that this transition is best illuminated by the very factor which is meant to hinder it, namely the incessant pounding of the rigid and inflexible statements on sexuality by the Roman Catholic authorities and particularly by the present pope John Paul II.

The hardening and ineffectiveness of papal teaching

In fact, if one thing has changed in papal teaching since Paul VI dashed the hopes of all those men and women who believed that they would soon see a development in this teaching with his 1968 encyclical on the pill (*Humanae Vitae*), it is not its content but the force and frequency with which the last pope has reaffirmed it in season and out of season. Paul VI had been very worried at the upsets caused by his 1968 encyclical. He could hardly have been very enthusiastic at the indifference or bitterness with which the conclusions of the 1971 synod on the obligation to celibacy in the priesthood were often received. As for the documents of other Roman authorities, for example the various interventions of the Holy Office (rechristened, in an optimistic way, the Congregation for the Doctrine of the Faith), they aroused either indifference or derision, the palm here going to the priceless declaration by the Holy Office on certain questions of sexual ethics published in 1976 under the title *Personna Humana*. Amazing or disturbing though the Roman interventions on sexuality may have been, they were nevertheless relatively episodic, and their authors did not give the impression that they represented one of the most constant and essential elements of their action.

Since the arrival of Karol Wojtyla, things have been very different. As we know, this pope travels a good deal. The force of his personality and his extraordinary gift for meeting the demands of the mass media mean that all that he says and does is immediately passed on and amplified; in France, at any rate, thanks to television he is certainly the only priest – and *a fortiori* the only bishop – who can enter every home, whether of believers or of non-believers. We also know that in whatever circumstances, John Paul II has restated in the firmest way possible the most intransigent positions on contraception, abortion, divorce, celibacy of the priesthood, young people living together, and so on. So no one can ignore that this pope makes the defence of these intransigent positions one of the essential and constant features of his activity.

What makes it easier to measure the fact that believers are in process of going over to the other side in connection with these matters is the total failure in this sphere of this successful pope. The Catholic women of France and the United States have welcomed the pope in such large numbers that they must include women who take the pill or wear an IUD; nevertheless, none of them has stopped doing this as a result. Many Polish women have welcomed their Polish pope: none of them has stopped practising abortion, and Poland is the Catholic country where abortion is practised most widely in the most official way. So high is the number of women involved that abortion cannot be supposed to be limited to the small minority of non-Catholic Polish women. Moreover, since the number of practising women Catholics in Poland is the highest in the world, Poland is the country which has the largest number of practising Catholic women who resort to abortion. Karol Wojtyla has not changed that by having himself acclaimed pope any more than when he did as archbishop of Cracow. African men and women joyfully gathered round this pope, who severely rebuked them for their family and sexual practices; they continued to applaud and chant, but there is nothing to indicate that they have changed their way of behaving, which among other consequences deprives them of any possible involvement in the sacraments, and particularly in the eucharist. They listened with great devotion while this same pope presented this sacrament to them as the centre of their individual and collective Christian life, though he must have known that eighty per cent of them had no access to it and had no intention of changing the family and sexual customs which stood in the way of their involvement. It would be cruel to ask if the pontifical objurgations at Manila and the magnitude of the popular success which the pope encountered there has lowered by a decimal point the level of child prostitution, which is one of the highest in the world.

What must be stressed here is not the possible ineffectiveness of the words of John Paul II; which of us could stand up to an examination of this sort? The important thing is that the believers who are so interested in this pope are not interested in what he teaches about sexuality, however important it might seem to be to him. A journalist who covered the pope's visit to Ireland and joined in the young people's night told me that the young Irish men and women sang, danced, drank, smoked (and not just tobacco), flirted, not to say made love while waiting for the pope to arrive: when he arrived, they got up to acclaim him madly, played the guitar for him, interrupted what he said with applause, gave him another ovation when he left them, and then went on with their night of relaxation and festivities just as before.

I am not interested here – fascinating though it might be – in knowing how the brand image of John Paul II in the media will stand up to the constant failure of one element in his activity to which he attaches so much importance. Nor am I interested – important though it might be – in knowing how a pastoral and doctrinal authority like that of a pope can be exercised when believers flatly refuse him the hearing in this sphere without which (as the most serious theologians and canon lawyers have shown only too well) no word – even a pontifical word – can have the force of law in the community of believers. I am only interested here in the way in which the very spectacular action of this very spectacular pope meets with such obvious failure in this sphere that he does not even provoke the slightest discussion and disturbance among the believers who are so interested in him. The combination of this spectacular activity and this failure as a result of indifference is one of the best indications of something that might not perhaps emerge otherwise (so many facts are so ordinary as to be neither proclaimed nor defended), namely that in matters relating to sexuality, believers are in process of changing sides. If the believers in question belonged to the impressive ranks of those who have withdrawn on tiptoe from church life and have more or less given up trying to say what they believe in, this change of sides – while being important – would not be so significant. But the men and women whom I have just mentioned are still involved in the life of the church. They often play an active role in it and often try to deepen their faith, both individually and collectively; they pray, practise the sacraments and read the Bible. So what do we make of that?

Contraception and abortion

A significant proportion of these women take the pill, wear an IUD or practise one of the forms of contraception that the Roman Catholic hierarchy censures. They do not do it shamefully, in an underhand and neurotic way, but with full awareness and understanding, convinced that this is in no way contradictory to the best of their Christian life (after all, is not this what a number of lay people, theologians, priests and even bishops wrote before *Humanae Vitae*?). They do not even accept the somewhat spurious – not to say hypocritical – way of posing the problem worked out by clergy seeking to respect the encyclical while at the same time getting round it, according to which abstention from such contraceptive practices was obviously the ideal (since the pope had said so) but until it was possible to attain such a level of perfection it had to be accepted – here as elsewhere – that believers lived, with greater or lesser remorse, on a lower level of perfection, and therefore resorted to these practices. No, if these women find, as do many other women, that contraceptive methods present real inconveniences, this has nothing to do with their compatibility with Christian life. When their daughters become sexually mature, if this poses different problems for them – as it does for all mothers – these problems are not of the order of Christian morality and it is not this that makes them hesitate over suggesting the pill.

When contraception fails, the question of abortion may come up. This is a serious problem for these women – as for all women – and for their husbands, since abortion is not primarily something practised by 'those little bitches who fuck around here, there and everywhere'. When these women think that they have to resort to abortion, they do so, like most women, with death in their soul, or at any rate, having two minds about it. And like most women, they feel guilty (consciously or unconsciously). But when they think about it, they do not attribute this guilt to the fact that no matter what, abortion is as sinful before God as the Roman Catholic hierarchy claims. And when they speak of it to a priest it is not so much to confess it sacramentally as because they are in the habit of talking to a priest, or have the chance to talk to a priest about the problem (often within a group, and often to this group because a priest is in it).

Marriage and divorce

When these women and their husbands see their children beginning to have a sexual life of their own, they experience the more or less contradictory sentiments that this always arouses among parents. But they think of the good side of sexuality, they love it, as one loves justice, truth, intelligence... and faith. They are also happy to see their children arrive at this stage, even if they know that, like justice, truth, intelligence... and faith, sexuality calls for an apprenticeship which, like all vitally important apprenticeships, takes place (as I have learned from experimental psychology) by trial and error, and involves hard work, setbacks and sufferings, for the children themselves and for others. When after these trials and errors a child begins to live with someone before getting married, they see this more as a prudent step, not to say an understandable hesitation, than as fundamentally immoral. And when their children get married – often after deciding to have a child – they see no reason why they should not celebrate their marriage sacramentally if they want to. I am struck by the increasing number of religious marriages celebrated in these circumstances in the most varied circles; they do not provoke more or less outraged or scandalized comments in the communities concerned, but on the contrary unite these communities in prayer and delight. It must be said that often the couple getting married and the priest involved themselves put things with frankness and simplicity. Several years ago now I noted in the window of a printer in the Place des Vosges in Paris an invitation to a wedding which went like this: 'A and B, having lived together for several years and brought C, their child, into the world, have decided to marry sacramentally. They invite you to join in their prayer and their delight in the church of D, on..., where the nuptial benediction, followed by mass, will be given by Fr E...' I was somewhat surprised to recognize the last name on the card as that of one of my Dominican brothers, professor in a pontifical university in Rome, who was hardly known best for his laxity; as a specialist on Marx he had been used more or less against his will by the most reactionary part of the Roman

Catholic church of Southern America against liberation theology and against the Latin American basic communities. Thus even a man like him agreed to celebrate a wedding in these conditions which was announced in these terms.

A similar development has taken place almost more rapidly in the attitude of an important proportion of believers over the remarriage of those who have been divorced. Fifty years ago such people were ostracized from the Christian community as from all good society, and there are still enclaves where that continues. But an increasing proportion of Christian communities behave differently. The fact of knowing that the Protestant and Orthodox churches have long had a different practice from that of the Roman Catholic church has some significance here. However, other factors are involved, and these are not so much a matter of laxity as of a deepening of the faith. Moreover, it is important to do justice to the French bishops, who, in recent years, have published two remarkable texts on the attitude that Catholic communities ought to have to divorced people. The bishops did not go so far as to recommend that divorced persons who had remarried should be admitted to the eucharist, which is something that has long been wanted by the majority of moral theologians in France, and by a number of the faithful and many priests. But they recognized them as not just passive but active members of the community, stressing that they could well be entrusted with pastoral and catechetical responsibilities. Some French bishops had even authorized the celebration, if not of a sacrament, at any rate of a religious rite of prayer in church for the remarriage of certain divorced persons. Since John Paul II, the Vatican has put its foot down, as it earlier gritted its teeth over the documents in question. The French bishops have not disowned these documents and have made a tactical withdrawal over the rites. But look what is happening in the countryside around Autun! At all events, the number of eucharistic gatherings at which, with the full awareness of the clergy and a large number of practising Christians, divorced men and women who have remarried take communion, is increasing. After all, did not the man of Nazareth love open tables, and are we not gathering in his name so that he can be in our midst?

More than just the way in which believing men and women perceive the question of extra-marital relationshps bears witness to a change of sides here. It is no more proclaimed, theorized about or defended than the others we have considered, but like them is happening almost imperceptibly on an everyday level. Fidelity and the promise that love will last – if possible – for ever remain highly esteemed values, well appreciated beyond the narrow circle of believers. The misunderstandings, the conflicts, the failures are felt as keenly in this circle as outside it. It has to be said that these conflicts are all the more trying since they test not only the relationship between the two partners but also the awareness that each of them has of his or her own identity. There is nothing new here, except that a certain ideology of the couple, which has both lay and Christian variants, comes to complicate what was already by no means a simple matter, calling for even higher ideals in a relationship in which a great deal is already being asked. What is new is for believers to discover that fidelity is like all the other great human values; one can grow oneself and make others grow by serving them, but one can also degrade and destroy oneself and degrade and destroy others by being enslaved to certain forms of fidelity, just as one can do the same thing by being enslaved to certain figures of justice, truth ... and even faith. After all, religious faith has produced as many corpses or petrified at least as many living dead as any other great human value. The new development is that believers no longer feel that they have to use their faith or the sacramental character of their marriage to justify and canonize the pernicious forms of fidelity.

Equally new is the fact that they do not just think in those terms about what may end up in the breakdown of their relationship, or even in its degradation. Men and women with profound beliefs and often involved in the life of the Christian community discover that an emotional monolith is not necessarily the ideal form for a marital relationship, and that while the existence of other emotional commitments can indeed sometimes break up their own relationship, it can also sometimes further it, and at all events enrich first themselves and then their relationship and their partner. Granted, perhaps their relationship may have to undergo a degree of restructuring, since sometimes social or psychological forces of more or less doubtful quality combine to present as the only alternative this monolithic emotional character, claiming that it is the ideal status, outside which the couple and each of the individuals involved would be doomed. But here again – and this is the point at which a changing of sides is most evident – these believers do not use their Christian faith or the sacramental character of their marriage to justify and canonize what they discover to be the illusory features in the imposition of this monolithic character. This is not a Christian variation on the stock vaudeville situation which shows how a liaison or a passing adventure has benefitted one or other of the spouses who afterwards is all the more loving as a result; far less is it the case that this monolithic character is found to be damaging, necessarily or uniquely, as a result of involvement in other amorous relationships. Nor do we have here a Christian variety of the experience well known in an earlier period of our society to doctors, lawyers, priests and all those who were on the receiving end of confidences, namely, as one of them cheerfully said, that when one knows people's secret lives, one sees that the old couples who get on best are often like favourite pieces of underwear: they have patches and darns everywhere, but the important thing is not so much that the patches and darns in question are the result of what were then called breaches of contract but that they are the result of developments in the personalities of each of the partners, and can well be of a very different order from the friendly or amorous relationships which imperil the equilibrium of each individual or their relationship.

It is a much more important – and much more decisive – matter that believers should discover that their marital relationship is not the whole of their emotional lives and that what is nevertheless irreplaceable about it in their lives may not find its best expression in that monolithic character which society, including religious society, has so many reasons for imposing on them. What we have here is the fact – the decisive fact – that believers discover that the role of their faith in the God of Jesus Christ in their lives is not primarily to canonize a totalitarian conjugal life or its monolithic character; what they expect from this faith is rather that it should help them to build up their life, in this sphere as in others, no more and no less, refusing to make an exception here to what would normally be the function of faith in all the other spheres: that of helping to live life, one's own and that of others, rather than serving first and above all to maintain certain fixed patterns of life.

The 'affective' life of priests and religious

It is not surprising that a somewhat analogous development should have taken place among priests and religious, male and female, over the significance and the practice of their vow of chastity. Beyond question, in France at any rate, the century between 1850 and 1950 was one of those periods when the vow of chastity was observed in the best and richest way. For more than thirty years I lived the religious life, among others who were doing the same thing. I have seen some marvellous successes in fulfilling the vow of chastity. I have seen some more or less successful sublimations and some more or less destructive repressions. I have also come across some amazing examples of silence: I have known very eminent religious who thought they had no sexual life because they had the sexual life of a boy of eight, working hard and well, and thinking of mummy every day. But there is nothing new in that, any more than there is anything new in the more or less notorious instances of concubinage embroidered down the centuries by popular retelling, or the torments into which noble or timorous souls have been plunged by budding love or the temptation of solitary practices. What is new is that an increasing proportion among priests and men and women religious under sixty-five, albeit a constantly diminishing number, feel quite differently about the sort of affective, not to say sexual life, that is compatible with the aims of their religious or priestly life. (Because it is the custom in such circles, I am acting here as though the distinction between the two could be clearly defined, which is certainly not the case; there can be no affective life without sexuality, even if there is no sexual behaviour in the classical sense of the word.) The new development is that an increasing number of priests and religious of both sexes no longer feel that to abstain from all affective and sexual life or to repress it is a privileged means of achieving the religious or priestly goal to which they still want to devote their lives. So they no longer experience their activity in these spheres as being a lack, a fault, a setback to their aims or their service of God, faith and the church (of course that can still be the case, but it need not necessarily be so). These men and women, like their partners, are certainly in a difficult situation, since the Roman hierarchy and a by no means negligible part of the community of believers regard their status otherwise and continue to consider abstention and the repression of all affective – and at all events all sexual – life as such a necessary means in the priestly or religious life that it comes to be part of the end itself. So from a social perspective, their life in these spheres is inevitably condemned to being lived out under the sign of conflict and contradiction.

However, what is new is above all that an increasing number of these women and men no longer blame this conflict and contradiction on themselves, their weakness or their setbacks; they blame it on the church society which has wronged them in this way. Another new thing is that a growing part of the community of believers is doing more than tolerating the situation by closing their eyes to it: they approve the fact that priests and religious live in this way and, like them, think that serving the faith, the church and God (a service which they recognize as being the one to which these men and women still want to consecrate themselves) does not require them to abstain from all affective and sexual life. Besides, this is a situation against which the bishops and superiors of male and female religious Orders have given up struggling. This is not because they approve, even if they tolerate the position with more or less good will. It is because they are aware that they are dealing with a new phenomenon, quite different from the proverbial failure to observe the vow of chastity in certain periods in the history of the church or, today, in certain countries like Africa or Latin America. What we have now is not a *de facto* situation but one in which rights are involved. It is right – not because the fact is tolerated or because laxity has crept in with a decline in moral standards – that these men and women should conceive of their emotional and sexual life as being quite compatible with (not to say favourable to) their serving the faith, God and the community of believers. Even yesterday, the majority would have seen their affective life as being in principle incompatible with their calling and would have resolved to abandon their religious or priestly state, or to mortify their affectivity and sexuality, or to live on scraps of it in inner torment, guilt and secrecy, in a manner as unsatisfactory to them as to their partners (since their partners often suffer more than they do). Today, the compatibility is affirmed and lived out, certainly not without pain, because of the social situation and our individual and collective heritage, but in a conscious and determined way, in both human and Christian terms.

The change of side is all the more noteworthy, since these men and women, these priests, these religious of both sexes certainly do not fail to recognize that other men and women can express their service of the faith, of God and of the community of believers in another way; they accept that abstention from all sexual and affective life might seem to others to be such an essential means to that end that it was an integral part of it. They do not deny the value of the vow of chastity for certain men and certain women, either theoretically or in practice. But they do refuse to make it the only, or even the best, way of devoting oneself in a particular way to God and the life of the community of believers; and they simply want to live in accordance with their convictions, without a fuss and without being debarred. While such a change of sides may not be particularly spectacular or proclaimed from the rooftops, it is particularly significant because of the considerable – indeed often excessive – symbolic value that Catholicism has long attached to religious life and the priestly state.

Homosexuality

We ought also to discuss homosexuality. I shall do not do so as though this were necessary for strictly personal reasons: only very recently has the unconscious resistance that prevented any under-standing of homosexuality and inspired me with a certain fear of homosexuals, whether men or women, lightened a little. So I do not have the long familiarity with homosexuality or with homosexuals that I have acquired over more than twenty years with the various situations that I have just been describing, and I have always thought a long familiarity of this kind to be a necessary epistemological prelude to discussing a question. For the same reason, I find it very difficult to see the facts of a problem that I nevertheless sense to be of vital importance, namely the ambiguity of the position of the Roman Catholic church towards homosexuality. Certainly the church has condemned homosexuality outright from the beginning, but on the one hand it is more clement than one might have supposed towards certain of its forms and on the other hand it practises homosexuality to a degree which cannot be disregarded.

This relative clemency appears in several circumstances. In 1960 I had occasion to review a manual on vocations and the training of priests produced by a Roman prelate. In it, this expert wrote, in full conformity with traditional practice and doctrine, that candidates who had practised masturbation or homosexuality could be admitted to the first degrees of priesthood on condition that they had undergone a probationary period of victorious abstention for a period of one year. However, it was absolutely forbidden to accept for the priesthood any candidate who had had sexual relations with a woman, apart from the exceptional case of elderly men who had already been widowed for a long period. Besides, we know that often it is only when certain practices break out as scandals that superiors of colleges decide to displace a religious or a priest who is too sensitive to the charms of young boys; again, such men are often sent to other colleges, for fear that they might be still more dangerous in a parish. The stability of those who live in the great monasteries and the distinction of those who visit them mean that people do not feel the same urgency in connection with certain religious superiors or teachers (and here I am speaking only of inestimable people who justly have a high reputation); the slightest heterosexual conduct along these lines would have had quite different consequences.

This is perhaps not unrelated to the other point that I confessed to have felt but not yet to have understood sufficiently, namely the monosexual – not to say homosexual – character of Catholic ecclesiastical institutions. The religious Orders, for men or women, are monosexual, the male clergy is monosexual, the ecclesiastical hierarchy is monosexual, theology has been monosexual until very recently, and so on. To talk of the church's practice of homosexuality is an abuse of this word if by that one mean an explicit practice. But it is not an abuse of the word if by it one understands on the one hand the kind of attitude to women and to femininity that is engendered by spending all one's everyday life in a universe where there are only men, and on the other hand the kind of attitude to men and to masculinity which is engendered by the fact that all important human relationships are exclusively made with men: the relationships of the superior to those under him, of the spiritual director to the disciple, of the teacher to the pupil, of work and collaboration in prayer, the common life, the intellectual life, the apostolic life, ordinary everyday life, 'brotherly' relationships, with all the emotional content that they involve, without even mentioning the inevitable role played in them by sexuality in the broad sense of the word and (much more rarely than one might suppose) in the classical sense of the term. This monosexual, not to say homosexual, character of religious and priestly life seems to me to play such a major role in the life and mentality of the men and women who live in this way, as in the discourse, practices, institutions and mentalities that they contribute so markedly towards shaping in a Catholic setting, that the Catholic church certainly could not state outright its position on homosexuality without having first brought out what is implied by the monosexual character of its structures.

However, as I have said, my inner resistances have for too long kept me from a correct understanding of the situation for me to venture on doing that kind of work here. All I can note, here as elsewhere, is that some believers, men and women, no longer see their homosexuality in the same way, nor do they think it incompatible with their faith. Certainly being a homosexual almost always entails difficult personal and social experiences, and the believers, the men and women of whom I am speaking, are no more free from this than their fellows who are not believers – on the contrary. But I note that some of them no longer use their faith to authenticate and canonize their fluctuating experiences now that they understand better that these do not necessarily coincide with the vicissitudes of grace and sin. I have also noted that the attitude of an increasing proportion of communities of believers to homosexuals is developing: they are no longer necessarily and *a priori* deprived of the possibility of playing an active role in the life of the communities, even when their homosexuality is known. And this happens, not through laxity or hypocrisy, but through a different appreciation of homosexuality and homosexuals – as also from an ethical and Christian point of view.

Contraception, abortion, sex before marriage, divorce, extra-marital relations, the affective and sexual life of priests and religious of both sexes, homosexuality, these are a whole series of essential issues related to sexuality over which a certain number of men and women believers seem to be changing sides. These points are so essential in the image that a certain kind of Catholicism wants to give of itself that in the eyes of external observers this Catholicism often seems to define itself by its positions in these spheres, rather than by its specific message about God and Jesus Christ. So the development is decisive, and I must stress some of its general characteristics here.

A development which is neither lax nor clerical

The first thing to note is that this development is the work of men and women whose faith in and commitment to the life of communities of believers are profound and active. Granted, one could find an analogous process among the much larger number of believers who have left the church on tiptoe and can no longer be asked questions about their belief – and in any case would not feel like answering them; one could also find a similar change among non-Christians or non-believers, and no one will want to attribute this to the debasement of faith and its corruption by the 'spirit of the world'. It is enough to know these men and women to see that that is not the case. This development has not come about through laxity or superficiality, but as a result of reflection, conversation, prayer and often personal difficulties and conflicts. As to my own experience, in all these spheres, not only were the traditional views inculcated in me by my family circle and my Christian education; in the first phase of my life as a religious and a theologian I had deepened my understanding of the doctrinal and pastoral reasons which lay behind them and made them my own. I have not changed my mind in a sweeping way, or lightly, but problem by problem, reason by reason, with scrupulosity and inner debate, in discussions with those who were looking in the same direction and in loyal confrontation with others. The men and women who have begun to change sides on questions connected with sexuality do not give the impression of having given in or truncated their Christian life; on the contrary, they seem to have progressed and to have enriched their lives as human beings and as Christians. Only if one knows nothing of the questions they ask themselves and their clashes, sometimes with those closest to them, will one fail to recognize the serious dimension of their move – in human as well as in Christian terms.

Another point is worth stressing: of all the developments which have taken place in Western Catholicism over the last twenty years, that in connection with sexuality is the least clerical. I want to stress that it is less the work of clerics, in the twofold sense of churchmen and intellectuals, than any other. Of course the liturgical, biblical, catechetical and ecumenical renewals would have got nowhere had they not been passed on rapidly and powerfully by lay people, men and women; but their origin was clerical, they were prompted, thought about, articulated by clergy, pastors and theologians. Developments in connection with sexuality are much more substantially non-clerical. I do not mean that clergy, pastors or theologians have not shared in them, still less that they have been the work of all the laity, some of whom could teach the clergy a thing or two about clericalism. But however close the Catholic clergy would like to be to the problems of the laity, the fact remains that this transformation was not primarily the work of the clergy, either in the way in which it began or in its development and orientation. That perhaps explains why it is also less orchestrated, less proclaimed and perhaps less articulated with the other Christian dimensions of life and doctrine, though that does not mean that it is less reflective or less serious. I shall return shortly to the risks that this may bring, but first of all I must stress the advantage which follows. For once, in Catholicism, if I dare put it that way, the consumers are the producers; those with a particular experience are trying to find human and Christian truth in it. The clergy – men of the church or intellectuals – have their part to play, as befits a church; it is a role which is not secondary but second. Hence perhaps the difficulty certain clergy – and in any case the clerical hierarchy – have in understanding this development, since it not only disturbs them in a sensitive area but also lessens their power and its effects.

Although it is not my main focus of interest here, we must consider the ecclesiological problem which arises out of this. In ecclesiological terms, what is the significance of the constant contradiction between what the hierarchy says and the practice and convictions, not just of the very great majority of the more or less lukewarm faithful, but of a majority of believers of both sexes whose faith and practice are alive? The seriousness of the problem is not lessened by the fact that the present pope has been familiar with it for a long time: when Karol Wojtyla became John-Paul II, a journalist and theologian whose atttachment to the Holy See and the person of the pope are well known, Abbé René Laurentin, published (in *Le Figaro*, 18 December 1978) the results of a very serious sociological enquiry according to which seventy per cent of Polish Catholics are opposed to the position of the hierarchy on contraception and fifty per cent to its position on abortion and premarital relations. I must stress here that these percentages relate to Catholics, of whom seventy per cent are practising. In no other Catholic country in the world would one have obtained such high percentages among Catholics, including such a large number of practising Catholics, particularly over abortion (I have already indicated that Poland is the country with the largest number of practising Catholic women who resort to it).

Let us again leave aside the fact that a church like the Polish church can tolerate such a dichotomy, since its force is not based on a doctrinal or moral accord between the hierarchy and the grass roots but on its historical and political role in the survival of the nation. However, in the majority of other local churches, and throughout the universal church, a minimum of agreement between the hierarchy and the Christian people is indispensable. The need for it is even greater when one is no longer dealing with the easy-going pragmatism of John XXIII or the complex and sophisticated thought of Paul VI but with the constant unrelenting self-affirmation of a John-Paul II. What authority, particularly when it is so spontaneous and seeks to be so powerful, can ultimately resist a madness which is so constant and so regularly experienced in practice, above all if this madness does not even feel the need to formulate and affirm itself? This is a difficult problem for the exercising of authority by Rome as it now conceives of itself. But there is an even more serious problem, namely that this contradiction prevents Christian people from receiving what it rightly expects of a pastoral authority without which I personally cannot conceive the church, and that this authority thus sees itself deprived of the minimum of receptivity without which it could not exercise itself legitimately in an authentically Christian way. That having been said, as far as I am concerned, if I had to choose between two evils, a hierarchy which moved and a Christian people which did not, or a hierarchy which did not move and a Christian people which did, beyond question I would choose the second, which seems to me less of a problem because it preserves the essentials. However, I maintain that this is a bad thing, not just for the structure of the people of God but for a matter which is directly connected with my immediate concern.

The reason why changes in ideas and practices connected with sexuality are of interest to me is that, like those related to death, they are bound up with certain ideas of God and certain practices of faith which have a reciprocal effect on one another. In the first part of this book, I wanted to bring out what I have called the decomposition of certain practices of faith and certain ideas about God. I have stated my conviction that recomposition presupposes that in the matter of some anthropological realities which have always played a major role in Christianity, believing men and women should pass over to what I have called the other side. It is, for example, because some of these views and some of these practices seem to me to be inextricably mixed up with views about death or sexuality which from now on are impossible for us that they have to be transformed or disappear in order to give place to more adequate ones. That will not happen without much long and patient work on the part of both individuals and communities of believers.

Those men and women who have done the hard work presupposed by this change of side over sexuality risk failing to understand the consequences of the change for their faith. In the worst case, supposing that no views of God or practices of faith are possible other than those which were associated with the views and practices of sexuality that they have legitimately abandoned, they will reject both together and their faith will weaken and end up by disappearing. In other cases they will be well aware that other courses are possible in Christianity, but because the attitudes of the church – and *a fortiori* the ecclesiastical hierarchy – have not yet undergone the same change, they will find themselves isolated and ill at ease over Christian views and practices where their own approach has no place and has made no impact. It is amazing to see how many men and women who have undertaken this change of sides practise the eucharist, baptism, marriage, reconciliation and even the religious life and the priesthood, while the structure of these sacraments or these forms of life remain unchanged and should really be hostile to them and reject them. Such a situation cannot be prolonged indefinitely without grave damage not only to the Christian life of those involved, but also to the life of the church communities and the truth of the sacraments themselves. I admire the courage of women who, while formally going against the statements of the hierarchy on sexuality, think that they must continue both to live in the way that they have chosen and participate in the eucharist, saying, 'It's donkey's years since I bothered about what they (the parish priests) said.' This unfortunate dichotomy is better than abandoning one or other of what are thought to be contradictory poles, but it would be better still if the consequences of their legitimate options over the views that men and women can have today about God and the way in which God can be a 'God with them' could be brought out to better effect.

That is why, while it is perhaps not very important that they should succeed in convincing everyone (it is inevitable that a certain fringe of the population will reject these changes: even if this fringe were no more than ten per cent, in France it would include five million Catholics, which would allow the formation of a community who should be left to live as they want), it would be vital for these believers to be able to put their views into practice in a less solitary way and to be allowed to share in the indispensable development of new ideas about God and new practices of faith. Failing that, this change of side will have been beneficial for their sexuality and their human life, and that is something, but it will prove disastrous or fatal to their faith, and that would be catastrophic. This is where the ministry (in the strict sense of the term) of pastors or of men and women theologians (which is rather different) could be useful – the role of the latter, while remaining second, would be no less essential. One must hope that the present ecclesiastical context does not prove a final discouragement to the men and women who could fulfil these ministries; it does seem to me eminently desirable that these believers should benefit from such a service so that the realization of the God of Jesus Christ can be more sure and more lively in the form in which he can and wills to be the 'God with us'.

4. Our experience of sexuality is changing

Conditions in the church would be more favourable to the quest of believers in process of passing over to the other side in connection with the way in which their views of God and sexuality are linked if only it allowed them to move rapidly to a clear and well articulated vision, from which they could define institutions and regulate behaviour in complete security. The impossibility of doing this is not connected with factors peculiar to Christianity but with more general factors which affect the whole of our Western society: sexuality is in process of changing, at least as radically as death, without people knowing very well why or how, and still less towards what. If we do not have a very good idea of what sexuality is today, we know still less about what it was yesterday and less again about what it will be tomorrow. It is also difficult for us to foresee and therefore to orientate a development the features of which are only evident to us afterwards. I would not pretend here to forecast the future of sexuality. However, to end this chapter I must give some examples of the little that we do know about recent changes, since it is important that believers going over to the other side in this connection should not live with their problems in a vacuum as though they were the only ones to have them. Their problems are indeed special in so far as they involve their faith or the link between God and sexuality. But they are part of an overall situation which forces itself on them from all sides and which involves the whole of our Western society, since in one sense the whole of this society is engaged in changing sides in matters of sexuality.

The increase in longevity and birth control

As with the changes I mentioned earlier in the significance of death and what that involves, the paradox is that some of the most radical changes over sexuality came about by chance, without having been intended, without even having been foreseen, and were an established fact well before people became aware of them. It would have surprised Pasteur and researchers in his day had they been told that their work would completely revolutionize the nuclear family, the structure of marriage and sexual experience. However, that indeed happened, and for the same reason as with death: quite simply through the staggering increase, in a century, in human longevity. For many centuries, as I have already said, half the human beings who were born did not reach the age of fifteen, and half of those who passed this age did not reach thirty-five. That means that only a quarter of the babies who were born would be concerned with problems that might be posed by life after the age of thirty-five and only half of them by the problems of life between fifteen and thirty-five. Half the baby girls would die too young ever to achieve marriage or motherhood, and less than a quarter would have experience of the menopause. In the middle of the nineteenth century, i.e. well after longevity had already begun to increase slowly, essentially for social and economic reasons, a marriage (for example, in the United States) would last on average thirty-four years. The first third of it would be taken up by pregnancy and breast-feeding six children (on average); the husband would die before the last child got married. However, for numerous centuries the average length of a marriage was no more than twelve years, a period which was taken up with the pregnancies and breast-feeding of six children. French women who married in 1900 had a fifteen per cent chance of celebrating their golden wedding; for those who married in 1980, the chances (divorce apart) are fifty-four per cent. The considerable increase in longevity, combined with the fact that thanks to a decrease in child mortality, two or three pregnancies (instead of seven) are enough for at least two children of a couple to reach adulthood; this means that the life of a Western woman is divided into a different number of stages of a different kind from those which marked the life of her forbears. Four years elapse between her wedding and her last pregnancy; then there is a much longer period, when the education of her children gives her a chance of working again much sooner, whether by necessity or by choice; then there is a long period in the marriage when the children have left home but she, and certainly her husband, is still working; then there is a period (which will soon be an average of fifteen years) when she and her husband will both be retired and alone at home; finally there will be a period of widowhood, which in France will be on average between seven and ten years, since in France more than elsewhere male longevity is significantly lower than female. So over the centuries, the sexual life of a woman will on average have lasted less than twenty years, almost all of which will have coincided with the years taken up with her six pregnancies. However, the sex life of a married Western woman at the end of the twentieth century will last on average more than fifty years, only six or eight of which will have been taken up with two or three pregnancies: again, more often than with her forbears, this sexual life will have begun several years before marriage. Such changes, even if they are not those which most attract the attention of ideologists, have a considerable effect on sexual experience; quite apart from any theory, any choice or any reflection, the function of reproduction moves into the background, while the forefront is occupied by personal relationships and personal development.

The reproductive function of sex has been profoundly changed by the control over it allowed by contraception (quite a different kind of control from the savage, albeit widespread practice of birth control by means of abortion, the exposure of children or infanticide which has gone on down the centuries). Another step in our control of reproduction is imminent: several days before I wrote these lines, a team of American scientists announced that a pregnancy obtained by the implantation in the uterus of a sterile woman of an embryo obtained by the fertilization of an ovum of another woman with sperm coming from the husband of the sterile woman had already gone to four months. Similarly, one can see the possibility of exercising a degree of control not only over the reproductive processes but also over their results, by genetic manipulation. I am not a futurologist, and I would suppose that the usual methods of fertilization will continue to be used most. But for too long reproduction has played too great a role in ideas of sexuality for all the changes in its forms and significance not to have a considerable – and *a priori* unforeseeable – effect on of the significance of sexuality itself.

Social and economic factors in the transformation of married life

The results of progress in biology – whether or not that progress was sought – are far from being the only factors to bring about a profound transformation of sexuality in our Western society. Another series of factors has been no less determinative, all the more since those who set them in motion found it impossible to foresee their results: here I am talking about the development in the West of industry and the urban environment. Sociologists are unanimous in their view that the conditions of life and work resulting from the industrial and urban revolution have changed the structure of the family, the function of marriage and the married couple, for the man and woman who make it up, both profoundly and unintentionally. One of these changes is that special importance is attached to the nuclear family as a result of the disintegration of other family and social structures and relationships. Each of the partners becomes almost the only possible pole of affective relationships, and the child itself becomes more a prolongation and an emotional need of the couple than the new being that the parents have a mission to provide in order to secure the survival of the family, the city, the nation or the race. There are good reasons for supposing that the result is an excess of emotion and an over-valuation by both the individual and society of the couple, the partner and the child. It should also be pointed out that a certain Catholic pastoral view of marriage, a certain type of marital spirituality, a certain Catholic exaltation of the child, of motherhood and fatherhood, contribute towards making this excess and over-valuation even worse, so that the couple risk being crushed under their weight. The youngest generations are hesitating to follow this course, not only because the staggering increase in longevity now makes marriage a state which lasts for more than fifty years and which has very different stages, each demanding very different qualities if it is to be surmounted successfully; it is also because the ever-increasing number of objectives imposed by a certain view of marriage seems to them impossible to realize. That is why the solution of the crisis in marriage of which people speak so much does not seem to lie in an even greater concentration of even more numerous objectives and even greater demands in this connection, but on the contrary in a struggle against this excessive value attached to marriage by the relocation of the married couple and of marriage itself in a broader context of social relationships and emotional commitments.

Even on this hypothesis, it would remain true that what love and marriage have become in our Western industrial and urban society are so different from what they were formerly that historians of the family and of sexuality do not hesitate to say – do they exaggerate or not? – that love and sexuality in the sense in which we understand them now are inventions of nineteenth-century civilization. At all events, marriage and the married couple have so long been the place, the context and the model for sexual life that it is inevitable that the radical transformations of marriage and the family will have profound consequences for our views of sexuality and on our way of life. It might not seem very romantic – or very theological – to attach so much importance to social and economic factors like the development of industry, salaried work and the urban environment in matters of love, sex and the family. Similarly, it might seem surprising that with my rather psychological training I attach so much importance to biological, demographic or social and economic factors. However, quite apart from their considerable importance, these factors are the ones which a certain Christian view of love, marriage and sex too often and too systematically fails to recognize: so they are well worth stressing. Finally, they are of such considerable magnitude and importance, and concern so many hundreds of millions of human beings, that they are a particularly good way of showing how in sexual matters our Western society is in process of going over to another side from that on which it has lived over the centuries, the context where the traditional Christian view of sexuality has come into being along with its connection with a certain view of God.

Stressing the importance of these social and economic factors obviously does not dispense us from stressing the importance of other factors. It is very probable that the knowledge of sexuality that we have been in process of acquiring over the last century or so will have notable consequences for our ideas of sexuality and sexual behaviour:

biological, psychological, psychoanalytical, ethnological, historical, and so on. I indicated at the beginning of this chapter the impact that contact with these various disciplines had on me. It is also very probable that the transformation of sexual behaviour and of the image and place that it has in the mass media will also have important consequences. I feel quite incapable of describing them, since I feel quite incapable of foreseeing them. Above all I want to avoid what would be a twofold error, supposing that the essential feature of our contemporary task was to foresee this evolution in sexuality and draw normative consequences from it, thus deciding *a priori* and from the side which we occupy at present what the other side might be, and above all what it should or should not be.

Predetermine or participate?

That would be a mistake first of all in connection with the actual course of development. Who could foresee the formidable consequences which would result from the work of doctors at the end of the nineteenth century or from the development of industry, wage-earning and the urban environment? Sexuality was a million miles away from the preoccupations of those who furthered, were involved in and became the victims of these revolutions. Whether they wanted to or not, however, they have transformed love far more radically than all the popes, the theologians, the philosophers and the writers of love songs. Recently a young and very brilliant American specialist on computer sciences living in Silicon Valley said on television of his three-year-old son: 'I am involved in research and knowledge in a sector which is going to transform our way of living, and the only thing that this enables me to foresee about my son is that he will live in a universe of techniques, models and concepts which are beyond my imagining, since the only thing I know about them is that they will be different from mine: I know that I do not know who my son will be in thirty years, nor how he will live, think and function.' Such a statement is even more true of what sexuality will be when our society is on the other side. The important thing is not to predict it: on the contrary, we can be certain that if we try to, we shall be wrong and do damage to the process and those involved in it. The important thing is to work on the other side and live there, individually and as a society, as well as possible.

The mistake that we would make if we wanted to foresee and prejudge the future would also be a mistake from a Christian point of view. The task of believers is not to decide on behalf of all human beings what sexuality must be on the other side, as if their status as believers gave them special insights. Even if history did not prove that over twenty centuries believers have inferred almost everything and its opposite from the gospel and tradition, the gospel and tradition are not primarily instruments for forecasting or theories from which one can deduce *a priori* models for societies to come. They allow believers to help God make himself present to men and women in a given situation, to help the Spirit of Jesus Christ introduce the 'God with us' among them and to ensure that a new form of human history can become a new form of the kingdom of God. That certainly does not mean that believers should systematically absorb everything that comes into their world; faith is also judgment, criticism of the world. However, even this function of criticism and judgment does not proceed by *a priori* inference from a model; it lies at the very heart of the development and the processes in which the gospel and the tradition are light and company, warmth and power, joy and toil, searching and patience, support and rejection, courage to go forward but also deviations and setbacks. That is why believers, even when they are theologians, do not primarily have the task of foreseeing what sexuality will be on the other side; their task is to go over there with the men and women who experience today's society in order to prepare tomorrow's society there and thus contribute towards shaping, constructing tomorrow's sexuality and making what contribution they can through the God of Jesus Christ and with him. As he has said to us, 'Do not be afraid.'

III

Guilt*

With no further interlude

How can we avoid asking ourselves about the interconnection between certain views of God, certain practices of faith and guilt? How can we avoid asking what would happen to these views and these practices if, in connection with guilt, too, our Western civilization was in process of changing sides? Once we note the real slavery in which guilt entangles human beings and the way in which it deforms and vitiates so much of our behaviour and our ideas, how can we not desire with all our strength as believers and human beings to 'liberate' God, at all events to liberate the ideas we have of him? How can we not want to let go of this God who is so steeped in our guilt that he is an idol set up by it, and how can we not seek to rediscover the true countenance of God and our own true countenance?

At all events, guilt is a very different matter from death and sexuality. Even if death and sexuality are changing substantially, as I have sought to show, strictly speaking they are nothing new. That is the least one could say. Guilt, on the other hand, must be said to be a recent discovery. Certainly, over the millennia, legal institutions, morality, religion and simply common sense are very well aware of moral failings and have set out to assess them as accurately as possible in order to punish them as fairly as possible and combat them as effectively as possible. However, two men at the beginning of the twentieth century made us understand and feel that guilt is something rather different: Nietzsche and Freud. The considerable importance of psychoanalysis here must not make us forget the irreplaceable contribution made by Nietzsche. From now on, whether or not one has read Nietzsche and Freud, whether or not one has had experience

---

* This chapter on guilt was written in August 1983 at Parc-Trihorn.

of psychoanalysis, what these men have shown us has become more or less common property.

Despite my experience and my knowledge of psychoanalysis, I am personally not very sure how guilt works. But strangely I sense it, I smell it. Granted, the way in which I do so is still rudimentary; it must escape me and act without my being able to grasp it. But what I see of it and what others who have nothing to do with psychoanalysis but discover guilt in different ways see of it is already enough to bring about a considerable change in our views of God and our practices as believers. These are the transformations that I want to describe here. I am not a psychoanalyst, I am not writing for psychoanalysts and I would be incapable of writing a treatise on guilt: many psychoanalysts would in fact feel equally incapable. I am in search of what would allow us to free God from the more or less distorted views that we have of him; I am trying to encourage the decomposition of our idolatrous enterprises; I want to discover those mutations of our chief human experiences which are making us move over to another side. It is on this other side that God will be 'God with us' in a specific historical form which will certainly be new, as each of the specific historical forms of God down the centuries have always been new. After long years of work which has been just as difficult and costly as that on death and sexuality, but finally no less fruitful nor less beneficial, I have become convinced that what we have discovered about guilt entails a radical change of side: some views of God and some practices of faith are so inextricably bound up with a kind of experience of guilt that is becoming alien to us that these views and practices will have to undergo a change the radical character of which will be proportional to that of the change which this new perception of guilt entails.

I have called it a new perception. For it is not, as certain fanatical supporters or certain critics of psychoanalysis, each as ignorant as the others, have said, a matter of ridding the human being of guilt altogether (though often it is necessary to rid people of guilt in some ways); it is not a matter of suppressing failings, evil, sin. This is a new perception of failing, evil and sin arising out of our new perception of guilt. So it also entails a new view of the God who judges and punishes, the God who saves and has mercy, the God from whom we beg pity and pardon, and whose goodness and grace we sing. It is a new view which necessarily arises from our new perception of guilt. When one is open to this new perception, one often does not even think of guilt, does not even mention it by name or identify it, but begins to understand what is said, what we say, in a different way. One begins to feel differently about what happens or does not happen, what we do and do not do. The only way in which I can explain is to describe here how for the first time I dared to allow the first elements of this new perception to develop and how I ventured to put them to others. You will see that the word guilt does not occur, nor does any theory of it; it was simply that I suddenly 'understood' in a different way words or practices that I had already come across a hundred, a thousand times before, but never like that.

1. A Holy Week, or 'Is sin important like that?'

This happened exactly ten years ago. Our Dominican faculty of theology at Le Saulchoir was in its last days, but the teaching body still had some style and the teachers met regularly for a working week which we called the 'internal week'. During that time we spent at least half of every weekday working together on a theme and invited several other Dominican theologians or philosophers to enrich our reflections. Some of the great names of theology or French religious study came, and the youngest and least known were by no means inferior. The theme discussed on this occasion (spring 1973) was in fact guilt: I had been asked to give a theological paper which came after a psychoanalytical paper given by one of our number, who was at that time interested in the practice of psychoanalysis, something to which he has since devoted himself more exclusively. At that time I had already been teaching for more than fifteen years; I had had several articles and two books published in which I had brought together theological theory and psychoanalytic theory to study the problem of sin, guilt and so on. So people expected that I would give quite a theoretical theological paper, and that is what I planned to do. However, quite a different approach forced itself on me in an unexpected and irresistible way. I had just spent Holy Week in a village in south Finistère to which I had been going for almost ten years. I would work there gently, rest, perform whatever ministries the rector asked of me on Sunday or during the week, confidently and without any fuss. To deal with my topic I simply told this eminent gathering about three new 'perceptions' which had forced themselves on me during these recent celebrations and which had made me ask: 'Is sin as important as that?', or rather, 'Is sin important like that?'; in other words, 'Is that how sin matters to God and to humanity?'

Maundy Thursday

I followed the liturgical order of the celebrations and began with what had occurred to me on Maundy Thursday. I had been asked to preach, and I had prepared a sermon on the theme of a God who shares himself with human beings. In fact I have never seen Maundy Thursday so much as a commemoration of the eucharist and its ministers, the priests, though that is the way in which a certain Catholic mentality sees it ; for me it is the feast of that of which the eucharist and the priesthood are only the instruments and the symbols: it symbolizes the fact that God wants to share himself as really (and the presence is real primarily in this sense) and as simply as we human beings share the bread and the wine. The life that God comes to inaugurate among us is a life of sharing and service, like that of Jesus, as is evidenced by the story of Jesus' washing of his disciples' feet which is included in the liturgy for this day. These are the themes over which I never cease to marvel: for several days, I was steeped in them, turning them over in my mind all day, letting them 'simmer on the hob' as I used to do when I was preparing a sermon. I never wrote anything down in advance (how I used to love that way of doing things!) and in the seconds before this celebration on Maundy Thursday I concentrated and relaxed as athletes do before a race. At the beginning of the celebration I never had any trouble in saying, 'Look, we have the good fortune to be gathered together for a splendid festival and what we are going to celebrate we shall celebrate *in the name of the Father, and of the Son, and of the Holy Spirit.*' That in effect is how mass began from then on. And the vigorous response came back, 'Amen'. I kept to the classical liturgy after Vatican II, observing the wish which the celebrant then expressed because it is the wish not only of the whole community but also of God himself, and the least one can do when one invites and receives people in someone's name is to introduce that someone and to give the reasons for the invitation. That is what I did, making my comment in this spirit and then pronouncing the phrase provided for by the ritual: '*The grace of our Lord Jesus Christ and the love of God and the fellowship of the Holy Spirit be with you always.*' And they would reply very politely, according to the liturgy, '*And also with you.*' It was a lively yet tranquil Breton parish, where the liturgy of Vatican II had been well received and was performed well, largely because people had taken the trouble to explain it to the fishermen, the farmers, the workers and the small businessmen, who could now pray as well in French as in Breton or in Latin. So it was not a matter

of making unexpected innovations, and at that time I had no reason
to want to innovate at this point of the liturgy. Then I immediately
went on to what the liturgy provides for after what I have just recalled:
'*Let us prepare for the celebration of the eucharist recognizing that
we are sinners*', and I intoned one of the penitential formulas
provided.

It was then that I suddenly felt that something was wrong, that
what I was doing was not right, that it did not fit. Why? I had just
welcomed the participants in the name of God, given them God's
welcome and introduced God and his wishes to them. Now that we
were introducing ourselves in turn, what did we find to say to God,
what did we think we had to say to him before anything else? We
had to talk about our sin, the fact that we were sinners! No doubt
the fact that it was Maundy Thursday and the themes that I had
prepared for my sermon emphasized this impression, but reflecting
on it later in the day I told myself that the whole thing was wrong.
That is not the way in which you behave when friends invite you to
a party; indeed to behave in such a way would be impolite, out of
place. When friends invite you and welcome you, you say, 'What a
splendid meal', or even 'I'm hungry', or 'What I like about you is...'
Or you talk about them, ask how they are; or you talk about yourself,
tell them what a pleasure it is to be with them, how delighted you are
about the occasion for the invitation, in short express your pleasure.
So why, when God invites us to his meal, do we feel it necessary and
find it normal to begin by telling him that we are sinners? Why is it
that the way to 'prepare ourselves for the celebration of the eucharist',
is to acknowledge that we are sinners and not first of all to tell God
that we are happy to be there, that we are happy because of him,
because he is who he is? Why not begin by singing the Gloria? Would
that not be a better way of preparing for the eucharist, leaving the
confession of our sins until later? It is not a matter of removing sin
and confession altogther; it is simply a matter of their place, the
importance attached to this confession. So I asked myself: 'Is sin as
important as that?', or rather, 'Is that the way in which sin is
important?'

I immediately told myself by way of objection that according to a
fine old expression the eucharist is the table of sinners, and I recalled
that Jesus had been censured for having shared meals with them. But
the point is that never in the gospel is Jesus said to have required
sinners first and before all else to recognize their own sin, so that he
could then listen to them or accept an invitation from them. Besides,
what does the fact that the eucharist is the table of sinners tell us

about God? Many of the penitential formulas which follow the exhortation 'Let us prepare to celebrate the eucharist by recognizing that we are sinners' repeat the phrase, 'Lord have mercy'. Granted, our human life is often miserable and wretched, not to say intolerable enough for us to deserve pity. But what are we saying about God when we think that this must be the first word that we address to him when we celebrate the eucharist? Is God someone whose way of being interested in us and reason for this interest are such that the first thing we must say to him, the best way of greeting him, of responding to his salvation, the best way of interesting him in us is, 'We are sinners, have mercy on us'? Is God going to be a better God, is he going to be more God because the first thing that we have invited him to do has been to pardon us for our sins? It is enough to imagine the situation with anyone other than God to see that we would not behave in this way with anyone who invited us to his table, even if this person had some offence to forgive us.

So I discovered that it was out of place to treat God in this way, out of place to encourage this way of meeting on the basis of our condition as sinners, out of place in relation to God, ourselves and sin: indeed sin was important, but not in this way. The fact that God pardons us was important, but not in this way. What was it that happened to upset the apple cart, distort faces, spoil relationships? What was it that found fulfilment in this shift of emphasis? I did not say more to my colleagues of ten years ago, because I did not say more to myself: I was just becoming aware of the question. I simply stressed the phrase 'out of place', which I used in its two current senses of a change of place and impoliteness, because my colleague – who had spoken before me about guilt in the psychological sense – had used the same term in its psychoanalytical meaning of displacement. But I did not press it further because I could not see more clearly myself; I preferred to describe other experiences which had come up on subsequent days and which reinforced this impression of the sense of the importance of sin being out of place.

Good Friday

The day after Maundy Thursday is Good Friday. Of all the offices of Holy Week, the great office of the veneration of the cross on the Friday afternoon is the one which has always seemed to me to be the most sombre and the most solemn; besides, it is one of the earliest monuments of the Roman liturgy, and some of its hymns are among the masterpieces of Gregorian chant. It was my good fortune from the first year of my life as a Dominican that the novice master, a man of the gospel to whom I owe a great deal, put all my Good Fridays to come in a remarkably different light from that which had cast shadows on the Good Fridays of my Christian childhood, although this was a day of almost complete fasting and total silence (the offices apart), marked out by weariness after a nocturnal vigil. He said to us: 'My brothers, you must not confuse meditation and sadness: today it is wrong to be sad, since it is the festival of man's salvation through Jesus Christ; it is the festival of Christ the saviour, the festival of a victorious death.' I was to take that up much later in my own way when I preached on Good Friday: 'It's a good thing for a man to die for God; it's a good thing for a God to die for man.' In fact the liturgy was not sad but glorious, including the long procession of the veneration of the cross, an Eastern inspiration, in which each of us approached the cross, prostrated ourselves before it three times and then kissed it, during the singing of a splendid hymn, *Crux fidelis*, which I can always remember.

After two introductory biblical readings, the first high point of this liturgy is the reading of the text of the passion according to the Gospel of John. As the community's cantor, I have sung or read this passion in Latin or in French about twenty-five times. Being neither a real bass nor a real tenor, but able to sing higher than most basses and lower than most tenors, I would vary which of the parts that I sang; sometimes I would have the part of the narrator, which is better suited to a baritone; sometimes that of the crowd, which is better suited to a tenor; and sometimes that of Christ, which is better suited to a bass. While singing the other parts, or singing that of Christ, I was able to note something that is not perhaps so obvious if one is not actually involved. The Christ says virtually nothing; he undergoes his passion silently, almost as if he were dumb; the din of the crowd or the long hesitations of Pilate have a far more prominent place. I had noticed this for a long time, and in the days when we were reading the Gospel as though it gave us direct access to the personality of Jesus and his behaviour, I had meditated on this attitude of Jesus long enough to be amazed at it. The reading of the passion was followed by a series of prayers, the 'great catholic prayers', addressed to God for all conditions of human beings and for all their needs (hence the name catholic, in the original sense of the word: that which concerns everyone, including those whom this liturgy called the 'perfidious Jews', until Pope John XXIII suppressed this designation), each of these prayers being preceded by a long admonition from the deacon which almost doubled its length. Then came the central

ceremony, that of the veneration of the cross. We all took our shoes
off and walked in bare feet towards the cross, stopping three times
to prostrate ourselves; the veneration began with a prayer called
known as the 'reproaches' (Latin *improperia*). Two officiants held
the cross in their hand and presented it to us, singing a long entreaty
placed in the mouth of God and punctuated by a refrain, 'O my
people, what have I done? How have I grieved you? Tell me.' The
couplets which came between the refrain made God enumerate one
or other of the benefits which he had heaped on his people (that is to
say, all of us, not just the Jews), and each time the reminder was
followed by the description of ill-treatment or insults which human
beings had inflicted on Jesus of Nazareth: 'For love of you, I smote
the Egyptians... and you scourged me before delivering me up... I
opened the waters of the river before you. And with a spear-thrust
you opened my heart. I gave you living water which sprang from the
rock, and you gave me gall and vinegar to drink... I raised you above
the others by my omnipotence; and you raised me up on the tree of
the cross.' 'O my people, what have I done for you... O my people,
what have I done for you!' I sang, directed or heard this dialogue
dozens of times; it was the best part of the office not only musically
but also dramatically. Dozens of times I prayed this dialogue in which
everything possible was done to evoke both compassion towards
Christ and consternation at the way in which we treated him through
our lives as a result of our sin (for it was more a matter of blaming
ourselves for all this rather than the 'perfidious Jews'; we were the
ones who were perfidious, in the etymological sense of the word, the
ones who betrayed the faith).

That Good Friday, as on the day before, suddenly, hearing these
reproaches once more, I had the vivid impression that something was
wrong, that something was out of place, was displaced. I discovered
for the first time that these reproaches put in the mouth of God were
not at all like what we had heard half an hour earlier in those few
words which the evangelist had put on the lips of Jesus, not to
mention the silence which he had made him observe. Certainly, I no
longer read the Gospels as if they gave me direct access to the person
of Jesus, his behaviour and his psychology. But the fact remains that
the first Christians, whose worship and faith underlie the writing of
the Gospels, wanted to celebrate the Christ in this way, because that
was the way in which they perceived him; the fact remains that Jesus
of Nazareth existed and behaved in such a way that these first
Christians could not just invent any way of celebrating him. The
passion narratives are certainly the most 'historical' and at all events

the earliest part of the Gospels: if Jesus had suffered and died uttering a flood of words and constantly interrupting each and every one, the passion narratives would not be like the ones that we possess.

Each reading of the passion had confirmed this impression for me: Jesus had been silent; he had not complained by constantly saying, 'O my people, what have I done to you?'; he had not made a catalogue of all his good deeds in order to overwhelm us with shame by cataloguing all our misdeeds. He did not humiliate us; he was himself humiliated, and in a far different way from that which we associate with him. Certainly, he had complained, but as a man who was suffering, not as a man giving a lesson or listing what his debtors owe him: 'I hunger... Why do you strike me?... If possible, let this cup pass from me... My God, why have you forsaken me?... It is finished...' So where did these reproaches come from? Raising the question compelled me to return to the rest of the Gospel. Nowhere did I see Jesus behaving in this way towards sinners, nowhere did I see him presenting God in this way because human beings are sinners. Never did I see Jesus utterly complacent over sin, but he never moaned, never (if you will pardon the familiarity, which I need to stress what I want to say), never said, 'Why have you done that to me after all I did for you? Aren't you ashamed?' If Jesus had never used the language which the reproaches attributed to him, if he had never presented his God as using this language, who was speaking? Who was allowing himself to attribute to Christ, to God, a language alien to that which the Gospels recall? Who displaced this divine language, who was so out of place as to displace God?

Reflecting on this displacement, I noted – as I did with the 'Let us prepare to celebrate the ￿ucharist by recognizing that we are sinners' – that in attributing to God and to Christ this language and this attitude, this moaning aimed at obtaining a distressed acknowledgment of guilt, we were treating God as we would not dare to treat a human being, and attributing to him attitudes which we would not like anyone to have towards us or which we would be ashamed of if we had wronged anyone or they had wronged us. Of course we sometimes say or are told, 'What do you think you're up to, how could you have done that to me after all I've done for you, I must be fond of you to forgive you after doing all that to me', or, 'I must have been awful to have treated you like that after all you've done for me, you must be fond of me and be an extraordinary person to pardon me when I am so unworthy.' Yes, we sometimes talk like that and even mean it: it makes a good scene, like those in novels, the theatre or the cinema. But we are well aware that when we talk like this we are not showing our best side, and we hope that the best side of other people will be rather different. We feel that when we find real forgiveness possible it is more profound and more silent. It gropes for words and gestures; in such cases it is enough to have found something – which emerges tentatively and with difficulty and from deep within us – for the other and ourselves to hang on to. We know that, like charity according to I Corinthians 13, real forgiveness does not take account of evil, that it does not reckon up good and bad in order to calculate debts and credits. Real forgiveness does not give lessons, it is too concerned to remain, almost unable to believe it, on the threshold of the renewed encounter, to get used to the fact that the other person is there again, that the separation is over, that the relationship is restored, however bruised. So who is introducing God in another guise? Who is interested in making us have such a scene by reproaching God, a scene as out of place given all we know of God as it is out of place given the little we know about genuine forgiveness? Again, I did not say more to my colleagues of ten years ago, because I had no more answers to the questions which were only just emerging and which not only filled me with trepidation but also provoked considerable resistance in me. But there again, I stressed the phrase 'out of place', the idea and the mechanism of displacement, since my colleague had spoken of displacements in connection with guilt. And again, I preferred to go on to a similar experience which had raised analogous questions for me.

Holy Saturday

After Good Friday it was Holy Saturday. The Christians of this village in South Finistère were good Christians; so they made their confessions before their Easter communion (that was ten years ago; since then, even in this area, the practice of confession has diminished a lot). There were four of us priests to hear confessions: I was the only one unable to speak Breton, but that was hardly a problem since the Bretons preferred to make their confession to me in French rather than spend a long time queueing at another confessional. I may perhaps have occasion later to describe my personal practice at confession as a penitent, but I have no difficulty, as a minister, indeed quite the opposite, in hearing the confession of believers who seem full of good faith, provided that this good faith is not too contaminated by bad conscience – in which case I try to invite them to make another kind of approach. So I heard confessions for several hours that Holy Saturday, as I had done in many other circumstances, with the mixture of attention, respect, monotony and weariness that this ministry involves.

Then suddenly, as on the previous day, and the day before that, I began to see what was happening in a different way. These men and these women, these old people, adults and children made their confessions very well, as they had learned to, and their whole heart was in it. As required, they began by saying, 'My father, bless me, for I have sinned.' But I noted for the first time – though it had certainly happened before – that immediately after that they went on to what they had to say next without even waiting for me to give the blessing that they had just asked of me. As I began to notice that, I decided to vary the words of the blessing in one way or another or to give a brief commentary on it. Those to whom I was giving it did not even notice, or if they did, they stopped on being interrupted, as if I had not respected the rules of the game, as if I had departed from my role: I was not there to speak to them, or at any rate to speak to them like that at that moment. I am not stressing this point as a criticism of them or of those who had trained them, but to indicate how and why my astonishment grew. It is precisely because these Christians made their confessions well and their clergy had trained them well that the incongruity of my interventions appeared all the more clearly, and I was led to ask myself what was out of place in blessing people when they asked you, or rather what was out of place in what they were asking of me without actually asking me for it.

The hours went by. My disquiet increased to such an extent that I stopped hearing confessions for a while – as the call of nature sometimes demands. In fact I was beginning to be disturbed, asking myself what I and the penitents were doing. Sometimes, on the basis of what I thought I could perceive of them from what they said to me and what I could read in their faces through the grille of the confessional, I would risk talking to them, after they had confessed their sins to me and asked absolution of me, 'If I thought them worthy'. I did not talk first of all about their sin or about the penance that they were waiting to be given, but about Easter. Just Easter. After all, it was Holy Saturday; they had come to confess because of Easter; it was not improper for me to talk to them about Easter. However, they were completely nonplussed. When they had finished and done their part, I sometimes said, quite simply, 'Well, so tomorrow's Easter.' Amazed silence. I said again, 'Have you come to make your confession because tomorrow is Easter?' Embarrassed and affirmative reply after several moments of astonishment. So I went on: 'How do you feel about Easter?' Silence. Embarrassment.

Panic. I must stress that I do not hold this reaction against those with whom I was speaking or those who had trained them. Besides, most of them worked hard and had taken the trouble to add a long wait on to the end of their day in order to make their confession, and if the priest had to add to that... But I would stress that precisely because they were good Christians and made their confessions well, my interventions seemed even more out of place, or it became even more evident that it was out out of place to talk to them about anything that was not directly related to their sin, its forgiveness and their penance.

After the embarrassed silence of one woman following my question, 'So, tomorrow is Easter. What does that mean for you?', what she had said earlier prompted me to add – and this was clearly not in order to get back on the right wavelength – 'Do you have television?' A period of silence, then this time a clear and calm answer, 'Yes, of course.' So I said, 'Well, you will have seen reporters interviewing people in the street, asking their impressions. Suppose for a moment that when you came out of church someone from radio or television stopped you and asked you, microphone in hand, "Madame, tomorrow is Easter, what do you think about that?".' Silence. I was afraid I had gone too far; it seemed unfair to ask this women a question like that, but at the same time I was looking for a way in which Easter, the God of Easter, could be involved. Then, slowly, this woman began to talk. In her own words. Not naturally, because it is not natural to talk about such things. But truly, and simply. About God, about herself, about Easter. Very briefly: people are not very chatty in that part of the world. But truly. I was embarrassed. I could have wept.

I went out for a few moments. I walked in the large square behind the apse of the church while my three colleagues continued to hear confessions until I had pulled myself together. And I asked myself, 'What is all this din rising up to God today from all the churches in the world? What is all this talk? What are people talking about? Is it what they ought to be talking about today? If a din has to rise up from the churches today in this silence of Holy Saturday, between the death of Good Friday and the dawn of Sunday, should it be this din? Is sin as important as that? Or rather, is that how sin is important? What is it that displaces the importance of sin, that displaces God, that displaces man, in such a way that even people of such good will have to think so badly of themselves, bring up misunderstandings, incidents or quarrels in order to take their place in the blessing they want from you, to take their place at Easter, with the God of Easter they come to celebrate? Couldn't people stop all this noise for a moment, to prepare themselves, in the silence of Holy Saturday, for the dawning of Easter, for the rustling in the garden, the journey of the women, Peter's heart pounding, the running of the younger man, the tears, the false doubts, the trembling joys... What is it that changes God and human beings, what is it that displaces them so much that they are displaced from a place that is theirs by right?'

There too, I did not pursue the matter further with my colleagues of ten years ago, for the good reason that I myself had not gone further during the few weeks which separated my telling of it from this Holy Saturday. I was still too embarrassed by the resistances which asking such questions aroused in me, the way in which they disturbed me; these questions seemed to go against a current the power of which I had not hitherto experienced. I do not know what effect my account had on these Dominican theologians and philosophers; none of them said a word about it, apart from one person who spoke one phrase as we were leaving. Since they were expecting me to give a theoretical theological and psychoanalytical account, I suppose that several of them would have thought that I had not had time to prepare a serious paper. That happens to me, as it does to everyone, and perhaps to me more than most. So they might have thought that I had got round the problem by giving them lived experience, a first-person account; they might have thought that all right for a less posh audience, but not good enough for them. As far as I was concerned, while I was doubtless wrong to entitle this account 'Is sin important in that way?' without any further explanation, it marks the first elements in what was still a very embryonic awareness of the way in which the displacements of guilt ravage faith, our views of God and our practices as believers, and of the monstrously parasitic way in which individual and social systems of guilt feed on the best of Christian faith and pervert it.

2. Some processes where guilt is at work

Focus on the status of the sinner

Thoughts of this kind do not develop all at once: they ebb and flow, disappear and return. Others arise. You may feel that they are in the same family but you cannot discern their effect and their origin: some do not hang together, but are rather like the diffuse elements of a nebula. Besides, what we have here is the result of two forces acting in opposite directions: something unfolds and rises to the level of awareness, something else works to repress this process of becoming aware. But it seems as if when a first thought of this kind has occurred, a new kind of attention is aroused, so that, despite the interplay of anxiety and resistance, you begin to hear and perceive what you had not heard before.

So it was that I came to note, progressively, bit by bit, the amazing number of prayers addressed to God which are concerned to highlight a situation of estrangement between God and man, a situation in which God is *ex hypothesi* ill-disposed to human beings, as it were fed up with them and on the point of punishing them because these human beings, *ex hypothesi*, have wounded and saddened him and deserve, *ex hypothesi*, his punishment. All these prayers begin with 'Be favourable to us', 'Spare us', 'Abate your anger', 'Have mercy', 'Do not remember our faults', and so on. For years and years, over the hours ('hours' here being the term for the different offices which punctuate the communal prayer of the monastic or canonical orders), I have said such words, and at one time – distractions apart – I used them seriously and deeply in my prayers. In fact I saw this as one of the most normal and necessary ways of addressing God, understanding our relationship to him and starting a dialogue which everything suggested I was constantly in danger of interrupting. Do not suppose that this type of prayer is the arbitrary choice of an isolated period within the Christian tradition or a spirituality marginal to it. Whether we look at the earliest or the latest psalms that Christianity took over from Judaism, at liturgical prayers composed in the patristic period or at mediaeval prayers, at more modern devotions or even the first liturgies in French composed from 1965 on in the wake of the liturgical reform of Vatican II, this a theme which, if not unique, is always dominant. Above all, it is almost always the one which comes first, as if it were the one with which prayers should begin, as if it were the one that set the scene and laid the foundation for all that could enter into prayer between God and humanity.

Nor is this a set of problems restricted to devotion which does not reappear outside that sphere. As first a student theologian and then a professor of theology who has had to lecture on the treatise on sin (which, in the Thomistic tradition, comes in ethics rather than dogmatics), trained in exegesis, patristics and the history of doctrines, classical and modern, and continuing to keep up my knowledge of these various areas as well as possible, I was well aware that there are two great families of thought in Christianity (to over-simplify matters). One makes human sin and the forgiveness which brings salvation from this sin through God and Jesus Christ the two poles around which it is possible to define both the human condition and the salvation brought by God. This is a very dramatic conception of human existence, of the Christian condition and the destiny of Jesus Christ as saviour, in which man is essentially defined by his status as a sinner and Jesus Christ is virtually defined as one who saves from sin. Another family of thought sees the relationship between God and man less in terms of conflict: God is the living one whose saving work consists in giving human beings a surplus of life, a 'spiritual extra' over and above the life that they can already live by virtue of being human beings (a condition which is itself a gift of God). So Jesus Christ is primarily the one who has revealed to us, by his incarnation of it, this richer form of relationship with God and of relationships among human beings and this spiritual extra. In such a perspective, sin is certainly not eliminated; its status, if I might put it that way, is that of an accident which can happen to human existence and degrade, not to say shatter, the life which God seeks to give to humanity. On this view sin can be 'mortal', and deserves as much attention as anything which runs the risk of killing biological, ecological, social and individual life. So it calls for a corrective action and a preventive action, just as all life needs to be warned about and healed from all that could kill it. But here life and the gift of life are the poles around which everything is organized and by which God, human beings and their relations are defined. Here, while sin is neither unimportant nor secondary, it comes second. This is a less dramatic conception of human existence, God and Jesus Christ, which involves less conflict.

With twenty years' experience of theology, I knew that these attitudes are just as old and just as Christian as each other: we find them both in the New Testament. I knew that each of them had been illustrated by venerable forms of piety, spirituality, theology and sanctity. I also knew that, at least in our Western world, the dramatic conception of Christian existence and the quasi-definition of man in terms of sin have gained the upper hand. For example, while we find a basis for both these views in the letters of Paul, it is the passages which support the dramatic conception that make the most impression (perhaps they are in fact most characteristic of Paul's gospel). Of the long line of those men and women who have felt more at home with these ideas I need only mention the names of St Augustine and Luther to indicate how far it has fashioned Western Christianity; the theological weight of St Thomas Aquinas – who attempted one of the rare syntheses between these two families – was not enough to overthrow this primacy. In France one might recall Pascal and Jansenism, and also the most influential French Catholic writers of the twentieth century: for example, Mauriac and Bernanos. As for the theology of the past forty years, it has been so strongly dominated – at least in Europe – by the great Protestant theologians, Karl Barth, Bultmann, Pannenberg, Moltmann and so on, because of their great status and the wider intellectual freedom that they enjoy in their churches, that we should not be surprised to see this view more alive and evocative than ever: the voice of some Catholic theologians orientated in a rather different direction is not strong enough to counterbalance them, and the theology of the Orthodox churches, which is much closer to the other vision of things, has virtually no influence at all.

So you can understand that it took a lot of time and deep and difficult inner questioning, both conscious and unconscious, in the face of the weight and authority of such institutions, for the first inklings to appear of a question which was new to me and was not echoed in any way from outside (except by those who asked it in a way that proved to their satisfaction the illusory and alienating character of Christianity). Why is sin accorded this privileged position, so that in fact it serves as the point of reference for the definition of man before God, the status of God himself and that of Jesus Christ as saviour? Why do we have to put sin first? Why do we make it the touchstone of all prayer, all spirituality, all theology? Is sin as important as that, or rather, is that how sin is important?

The failure to recognize sin and the exaggeration of its effects

So I found the same question coming up with growing insistence in several ways. One attitude would have been possible, the one adopted by most of my friends who were non-believers or had become non-believers: to get rid, if not of guilt, at least of sin. I could not do that, not only because of the traditions in which I was so deeply steeped or the power – in me as in anyone else – of the obscure forces which ensure the success of the displacements of which I was aware. In fact, following another development which is clearly related to the one of which I am speaking here, I came progressively to feel that our life does not have any other survival than the traces it leaves in the memory of other human beings; in the memory of our earth, which is itself mortal; or in the memory of God, if there is a God. All that relates to life is mortal. Now that also means – though this is just as hard to accept – that even before coming to its term, every form of human life is exposed to death and can die, not naturally, because its end has come, but accidentally. Now whether we like it or not, we are the principal instruments of death, foremost in spoiling life: every day, throughout the world, in millions of ways, life is spoilt, as are love, intelligence, justice, beauty, work, effort and pleasure, and living beings are mocked and trampled underfoot. I am not stressing this now to attest the reality of sin but in order to say that if all life seems to me not only mortal by nature but susceptible of being put to death 'accidentally', the same must be true of what life there could be between God and human beings. Or perhaps there is no God and there are no relations between God and humanity, or, if there are, they too are necessarily mortal and under the threat of death: this life too can be damaged, shattered, broken. That is what I call sin, and how could it too be prevented from possibly being fatal? Certainly not by anything that God could do, though he was presented to me as one who could withhold from us the favour that we had so often to implore; the action had to be that of human beings. Since – rightly or wrongly - I persisted in thinking that there was a God and that he had initiated a certain relationship between himself and us, I could only claim for this relationship what seemed to me to be essential to all form of life we know of, namely that it is naturally and accidentally mortal. For me the non-existence of sin would have been anthropological non-sense even before it was theological non-sense.

If it was impossible for me to subscribe to the view that sin did not exist, it was also impossible for me to regard sin as being as important as certain forms of Christianity so often suppose. I was indeed convinced – even now people still refuse to recognize the fact – that every day, millions of times over, life has been mocked, spoilt, destroyed by human beings. But it seemed to me wrong – and incorrect – to attribute it to their sin. St Thomas Aquinas, who exalts freedom to the point of seeing it as the way in which human beings are most in the image of God, also taught me that 'free actions' are rare in the life of human beings; those of a lifetime can sometimes be counted on the fingers of one hand. He did not stress how rarely they occur out of élitism or pessimism, or with reference to the devastating role of sin (which is in itself a free act), but rather arise out of an acute awareness of the magnitude of our freedom and the demands which need to be fulfilled for us to be free. So I could not attribute to sin, to that rare thing which is real sin (since I stress, with Thomas, that sin can only be sin if it is a free act), this interminable train of damage to life over the centuries.

My other studies led me progressively to discover all that governs the behaviour of human beings, all their conditioning (not in the pejorative sense of the word, but as a term for basic and formative elements), whether economic, social, psychological, biological or even cosmological, all those threads of which we are woven by the forces which go before us and affect us, and of which we are usually ignorant or unaware. So I could not claim to think – as a certain form of Catholicism does with such passion – that all of us, individually and communally, are the source of all the evil that we do as a result of our continual sins, but that sin cannot be designated its cause. There again I had to ask whether sin was as important as that: unhappiness, evil, death are very important quantitatively and qualitatively, but must we regard the importance of sin as being of a similar magnitude? I began by noting the element of megalomania in such an affirmation by the subject of his or her fundamental guilt, but I would be anticipating too much if I developed it further at this stage of my itinerary. I shall come back to it later.

Contempt for Jesus' attitude to sinners and sin

So I was in a difficult position at that time: on the one hand to say that sin was not real was to reject the possibility of any relationship between God and us and therefore in effect to say that the existence of God had no meaning. At the same time, if such a relationship did exist, to say that was anthropological nonsense. But on the other hand it was also anthropological nonsense to attribute to human freedom all the misfortunes of the world and humanity, since to attribute them to sin is to attribute them to human freedom. The difficulty I found myself in was reinforced by a similar difficulty when I turned to the image of Jesus Christ presented to us in the Gospels and to the God whom, according to these Gospels, Jesus proclaimed to us. Jesus was not in any way presented as having neglected sin, having treated it with false indulgence or complicity. Indeed, he was presented as having been even more demanding on many points than the scribes and Pharisees of his time, since 'They have said to you... but I say...' is not just concerned with blessings and liberation, and the Beatitudes have another side: the Woes. But in addition – and this point might seem more difficult to grasp than the earlier one, even if it is just as vigorously attested, everything suggests that Jesus sought to make his contemporaries understand that sin did not have the kind of importance that they attributed to it, and that he himself and his God attached a different importance to it from that which they were supposed to attach to it. One could be the emissary of God and eat with sinners; one could be the emissary of God and keep company with publicans, prostitutes, Samaritans or those whose infirmities and misfortunes were supposed to have something to do with sin: the lepers, the deaf, the blind, the lame, the paralysed, or even the second-class citizens among the people of God – the women and children.

So everything suggests that Jesus had sought to tame, calm, sort out all the complications felt by the sinner with his view of himself as a sinner before God: he did not deny sin or neglect it, but rather, even before forgiving it he sought to disentangle the bonds through which the sinners were caught up in their sin, to open up a gap in the wall that the believer thought had to be built to testify to his exclusion. Everything suggests that Jesus said: 'You do not need to be afraid of being a sinner like that; look at me, I am not afraid of you because you are sinners. You don't die from being a sinner, you die if you think you are going to die from it; let me come, let me eat with you, and then we'll see. But that's not the first problem to settle; we must not begin there; you and I have other things to do; we have to be together. I want to dine with you this evening.' After that, he evidently had to make up a parable to explain to the others what he was about, since, in a bizarre way, those men and women who were directly involved (Zacchaeus, the woman taken in adultery, and so on) knew straight away and did not ask for an explanation. So when it came to the Jesus whom the Gospels showed me there were complications: there was no question of dismissing sin without leaving Jesus and his following (in the sense of being a disciple of Jesus, the imitation of Jesus Christ), but at the same time there was no question – this was more difficult but more decisive – of attaching the kind of importance to sin that the Jesus of the Gospels had constantly fought against because it deformed the image of his God and that of humanity.

Besides, thinking of Christ and the ideas one has of his role as saviour made me see more rapidly and more clearly than in other contexts the strategies of the forces which in this way displace the importance of sin and thus distort at the same time God's image and our own. Here again it took me several years of plodding and timorous evasion, but the nebula ended by taking some shape. And if there are points in *When I say God* which I would now have made differently or parts that I would have written differently, I am quite sure that the basic details of the part devoted to the death of Jesus of Nazareth and his significance and the way in which I presented them are the best part of the book. Of course, my Roman censors found a way of discovering heresies, and that was all the easier for them since they attributed to me views which were the opposite of what I said in order to condemn them, a procedure over which I could have won a libel suit against them under any normal legal system. I must grant them that my view of the death of Jesus does not allow them to be as sure of their power as they are; so their preference is very understandable. This comment is less irrelevant than it might seem, since the more authoritarian those in power are, the more they find it useful, indeed a prime advantage, to exploit the forces that are mobilized by guilt. So it is not surprising that, in order to secure their power, the scribes and the princes among the priests have always wanted to encourage a view of Christ and his death which conferred on them absolute power over the management of this guilt.

Be this as it may, we know the place occupied, in a great many forms of Christianity, by the idea that for human sinners to be reconciled with God a price has to be paid and an expiatory sacrifice has to be offered; otherwise God would be in some way bound by his own justice and would not be able to forgive man even if he wanted to. Since it is out of the question for humanity, sinful as it is, to offer God a sacrifice proportional to his holiness and to the wrong that he has suffered, God has to provide it. For example, it may be thought that in Jesus Christ God has made a gift to humanity of someone who, because he is truly man and truly God, will be able to offer in the name of humanity, from the depths of his being, the redemptive sacrifice which will appease the righteous anger of God and free his love from the legitimate demands that his justice imposes on him. Jesus Christ is glorified because he who had a divine state was degraded to the humility of the human condition in such a way that sinful humanity could be represented by one who committed no sin but was made sin for us – since he was made man – and whose death tore up in God's presence the writ of our condemnation and made us free.

Those familiar with the New Testament will have recognized in the phrases I have just used formulae which can be found there often. By helping us to discover or rediscover a considerable number of texts from the so-called inter-testamental period (between the first century BC and the first century AD), research over the last thirty years has allowed us to understand in what context and for what reasons the authors of the later strata of the New Testament literally engendered forms of Christianity rather different from those evidenced in the earliest strata, which indeed proved more successful than the latter. This difference in success can partly be explained by the difference in the importance attached to sin in each of these strata. With Ernst Käsemann, I think that there is no reason to declare *a priori* any text of the New Testament to be necessarily free from heresy (except for a 'political' reason, when an authority seeks to base the absoluteness of its power on the absolute inerrancy of the text of which it claims to be the only official intepreter). So I do not want to dwell here on the reasons for the development of some of these New Testament constructions, which are more closely connected with the preoccupations of the circles in which they arose than with the individual personality of their authors, though I must point out that commentators on primitive Christianity and historians concerned with it were a great help to me here (Käsemann belongs as much in one category as in the other). In fact they allowed me at the same time to understand why these great religious geniuses had acted as they did and why we need not follow them today, because our situation as human beings and believers calls for something different.

That having been said, there is no need to be an expert in exegesis, still less a psychoanalyst, to note the incredibly infantile (I do not say childlike) views of God and sin which are encouraged by the popularized forms of these venerable theologies: an exasperated God who has to be offered a sacrifice to appease his anger and set free his mercy which is bound by his own justice; a Son whose role as Son consists in effacing himself before his Father to the point of death, but who will be recompensed by this Father, who will make him Lord, establishing him at his right hand; human beings from henceforth ransomed, but nevertheless – as if by chance – by no means freed from their guilt, since each of their sins, up to the last moment of their life (and how can they stop sinning?), exposes them again to the just punishment of God and again calls for the intervention of the redemptive Christ and, for good measure, that of his Mother, who has become our mother, along with the whole cohort of saints. Here the fault of these sinners is heightened to such a degree that from now on it represents an insult to this Son who is given over to death for us and this Father who has loved us to the point of sacrificing his Son for us. Here again, for those who begin to 'hear' what is being said by such a system of views, there would seem to be no alternative than to call all this by its proper name, which is not the name of God, and to consider God as a variation of what we now know better under another name.

I cannot make up my mind here, doubtless for reasons connected with my past and the make-up of my personality, but also for reasons which seem to me to be connected with the faith. As well as understanding better why these forms of Christianity had been developed and why they were not necessarily called for, I also discovered that there had been quite different ways of being a Christian, and I could read most of the Gospels without finding in them traces of such a conception of the death of Jesus Christ, of the wrath of God and and the need to offer him a sacrifice of this kind in order finally to let his justice leave his love free to operate. The Jesus whose features other Christian communities had constructed by remembering what he had been and celebrating what he would be from now on down the centuries was in fact dead, he had been assassinated, he had not avoided death and had accepted it as his destiny when it proved to be necessary. But one of the main reasons for his being put to death by the religious authorities of the period was precisely that he said and did things in connection with sin, the nature of the sinner and the relationship between God and the sinner which abolished the religious structures human beings had made in connection with sin. That is why he is our saviour, the servant of God and man, the revealer of God and of what we are. He shifted the foundations of these constructions, just as he destroyed the foundations of the temple and of its priests. It was this shift that they had at all costs to prevent: this man had to die for the general good, for the good that all people thought they could find in what this Jesus had displaced.

The extraordinary thing – as I noted in *When I say God* – is that from the beginning numerous forms of Christianity have done away with the displacement that Jesus brought about and that caused his death. From the beginning they have managed this *tour de force* by displacing Jesus in order to reintegrate him into the system from which he had wanted to free human beings and to make him the guarantor and high priest of what he had rejected to the point of preferring death rather than subscribing to it and enslaving us to it. Many representations of redemption, of satisfaction, of expiation and of substitution, and the whole complex of certain views of God the Father, the Son, and humanity which are tied up with them, amount to the most gigantic displacement that has ever been achieved by the forces mobilized by guilt. When one becomes aware of this, one is almost terrified by the infernal power presupposed by the success of such a displacement. One hardly dares to go on asking, 'Is sin as important as that?', or rather, 'Is sin important in that way?', since one hesitates to confront such powers. However, in the end one has no choice. If we did otherwise, think how they would mutilate human beings, enslave us, disfigure the face of God and of Jesus Christ!

3. Hatred of God

In the environs of hate

Another theme took much longer to come home to me: I have to say that it was even more disconcerting than the earlier ones, since even more than the others it seemed to take me off what seemed to be the only possible way in Christianity; there was even something odious about it, in the literal sense of the word, as it was to do with hate. Since my first contacts with psychology and psychoanalysis more than twenty-five years ago – at that time purely through books – I had learned that there is no love without hate. The clinical demonstration and theoretical study which followed convinced me of this, but only in a rather abstract way. I accepted this truth, but I was not quite sure what to do with it, as though it hardly concerned me.

I was further helped in this resistance by what St Thomas Aquinas had taught me about hate some years earlier. Speaking of the passions of the soul, and much inspired by Aristotle, he distinguished – as I have said – two families of passion: those in the sphere of the concupiscible and those in the sphere of the irascible. Love belonged to the first family, but contrary to what one might expect, hate did not belong to the second family but to the first, like love. In fact, St Thomas stressed, hate is simply the movement by which love turns against what robs it of its object, though it may be this very object of which it robs itself. That is why, with his usual calm assurance in these matters, St Thomas regarded hate as being just as normal, healthy and necessary for the life of the psyche as love, for what would a love be that did not rise up against anything that deprived it of its object? So St Thomas did not find that hate was intrinsically immoral; it could be sometimes virtuous and sometimes sinful, like all other human behaviour.

This was already a quite diffent conception from that of the Christian moral tradition, which otherwise would have been enough to compel me – like any other person – to recognize my personal anguish at the least stirrings of hate. On this point, as on others, the morality of St Thomas had no success in Christianity, still less when he went so far as to maintain this conception of hate in connection with the gospel commandment to love one's enemies. According to him, the fact that we have to love our enemies because God has loved us does not in any way alter the fact that our enemies remain our enemies, our adversaries (*ad versus* – turning against), and that as such they cannot but arouse in us stirrings of hatred which are quite natural and do not disappear because in other respects – i.e. through God – we should love them. So my mind was not closed to the idea that there is a certain relationship between hate and love, and that perhaps helped me to be less hostile to what psychoanalysis taught me of other relationships, though it doubtless encouraged a resistance to discovering that their proximity as demonstrated by psychoanalysis is far greater, and disconcerting in a different way from that of which I had been convinced by St Thomas.

For a while this psychoanalytic theory, too, remained somewhat outside my preoccupations; it might be true, but it did not greatly concern me. I am incapable of describing how my own analysis made the psychoanalytical theory more real, and how as it were tremors began which were later to end up in a modification of my inner landscape and my external horizons. However, whatever happened hardly came about explicitly. In the years which followed I continued with a real but somewhat detached interest to listen to psychoanalysts talking (*à propos* of patients, themselves or in a more theoretical way) about the ambivalence of love and hate. Now that I am less detached I feel incapable of recreating after the event the first signs or events which provoked this change. I vaguely remember a conversation with a psychoanalyst friend, Jewish by family and tradition, whom I see all too rarely: he had just read *When I say God* and spoke to me of the different feelings that Jews express to their God, the words and injunctions which they address to him. Beside these, Christian prayers seemed to him to be very pale. It was then, or at another moment, that an idea formed in me with that conviction that the conscious has about the unconscious, an idea at that time a hundred miles ahead of my conscious awareness which, moreover, had no context because everything was organized in such a way as to exclude it. It came home to me directly with a certainty that was more calm and beneficent than upsetting and divisive (people talk a good deal of nonsense about the 'reductionist' or 'suspicious' character of analytical interpretation). Anyway, at that moment or another, I knew something that I had never known, though it was as if I had always known it: there had to be as much room for the hatred of God as for the love of God. The use of the genitive is ambiguous here; I restrict myself to the two possible meanings which came to mind then: it was necessary for our hatred for God, our hatred against God, to have as great a place as that of our love of God, our love for God. And on that day I felt that one of the tasks I had in connection with God, but also in connection with myself, was to discover the status of this hatred of God.

I noted afterwards that the dawning of this thought had been held back in a way which was particularly characteristic of the workings of resistances in such matters: this thought had been prevented from arising by the very way in which it was already present in my field of consciousness, in the practice of my faith, in my theological knowledge and teaching. The notion of 'hatred' of God in fact appeared there, on every page and in its right context. It has biblical foundations, not only as an idea but even in the vocabulary of the Bible. However – at all events in the area I was concerned with – it owed its weight to St Augustine. We know that St Augustine was what one might dare to call a master where sin was concerned. By this somewhat provocative turn of phrase I want to indicate that he not only bequeathed to us a theology of sin which was to weigh heavily – for better or for worse – on all the later development of Western Christianity but that he also bequeathed us, in his *Confessions*, one of the most extraordinary psychological legacies, telling us what he felt about his sins, his condition as a sinner, and the God of whom he found a manifestation at the very heart of his condition. What I have written so far doubtless indicates that I am far from feeling at ease in all the characteristics of the Augustinian variant of Christianity. However, genius is genius – even when it has morbid aspects – and the *Confessions* remain a masterpiece. Now St Augustine had defined sin as hatred of God and had used all his theological, psychological and literary genius to develop the implications of this definition. I had read, worked on, and mediated on all that.

Like far more eminent theologians than myself, beginning with Thomas Aquinas, I found some difficulty in defining sin in terms of a hatred of God which was not as it were present in the consciousness of the sinner and which in any case we almost never give as the goal of our sinful actions. The man or woman who commits murder, theft or adultery does not give hatred of God as his or her purpose and is not primarily motivated by hatred of God. Had I not read Husserl, and had I not known about intentionality, my Aristotelian and Thomistic background would have been enough to prevent me from defining a human act in terms of a purpose and a motivation absent from it. But Augustine's rhetorical virtuosity and dramatic power succeeded in reintroducing hatred of God as the defining factor in sin because its effects and aspects were the most decisive (since they related to God), even if this hatred was not the most apparent motivation or purpose.

So this concept of hatred of God was very much present in my awareness; hatred of God had its place. And what a place! That of sin. In order to settle everything, or to hide everything, even though it was of Augustine's making, this hatred presented itself in a way which was not incompatible with what I had learned from St Thomas about the relationship between hatred and love. Certainly, in sin, hatred of God was not a movement triggered off by a love for God which saw its object slipping away and turned against the one who was the source of its deprivation. But it was a touch of genius to show that God was hated to the degree that he was felt to be depriving the sinner of the object of love that he was giving himself in a guilty fashion, namely his own self. When the sinner steals, when he kills, when he commits adultery, it is himself whom he is loving in a disordered way. And it is of the self whom he loves in this way that the sinner risks seeing himself deprived by the God who seeks to turn him from his sin: thus the sinner hates God with a hatred proportional to (and arising out of) the love which he has for himself, a love which risks seeing its object, namely itself, being taken away. So hatred of God had a place, and indeed a prime place, in my mental universe. However, as is often the case with resistance, the place it occupied was ideal for preventing quite a different significance and quite a different status of hatred of God from emerging. That is why, when it ultimately proved absolutely necessary for me to discover this status, I had a feeling that I was on to something radically new. The fact is that the relationship in our unconscious between hatred and love brought out by psychoanalysis is very different from the status of hatred which had been taught me by Thomas Aquinas; the unconscious hatred involved in our ambivalence towards God is radically and undoubtedly nearer to love of God than the hatred of God which St Augustine, that doctor in sin, has described so well.

That is why I feel incapable of expressing myself in a very articulate way, first of all because these thoughts have been going through my mind for far too short a time, and also because these are telluric matters of the unconscious about which even the most expert psychoanalysts would not venture to talk other than in metaphor. Besides, many people prefer to distance themselves from them for theoretical reasons which are often quite interesting. I think that it will be better for me to try to describe some of the effects that this very radical matter of hatred of God had on me – and more in keeping with my competence and my personal experience. To begin with, I was (and in a way still remain) completely defenceless before this question. Not only did I not have the slightest reply to it, but the question itself was too disconcerting, too out of place in my individual and social religious world, for it not to stand there like a monolith from another planet, as massive, as incontestably present and as impenetrably mysterious as the statues on Easter Island. However, little by little, relationships began to appear between this maverick question and other questions or elements of answers which were more familiar and more intelligible to me.

The mechanism of rechannelling

For example, some years ago now I read with great profit a text in which Freud gave an account of one of the strategies used by the superego towards the drives. I will not bother to explain here the concepts that he uses, since they are now far better known to the general public than the concepts of St Augustine or St Thomas to which I referred earlier. Besides, I am not persuaded that this way of representing the workings of the psyche is the best way of doing justice to the chaotic character of the world of the unconscious, above all in the version given by popular psychology. However, quite apart from the fact that it has the advantage of simplicity, doubtful though that may be, it is far from being without truth. Anyway, Freud explains that when the superego forbids the drives – i.e. sexuality and aggression – to fix themselves on external objects, it nevertheless has to tolerate some expression of them; it does this in the form of compromise, providing them with an object to which they can devote themselves, and in this way preventing them from being involved in other directions: this permitted object is the subject itself. So sexuality finds itself forbidden to fix itself on another object, but it is authorized, by rechannelling itself towards the subject, to fix itself on the ideal of the self that the superego offers it. The subject can invest itself in this ideal all the more easily in that it is capable of satisfying not only the superego but all the persons and institutions that it represents. There is no limit to this investment of self, and the ideal of the self thus cherished can be cherished all the more since because the ideal relates to the persons and institutions represented by the superego it can pass as being less egocentric than it is in reality. So in its own eyes, as in those of others. the love of the subject can pass as a love of these persons and these institutions.

This mechanism of rechannelling not only happens with sexuality:

Freud shows that it also happens with aggression. If the superego does not authorize aggression to attack an external object, here again it has to tolerate a certain amount of free play, which again it does through compromise. It offers this aggression an object to which it can relate with impunity, namely here again the subject itself, under the species of the bad self that the superego denounces. So there is a shift in the direction of aggression against external objects in that it is rechannelled and directed at the subject itself. The subject can attack its bad self all the more fiercely when, in so doing, it can legitimately feel that it is obeying the wishes of the persons and the institutions represented by the superego and, by attacking itself in this way, it is bearing witness to its love and respect for these external authorities. Like the libidinal investment of the ego in the ideal, the fixation of aggression on the bad self can thus be boundless. We see that in such a configuration the drives of the subject are very intense, even if he or she would be surprised and profoundly indignant if this were pointed out (though that would be as stupid as it would be ineffective). However, this intense activity of the drives is entirely centred on the subject itself and can be exercised with all the more intensity in that it respects the prohibition against external objects and presents itself as homage to individuals and authorities which in origin are as much the ideal of the ego which is thus adulated as of the bad self which is thus execrated.

On my first reading of this text, more than twenty-five years ago, despite what was then the very rudimentary and exclusively bookish nature of my understanding of psychoanalysis, I was literally dazzled by the light which it shed on certain attitudes in the religious life (meaning the life of religious) of which I was well aware in myself and in the religious mileu which had so deeply impregnated me with its ideals, so skilful and powerful was the method of training. Obviously this training would not have been so successful had it not met with active complicity on my part and that of a certain number of my friends. So profoundly were we steeped in it that I am not sure whether anyone who has not experienced it can measure its dimensions, just as they will not perhaps be able to understand at what point the Freud text which I have just mentioned applies admirably to what was asked of us and what we tried to achieve.

The prohibition against sexuality being related to external objects was self-evident: it is even surprising to note how much it went without saying. I have already said that it was scarcely spoken of, far less so than obedience, poverty or the common life. For many of us, as for the institution (I am speaking here only of the male religious life, having virtually no experience of the female), that went almost without saying. It is obvious that such a facile acceptance – though there were the ups and downs of temptation, which were not always displeasing – depended far more on our previous personal history than on the training we were going to receive. However, I think that this acceptance – at first sight disconcerting for men between twenty and thirty years of age, many of whom had already shown that they had strong and relatively normal personalities – was so easy only because we had already made a heavy investment in this kind of individual and collective ideal of the self. In fact, in order to divert our sexuality to fixate on other objects, it was both easier and more effective to consolidate this investment and take it to its climax, evoking the thought of God and humanity, the figure of Christ, the apostles, the prophets, St Dominic and so on, and to do so with such intensity that it became in effect almost useless and as it were flippant to dwell on the temptations of the flesh. We had more and better things to do, in the sphere of sexuality, too: to go ever further and more deeply in our investment in this ideal.

Of course, we did not succeed sufficiently, and this was drawn to our attention in a way which did not need to be very demanding. We were as aware of it ourselves as we were sorry. But there again, the other form of rechannelling could be basically involved, namely that of directing our aggresion against our bad self. Yes, we were bad religious; yes, we were unfaithful to the spirit of our father St Dominic; yes, we were betraying our apostolic vocation, our call to the life of the gospel; yes, like the rich young man in the Gospel we were responding badly to the call of Christ, and like him we grieved Christ, as we grieved his Father, who was also our Father; his Mother, who was also the guardian of our Order (all Orders say that she is their special guardian, but were we not the inventors and promoters of the Rosary?); and all the cohort of the saints and holy Dominicans. We wept, we were distressed about it, we chastized ourselves. (I belong to the generation of religious who were taught to chastize themselves in the strict sense of the word, i.e. we beat ourselves at least twice a week with a kind of scourge, not of leather but of knotted cords, which bore the well-chosen name of 'discipline'.) And we very soon came to find such conduct normal, like everything else, not primarily through masochism, perversity or weakness of character (most of us did not lack character, and that is the least that one could say), but because it seemed to us to be as holy as healthy to get to grips with our bad self.

This fixation of our aggression meant that a very vigilant control was exercised on any temptation that we might have had to relate to others than ourselves, our companions, our brothers. Centuries of experience have allowed the religious life to bring to perfection ways of allowing and controlling aggression between 'brothers' which border on genius. The aggression was exercised far better, controlled better and repressed better than sexuality. We steeped ourselves progressively in fraternal customs the gentleness of which has made the peace of the cloisters and the affability of their inhabitants famous. But we could resort to staggering savagery when we were attacking the bad self of others and struggling for respect to be given to the ideal which was the heart of both our personality and our community. Here we saw ourselves clearly as showing not so much aggression towards others as a burning love of this ideal, even a burning love for our brothers, whose good we sought, a good which – for them as for us – was the common ideal. After more than thirty years of religious life I could fill numerous volumes with facts and anecdotes illustrating this behaviour and its mechanisms. That is not my aim here. Far less is it my aim to make us seem ridiculous for having behaved in such a way: moreover, one finds such behaviour elsewhere, in more or less analogous forms, among men of equally high quality and in much-respected groups. My aim is solely to stress the formidable efficacy of the system in question, and the great variety which its reference to God produces in it.

In fact, each step forward, each piece of progress by the group or an individual, reinforced the system. On the one hand it increased the investment in the ideal of self at the same time as it reduced the risk that sexuality would become fixated on another object than this ideal. On the other hand, it allowed aggression to vent itself more strictly on the bad self (its own or that of others) since while the ideal of self had been elevated by an even greater investment, the gap between this ideal and what one made of it, individually or collectively, appeared all the greater. Thus the judgment to be made could only be that much more severe and the combat more determined. Had we achieved holiness, nothing would have changed; on the contrary, everything would have been reinforced: for if someone made us admire the extraordinary intensity of the way in which the saints had invested in their ideal, we would have been told that only the saints knew at what points they were sinners and we would have been made to meditate on the witness and the writings in which some of them had spoken about this in an astonishing way. What the reference to God introduces into such a process is absolutely vital: once God is involved there is no limit. Any other point of reference would have involved a limit, since any other object than God would not merit an investment of such intensity. But since God is the point of reference for the whole process, not only is there no limit but there is not even a trace of one. That is why the temptation to invest one's sexuality in another object than this ideal, or one's aggression elsewhere than in this bad self (one's own or that of others), was not so strong, since the reference to God allowed sexuality and aggression to be attributed an object which did not impose any quantitative limit on their exercise. More than any other, this same point of reference to God allows an unlimited expression of sexuality and aggression with the blessing – and this has to be said – of the superego, since it is for God, for love of him, in his name and with his blessing. What would one not give to become patron of such an orgy of investments!

At this point, then, we do not seem to be far from hatred of God. However, over the years, I have been able to discover, explore and then explain, discuss and teach all this (though I obviously would not claim that the religious life could be reduced to it) without it seeming to have the least connection with the concept of hatred of God, though I have pointed out that in any case that played quite an important role in my mental universe. One of the first effects that the incontestable appearance of my new acceptance of this concept had on me was in fact to establish a connection between it and what I have just mentioned. That was more familiar to me and gave me the first glimpse of how this indecipherable hatred of God might be understood, though for so long the two had seemed quite unconnected. In fact, if there were hatred of God to the same degree that there was love of God and because there was love of God, this hatred had to be at work, it had to be in action. Evidently that could only happen indirectly, since this is as unacceptable a sentiment for each individual believer as it is for the believing community. One might even predict that the despicable aspects of it would require evasions and transformations complex enough to mask its true face under acceptable or even very respectable appearances. However, it could also be foreseen that its power – which, I repeat, is identical to that of the love of God – would be great enough to give it a choice place in individual and collective Christian behaviour. Of that at least I was certain, but of nothing else.

That was when what I had observed and understood about the rechannelling of aggression had proved to be connected with this line of questioning. A first piece of evidence came home to me, in such a way that – despite the fear inspired in me by the upheavals which I knew it would cause, and which I was aware would be very burden-some – I had no doubt about its truth once it appeared: short of being able to express against God himself the hate that he felt for him, the believer necessarily directed it against himself by proclaiming himself to be a sinner. He (or she) proclaimed himself wicked and deserving of the hatred of God, of himself and of others, and in so doing clearly proclaimed that – since he was a sinner – he hated God (as St Augustine was well aware). If the proclamation by Christians of their sin was so important and so urgent that in preparing for the eucharist it had to come immediately after a recollection of the love of God for humanity, it was because one of the functions of this proclamation was to provide an escape for hatred of God by altering its direction, by transforming it into an accusation directed at the self for hating God, a mechanism of which the unconscious provides us with thousands of examples in equally decisive matters (though I do not pretend to reduce it to that alone). I had also just discovered other functions of this proclamation, of which I shall speak later, but I must now stress just how powerful are the reasons we have for hating God and what their nature is.

Hatred of the father

Some reasons are almost self-evident, that is, as far as this can be said of any ideas which are barely established. We need only recall the element of conflict in the character of the relationships between God and humanity as they have been dramatically brought into the foreground by the whole of the Christian tradition that I evoked earlier: the jealous love of the Father for his sons, the envious love of the sons for the Father, the paternal privileges which the sons want to seize, the aim of the sons to eliminate the Father less by killing him than by becoming identical to him ('Do this and you will be like gods'), the just anger of the Father against this claim, the punishment of the sons, the sacrifice offered by the Son and reconciliation ending with the Father himself, in his mercy, giving his sons the privileges which they had wanted to take away through sin ('God is made what we are so that we may become what he is'). Some Christians who despise psychoanalysis mock the somewhat basic character of the Freudian drama of the Oedipus complex: the summary I have just made of a view which is quite classic in Christianity shows that here Freud hardly went quite so far in the divine simplicity of the scenario. This style of relations between father and son is steeped in sentiments in which the ambivalence of love and hate is only equalled by its power.

There is insufficient indication here of one of the most radical causes of the love-hate of the son towards the father, which does not have an exact parallel in the love-hate of the father for the son, namely that the son sees the father as someone with an attribute the possession of which would fulfil all his desires. Here psychoanalysts speak in terms of the penis and above all the phallus, but some have understood very well that the word can be one of the configurations of this attribute. It is easy to see that this configuration is favoured in Christianity: for if the Son has actually been called the word (he is the Word of God), it is the Father who bestows this word. The Son is only the Son through being uttered by the Father. The love-hate of the Son for this Father who utters him and its ambivalence would appear in the fact that the naming of the Son sometimes goes so far as to make the Son the one who has this word, though he is only its effect. Even if we do not share Freud's view, that Christianity substituted a religion of the Son for a religion of the Father (Judaism), we have to note that sometimes Christianity leans more towards a christocentrism than a theocentrism, indeed to such an extent that the two other great monotheistic religions (Judaism and Islam) consider this promotion of the Son and the sons as idolatrous and injurious to the lordship of God. It is very true that in Christianity, it is the Son who is called Lord. One way of representing God as Father, Jesus as the Son and human beings as the children of God is close to that which, in the unconscious, produces what are at the same time both the most ambivalent and the most powerful relationships, all this happening as if the most archaic imagos, and the stirrings of love and hate which they arouse in us, were taking over the most central elements of the Christian faith to subject them to their vicissitudes, while profiting from their prestige.

Here again the reference to God allows these vicissitudes almost complete free play. If there has to be an attribute the possession of which would assure the realization of omnipotence, what more certain basis could one find for it than God himself? If we have to be able to hope to participate in the possession of this attribute by a guilty appropriation or a merciful act of grace, from what or whom can we hope, expect and receive more than from God? If we have to love-hate someone for having what we do not have and above all for being what we are not, whom could we love-hate better than God? And if we have to repress our hatred because it would be too dangerous, not to say too devastating, to express it to someone on whom we depend so much and whom we love so much, what hate can be more repressed than the hate of this God on whom we depend so much and whom we love so much?

Over the years during which I devoted the main part of my work to dealing with a corpus of psychoanalytical theory and a corpus of theological theory in connection with themes like the fatherhood of God, sin and so on, I was aware of the majority of aspects of the conflictual relationship between father and son, but I did not allow the same amount of space for hatred of God. Now that I had allowed this reality to appear in me, looking back I was amazed that I had not become aware of everything that showed its evidence and nature in what I had nevertheless clearly perceived of the relationship between father and son. Perhaps I could only let it surface when I was close to discovering the way out that this hatred had to find and the way in which it had the power to express itself. That is doubtless why, once I began to ask myself about it, I did not take long to see the route and the procedure provided for it through such a massive proclamation by Christians of their sin.

The extraordinary effectiveness of the rechannelling of hatred of God so that it becomes hatred of oneself because one is a sinner derives from the fact that it allows one to accept that one hates God, but displaces this hatred and its object. By calling sin hatred of God and confessing sin as such, people recognize that they hate God, and this does not seem to be a displacement or direction for their hate. But it is, since in that case one is reducing this hatred to being the characteristic of only some of our behaviour, namely our sins. This allows us to obliterate and deny its radical and determinative character, inscribed in the very nature of the relationship of humanity to God as we present it to ourselves. This radical and determinative character cannot be acknowledged and must be rechannelled, since it does not find any way out in a proclamation of sin, where hatred of God is only acknowledged as being in some way occasional. So it is necessary to look for another way: directing hatred back on oneself tries to provide it, and with some degree of effectiveness – which ensures its success in Christianity – but without being able to alleviate or exhaust a hatred the source of which is so radical. And that compels people to begin the process of self-accusation all over again *ad infinitum.*

Hatred of the mother

You will have noticed that there has been no mention so far of the figure of the mother. However, she occupies an important part in the Freudian drama of the Oedipus complex, if only as the sexual object reserved for the father, and by virtue of this fact becomes the object whose possession would allow the son to eliminate the father, again more by becoming identical with him than by killing him. Those more learned than I in psychoanalysis have commented for a long time that in fact, while the figure of the mother plays an important role in Freud's account of the life of the psyche, she led to retreat and side-stepping on Freud's part. Psychoanalytical theory has only quite recently ventured into the abyss of this mother figure, who is in fact more important – and therefore far more masked – than the figures of the Oedipus conplex. I leave psychoanalysts to discuss that. As to my concerns, I subsequently discovered why, in order to keep out of this abyss, I was so ready to maintain the exclusively masculine character of the Christian drama: Father, Son and Spirit. Granted, the figure of Mary seems to some people to introduce a feminine principle into this monosexual universe. Jung stressed this point a great deal, but the way in which he did it was all the less convincing in so far as the sweetness and benevolence of the figure of Mary proved more radically to be the reversal and the denial of the most terrifying characteristics of the mother figure. Be this as it may, I too, in my own way and for my own reasons, confined the mother to a quite secondary role, that of the Oedipan symbol of the fulfilment of desire and rivalry with the father.

When a psychoanalyst friend, whose work I have followed for almost twenty years, began to attach increasing importance to the mother figure and to develop the different aspects of what another psychoanalyst friend came to call the 'maternal monster', I felt, like some of his audience, that he was exaggerating somewhat. It took me a number of years to catch up – still only very partially – with what he was trying to express. I shall not undertake here to outline the essential features: these psychoanalysts themselves have great difficulty in arriving at them, and their written work has been going much more slowly or has become far less coherent since it has been devoted to this object. I will content myself here with saying something that might be of some importance for hatred of God. In fact, as the vertiginous character of the abyss that the mother figure covers becomes evident, we find not only fear or repulsion at the risk of losing oneself in this gulf, but literally hatred of the mother. This hate does not relate only or primarily to the risk that the mother forces on us, but more radically to that which makes the mother loved, the fact that the mother is mother. What makes a person inalienably attached to her and radically dependent on her also makes that person hate her with a hatred which produces an equally inalienable bond and equally radical dependence. As one of these psychoanalyst friends said, only half-smiling: 'Killing the father is nothing, the first one to come along can do that. But mothers are indestructible!' So it is because the mother has this unique role as origin, in both the biological order and the order of desire, that she is the object who is at the same time the most loved and the most hated, the one *à propos* of whom the radical ambivalence of love and hate appears most strongly, even if this appearance comes up against considerable resistance which is proportionate to its object. It is worth while pointing out, above all to readers who may be unfamiliar with psychoanalysis, that this radical ambivalence of love and hatred towards the mother has no pathological content, even if some of its configurations and some of its denials are beyond question among the most pathogenic factors possible.

When these psychoanalyst friends began to bring out various facets of the 'maternal monster', the perverse and persecuting seductress, I began to ask about hatred of God – as will have been evident, from quite a different direction. How could their research not shed some light on my question? If someone is even more our origin than our mother, it is God as represented by a certain type of Christianity. If someone is even more than our mother the womb to which we return to in order to find eternal happiness, it is God. If someone is even more concerned than our mother to show us unfailing love it is the one of whom we expect even more than we expect of our mother, even if we are not worthy of it, and therefore the one on whom we are even more dependent than our mother. In other words, it is God as a certain type of Christianity presents him to us. So if there is someone who, precisely because of all that, is more formidable and hatable than our mother, it is God.

It took me a long time to note the hatred of God engendered and disguised by the representation of him through the figures of Father and Son. It took me more effort, and involved more setbacks and evasions, to accept that the representation of God as the radical origin and the ultimate and unique goal of our existence engendered and disguised a hatred towards him for which only hatred of the mother could provide a relatively adequate image. I was flabbergasted, horrified, sometimes obsessed with it, since as I had been able to see among my analyst friends, bringing out this kind of sentiment overthrows so many established orders, both outside and within ourselves, that the energy it requires leaves one exhausted or makes one stand still in front of the obstacle, transfixing and gnawing away at one in a state which borders on both paralysis and trembling. Is this not the *tremendum* which is spoken of in connection with the sacred? To what are we exposing ourselves if, like me, we have to turn my friend's half-jest round and say: 'All right, mothers may be indestructible, but God is miles ahead of them; he is indestructible by definition'?

Hatred of the mother (here again, I am envisaging only one of the two possible senses of the genitive, hatred directed against the mother: the other possible sense, the hatred felt by the mother, is still too much unknown territory for me) is not an established feeling. I have pointed out that even in psychoanalysis it had difficulty in gaining any ground. Everything is against it, beginning with the radical degree of the love that we have for our mothers. That is doubtless why the popularized forms of psychoanalysis which have had most success are those which are silent about the mother figure and confine her to the quite secondary role which is given her by the devalued version of the Oedipus complex in which, after all, it is never more than a matter of wanting to lie with her. But this is doubtless also why the forms of Christianity which have had the most success are those which bring to the fore the dramatic conflict between God the Father and the human beings who are his children, a conflict centred on the sin of the latter and the redemptive sacrifice of the Son of God. If I may put it that way, it is enough to rechannel on to oneself the hatred of God implied by such a situation through the procedure that I have described, namely by the proclamation of one's sin and by maintaining hatred of oneself as a sinner.

To stress these themes to the point of obsession in fact allows one to conceal and muzzle all that would come to light if one allowed oneself to evoke in connection with God something more radical than the caricature version of the conflict between father and son, namely relations with one's mother and the fact that she is a maternal monster who arouses the most indelible of our hatreds. I now understand why I was favourably impressed more than ten years ago – though without understanding why – by reading an article written by a French psychoanalyst, even though I differ a good deal from her. She depicted in it how one of her patients, a believer, had progressively lost faith in the course of his analysis to the degree it was changing his relationship to his mother figure. In his case his religious faith in a Father God was only a defensive protection against the terrifying and morbid aspects of this figure, a protection which was becoming useless, not because the ambivalence of his relationship to his mother was disappearing, but because a less onerous way of experiencing this ambivalence was appearing. I knew what this analyst thought about religion, and I suppose that she was quite ready to generalize from her observation to all religious attitudes, as she has done in several other of her books. I am not at all inclined to follow her in this generalization, but her observation has a significance which goes beyond the case in question. The strong point of her work lies in showing how and why Christianity has to organize itself in order to bring to the fore the least intolerable conflicts and feelings, in order to conceal the likeness between maternal imagos and certain views of God which have had so much success in Christianity. These views can only be maintained by rechannelling the hatred of God inevitably aroused by the assimilation of God to these maternal imagos. Some forms of Christianity stress this assimilation so strongly that they cannot but trigger off this ineradicable hatred of God, but at the same time they can only rechannel it, because to express it would be so intolerable. There is only one way out, that of directing this hatred which will not acknowledge its object against oneself. I must have been very naive – but who is not in these areas? – to be surprised that the majority of prayers, beginning with the eucharistic liturgy, are so quick to stress the proclamation by human beings of their sin above all else. A hatred like that of the mother can bear even less to wait to be repressed; it has to emerge quickly in the form in which it is rechannelled, and there has to be a speedy proclamation of the point at which we are hateful because we are sinners.

A difficult way

As I noted the way in which the proclamation by believers of their sin served to let out a hatred against a God which was bound up with the paternal and maternal imagos with which Christianity too often associates him, my situation became both more simple and more complicated. It became more simple because it gave me the means of answering the double question that I raised in the course of this chapter. It is not a matter of denying the existence of moral evil or the guilt of human beings, but of asking about the forces which move them to attribute to their failings consequences the individual, collective and even cosmic magnitude of which far surpasses the degree of freedom which it is anthropologically reasonable to recog-

nize in the human condition. It is not so much a question of denying
the exsitence of sin or the fact that human beings are sinners and that
God saves the sinner in Jesus Christ, as of investigating the force
which impels believers to attribute to their sin consequences which
deform and pervert the actions and the words of Jesus about sin and
his revelation of the attitude of his God – who is our God – to sin.
What is the origin of all these 'displacements'? What is it that
engenders them and applies them with such force that they transform
our greatest certainties about Christ and God into their opposites
and end up by establishing these idolatrous opposites at the heart of
the very forms of Christianity which have had most success? If the
rechannelling of hatred of God so that it becomes self-accusation
plays an analogous role to the one that I have tried to sketch, the
motive power of this hatred is largely enough to explain the magnitude
and the power of these displacements. So my situation was simpler
since my questioning had found the beginnings of an answer.

But my situation was complicated in so far as these beginnings of
an answer shed a light on certain Christian practices, views and
affirmations which made them almost intolerable for me: I could no
longer feel at ease in these practices and views which seemed to be
those to which many believing men and women were most attached
and in connection which they found the most happiness and benefit
in being believers. The more I thought that I had a better understanding of why the teaching and practice of Jesus on sin had been
deformed, the more I felt myself at ease with this teaching as I had
received it, not primarily from my personal explorations, but from
the best of exegesis and contemporary theology. I also felt myself
increasingly alienated from so many practices and views because I
could see the displacements which were at work in them.

I shall soon be pointing out how I found help in noting that
however original my personal pilgrimage might be, I was not the only
one to find myself in such a situation. A number of other believers,
men and women, found themselves in a similar situation, for if many
of them are in process of passing to the other side in matters of
sexuality, many are equally in process of passing to the other side in
connection with the proclamation of their sin. One has only to see
the almost vertical drop in the practice of individual confession
(including that among the most practising Catholics) to note this,
though it must also be noted that the Roman hierarchy is hardening
its position against this change just as much as it is over sexuality. As
I write these lines, while Pope John-Paul II is at Lourdes, preparations
are being made for a synod on reconciliation and penitence to be held

in October 1983, one of the more or less avowed objectives of which is to bring into line groups of Catholics who are trying not so much to do away with sin and the confession of sin – which is what they are wrongly accused of doing – as to develop ways of proclaiming it which are less dependent on the various mechanisms, some of which I have cited (different pilgrimages from mine show other equally powerful forms which distort the face of God and humanity just as much).

Nevertheless, I felt quite alone on the roads along which I was taken by my question 'Is sin as important as that?', or rather, 'Is sin important in that way?' I must now describe others of these roads: they might have seemed less rugged, since they no longer involve hatred of God but rather love of God. However, they were no less so, since they led me to discover that while certain forms of the proclamation by believers of their sin might be centred on love of God and not on hate, they ended up in representing this loving relationship with God or this love of God for us in a way which was again subtly but decisively out of place in comparison with what had been shown us in Jesus Christ.

4. Guilt as a strategy of love

The proclamation of guilt, a demand of love

No one has explained better than Conrad Stein why, in the analytical situation, the patient takes so much trouble to get the psychoanalyst to find him guilty. The pages that he has devoted to this subject are among the best of his work *L'Enfant Imaginaire*, which I have already mentioned. A very popularized, even vulgar, version of psychoanalysis tries to argue that when it comes to guilt the only concern of psychology is to eliminate it. Nothing could be more wrong. It is of course true that the cure, or quite simply the interpretation, can have the secondary effect of ridding the subject of illusory guilt. However, the real problem of guilt in psychoanalysis does not lie there, and the nature of guilt appears much better in the reiterated demand of the patient to the analyst to find fault with him and thus allow him to hold himself responsible for the guilt of which he has secured recognition from the analyst.

The amazing thing is that such a procedure does not end up only in allowing the patient to set himself up as a subject in so far as he is guilty. It also allows him (though the one thing does not go without the other) to assure himself that the analyst has the feelings for him that he might expect from a judge, namely a mixture of severity and mercy, justice and leniency, a mixture which represents a form of love which the patient requires from his analyst and which sets up an indestructible relationship, since the guilty person needs a judge, and the judge needs a guilty person. If the establishment of this relationship is a necessary transition in the analytical situation, the progress of the cure brings about a shift in the respective positions of the patient and the analyst. In fact, securing the acknowledgment of one's guilt is not the most constructive way of setting oneself up as a subject or assuring oneself of the love of others, certainly not the type of love of which one might desire to be the object. However, what happens in the analytical situation indicates that we are very concerned to cling to this kind of make-up as subjects, this form of the demands of love, this way of assuring ourselves that we are loved and asking to be given this kind of love. What happens in the analytical situation allows a better understanding of the ravages that this way of setting ourselves up as subjects and assuring ourselves of the love of others makes in our personal lives, our relationships and our societies.

I have been aware of these discoveries now for more than ten years; first of all I made them through books, and then I began to experience their profound truth in a less abstract way. The more they began to convince me, the more I had to note the light they shed on something of what was involved in the proclamation by believers of their sin. At the very beginning of my life as a Dominican, when I regularly went to complain to the novice master that I was a bad religious, that I was a bad Christian, that I lacked faith, charity, hope, obedience, chastity and so on, did not this man reply to me, 'Are you a sinner? Do not complain, that is your claim to glory before God'? Was not the *Miserere* (Psalm 51) the psalm that we recited most often, sometimes several times a day, the length of which marked the duration of the discipline that we had to administer to ourselves, the psalm which liturgy and religious observances put most often on our lips, all of which implied that this was the psalm which said most about God and that he most liked to hear? 'Be merciful to me, O God, because of your constant love. Because of your great mercy wipe away my sins. Wash away all my evil and make me clean from my sin. I recognize my faults; I am always conscious of my sins. I have sinned against you – only against you – and done what you consider evil. So you are right in judging me, you are justified in condemning me. I have been evil from the day I was born, from the time I was conceived I have been sinful,' and so on. Yes, hundreds of times, thousands of times, I have said that to God from the bottom of my heart, convinced that I was speaking to the bottom of his. Hundreds of millions of times, millions of Christian men and women have said to God, 'I have been evil from the day I was born, from the time I was conceived I have been sinful', and they have told him, 'that you are right in judging me, you are justified in condemning me.'

Here again, the reference to God sets no limit on what can be accomplished through such a mechanism. If it is by having one's guilt recognized (forgiveness itself amounts to such recognition) that one can be assured of being established as a subject, how better to be assured of this than by being recognized as guilty by none other than God? If it is because someone declares us guilty (albeit to pardon us) that we can be assured of his or her love, of whose love do we need more assurance than that of God, and by whom is it more important for us to be declared guilty? What other judgment would assure a greater love and establish the object of this judgment more fully while showing the greatness that there is in being so judged, 'that you may be right in judging me...' (The French edition of the Jerusalem Bible has the following note on this verse, 6b, 'Utterly pure and with integrity, by forgiving God shows his power over evil and his victory over sin.')

I could multiply *ad infinitum* the examples of the importance and efficacy of this procedure in Christianity. Suffice it to say that each time I discovered a new one I was both reassured, since it brought confirmation of my hypothesis, and almost incredulous, so surprised was I at seeing almost everywhere what formerly I had been unable to see anywhere. My astonishment did not come from noting the importance of this mechanism in the specific functioning of Christianity or even in its dogmatics, since I had just discovered its place throughout the processes of the psyche. What I also discovered – the analytic situation provided the evidence for this, but it was confirmed by experiences of quite a different type – was that one did not have to give up hope that humans could find less onerous, less enslaving and less illusory forms of establishing themselves as subjects, of assuring themselves of the love of others, of sometimes allowing its fragile victory and the appearance – even if only in a flash – of the reflections of its glory. So I hoped that in Christianity, too, it would prove possible to resort to other procedures and that the existing ones would not continue to merit such a prominent place, even if it became easier for me to understand why they had had it in the past.

I hoped that this would happen all the more since, while I could see clearly why and how Paul of Tarsus had attached so much importance in the variant of Christianity which he founded to this way of setting up the sinner as subject and the God of love as judge and saviour, I noted that a conception with a very different nuance was dominant in the Synoptic Gospels. I discovered what had been literally scandalous (*skandalon* = the stumbling block: Jesus died because of it) in the behaviour and the words that the believing communities which stand at the beginning of the Synoptic Gospels had attributed to Jesus, or those which, on the contrary, they had carefully abstained from attributing to him, even though they were so natural and so obligatory in the society of the time. As I have done so often in preaching, celebrating, teaching and writing, I must recall once again the mass of men and women whose encounter with Jesus the Gospels have remembered and celebrated: Zacchaeus, the Samaritan woman, the Syro-Phoenician woman, Matthew, Peter, Mary Magdalene, the woman taken in adultery, the paralysed man, the lame, the blind, and so on. Certainly we are told that some of them, when they saw him, cried out, 'Son of David, have mercy on me.' What else does one say to an emissary of God when that is what you think he wants to hear from you? But when Jesus takes the initiative in the encounter, or in the majority of the encounters in which his various conversation partners take the initiative, he never asks the other person to recognize that he or she is a sinner so that they may claim the right to speak with him, to become the object of his attention. Jesus never presents himself as occupying a position which he only holds to the degree that people confess their sin to him and ask him for forgiveness. So, to take up the words of the *Miserere* again, this is not the way in which he proved to be right, nor is it the attitude that he wanted to have towards human beings. He had other and better things to do; he had other and better things to bring out in others; he was in more of a hurry: 'Zacchaeus, I want to eat with you this evening.' Afterwards, and only afterwards, and precisely because it had not been asked of him in the first place, Zacchaeus understood. And he redistributed the fortune that he had so greedily acquired.

So once more it proved that a displacement had taken place, so powerful a displacement that it had perverted and reversed the way in which Jesus had allowed human sinners to set themselves up as subjects and what he had shown to be at stake in the love of God for human beings. Once more it proved that the mechanisms of guilt had been taken over and appropriated by Christian faith: to dare to guarantee in the name of Christ himself and his God that proclaiming oneself guilty was the most certain way of setting oneself up as subject, and that to ask God to pronounce a verdict of guilty and to give pardon was the best assurance of his love, because the greatest assurance of God's love lay in God himself: 'that you are right in judging me.' In my view, one of the most certain indications that death did not reduce Jesus to nothing and that his Spirit is capable of raising him up among us is that the power of this displacement has not proved victorious, that its extraordinary success has not succeeded in effacing the significance of the revelation of Jesus in this respect, and that (thanks to the Spirit and – it must be said – through the majority of the historical forms of Christianity) men and women have been found to remember him, to raise him up and to hand him on to us. When we become aware of the power of the mechanisms which are at work in this kind of displacement, we can see that the achievement of Jesus is almost incredible.

The proclamation of guilt, imprisonment for love

Another way for the subject to set itself up as such and to assure itself of the love it needs by declaring itself guilty is just as powerful as the one I have just mentioned. This relates to the wound that we inflict by our own fault on the one whose love we claim and to the status of which we assure ourselves by obtaining his or her pardon. To fail someone who loves us puts this person in the position either of abandoning us (that is why the manoeuvre is risky) or on the contrary of suffering from our failure and seeking to rediscover us (that is why the manoeuvre is worth trying). We can often see this mechanism at work in some families where the mother's favourite child is in fact the black sheep who does all the damage, certain that he will not only have the benefit of his mother's indulgence but that he will also be her privileged object of love, to the precise degree that he makes her suffer or spend most of time, with brief respites, trembling for him. The other brothers or sisters, or the husband, are by no means the last to be aware of the power and exclusiveness of the bond which is created in this way. The impossibility of setting themselves up as subjects or assuring themselves that they are the object of an unfailing love in any other way pushes some people into delinquency. This kind of delinquent keeps on committing misdemeanours and crimes in order to satisfy this need outside which he or she feels that there is no salvation.

To describe a more general phenomenon in psychoanalytical

terms: by declaring himself guilty – not to mention actually making himself guilty in order to be better able to affirm that he is – the subject sets himself up as an object lacking in the desire of the one whose love he claims, and thus obtains a love which will give no respite to the person who has been both wounded and called on in this way. Reconciliations following on forgiveness do not restore this love to its former state: it remains definitively scarred by this wound and this quest and thus will be all the greater by virtue of the fault and its forgiveness. So here the declaration of guilt is a real attempt at seduction, but it is also a bid for power where love is concerned. It is aimed at putting under an obligation the man or women to whom it is made, calling on them to regard the guilty party as a privileged object because he or she has failed and because he or she is forgiven. This procedure is so manifest and widespread that we hardly need psychoanalysis in order to become aware of it. Be this as it may, above all because of what the situation of analysis brings up, psychoanalysis allows us to discover the magnitude and the virulence of this procedure, the extent to which it is present in the most varied human societies and relationships, and the degree to which its radical and archaic elements make human beings resort to it so readily and find in it so many more or less short-term delights, or present them with so many difficulties in transcending this extremely rudimentary way of securing the love of another.

There is no need to be overly familiar with Christian practices or biblical texts to note the place held by this procedure in the way in which numerous varied historical forms of Christianity invite human beings to present themselves before God and suppose that this way of loving is the one that best characterizes the love of God for them. The Old Testament and the Gospels are so full of texts which glorify this way of behaving towards God or this behaviour of God towards us that I cannot help feeling that they are almost blasphemous when I begin to read them in this light. To think of the happiness I felt in reading, meditating on, praying with, texts like the lost sheep, the lost coin, the prodigal son and so many others! In the Old Testament, particularly in the prophets, think of all the marvellous texts about the love of the Lord for his people, the ups and downs in their relationships of love, the splendid descriptions of the shame of the daughter of Jerusalem and her blemishes, the way in which the Lord suffers from her infidelity and she fails him, the way in which he will lead her into the desert to wash her stains from her and be betrothed to her anew. Think of the marvellous descriptions of the beauty of Zion forgiven and the rule that she will exercise over the nations!

Everyone knows that there is more joy in heaven over a repentant sinner than over the ninety-nine just people who observe the law. Everyone knows that it is better to be the prodigal son than his older brother, for while it is true that the latter is always with his father and that everything his father has is his, it is also true that his father never offered him even the smallest kid for a celebration and that he worked hard in the fields while they were killing the fatted calf and celebrating the return of the prodigal. It is certainly true that in making himself the object his father lacks, the prodigal son puts the father in the position of having to wait for him and run to embrace him before he can even end his declaration of guilt. It is also true that the son, by becoming a prodigal, at the same time assures himself of being the favourite son.

When I began to note how important the psychological process that I am emphasizing here was in the texts, I was frightened, because I had the feeling that suddenly no stone remained standing on another. These texts had been the very substance of my faith. Since then I have rediscovered that this was not their chief meaning. I did not rediscover this by underestimating the place held by this procedure or by rejecting the importance attached to it by psychoanalysis, but in more classical ways, in particular through exegesis (albeit more recent forms of exegesis, like semiotics). The question nevertheless stands, and is disturbing. These texts owe some of their success to the way in which they are utilized by this procedure, if not the way in which they are more or less the product of it. Besides, so many Christian practices, so many propositions or forms of behaviour encouraged by spirituality and theology, employ this process so crudely that here I find myself in a complex situation. On the one hand I understand better why and how the proclamation of guilt had an importance disproportionate to the importance that it is anthropologically reasonable to attribute to human sin and to the attitude towards sin and sinners which the Gospels claim to have been that of Jesus. On the other hand, here again it was increasingly difficult for me to feel at home in practices and conceptions which suggested that the love of God had to be secured by this kind of process and that God had to be paid the greatest possible homage by our making ourselves the object he needed to such a degree that he would be restless without it.

This procedure affirms a somewhat banal megalomania: here the human being confers on himself a kind of omnipotence over God, since by his failing and God's need to pardon it God is thought to have sealed an irrevocable contract that he cannot break without denying himself and without continuing to be the best that he is thought to be. By proclaiming our sin we imprison God's love. I can understand better what leads one of the most talented modern French writers on spirituality to exclaim: 'People want sinners.' I have also found a better explanation of why this author is one of the most effective writers of his generation. But I would continue to stress that the evangelists did not think that they should attribute this kind of dramatic exclamation to Jesus, though they took such care to stress the paradoxical and unheard-of features in his behaviour towards sinners. Is it a cause for despair that this behaviour cannot be effaced by the type of omnipotence and love that such a way of proclaiming sin claims to guarantee? At all events, it is a fact that over the twenty centuries of processes of this kind there have always been men and women who, by the grace of God, have made it possible for new witness and new life to be given to the behaviour of Jesus and for this witness to succeed in slipping through the very close-knit mesh which the various forms of guilt weave in us and around us.

Difficulty in writing

Love, hate, the strategies of love, the strategies of hate... Was this not an explanation of the different displacements that I had noticed when I began to ask myself, 'Is sin as important as that?', or rather, 'Is sin important in that way?' In fact there was no question, nor is there ever, of an explanation in the strict sense. Each of the themes of this chapter on guilt has only appeared to me very slowly, first in an intermittent and wavering way, and most of them are far from seeming clear and certain to me even today. The fact that love and hate are involved, and more specifically love and hate of God, is sufficient explanation of the intensity of my resistance to the emergence of these ideas. It must be added that these ideas seemed to shake whole areas of the Christian edifice, entailing a real decomposition of my being as a believer and making it more and more difficult for me to live with those men and women who found benefit in what I could no longer make my own. Granted, I have since discovered, within myself and around me, that there were other ways of interpreting and living out Christianity, and indeed living out the reality of sin and guilt. But this discovery, too, is recent and uncertain, and seems very fragile in the face of the formidable edifice that guilt has built up from Christianity.

Moreover, the simple fact of putting down these different themes in writing and in a certain order gives the deceptive impression that they are a coherent group of experiences and arguments: that was not the case at the beginning, nor is it yet. These different themes emerged in my consciousness in a completely random way. Everything happened as though the beginnings of a condensation, a crystallization, were taking place somewhere at the heart of a great nebula. After a number of movements and transformations within me which were most often completely unconscious (their only conscious manifestations were anguish and disarray), a hitherto unsuspected idea came into being. Certainly its nucleus provided some light, substance and relief; but it soon transpired that this would progressively involve a series of consequences which I felt would be very disturbing to me and to my relationship with the believing community. Some weeks or months later another nucleus appeared in another corner of the nebula, itself also a source of light and comfort, but also pregnant with an aura of disturbing consequences. The relationship between the first and the second nucleus often only appeared much later, sometimes when other nuclei formed elsewhere and a constellation began to take shape. But where a degree of intelligibility, substance and relief took shape, disquiet grew over what the elements of the newly acquired truth were going to demand.

This led me to a completely new attitude to writing. I had once written a good deal, very easily: theses, memoranda, articles. Writing simply helped me to fix on paper ideas which were clearly formed in my mind or commentaries which the various monuments of theology inspired me to produce (since theology is always done by commenting on the thought of others: biblical writers, church fathers, great theologians, documents of the *magisterium*, and so on). I wrote my earlier book *When I say God* (as I pointed out in the preface, written – exceptionally – before the book itself) 'for my pleasure and in order to be able to go on living'. This time, however, writing was a torture. It took months and months for the word decomposition to emerge and almost a year for me to set to work on what had thus come to light, which forms the first part of this book. As for this chapter on guilt, I was blocked for months on end before getting to work, incapable of doing anything else but incapable of writing it, completely stuck in a vague but omnipresent anguish. In order to reassure myself and those around me I thought up a comparison with the formation of petroleum. I said, just managing not to smile, that it took millions of years of enormous subterranean pressure to make petroleum, so it was quite normal that I should experience and produce important internal upheavals in order that what I had to write could take shape. However, this last time, I could do no more;

I had more the impression of bearing within myself a child who was going to die before even being formed and who would kill me in turn by decaying within me.

I mention this not so much to communicate my own state of mind as to tell those men and women who experience the same difficulties not to be discouraged. You don't die of it. At least, you don't always die, or you don't die entirely. Why should creation, why should quest and discovery, be less difficult, less laborious, less crucifying in connection with God than in any other sphere? Why, when we have to face the whole gamut of the effects of guilt, in us and around us, should we not be indwelt and threatened by the most archaic, the most fascinating and the most terrifying figures of the pantheon of our psyche because God is involved? I have another reason for taking stock of these problems over writing: for various different but converging reasons, believers on the one hand and theologians on the other, and finally the church authorities, want to have clear, well-constructed and completely relevant proposals made to them. They need to know that in these spheres this is impossible: guilt cannot be put neatly in a cupboard with well arranged and clearly labelled pigeon holes; it cannot be dealt with from a chair, academic or ecclesiastical; it does not bend easily to the laws of thought; it is not easy to conceive; it is not easy to express clearly and the words for it do not come easily.

That is why I am not disturbed at the formal imperfections of the previous pages. It is also why I am convinced that they could have been better if I had written them, but at another time. The essential thing is that something should emerge, and I have good reasons for thinking that this is the case, if only because I have stirred up all the symptoms which guilt displays when it is deranged. That is also why I am reasssured not so much by the formal perfection, correctness and cohesion of my analyses as by the way in which my approach coheres with that of believers who set off from another starting point. For I am not the only one to 'change sides' over guilt: others also do so, and in a more significant and beneficial way than they do in any other respect, and for quite different reasons.

5. Believers begin to change sides

I have already given one of the most obvious indications of this by showing how believers are 'changing sides' over matters of sexuality. In fact sexuality is the privileged theatre of guilt. Even if psychoanalysis does not allow us to understand why, we need only recall the extraordinary attention, sometimes amounting to obsession, that the Catholic moral tradition, the priests and the faithful have paid in certain periods to failings connected with chastity. To change sides over sexuality is therefore necessarily to change sides over guilt. But there are other more directly significant signs.

Communal expressions of penitence

One of them is the welcome which some communities of believers have given to various attempts to develop a communal expression of penitence. I have mentioned the disfavour to which the individual confession learned and often practised by my generation has sunk, and to which Catholics have been used since its invention in the seventh century and its consolidation up to the twelfth century (for this form did not exist earlier and for a long time was frowned on by many responsible pastors). Very damning reasons are often given to explain this disfavour: the loss of a sense of sin, the loss of the sense of the priestly power to absolve sin, the loss of the sense of the moral authority of the family and civil and religious institutions, the decline in the number of priests capable of hearing confessions and finally – I almost forgot! – the pernicious and reductionist influence of psychoanalysis. It is also argued that communal expressions of penitence would have one great advantage: that of freeing the faithful from what is often the embarrassing business of having to confess one's sins explicitly to a given individual.

The trouble is that none of these objections tallies with basic experience; moreover, they are most often put forward by those who have hardly been involved in them. I do not claim to have a great deal of experience myself, but I have carefully read what has been published on this subject, including what has appeared in the reviews of pastoral theology and liturgy. I also know the form that Catholicism takes in a region with a very strong Catholic and even clerical tradition, namely Brittany, having gone there myself several times a year for twenty years. Now it so happens that in some regions of Brittany, communal expressions of penitence are in great favour. Why? Brittany still has no lack of priests to hear confessions; it has not been particularly ravaged – as far as I know – by the misdeeds of psychoanalysis, and finally, and above all, the Christian men and women who welcome these expressions of penitence also continue to practise individual confession, albeit more rarely. So what is going on?

Various factors are at work: the biblical and liturgical renewals have allowed these believers to discover that hearing the word of God together, possibly discussing and looking for its meaning together, and celebrating the forgiveness and the salvation of God together were far from being less effective ways of entering the presence of God and being judged by his word, asking, receiving and celebrating his forgiveness, than an examination of conscience made individually and in the *tête à tête* of the confessional. They also discovered – as with the eucharist – that the sacrament of penance, like all the sacraments, is primarily an act of the church, of living in the church, i.e. in community. They have discovered that, as with all sacraments, the community had a role which, while certainly not doing away with that of the priest (who at least presides over this observance as over all celebrations), is not reduced to that of the passive witness to which it had been progressively confined and which in the case of the sacrament of penance it was even denied. Finally, they also discovered that God was not the only conversation partner in matters of sin, but that it was all the more important to accuse themselves before the community which they might have harmed and ask its pardon, and that this was sometimes more difficult than to accuse oneself anonymously before an invisible priest. All these changes are essentially ecclesiological in nature, completely in line with what Vatican II wanted to promote, and at first sight have nothing to do with a change of sides over guilt. However, such changes of an ecclesiological kind could not have happened had they come up against too rigid forms of the various displacement mechanisms that I have mentioned (and cannot happen if they do come up against such mechanisms). Besides, where they can happen, these changes in turn evoke or encourage a palliation and weakening of these mechanisms and a way of coping with the vagaries of guilt.

Those whose power is based to a large extent on the strength of these displacements know this very well and proclaim it with an astounding freedom. Three days before I wrote these lines, John-Paul II was at Lourdes: one of the eleven speeches which he gave in less than forty-eight hours was aimed at preparing for the next synod on penitence and reconciliation, one of whose avowed aims is to limit, not to say suppress, communal forms of expressing penitence. Reading the account of his proposals as I was preparing to work on these pages, I was amazed to see how what I was getting ready to explain had been formulated in a phrase of almost incredible crudity: the pope denounced 'those currents of thought which relativize the nature of sin and by virtue of this fact devalue the power conferred (on priests) by ordination to pardon it'. Those who exercise power and want it to be absolute are often particularly acute in discerning what might threaten this power. Besides, it is significant to compare two features of the terminology: the pope says that the priest has the power to forgive sin, when in the strict sense it is God and God alone who forgives sin, as the priest is only the minister of forgiveness. Obviously John-Paul II would not deny that, but he does not stress it, since he wants above all to reinforce the power of the priest. An inverse and symmetrical change has taken place in connection with communal observations of penitence: to begin with, there was talk of collective absolution, which meant that these observations were still being defined by the power which the priest was alone capable of exercising there, namely absolution: progressively (and for various reasons), the expression of collective absolution was replaced by the communal expression of penitence. One unintended but nevertheless certain result of this change is that it is the act of the community (albeit presided over by the priest) which serves to define what is involved, and not that of the priest.

It is no coincidence that those who want to prevent these developments and keep their powers should use as their bogey-man the loss of a sense of sin and of a sense of God. While such an observation may well be true of a large part of our Western world, on the other hand it is defamatory and injurious to level an accusation of this kind against communities of believers who are seeking to develop the most satisfactory forms for the communal expression of penitence. Only if one has never shared in the life of these groups, never joined them in looking for the meaning that the word of God might have for their life, never engaged with them in their struggle against evil and sin in society, in the church and in themselves, can one dare to accuse them of having lost the sense of God and of sin, and attribute to this double loss a quest for forms of celebration the main effect of which is to change the type of power that some strategies of guilt are compelled to attribute to the priest, and therefore to the prince of priests.

The mutations in our experience of conscience and the law

That having been said, it would be just as fallacious to fail to recognize that while believers may in no way have lost the sense of God or the sense of sin, they find great difficulty in discovering and describing this sin. This great difficulty is in no way connected with a weakening of their faith but rather with the cultural mutations to the effects of which they have been just as subject as non-believers. For several centuries, sin had been discovered and defined in terms of the combination of two kinds of criteria: individual judgment of the conscience on the one hand and the enunciation of a moral or religious law by society on the other. It is not the fault of believers if, for the past century, various scientific, sociological, psychological, historical, philosophical and even political approaches have led to the discovery that conscience and the law are very complex authorities which, while indeed expressing the best of a personality or a social group, at the same time also express a great many other realities of which most often we have been unaware. We have discovered that the judgments of our conscience were largely the product of psychological forces with quite different objectives from the moral conscience and using quite different means. We have discovered that the laws of our society are largely the product of social and economic forces which also have quite other objectives and use quite other means than the noblest civil or religious legislative functions. So these two kinds of criteria for locating sin, provided by the law and conscience, no longer have the kind of evidential value that has been attributed to them. Here lies the source of the disarray in which believers find themselves today, rather than in their loss of the sense of God or of sin.

When we come to realities which are as basic to individuals and societies as conscience and law, the mutations that they undergo are necessarily long, difficult and conflicting; the results of these mutations are impossible to deduce *a priori* from the way in which these realities were formerly conceived. I already said in connection with death and sexuality that we could not foresee what they will be tomorrow and the day after on the basis of what they were yesterday and still sometimes are today. The same is true of conscience and the law: we cannot see what they will become in tomorrow's society. That is why the role of theologians, pastors and the hierarchy is not to repeat and reinforce conceptions of sin bound up with experiences and views of the law and conscience which are no longer our own, far less to fulminate in the name of the loss of a sense of God and a sense of sin against believers whose sole failing in this matter is to be involved in new experiences and new views. The role of theologians, pastors and the hierarchy is to keep company with believers involved in this mutation and to go with them less as guides who know the way and the destination in advance than as travelling companions who are also involved in this mutation and change of sides, learning from other men and women what they may discover and invent. The function of theologians, pastors and the hierarchy is not to behave as proprietors of a truth they have the goodness and the desire to share with believers, but to put themselves at the service of this quest for truth which is also theirs.

However, we must not cherish illusions but have a firm faith: the forces which seek fulfilment in the displacement mechanisms I have mentioned are very jealous of their power and very concerned to conserve it. More than ten years ago, I had been invited to Rome by the cultural service of the French embassy near the Holy See to give a lecture. The subject I had chosen was these mutations in our experience of the law and conscience, and I had taken care to make it quite clear that there was no question of casting doubt on the idea of sin or its gravity. However, a minimum of intellectual honesty had forced me to say that neither theologians nor the hierarchy could foresee what would become of these mutations, though this impossibility was not too disturbing since – as I stressed to end with – in the end everything depended on the Holy Spirit. The result was a real diplomatic incident: the ambassador, who attended these lectures on principle, let me reply to a number of questions from the audience, but then took over and launched into a long refutation of my argument, something which had never happened in such circumstances before. This precedent and what was said by him caused echoes which resounded through the little world of Roman diplomacy for a very long time and gave me an even worse reputation among the ecclesiastical authorities than some of my theological views, though these were more dubious. Furthermore, the matter was so serious that the next day, after the ritual lunch at the embassy, the ambassador took me aside and gave me a long talking to in the fine gardens whose charms Pauline Borghese set off so well, going so far as to cancel a meeting with his fellow French ambassador at the Quirinal, who was involved in this lunch. I still wonder whose interests this ambassador was defending on that day, those of France or those of the Holy See. I incline towards the latter; besides, they were the only ones in question.

While it may be impossible to foresee what the sense of sin will look like when it has been remodelled by a new experience of conscience and the law, it is hardly rash to foresee that on at least one point its appearance will be different from that familiar to us and to numerous historical forms of Christianity. Beyond question the answer given to he the question 'Is sin as important as that?', or more precisely, 'Is sin important in that way?' will be quite different, both qualitatively and quantitatively. In fact the different changes of side which I which held such an important position in the way in which we have represented the importance of sin in our lives and our importance before God *qua* sinners. I have described how I became aware of a certain number of displacements which distort our perception of ourselves as sinners, of Christ as saviour from sin and of God as being offended by our sin and forgiving it. These distortions are translated into an excess and a turgidity which will disappear as we discover their causes. This disappearance will necessarily give the impression of a diminution in the sense of sin; the diminution will be real but it will also be beneficent, since the previous understanding of sin was an over-evaluation and not a more acute sense of what sin is.

When God is no longer identified in the same way with paternal and maternal imagos

Other factors will be even more important in this transformation of the sense of sin. I can only speak of them in strictly personal terms, for even if I have been able to note that very different pilgrimages from mine have led certain believers to similar opinions, I still can see these factors only in an ill-defined way, though their effects are important and already at work in my existence as a human being and a believer. Besides, they are too bound up with the most personal and most contingent parts of my pilgrimage for me already to be in a position to generalize from them. Nevertheless, for all that I cannot help noting that they involve factors and questions which largely relate to my situation.

To put it in two words, they essentially involve hate and love or, in four words, paternal imagos and maternal imagos, the violence of the hate and love aroused by these imagos, the radical nature of the ambivalence that they produce and the way in which this hate, this love and this ambivalence could be at work in certain Christian conceptions of human love and divine forgiveness, thus creating a considerable gap, not to say an unbridgeable gulf, between what we know of Jesus Christ and his God and the gigantic monuments that we erect to images of them deformed by the vicissitudes of guilt. Some psychoanalysts, and psychologists even more, while recognizing the archaic importance of these imagos and the type of love-hate that they arouse, think that they are primitive forms that a healthy development of the personality allows us to transcend, pathology by definition being the fact of succumbing to them. Others think quite differently, and although my first contacts with psychoanalysis were under the aegis of the former, I now think like the latter, namely that these imagos, this hate, this love and this ambivalence are the unavoidable parameters and paradigms of the human psyche. What can happen in a 'healthy' development or in the effects of a cure is not the disappearance or withdrawal of these figures and the emotions that go with them but a rearrangement of our relationship to them. It is certain that our relationship to these imagos can take on more or less morbid or fruitful forms, and also certain that there are more or less devastating and more or less creative forms of living out this love, this hatred and the radical quality of this ambivalence. However, the two remain essential poles in the arrangements of the fields of force in our psyches.

Since this is the way I think, there is clearly no way of thinking otherwise about our relationship with God. Paternal and maternal imagos, love, hate and radical ambivalence are also the essential poles which shape the field of forces in our faith, in this case in relation to God. There is no more question of wanting to establish faith in a space which would escape this field of force than there was in a debate which Paul Ricoeur once had with me in which he supposed that faith could exist in a space which escapes the unconscious and its structuring by the Oedipus complex. I do not in any way want to see the establishment of a new sense of sin which would escape the paternal and maternal imagos and the love-hate that they arouse; that would be to part company with human space and the human condition. I cannot conceive of any human way of experiencing any relationship – even with God – or any sense of sin which does not involve these figures and these emotions.

But there are ways and ways. To keep to my own case, it has become evident to me that my faith no longer expects of God what it expected of him when the image I had of him was – as it now seems to me – almost a carbon copy or a superimposition, pure and simple, of my paternal and maternal imagos. For example, rightly or wrongly, I no longer expect God to deliver me from death, I no longer expect him to fulfil all my desires, I no longer expect him to make me a god. That is what I tried to explain in *When I say God*, and I never denied that this would surprise a number of believers whom I certainly did not force to adopt my views. The love and hate that one has for an object of love are closely connected with what one expects of it, or more exactly, with the degree to which we identify this object with the maternal and paternal imagos, which make us expect of it what we expect of them. If I no longer expect God to fulfil the omnipotence of my desire or to deliver me from the characteristics of my contingency – death, wrongdoing, sexuality, it is natural that the love-hate

I bear him should no longer be the same as when I expected of him all that it was appropriate to expect. At the same time it is natural that my view of myself as a sinner and of God's attitude towards my sin should also be of another kind. I am convinced that the different nuclei which have appeared progressively in the nebula of my thoughts about sin would never have been regrouped in the embryonic constellation that I have tried to describe here had there not been, as a prelude, inklings of that other displacement in connection with what I expect or do not expect of God, with what I believe that he wants or does not want to share.

The change which ensues is both minimal and considerable: a slight displacement can be enough to change the whole perspective of a face, a body or a countryside. I have recently found it very difficult to use the word 'love' in connection with God, whether this is the love that he bears me or the love that I bear him. It is not that, like Aristotle, I think it would be crazy to suppose that God is concerned with human affairs: my God remains the one whom Jesus has shown to us. Nor do I feel that I am uninterested in God; the pilgrimage which I have retraced here is not that of a man to whom God is becoming indifferent; that is the least that one could say. But even if the question of an excessive psychologizing of our relations with a God whose 'personality' was conceived in too human a fashion did not arise (and it does arise, and I raised it in the first part of this book in connection with the necessary decomposition of a certain idea of God) we would still have the question posed to us by the way in which in Christianity the word love is used to designate the relationship between God and human beings. Very often the use of this word and the effects atributed to this love seem to me to be too directly dependent on the kind of love aroused in us by paternal and maternal imagos of the utmost antiquity. As I have said: no love can exist without reference to these imagos; not even our love of God. But there are ways and ways.

Beause I have come to be aware of this excessively direct dependence, I feel the need by a kind of epistemological hygiene, if only provisionally, to be more discreet in my use of this word love. It goes without saying that the same is true of hate. I hesitate to add something that follows from this but seems almost mad: the logical consequence would in fact be to say that my 'feelings' towards God are less ambivalent. It would be better to say that their ambivalence does not seem to me to have remained almost identical to the ambivalence of the emotions aroused in me by the representations and the representatives of my paternal and maternal imagos. Perhaps it may be understandable that, for the same reason, the rechannelling of my hatred of God into hatred of myself as a sinner, or my need to secure the love of God and to hold it captive by showing him that I am a sinner, play a much less important role than at the time when I delighted – and the word is not inappropriate – in making my confession once a week as provided for by canon law and our religious constitutions. I am also just as incapable of seeing what difference that will make to my life as I am incapable of seeing what will be the Christian sense of sin on the other side. I know only that here again we must begin by changing sides.

But whether it is a matter of death, sexuality or guilt, I also know that one discovery has played a decisive role in the awareness I have of this need to change sides and what I have noticed about people changing sides in our Western society. It is a discovery in connection with God, a discovery of God, which from now on is very important for what is God for me and what I would love him to be for so many others. So it is with that discovery that I must end this book, *confessing* (in the sense of faith proclaiming its object): God is God, so God is not Everything.

III

God is God, so God is not Everything

This last part was written in December 1983 and January 1984 at
Parc-Trihorn and in April 1984 at Tréon.

Another interlude

Although I said that I was eager to arrive at this theme, four months have gone by since I finished writing the previous pages. Certainly, I needed a rest: I had written half the section on sexuality and the whole of the section on guilt non-stop: the nature of this writing had been even more exhausting than the amount of it. One cannot write about the hate of God with impunity, and this was the very first time that I had ventured to do so. As was the case after I had written on decomposition, only part of me had been able to venture so far, and I had to wait for the rest of the forces to catch up with the scouts in these perilous advance-posts.

I hoped that that would not take too long. When I was on the point of beginning the second part, which I have called 'On the Other Side', I indicated, without saying more, that a conviction had come home to me one day at Christmas, just as at the previous Easter a conviction had come home to me that I had to 'let God go'. I added that I was going to need time to familiarize myself with the various consequences of this new conviction, and that in the meantime it would be better to go on to explore the other side, since on any hypothesis that was the place where life would be from then on. But I knew that I would have to come to this other distracting conviction – in the strict sense of the word: the fact of having to 'let God go'. I sensed that it had something to do with the theological theme with which I wanted to end, namely that God is not Everything and that since he is God he does not want to be Everything. But I did not know just how much the conviction and the theme were bound up with each other, and in a way which still in essentials continues to escape me.

The amazing thing is that the complexity and depth of this interconnection came to me in circumstances which for a long time I was obtuse enough to consider alien to my plans. Prosaically, it was a matter of the need to earn my living. As early as 1974, when it had been necessary to close the faculty of theology at Le Saulchoir and when any post as Professor of Theology at another Catholic theological institution was impossible because of the positions that I had taken on various matters, especially abortion, I had had to look for some way of earning a little money to contribute towards meeting the needs of my monastery and covering a minimum of personal expenses. I had the good fortune that this double demand did not call for considerable sums of money, and I had the further good fortune that a friend got me a job that was very interesting, relatively well paid, and left me plenty of free time to work at theology, preach and so on. Those were the conditions under which I wrote *When I say God*. But almost a year ago, say at the end of 1982, it became evident that this work could not go on and I had to look for something else. There was no urgency, and I waited, apparently more preoccupied with this book.

However, the situation became financially disturbing. I had no way of helping my community. My superiors accepted this in a very understanding way, but I felt it unworthy and dishonest, and I had to cut down on a very modest way of life (even if it is less so than that of many other Dominicans). Now to find work at fifty-seven with my kind of curriculum vitae and in present econom.ic circumstances is very difficult. Some of my Dominican friends were amazed with admirable candour that I was looking for 'secular work', forgetting that all theological or pastoral work of the kind that they were doing was forbidden to me.Some friends were amazed that I did not become a psychoanalyst. But I am not one of those who think that an analysis and relative familiarity with psychoanalysis are adequate credentials for becoming a psychoanalyst; and above all, it was evident that I did not really want to do that. Why? I was content to tell them what I told myself: that the 'God business' remained my essential preoccupation.

So I had to find work. In a bizarre way, I kept delaying for so long and with such inertia over the steps that had to be taken that I ended up telling myself that this was resistance (in the psychoanalytical sense of the word) to whatever I was banging my head against, the nature of which remained impenetrable. Months went by, with the interlude of the summer when I wrote half the section on sexuality and all that on guilt. Some friends, men and women, urged me on or exerted gentle pressure on me: why was I dithering so much? Another friend used the considerable authority of his position to intervene for me in various directions; I almost had to sabotage his efforts since I was so much caught up in inner contradictions, the power of which I knew from feeling their effects, though their content escaped me. And then there was this book which had to be finished: I was anxious to finish it and I was happy to be ending it on a theme which is dear to me and which seems good news about God and human beings, good news about God for human beings. God is God, so God is not Everything. However, I was not writing, and my progress in looking for a job was as slow and as oblique as that of a crab. These last months have not been funny: I was enraged at my impotence, I felt humiliated at being like that, at remaining like that. I thought I had allowed decomposition to do its work, I had devoted and dedicated the first part of this book to decomposition, and there I was, dumb and stuck like the mare in the psalm or like those little donkeys that one still used to find in the farms in the Bray area before the war, which sometimes transformed themselves into living monuments of the utmost obstinacy.

Little by little, a certainty emerged and was confirmed, the appearance of which makes it possible for me to take up my pen again today, 24 December 1983. It is two years after that Christmas which marked the emergence of a conviction the substance of which I shall mention shortly. This certainty was as follows: yes, I am intellectually convinced that God is not Everything since he is God. Yes, I am intellectually convinced that this is good news for human beings because they imagine that God wants to be Everything and in this way they do down both God and themselves. Yes, I am intellectually very happy and quite ready to end this book by developing this theme. But what stands in the way of my search for work and prevents my finishing this book is the fact that all my life I have conferred on God the status of being Everything. Theologically I have discovered that God is not Everything and does not want to be Everything. To discover this theologically, I have had to let this idea infiltrate into me bit by bit; I have had to allow forces in and around me to have free play, to allow a breach to be opened up. But in essentials my convictions have been quite opposite and my experience has continued to be the opposite. The reason why I found it so hard to accept the idea of looking for work was that working, having a 'secular' job, was opposed to everything in me that sought fulfilment in the 'God business' that defined me socially and psychologically, that was my identity, my specific character, both in my eyes and in those of others. Looking for work and working was the necessary but impossible practical confirmation that *for me* God was not Everything, but was, if I might put it that way, only God. Looking for work, working, was the necessary but impossible practice of a new way of giving the 'God business' a place in my life other than that in which I had wanted to construct my personal and social identity.

Now that after weeks and weeks of inner petrification (or putrefaction?) I have come to write these lines, I can see the link there was between the theological theme that God is God, so God is not

Everything, and the conviction that had dawned on me at Christmas exactly two years ago. As I came out of the mass of the day, there, all of a sudden, as I walked on the uneven granite cobblestones, it had come to me – with the same amazingly tranquil self-evident quality as at Easter, when I felt the need to 'let God go' – that I was going to have to 'let the Order go'. For that was the content of this second conviction that had previously escaped me: I, a Dominican to the marrow, had to 'let the Order go', in the same way and for the same reason that I had to let God go. Two years ago, I thought that it was only a matter – if I can put it that way – of letting the Dominican Order go. It took me all this time to discover that it was a matter of even more than that: I had to let the whole ordering of my life go. I had to let it all go as much for God's sake as for my own because this ordering in fact stamped on my life the fact that God was Everything. So God in my life was not God, but an idol. To become myself, to become human, I had to let go of what I believed to be more intimate to myself than myself: this order, in all senses of the word. Quite a venture! Did I then have to die in order to live a little?

I very much doubt whether by thus associating the theological theme that God is not Everything because he is God with the personal conviction that I had to 'let the Order go' I risk putting those who might be troubled by this conviction off the theme. I think I can tell them that, however great it may be, their disquiet can hardly exceed my own over all the months it took me to connect this conviction, which had dawned on me two years ago in a somewhat isolated and erratic fashion, with the theme. I certainly knew that the theme was not innocuous, but I would have preferred that the aspects of 'good news' it has for me should not have been affected by what seemed to be the sheerly negative harmonics of the conviction that I had to let the order go (I hope I need not repeat each time that this is not primarily or predominantly a matter of letting the Dominican Order go). So I hope that people will trust me, at least for the moment, and assent to discovering, as I have been led to discover, that the theological theme also has positive harmonies which arise from this disturbing conviction.

I have not forgotten that others, by contrast, will congratulate themselves that a theological theme like that of a God who is not Everything because he is God has not developed abstractly but in conjunction with praxis, indeed out of a praxis, namely the way in which one orders one's life depending on whether God is this more than that. Only a few months ago, when a Protestant theologian friend asked me what I was going to write about next, I told him: the fact that God is not Everything because he is God. This friend replied, as if it were a matter of course: 'Obviously God is not Everything and does not want to be Everything since he is Creator.' It has to be said that this friend recently wrote a theological book on creation. As I, too, had developed a similar conviction about God the Creator (which at the time was a somewhat neglected theological theme) in the second part of *When I say God*, I was intellectually as convinced as he was of this almost self-evident fact. But I was almost shocked by what I felt to be the levity of the way in which he considered the problem settled, when I myself was completely bogged down in it. I now simply tell myself that the way in which the life of this theologian was ordered – he was Reformed, married, father of a family, a professional writer as much as an academic theologian, was very different from the way in which mine was and that he could not begin from the same starting point in asking whether or not God is Everything because he is God.

Here I must stress one point which will remain extremely important for the pages which follow. When I speak of the ordering of my own life the qualification 'my own' is to be taken in the strictest sense. I am a Dominican, a religious, a priest: when I speak of the ordering of my life or of 'having to let the Order (or order) go', I shall be speaking of the way in which I personally ordered my own life around the fact of being a Dominican, a religious, a priest. So I shall not offer a general theory of the Dominican life, of the religious life, of the priestly life. Certainly, it may often happen that I discover in those around me, or in the past and present of the institutions in question, features analogous to those that I diagnosed in the ordering of my own life: I am not original enough to bear no traces of the extraordinarily effective training of which I was the consenting object. But I shall be writing about myself, about the way in which I personally interpreted and integrated the rules and objectives of the way of life to which I wanted to attach myself. I am not ignoring the fact that things could be otherwise for other men or other women (even if I know that it will be the same for many). I am not interested in a general critical examination of the Dominican, religious, priestly life in order to develop a theory. I am simply trying to face this theological 'good news' according to which God is not Everything since he is God, to face the way in which, in ordering my life as a Dominican, a religious, a priest, I had or had not claimed to make God what he is not and does not want to be, namely Everything.

I

God does not want to be Everything for love

Thomas Aquinas, Summa Theologiae *IIa IIae, qq.25-26*

I must now come to what seems to me after the event to be the first encounter that I had with the fact that God, because he is God, does not want to be and cannot be Everything. I must once again go back almost thirty years, back again to St Thomas Aquinas and my discovery of his theological writings on charity. With the lapse of time, I can no longer recall whether this discovery was made at the time of my first contact with these texts when I was a theological student, or some years later when I had to teach them as professor. I incline towards the latter, since this discovery certainly presupposes certain insights which would only have become possible for me as a result of the three years I spent studying psychology in the interval.

On this point as on others, Thomas Aquinas had to take part in the burning controversies of his time, and his positions were on the one hand original and on the other barely followed by Catholic tradition. The controversy in question could seem to be very remote from my subject, but it lies at its very heart. The question is whether charity's love does or does not have any other object than God, in other words (this time in my language) whether God is Everything for charity because he is its sole object or whether God is not Everything for charity. All the theologians involved in this controversy were excellent Christians (several, on both sides, were canonized and even proclaimed doctors of the church); all knew that Jesus had reduced the law to two commandments: love of God and love of one's neighbour. So no one dreamed of denying that charity had to be shown to the neighbour and not only to God. The point at issue was: who is the object of charity's love towards the neighbour: the person of the neighbour himself, or God?

The most mystical, the most enthusiastic of theologians involved immediately leapt at the object dearest to them, which was in any case the most important, and replied, 'God'. Since he was the source of this love of charity, being the embodiment of it (does not I John say that God is Love, *agape* = charity), how could God not ultimately be that of which he was the source? Did not everything come from God and go back to God? Certainly, charity was not limited to loving God, and consisted in loving the neighbour for the very sake of the love that God bears him, but in the end it is God himself whom charity loves in the form of the neighbour. God who is at the source of this love is also there again at its goal, rather as in the inner life of the Trinity, having in some way passed through the one who loves in charity and made him or her capable of loving, and also the one who is loved in charity by making him or her an image of God. The love that comes from God is therefore perfected by the movement which makes us pass from the neighbour whom we love to the one of whom he is the icon, God himself.

It is said that Thomas Aquinas weighed more than two hundred and twenty pounds and that he was sometimes so taciturn that they called him the dumb ox. He needed all that to resist such fine flights of thought and to dare to counter-attack by affirming that, despite their very mystical appearance, they fail to recognize the most original and most marvellous features of the work of God. In fact, St Thomas, said, if God creates beings different from him, the object of his creative movement must be these beings themselves, in the consistency which it is the specific aim of the creative movement to confer on them. (In the second part of *When I say God*, I stressed that belief in creation by God is not an explanation of the world but a confirmation of the difference between God and the world.) Thomas Aquinas even added that there was more perfection in creating beings who had consistency and autonomy than beings who would simply be the pale reflection or the copy of their creator (I translated this by saying that transparency is only a quality for window-panes). God, being more perfect than any human beings, creates more autonomous and more consistent beings than we could ever do. So Thomas Aquinas saw the autonomy and consistency of human freedom as one of the finest signs of the creative power of God and the divine character of this creative power.

What seemed to him to be true of the order of creation seemed to him even truer in the order of charity, not because he confused these two orders or put them on the same level, but precisely because the order of charity is even more eminent, worthy and perfect than that of creation. The movement of God's love of charity towards his human creatures thus confers even more consistency and autonomy on its object. Christians, too, would misunderstand this wonder if they thought that it was God whom they should love in their neighbour, since the neighbour is the object of the love of charity that God bears him, as he is the object of his creative movement. So Thomas Aquinas affirmed that we respect God less in loving him in our neighbour than in loving the neighbour himself in his autonomy and his consistency because of the love that God bears him. In matters of charity, God is the reason for loving, he is not the sole object of love.

Thomas Aquinas went even further: this reason for loving, who is God, is not our sole reason for loving. We have other reasons for loving than God: ties of blood, love, friendship, the nature of others, our own nature. These various reasons for loving are neither done away with nor absorbed by this other reason that we have for loving, namely God himself. That is why – think of the splendid questions 25 and 26 of *Summa Theologiae* IIa IIae – there is, said St Thomas, an order of priorities in charity, an order in the *multiple* and *diverse* objects of charity: God himself first, of course, but not only God; ourselves, whom Thomas Aquinas does not hesitate to put before anything else (the two hundred and twenty pounds of dumb ox were swept away by the Catholic tradition like a wisp of straw on this point, as on so many others, despite the biblical injunction to love your neighbour *as yourself*); then, after God and ourselves, the others. Again, these others are not all put on the same footing, on the grounds that God loves them all in the same way. For if this latter theme upsets the applecart of our loves by introducing our enemies into the sphere of charity, since God loves our enemies as much as he loves us, the reasons we have for loving one person more than another are not to be done away with or misunderstood on the pretext of charity.

To discover this doctrine of St Thomas was a real delight, a real liberation for me, but it called for a real revolution. In fact many things combined in my family or religious Christian tradition to make me somewhat reticent about any movement of love delighting in the very object of its love, finding its pleasure and its happiness there. Certainly one loved, not *only* out of duty but *above all* out of duty, including charity. Moreover – though perhaps I did not understand it very well – the whole apostolic and ascetical training that I was given in the religious life led to my preferring God as an object of love to such an extent that other objects were forced into the background, and sometimes completely removed from the field to which it was seemly to limit oneself. I was trained by Dominicans, some of whom I consider to have been almost saints: the extraordinary vigour of their apostolic zeal, their constant concern for God, their unparalleled devotion to human beings in the name of God, their fiery attachment to the person of St Dominic (who dreamed of dying a martyr and of going to evangelize the Cumani, and who spent his nights weeping and crying out, 'My God, my mercy, what will become of the sinners?'). All that was a force, an inspiration, an ideal for me. But I am not certain that I am the one and only person responsible for the fact that this extraordinary investment would seem to presuppose the divestment of all other reasons for loving and even – a horror for the brothers of Thomas Aquinas – that God was the object of our apostolic charity, even more than the neighbour himself.

The discovery of St Thomas' view was the beginning of what inevitably proved to be enormous changes. What, was God not the sole object of charity? Did he not want to be? Was God not the sole reason for loving? Did he not want to be? There were inevitably serious consequences in rediscovering others and oneself as worthy objects of our love and of a worth which does not offend the way in which God is the object of love but on the contrary pays it homage; in rediscovering the worth of other reasons for loving, other ways of loving; in rediscovering that their worth does not damage the worth of this reason for loving which is God but pays homage to it. To begin with, these consequences were positive and liberating: I often had the delight of seeing people opening up like flowers, when I enthusiastically taught them this concept of Thomas Aquinas. Over a greater period, I was led to discover – at least as far as I was concerned – that other consequences were more dangerous and could seem catastrophic. To say that God is not and does not want to be Everything for love, that it is greater for God not to want to be this, and that it is more loving for God not to make himself Everything for love than to make himself Everything would seem to have to be entirely positive and uniquely liberating.

It took me a good deal of time to begin to see the forces which resisted the recognition that this is the case: I may have some reason to return to it, but I must now make this point for the first time. Contrary to appearances, it is not to God's advantage to want to make him Everything for love. God does not want to be Everything for love, but human beings make him so, primarily to their own advantage, for in setting up God in this way they set themselves up as subjects (or believe that they are setting themselves up as subjects) in such a way as to be sheltered from all peril and all loss, or for love itself to be sheltered from all peril. Now where are human beings more in peril than in matters of love? And is not this peril so terrible, so radical, that to exorcise it we have to go so far as to make God something other than what he is and wants to be: Everything for love?

Genesis 2.18ff.

Another theme took more time to take shape and find a place in my thought, though it is true that it involved less innocent realities than the virtues of charity. I have already alluded to the difficulties that the religious of my generation encountered in the 1950s and even more in the 1960s in relating the religious life to the lay life. The whole religious tradition which we have inherited and integrated most deeply within ourselves presented religious life to us as the most perfect form of life, as much from the point of view of God, whose eminence it best honoured by devoting itself entirely to him, as from the anthropological point of view, since the most noble potential of the human being was devoted to the finest object possible; the least noble potential and the least noble objects were reduced to the most appropriate role possible, waiting to be finally eliminated in the blessed life to come, of which the religious life was the best possible anticipation on earth. And that was one more reason why this was anthropologically the most perfect life possible in this lower world. So we applied ourselves, to the best of our ability, to seeing that – in the best way possible – God was Everything in our life and that we aspire to making him Everything for others as well, waiting until one day (the day of the Lord?) he was Everything for everyone.

But, as I have already noted in another connection, in the 1950s and 1960s we also had to work with different lay movements whose concern was to make various aspects of life – professional, family, political, and so on – the object of what ultimately was also called a 'vocation'. The lay life became a field which was also that of the kingdom of God; the men and women who cultivated these fields also received from God a 'mission' which contributed just as much as the religious life towards realizing God's designs – but in a different way. In other words, in our ministry among the laity we were using a conception of God who did not want to be Everything in the life of these men and women, and we sang them the praises of professional, family, and political life in often lyrical terms which sometimes made our audiences smile or their minds boggle. But in our views of our own religious life we had a conception of God which made us think that he wanted to be Everything in our life and want to make him in fact as far as possible Everything in that life.

These two ways of talking and acting would have been compatible if we had made our choice of the religious life a choice relating uniquely to our own personality: since that is what we find ourselves to be, it suits *us* to express our relationship to God in this way. At the same time others, because they were different, could very well be expressing another kind of relationship to God of a quality equal to ours and as well fitted as ours to God and what he expects of human beings. But this was not our tradition, and it was not what one could call our ambition, either individual and collective. Down to our own day those leading the religious life have always thought it to be better suited to God and to what he expects of human beings, and to be a better indication of the true life of humanity with God when God is finally is all in all, and have tried to put that into practice. How do we reconcile this conviction with what we feel we have to say to lay people about lay life and the way in which God is equally radically involved there? I almost feel that this contradiction, which touches not only on many of us individually but also on the church as a whole, has played a major role in the 'departure' of a number of religious, male and female, and in what has been called the loss of identity among many others.

The very recent demands for a redefinition of the Christian identity, a redefinition of the religious and priestly identity, which emerge from the front line of the institutional church, are all associated with signs of a return to the old conception of the superiority of the religious and priestly life. Are they or are they not going to clash with what lay men and women have been able to discover about the depth of their existence before God? If I were one of these lay people, I would have my doubts; they risk being exploited, even if they are offered the bribe of participating in the liturgy, catechetics or theology on the same level as priests or religious. But I am neither a soothsayer nor a prophet. And rather than discover the lessons of a future of which I am utterly ignorant, here I prefer to learn the lesson of a personal discovery which at first sight might seem very banal (the term personal only indicating that no one had ever told me about it and that I made it one day, though it had always been there for the finding but had never occurred to me or been explained by those who had trained me).

It has to do with the first chapters of Genesis and the two accounts of the creation of the world by God that appear in them. Like the majority of Catholics of my generation, I had been trained in a more or less fundamentalist mentality. Like all the theologians of my generation, I had learned over the years to read these stories as magnificent poems the religious and human truth of which is not to be sought in their literal truth but in the original features which they display in comparison with other cosmogonies of neighbouring periods and cultures, and even more in the affinity of their religious themes to others which are no less essential to the Israelite experience of faith. I was very fond of these stories: I was particularly familiar with that of the six days (the first in the text as we read it but chronologically the second to be written) since it was read every year at the Paschal Vigil. As the cantor of our community, with considerable experience of the public recitation of texts, I had repeated it during the hours and sometimes read it myself: it is a very fine text. But my discovery was about the other story, that of Adam, and Eve taken from Adam's side while he slept. I was surprised to discover one day something that had been always clear but had been concealed from me by reasons as powerful, and as automatic, as those which explained why it had never been pointed out to me.

You will remember the text: the Lord created earth and heaven, then Adam whom he formed with the dust taken from the earth, and into whose nostrils he breathed the breath of life: 'And man became a living being.' Then the Lord planted a garden, took man and established him in this garden, Eden, to cultivate and keep it. He gave him every tree but forbade him to eat of the tree of the knowledge of good and evil. And the text continues: 'Then the Lord God said, It is not good that the man should be alone; I will make him a helper fit for him.' So the Lord created all the animals and the man gave them names, but 'For the man there was not found a helper fit for him.' So the Lord put Adam to sleep, took one of his ribs, made it into a woman and brought it to the man. 'Then the man said, This at last is bone of my bones and flesh of my flesh. She shall be called woman because she was taken out of man. Therefore a man leaves his father and his mother and cleaves to his wife, and they become one flesh. And the man and his wife were both naked, and were not ashamed.'

I have read, reread, studied and preached this text, and have learned from the commentaries the background to it and the perspective it adopts. But it took me many years to see that at one point the text moves in a direction which it would not have taken had it been written by authors who shared what was then my conception of the religious life and the conception of God that it implies. What does God say after creating Adam? 'It is not good for man to be alone.' But Adam was not alone. He was with God. He was very much with

God, not even alienated from him by sin, not even distracted from him by all these other animal and human creatures which did not yet exist. Here was the encounter with God, the one that I sought, the one that I had been taught to seek, the one that we had been told would be eternal bliss. And what was it that made God feel that Adam could not remain alone? If we had written it, the text would have been like this: 'And Adam got bored with being on the earth and only being with God. And God said to Adam, "Since you are not yet perfect enough to see that I am Everything for you and that you too should find complete fulfilment in the simple fact of being with me, and since I am a God who takes pity on your weakness as a poor human being and I do not want you not to have understood already that I must be enough for you since I am Everything, for the moment I am going to give you a helper who will make life less boring. You will go your way together. Obviously this is a digression; but I am good, I shall make this digression a way of learning, by no means devoid of charm, even if it is dangerous. When you get to that point, you will at last be ready for true life, life face to face; you will have learned that I am enough for you and that I am Everything for you. When you human beings get that far, you will not take either husband or wife, since you will be as angels." ' But that is not how the text was written. However, that is how it should have been written if God wanted to be Everything for man or if the religious life – with its vow of chastity – were best suited to the nature of God and human nature, if God's dream had been enough for human beings, if the life of human beings had to be shaped by the fact that their God was enough for them.

Familiarization with the other creation story, that of the six days followed by the seventh, confirms both the orientation of the other story and the questions that arise from it. On the sixth day, after everything else had been put in place, creation was given its crown in the creation of man: 'Let us make man in our image, according to our likeness... God created man in his image, in the image of God he created him; male and female he created them. God blessed them and said to them, Be fruitful and multiply, fill the earth and have dominion over it... God saw all that he had made. And behold it was very good.' Commentators had taught me that one of the original features of this text as compared with the majority of ancient cosmogonies with which it shares common features is that the creation of two different sexes is the outcome of the positive will of God and not – as in so many other cosmogonies or creation myths – an accident which happened to a creature who initially was unique, monosexual or asexual. The historians of doctrine had taught me that many great Christian theologians had been very embarrassed by this divine purpose and that several had not managed to believe it. For Origen, one of the pillars of Christian thought in East and West, there had been a first, completely successful, creation. Since out of pride the human being wanted to make himself equal with God, his sin had ruined creation: God was gracious enough to make another one, necessarily 'at second hand' and less perfect; sexuality had appeared in this second creation, and only there. Human sin had introduced it into a creation where originally it did not have a place and from which in any case it would be excluded when, in eternal life, things regained their true appearances: human beings would be as angels who, as everyone knows, have no sex. Did not the religious tradition, and with it some of those who trained me, call the religious life the 'angelic' life, *vita angelica*, playing on the assonance of the expression with the *vita evangelica*, the evangelical life, a term which was also often used to indicate that the religious life was most in accord with the gospel?

In *When I say God*, I spent some time stressing that creation is a matter of God establishing the creature in the difference between them. I could take up the same theme here by showing that the same thing happens in the difference between the sexes. However, even if it is not completely alien to this perspective, my present concern is different. What these texts tell me is that God does not want to be Everything in connection with sexuality, or women (since I am a man). Sexuality, the woman, are given by God; he is not jealous of them and they do not have to be done away with for God to be God. On the contrary, being God consists, among other things, in having instituted sexuality and given it to me. In a number of my earlier writings, out of theoretical theological and psychoanalytical considerations, I tried to show why sexuality – absolutized in a fallacious way – seemed to different forms of Christianity to be most opposed to a God who was himself represented in a fallacious way. Looking back after a number of years, I can see that several facts worked on me, each in a different way but ultimately converging to produce their result. These included the theoretical reflection that I have just mentioned, changes as a result of my analysis, developments in my personal existence and also the militancy and the practices that I mentioned in the earlier section of this book devoted to sexuality. It was just as important that the antinomy between God and sexuality that I had inherited from my family and religious tradition and that I had long put into practice and theorized about should be broken down in such a way that one day, reading the texts of Genesis, I noticed that they said something quite different. It is one thing to discover in connection with charity that God is not Everything and does not want to be Everything: it is something else to discover it in connection with sexuality. For the benefit of all those men and women who do not see how great the difference is, let me tell the following story.

A Dominican in my community, who had some experience and some theoretical knowledge of clinical psychology, wrote an article in which he discussed, among other works, my *When I say God*. Developing the theme – which is beyond dispute – that the real motivation of our actions often escapes us because it is unconscious, he discerned the secret motivation which had led me to write this book as being the need to justify the legitimacy of making love. He found traces of this unconscious motivation in the comparison that I made (on half a page out of two hundred and fifty, but we know how briefly and violently something that has been repressed can crop up again!) between the love of man and women, or more precisely between their sexual encounter, and the way in which God is present through the Shekinah. It would be wrong to tell this colleague that this comparison has been a classic one for more than twenty-five centuries, that for years the Jews read the Song of Songs at their great festivals, and that the Catholic liturgy also uses it in festivals of the Virgin Mary or the virgin Christian saints, and that mystical authors of all the great religions have often used this comparison more precisely and in a more developed way. He is well aware of all that, but he makes no mistake about the objective that he wants to defend because he feels it to be threatened. When a certain theory and certain practice of religious life proclaim that one does more honour to God by not having a sexual life (or, to be more precise, by not having an adult sexual life) and that this abstention is better suited to the nature of God and 'true' human nature as it will appear in all its purity in eternal life, one can indeed allow others the practice of sexual life, one can indeed use sexuality as a lyrical and mystical way of talking about God, but it is wrong, it is especially wrong, to give sexuality any place in one's own life other than a more or successful absence, a more or less successful lack. This colleague saw clearly that this was not my way of thinking or living.

It is not that I consider senseless the concern that impels certain men and women to give God such a place in their own life that they prefer not to have an explicit sexual life. But I feel that that is their business, related to their personal view of God and to the role that sexuality plays in their own personality. I am also well aware that such men and women come together to live out their own views of God and sexuality. But I think that such a way of living does not relate in any way to the very nature of God and the very nature of sexuality, and that it does not commend itself as being the best way of honouring the reality of God – in either this world or the next. Now people find quite a different conception in the traditional view of religious life and in the traditional views of God and sexuality prompted by the religious life, one according to which it is the very nature of God and the very nature of sexuality that favours such a view, and not ideas about God and sexuality which relate, for better or worse, to the personality of men and women who quite legitimately prefer to live in this way. So my colleague was not wrong in attributing to me a need to justify making love. Not being able to be judge and jury, I will not pronounce on the correctness of his diagnosis to the effect that the writing of my book was dictated by this need, nor on the validity of his judgment that such a need inevitably vitiates what it inspired. I prefer to evoke again the theme which came up at the end of the previous pages, that God does not want to be Everything for the love of charity or Everything in our reasons for loving.

I commented that it was not primarily for the benefit of God that human beings represented him as being and wanting to be Everything for love; they did it to provide a guarantee for themselves that they believed they could only provide in this way. It is no longer for God's benefit that some people represent him as the Everything in honour of which they renounce all sexual life. Rather it is for their own benefit, since by magnifying sexuality fallaciously to make it such a supreme reality that its sacrifice is the finest homage that one can pay to God, we keep ourselves from discovering it to be limited, contingent and affected by vicissitudes which must be denied in order to escape their dark power even more than their seduction. In this way people also protect themselves from the dependence on others and on themselves implied by expressions of sexuality (as by all dimensions of the human condition). Life sometimes shapes us in such a way that we do not consider the renunciation of all explicit expressions of sexuality too high a price to preserve ourselves from all that. Life sometimes shapes us in such a way that it does not seem too high a price to pay to transform God into someone to whom this operation would be particularly agreeable, even if it transforms him into the opposite to what we believe of him (in the credal sense) as Creator. Yet again – and I repeat this, even if I am well aware that this repetition will have no effect on those who do not want to listen; but perhaps that is true of all of us? – I have nothing against the fact that men or women prefer to express their relationship to God in such a way that they choose not to have a sexual life. Moreover, I have great admiration for beings capable of leaving everything, burning all their boats for a great passion. The only thing that I am against – and I am against it with all my strength as a human being and a believer – is what these men and women turn their choice and their theory about God and sexuality into, presenting this choice as if it were endorsed by the nature of God and the nature of sexuality.

II

The difficulties of detotalitarization

Even if it took longer and proved more difficult to discover that God did not want to be Everything in connection with sexuality than in connection with love, I had already been aware of this for some time when I wrote *When I say God*. I had also been able to devote the second part – that on creation – to the theme which at that time seemed to me to be most essential, namely that for human beings contingency is not a flaw but their very nature, and to the identification of the numerous mechanisms by which some forms of Christianity seem to me to pervert the Christian faith by making sin contingent and expecting salvation in Jesus Christ to deliver us from contingency. More recently, foreseeing that I would be ending this book with a part entitled, 'God is God, so God is not Everything', I cheered myself up in anticipation of concluding with what seemed to me might well be a hymn of praise to God and his creatures. If God does not wish to be Everything, but to be himself, God, if he wishes us to be ourselves, human beings, and if he wishes to be a God with us, it seems to me that we have something for which to praise him. That we want him to be God, that we want to be ourselves and that we want to be with him seemed to me and still seems to me to be good news, and a good way in which to end a book. But, as I have said, circumstances which seemed to have no connection with my concern have made it clear that at any rate for me personally, there is never an end to what impels us to make God everything, to turn him into an idol.

In fact, in my case – as I have already indicated – the problem was to find work for just a few years (given my present age and the labour market) in order to earn my living for a while and not be a complete parasite. My conviction that this was necessary did not present me with any intellectual problems, and was reinforced by increasingly pressing practical needs. Now as I have said, I resisted this with all my might. So what did I want to protect? What would I lose by finding work? To understand better what was involved and what escaped me for so long, I must describe what had happened to the conviction which had come home to me two years earlier as I came out of Christmas mass convinced that I had to 'let the Order go'.

The apparently favourable combination of a situation and a conviction

It is now four and a half years since the Vatican prohibited me to preach, preside at the eucharist and teach theology publicly. In the first part of this book, written by now two and a half years ago, I described the process of decomposition which followed, a decomposition which, despite its almost terrifying aspects, seemed to me ultimately a piece of good fortune from which I had to be able to profit. I had to 'let God go', to give him his freedom so that he could become what he is, even if that meant losing all that I thought I knew of him, even if it meant dying before the return of spring. But one knows that spring will return after winter, while I knew nothing of what season might come. During these hard years I was confined in a silence which led to my being forgotten, except by my superiors – at a local and a national level – who several times tried to get the Holy Office to mitigate the sanctions taken against me. Their lack of success was total. I have progressively become used to the idea that they will go on until my death. People denied this and pointed out that other theologians had been rehabilitated after being condemned. I retorted without great success that while this might be true, the sanctions had never been so heavy and the accusations of heresy had never been so grave or so numerous. Besides, the conditions in which I had been condemned meant that I had lost the little confidence I ever had in the kind of people who make their career at the Holy Office. As Lord Acton said before the discussion on papal infallibility in 1870, 'power corrupts, and absolute power corrupts absolutely'. In recent months, when the question has come up of retracting the condemnation of Galileo, these people have not hesitated to recall that after all, things were not as simple as all that and that their predecessors had not been so ill advised as had been claimed. Now unlike Galileo, I am not a genius, and while it is certain that the earth revolves around the sun, what I have written is not so certain. Besides, I have already acknowledged that I was wrong on one point or another. So I had to convince myself that I would never preach again, never preside at the eucharist again, never teach theology again.

In theory several solutions were possible: I could envelop myself in silent devotion, plunge myself into secular or sacred erudition, join Mother Teresa in Calcutta or some of my Dominican brothers among the starving peasants of Brazil, do jobs in Paris for Secours Catholique, or quite simply put myself at the service of my brothers, as several brothers – some priests and some not – do in my community in an admirable way. In fact there were many reasons of different kinds against that, but the most powerful was the very one that had led me to the Dominicans: I wanted to be able to speak of God, of faith, I wanted to be able to live with people and in conditions which allowed me to look for God and speak of him. For months and months I was completely stuck, hovering between these two arguments, neither of which I wanted to give up, without being able to resolve the impasse. On the one hand I certainly could not preach, celebrate, or do theology, and on the other I could certainly not live without speaking of God. So I did not so much live, as gently decompose, slowly but surely. My days were empty – incredibly empty. I have a variety of gifts and I was leading what one might call a good-for-nothing life. The only more tolerable moments were the periods of school holidays when I wrote this book: in the meantime, outside some weeks of occasional 'secular' work, nothing, nothing, nothing. At least in relation to what I am talking about here; what is essential in my life.

I asked myself what could be the meaning of the life of a Friar Preacher who no longer preached, a priest who no longer presided at the eucharist, a theologian who no longer taught theology publicly – and I told myself that this made no sense. But on the one hand I was attached to the Dominican Order by so many ties woven over more than thirty years that I did not envisage for a second – as I said at the beginning of this book – leaving the Order. On the other hand I saw no other way of living that could allow me to speak of God. One thing was no longer possible, but nothing else was possible than to rot where I was, trying not to stink too much. Yet inside me there was a stench, there was indeed a stench. Sometimes I told myself that I had been very lucky: up to my fiftieth birthday I had had a very good life, enthralling, and I regretted only a few errors or mistakes: many people had not had this opportunity. And at fifty-three I had been turned into a living corpse, as others are by an incurable disease, by a bereavement which breaks them up, or by unremitting professional failure.

Of course one always exaggerates when one says such things. In fact one almost always exaggerates when one thinks such things. But the suffering, the decomposition have the bad taste not to bother about the finer points. Or rather, finer points are a luxury that is impossible for them: you are out of it, you're saved, when finer points become possible again. But when you weep, you weep. When you sob, you sob. Still, I was not completely finished, because somewhere, work was going on, things were moving; from time to time the mists were breaking up. And a wisp of mist has a form, it is like something, it suggests something.

Several of these wisps reminded me of those features of religious life which seem so often to be inspired by the conviction that God is Everything, those features which seem so often to be organized, thought, intended to signify, to symbolize, that God is Everything. I would not claim to reduce the theory and practice of religious life to a proclamation that God is Everything and to be a human being is simply a matter of making God one's Everything. I am, however, obliged to note, in myself and around me, that this is the proclamation around which religious life is often organized and around which many of its adepts organize their existence. From this point of view, although the majority of current theological views on the significance of the religious life are less forthright than earlier ones, they imply in a more or less explicit way that the religious life derives its value from the fact that it signifies in another and better way than the lay life what God is and what is the true goal of human existence. What I have just said about sexuality and the way in which people think that they should sacrifice it to God, because to exercise it would be less worthy of him than to sacrifice it, is also very often true of the vows of poverty and obedience. I described in the first part of this book how the changes of the meaning within our culture of various anthropological factors relating to the vows necessarily entail a transformation of what these vows can signify about God and human beings. Once they claim to be a system signifying the nature of God and man instead of presenting themselves more modestly as the way in which men and women want to express their relationship to God for perfectly respectable reasons which are peculiar to them, religious vows cannot fail to suggest that they proclaim God as that Everything whose eminence and uniqueness are only truly honoured when human beings give themselves no other object than him.

Perhaps some people will say that it never comes to that. I would reply first that that is to treat too lightly views which, on the contrary, have been held quite explicitly over the centuries – and up to our days – by hundreds and thousands of religious, men and women, bishops and theologians, preachers and spiritual directors, or sometimes certain lay people like the incomparable Jean Guitton of the Académie Française, who declared *à propos* of the vow of chastity made by religious: 'To taste our deepest and most legitimate joys, we need to renouce some of them.' I would then add that we need to distinguish between theory and practice and that here, in contrast to other areas, practice is often stricter than theory. I want to say that I know a number of religious who, in their preaching and their writings, do not present in such a totalitarizing, not to say totalitarian, way the God to whom they invite men and women religious to dedicate themselves and who on the whole allow room for the Christian values of lay life. However, in their personal life they continue to behave as if God was such that it was improper to give oneself any other object of love, interest or activity; when they give themselves another object – which they consider to be a weakness or an accident – they feel really guilty, not so much about a quite understandable personal matter but about their relationship to God himself, whose love they have so grieved because this love demands that everything should be consecrated and sacrificed to it.

However, I should point out that I know men religious (the same thing is doubtless true of women religious, perhaps even more so but I know too few of them to be able to speak for them) who do make what they do match their theory in this sphere – and that is more difficult than it might seem. They do not believe that God wants to be totalizing and totalitarian; they do not believe that God wants to be the only object of love, the only reason for loving; they do not believe that God feels threatened or wounded when human beings express their sexuality, their autonomy, their interest in other things. They have arrived at that point not through weakness or laxity, but rather at the cost of hard work in faith, more constant attention to God and a courageous struggle against everything in us and around us that conspires to make God the Everything which leads human beings to think it is a good thing to set him up as an idol. They want to continue to lead a life in which the 'God business' has a predominant place, they want to continue to give an essential place in their life to prayer, celebration, preaching, theology, sharing faith and looking for God. They are seeking tenaciously, modestly, as far as this is possible without making God the Everything that he is not, without thinking that they have to make sacrifices to him by amputating what is the gift of God, a gift without repentance, like all the gifts of God. They come up against a great many difficulties: first and foremost in themselves, since most often they have been formed by, moulded to this totalizing and totalitarian conception of God which they now reject with all the strength of their faith: their training has often marked them so deeply that they sometimes have to do violence to themselves, not to say wound and mutilate themselves, to detach themselves from what had become so much part of them. But they also encounter a great many difficulties outside themselves, so powerful are the forces which conspire to make human beings believe that they fulfil themselves by making God Everything, so powerful are the institutions engendered by these forces or which feed on them.

I admire these men a great deal: for several years I tried to be one of them. But the situation in which I find myself as a result of my condemnation means that for me personally it no longer makes sense to remain among them. Even in its classical form, for me religious life was not an end but a means – at least, that is what I thought consciously. Taking vows, belonging to an Order, the observances, the organization of individual and communal prayer, and so on – for me all that was at least consciously just a means to an end, an end which, since St Dominic, the constitutions of our Order have defined as being the salvation of souls through preaching; this comprises far more than the act of preaching, though that remains its epicentre. From the moment when it proved that I would certainly not be able to preach any more, the end disappeared. And if the end had disappeared, what was the point of the means?

Don't misunderstand me. I do not claim that these means make no sense in themselves and could not be pursued independently of their end, which is preaching: a number of other religious Orders, a number of religious show that this can certainly be the case. But for me personally – and I stress the adverb personally, since my argument does not seek to be general – the means only make sense in relation to this end. I do not have the vocation of a Benedictine, a Trappist or a brother of the Christian Schools, but of a Dominican, and indeed a Dominican for whom the Dominican life makes sense only in connection with preaching. Since preaching was no longer possible for me, all the means became a body without a soul, a corpse. I took months and months to come to this conclusion, and perhaps I would never have made up my mind, had not, as I said, the body begun to rot away. The difficulty of becoming aware of this and making up my mind showed the real nature of my problem.

Theoretically, it was all very simple: since the end was no longer possible and the means had therefore ceased to make sense, it was appropriate to look for other means to serve the same end. Short of that, the end itself would disappear from my life. Service of the word of God, the salvation of souls by preaching, would disappear from my existence, and the corpse into which all my means had turned would become my own corpse. As I put it one day when explaining to my aged parents that I wanted to prepare for this eventuality: 'After all, if I leave the Order, it will be for the reason for which I entered it; since the service of the word of God by preaching which led me to it is no longer possible, this same service must make me leave it to find something else.' In theory that was very simple. Certainly it represented a radical upheaval in my existence, and the older one gets, the more difficult it is. But I had already experienced or caused several upheavals of this kind, and I know very well that as long as I live I shall have to know how to die to live, and the more important the cause, the more I shall have to know how to die in order to succeed in living a little. So in theory there was no insurmountable problem, especially as the *status quo* was proving increasingly sterile and fatal.

Yes. But I was as it were transfixed. I could not shift, I was deteriorating, and I was incapable of going towards the only possible way out, though it was a way out which I could take in theory and I could explain the necessity of it. I was entangled in a net the nature of which escaped me: it was as though my feet were both imprisoned in a concrete block. I raged, I felt humiliated to be like that. What was happening? Why could I not do something that was so clear, so evident, my sole chance of survival?

A growing paralysis

Certainly, elements of the diagnosis of my paralysis were plausible. On the one hand, the ties of all kinds woven with institutions and above all with people over more than thirty years, the friendship and confidence of so many, the companionship of even more... How could I come to separate myself from everything that had been my life, all the more since a number of people were in no way pressing me to leave. On the contrary, I knew that I would deeply wound a number of them by leaving. I had had enough experience of this wound myself to know what it represents, not only as the loss of a companion, but as a destruction of one's own way of living. Why inflict this suffering on them, why inflict it on myself, when I did not even know if anything else were possible? It was more a matter of letting go what I had for a more fanciful alternative; it was letting go of what had been life for what no doubt would only be death, in and around me.

Besides, people pointed out that while I was reduced to silence, the silence was not complete: I could still join in meetings of informal groups, accept rare invitations in France or abroad to speak, if not in public, at least in private. If I left the Order, I would be even more of a social outcast than I was already, I would lose the little that was still possible for me. I would be even less acceptable among many believers and no more acceptable among other believers or among non-believers as a result. Quite the contrary. At least I had a social status; I would lose it without gaining the right to speak or a context in which to speak. Whereas, as people pointed out, it was this word that I wanted to go on serving.

One day, a friend to whom I unburdened myself spoke to me of fidelity. She asked me, 'But what about fidelity?' I tried to show her that I was remaining faithful to the aim of my life, that I was even being more faithful than ever, since, in order to be able to serve this end, I was going to have to tear myself away from the whole of this body of means which had in practice become my own body. I added that for more than fifteen years, I had been pleading that the Catholic church should not burden divorced persons who remarried with the weight of their dead unions. It was not my union with the Order that was dead, it was the Dominican life that people had killed in me by making its aim impossible. Did I have to let its corpse poison me? Particularly as I was not leaving the Order to abandon the 'God business' but to try to find another way of serving the world, since what was dear and familiar to me was no longer possible? But one never uses the word fidelity in vain, and I could not avoid feeling guilty. So why leave, if leaving was also more or less treachery?

And then, prosaic or indecent though it might seem, there was the material aspect to consider. At fifty-seven years of age, my total possessions amounted to eight thousand francs in bank and post office accounts, some books, some clothes, a good radio and some cassettes, a small car more than five years old with 60,000 miles on the clock which needed new shock-absorbers and the replacement of its slipping clutch, neither of which I could afford. That was all, though it might seem to be an excessive, indeed scandalous, amount for a religious to own. Not much of a basis on which to rebuild one's life. In three and a half years, thirty-seven and a half years of religious life would give me the right to a retirement pension of about 1100 francs a month (value as at the end of 1983). My family has not come into great legacies. If I left the Order, having done only a little 'secular' work, I would not have the right to any protection against the effects of illness from social security and would not have the means to subscribe to a voluntary scheme. Certainly I would not find myself on the street, but I would be an utter parasite to anyone who might receive me. Finding a spot of work for a few years would improve the situation for the short time that it lasted. And then? Some more eccentric and better-known Dominicans than I or great theologians less heretical and also better known than I have been able to find rich patrons in Switzerland: they are still in the Order or incorporated into a diocese. The ultimate irony would be that the Order I was leaving is supposed to be a 'mendicant' Order.

'What,' said another friend to me one day, 'Do you dare to allow factors of this kind to influence your remaining in the Order?' Yes, I do. Not out of triviality but because I belong to the human condition. How many men and women (how many women, above all, because economically they are more dependent and more defenceless), well before they are sixty, have no possible choice in life because their material situation allows them no room for change! They have to stay in an unrewarding and badly-paid job, with a wife or a husband in a relationship which is virtually dead in every respect, in housing that they don't like, in a dull village, in an area where they are bored or there is an intolerable lack of freedom, work or even food... They have to put up with all that simply because they have no resources for doing otherwise. A little money, and everything would change. Why is it that so many millions of people play the lottery? We should not despise all these men and women; there is nothing contemptible in continuing to live in a certain way simply because one does not have the material means to live less badly. Why should that be false and scandalous in connection with the 'religious' life when it is true and respectable in connection with 'professional', 'family', 'cultural' life and so on? No one has ever seen a Dominican dying in wretched conditions or abandoned in the street. Even if many religious have no idea about the concern that finance causes their superiors, an even greater number does not take into account that belonging to a religious Order is the most extraordinary system of social security and old people's care that one could imagine. At all events, as far as I am concerned, the future looked so dark that - whether it seems too prosaic or not - I saw all this as a reason for resisting a change the need for which appeared to me very clearly in theory, but the consequences of which would be so catastrophic.

These reasons, and several others, cetainly carried a good deal of weight in my inability to change my way of life. However, there were other more considerable obstacles still, since in any case I had reasons for changing which urged me on considerably when I thought about them, so much so that they seemed to be far more convincing than the reasons for doing nothing. It is here that the circumstances resulting from my condemnation and the reflections prompted by the way in which the religious life is often too inclined to make God Everything were combined. Since my condemnation robbed me of the essentials of the Dominican life and nullified all its means, which only made sense to me in connection with these essentials, why should I not take advantage of the situation and try to see how to live a life in which I tried not to arrange my existence round a God idolatrously transformed into Everything? So it was not a matter either of continuing to go to pieces in a life which had become meaningless because it was deprived of its aim, or letting the 'God business' go, but rather of escaping this disintegration and remaining faithful to that without which my life might seem inconceivable: a kind of service of the word of God, albeit by and in silence.

Certainly I would have to leave companions and institutions which were dear to me, but it was possible for me to leave them without disowning them or condemning them. I know that many of them give the religious life the function of setting up God as Everything, but I also know that others do not do so, and live this life in a way which is fruitful for themselves, for others, and for God. I also know that the quite advanced age of the majority of the members of religious Orders and the quality of their past endeavours give them the right to grow old peacefully without having to turn their existence upside down. So as far as they were concerned, my departure would not look like a condemnation. I could not have borne that. They did not count for nothing in the fact that it no longer made any sense for me to try to live like them. They could not reasonably force me to rot where I was simply in order to stay with them. The best of them would understand that I was embarking on an venture which continued to be related to the one that we had shared.

On the other hand, I would indeed be leaving them, though I would be rejoining the far greater number of those men and women who have understood that if God is Everything, he is only an illusion, but who do not know that God is not Everything, far less that so much combines in Christian institutions to go on presenting God as though he were Everything. I was also joining the number, less substantial but not negligible, of those from whom I was less remote since they had 'let God go', let go a reduced God – yes, reduced, since a God reduced to Everything is a reduction – and were seeking to create a space in their life where this God who is God could have a place. I was going to try to learn to live with them and like them; I was going on a quest with them, deceiving myself a little as they were, and like them discovering something.

So a new life was appearing, the contours of which were certainly less assured or prestigious than those of my previous life, but a life in which a good deal was at stake. At all events, I did not have the choice: it was that or death, and not the death that life prepares for and engenders, but the death that ravages, kills and engenders nothing. Was it not an interesting way to spend the end of one's life to seek God, to seek to express God without setting him up in life as Everything, and not proclaim in the various sectors of life that he is Everything? Was it not good to look for the value of these different aspects of life, a value which they have in themselves and of themselves and which is destroyed if they are absorbed into a God who seeks to be Everything? I even told myself on some days that in a way misfortune was a good thing, and that if I had not been as it were decapitated by my condemnation, I would not have been led to try to live like this in a way which could even be as useful to others as the previous form of my life had sometimes been. So for me, for others and even for God, there was every advantage in the change I planned.

Despite all this, I did not budge an inch, although the decomposition entailed by the fact of remaining in one place was proving a little more degrading every day. So I was angry, with an impotent and humiliated rage. I continued to look for work, but in a very ambivalent way. I had said that I would prefer to work part-time, since I wanted to keep time to work, write and read, and I wanted to keep time for the 'God business'; besides, half-time work would satisfy my financial needs, which are modest, and would perhaps prove easier to find in the present state of the job market. But I also found that my material need for money and my psychological need to get out of my hole by some sort of external discipline were such that if only full-time work was possible, I would take a full-time job. That is what I said to those who interviewed me, without giving all the reasons.

Several weeks passed without anything happening. I was well received, and the authority and the prestige of the friend who recommended me did not go for nothing. Most often, despite their great good will and their desire to honour the request of this friend, those who interviewed me had nothing to offer: my age and my curriculum vitae made me difficult to place and the world is full of people looking for jobs who are younger, more experienced, more competent and more enterprising. Often, much more often than I would have expected, after the 'professional' interview had ended with a more or less explicit 'No', the person interviewing me added: 'I knew that I didn't have anything for you but I did want to meet you personally because of such and such that you wrote or such and such that you did.' There followed what was sometimes very vigorous praise of my gifts as a preacher, a theologian, not to say a celebrant. These men, who were often eminent and always over-busy, had spent time on me, less to try to help me (since in spite of their goodwill they could not) than to meet me. As one of them was going with me to the door of his office, he said, 'One way or another, keep going, do keep going; it's too important. We need people like you so much and there are so few of them.' I was amazed. I did not know I was known and esteemed by such men. To begin with, I was overjoyed, but then I was thrown back on the past by a request that brought home to me the impossibility of my continuing this past and the desperate search for a possible future. That was the sum of it. And the days kept passing.

There is a sequence which seems to work very well in some silent American or French comic films. Someone appears, and there is a piece of action, a gesture, a remark; only afterwards does one discover the unusual aspect of the situation; the action, the gesture, the remark is utterly incongruous. The same sort of thing happens in the life of the psyche, but while the lapse of time is only a fragment of a second for film gags, it may be hours, days or even months in the psyche. Or again, another significance of a familiar role or gesture only appears afterwards, and you wonder how you could have spoken or acted for so long without even noticing the enormous significance of what you were saying or doing, which has now become evident. Something very like this happened to me some weeks ago. It had been suggested that I should take a post as an administrative secretary for thirty-five hours a week for 6500 francs a month (value as at the end of 1983) in an organization which worked for a very interesting cause. But I exclaimed to myself, 'I don't want to clock in at the office every morning.' It was some time after that, above all thanks to friendly meetings with two married men who had once been Dominicans and now clocked in at the office every morning, that I saw the enormity of what I had said, an enormity which becomes significant or demonstrates its absurdity if it is compared with the objectives which I claimed to have in this search for a job and a new way of living.

However, before I go on to what I then realized, which will doubtless form the conclusion of this book, I must dwell on the reasons which impel one so strongly to make God the Everything that he does not want to be. In fact if I were to stress too one-sidedly the personal difficulties I felt in changing the way in which I had ordered my own life round the fact that God was Everything, I would give the impression that this totalitarizing of God was essentially part of my personal history. But while it is true that that is part of the problem, it is even more true that in this respect I am simply a particular instance of a much more general problem. So I would not want to leave that at a secondary level, even if I did not put it first in the ordering of my life. Just as the difficulty of finding work at fifty-seven in the present state of the job market and with my curriculum vitae is not solely or even primarily a result of my ambivalence towards what I felt the fact of working stood for (people of my age learn to retire early, or are taken more or less gracefully towards a pre-rirememt stage, or remain willingly or unwillingly out of work – and I could not count myself among these), so the difficulties of not letting oneself be caught up in all that leads one to make God Everything are associated with the power of all the psychological and sociological mechanisms which work in this direction. No doubt I made myself an accomplice, but their power does not depend very much on me and must be described independently of my concerns.

The forces which exert pressure towards totalitarization

God, totality of meaning?

One of the areas in which the totalitarization of God finds most fulfilment is that of meaning. The question of meaning is not just a philosophical question, or rather, it is only a fundamental philosophical question to the degree that it occupies a fundamental place in everyone's life. The existence of each one of us is too much the result of a thousand chance and inexplicable elements, and is too defenceless against a thousand equally chance and inexplicable events, for the question of meaning not to arise, not as an abstract or otiose question, but to enable us to cope with, or at least to make tolerable, the things that throw us off course or overwhelm us. Why? Why? Unlike other languages, French has only this word to designate two different but complementary kinds of question. Because of what? To what end? The uphill and downhill of our lives, the uphill and downhill of events. I have already said that I do not have much of a head for philosophy. So I will content myself by stressing the way in which these questions bear down on our lives, the way in which they bear down on the view that we may have of God as Everything: the Everything of meaning. This is a totalitarization which once again is not primarily the work of philosophers but above all that of the most elementary order of practice: by that let us understand that it helps us to sustain a certain relationship to our lives.

Do we understand nothing of our lives, of what happens to us? Can we not bear our lives to be meaningless or to become so? One way of imagining God allows us to suppose that to some degree things makes sense, even if that sense escapes us, that someone knows what it all means. Someone understands what we do not understand, someone guarantees the meaning that escapes us. Our lives are not absurd to everyone, nor are events meaningless to everyone. Someone, somewhere understands the absurdity of existence, the incoherence of this world of madmen. We must not go straight on to the next question that crops up: In that case why does he allow it, why does he do it, why doesn't he do it? Certainly it is an important question, and I shall return to it. But if we let ourselves be carried on too quickly we risk failing to see the consequences of the conviction that there is an Everything in meaning and that God is this Everything.

In this respect strict monotheism proves both more effective and more risky. In polytheistic religions, meaning can be in some way both fragmentary and conflicting. A particular sector of reality relates to a particular spirit or god, and another to another spirit or god. None represents the totality of meaning, and people have to approach several different authorities with limited competence, but they can explain the incoherence or the failure as much by the limits of this competence as by its plurality and the conflicts that can result from it. Strict monotheism centres the whole of meaning on one God; in theory it is therefore more effective. But it is more risky, and meaninglessness and absurdity become more difficult to explain, since every attempt at explanation derives meaning from this one unique and original God. Explanation then becomes so difficult that Manichaeanism is always a contemporary solution, even if it means not so much setting a God of Good and a God of Evil against each other, as being content to set God against a force of evil, sin. While God must be admitted to have allowed this sin, its origin can be said to go back far beyond any individual: Lucifer, Satan or original sin bore down on humanity long before there was any possibility of doing good or evil. However, the meaning of sin itself does not escape God. In him everything makes sense, including sin and evil.

It is only one step further to make God Everything in meaning, and that step is all the easier to take since one is not aware of the difference, and the problem to be resolved is too urgent for one to be bothered about epistemological nuances. When I was discussing the reflex which impels believers to think that without resurrection nothing makes sense, I already explained how Catholic apologetic loves to exploit the gaps, not to say the chasms, which confront the human quest for meaning and how much it loves to present God as the one who fills these gaps and chasms. In that case God is not only the one who gives true and ultimate meaning to what has only partial meaning, but the one who gives meaning to the nonsensical, the absurd. I have two difficulties, each of a different kind, over this view. One relates to intellectual developments in Western culture in this second half of the twentieth century. The other relates to what seems to me to be the way in which God has been manifested in Jesus Christ.

In connection with the first it is worth noting that the very idea of a meaning which would be the totality of meaning is an idea which is becoming increasingly alien to our present mentality, and becoming more and more suspect to it. Even the most exact sciences have given up the ambitions which Einstein and Heisenberg still had fifty years ago. They no longer seek a single explanation or a single theory, not because of a regression or lassitude in reason, but on the contrary because of a more profound understanding of the nature of reason and its relationship to what we call reality. What is true of the exact sciences is even more true of all our other intellectual approaches. We seek to discover the meaning – the well-founded but partial meaning – of each human enterprise or each aspect of reality, rather than attaching a partial significance to an overall meaning or an authority which might guarantee it. Even if the criticism of ideology has become less pressing and less totalitarian than it was, it has nevertheless forced us to establish a point of no return by showing both the power of such authorities and their ineffectiveness in connection with the question of meaning to which the establishment of these authorities claims to provide an answer. The setting up of a meaning which would be the totality of meaning would appear to do more damage than clarify or support whatever meaning might appear to us. People will say that in these conditions it is the very idea of God, the very idea of a God, which becomes meaningless. That is certainly the case if God is defined as being the totality of meaning in such a way as to make this reality more or less accessible to us to the degree that God makes himself accessible to us. It is here that I feel another difficulty which arises from what seems to me to be the manifestation of God in Jesus Christ, even if I know all the forces that impel us to give this description of a God who brings us salvation.

For a long time now, Catholic theological friends and colleagues have accused me of being Barthian. I dare not confess to them the exact number of volumes of Karl Barth that I have read and worked on closely; in any case that is not what counts, but rather the fact that I feel more at home in a view which looks for the meaning of God in what was and remains down the centuries his manifestation of himself in Jesus Christ, rather than in the answer God might give to the great human questions. What God shows us appears more in the question that God puts to us in Jesus Christ and in the response that Jesus Christ gives to this question (in short, what is called in theological jargon the self-manifestation of God in Jesus Christ) than in the way in which God might be thought to answer to our questions about meaning. The Gospels do not present Jesus as responding to the great questions that human beings asked in his time. Jesus hardly replied to the religious questions of his fellow religionists. On the contrary, we know the points at which he did not reply, the way in which he was evasive and parried the questions to the point where he had to be put to death by religious and political systems who claimed that these were the questions to put to God and that they were the guarantors of the answers to be given.

The resurrection of Jesus Christ and the Pentecost of his Spirit do not mean that Jesus Christ is henceforward the answer to everything ('Jesus or nothing') and that in him Christians from now on have the answer to everything. They indicate that God bears witness that the question raised by Jesus Christ is the one by which God manifests himself, that the reply given by God in Jesus Christ is what human beings can expect of God. It is useless to expect anything else of God, and to ask him anything else. God has no other meaning, gives no other meaning than that shown by the life, death and resurrection of Jesus Christ and the way in which the Pentecost of his Spirit makes him alive among us today. God does not show himself in Jesus Christ as being the totality of meaning, Jesus Christ does not manifest himself as being the totality of meaning. When they believe that this is nevertheless the case, Christians prevent meaning being found in the manifestation of God in Jesus Christ, which is not a manifestation of the significance of omnipotence. One could say, in a rough paraphrase of St Paul: We do not have the omnipotence of meaning; we do not proclaim to you the totality of meaning; we have nothing to proclaim but Jesus dead and risen; we have only this news which has no value as a response to everything or as the totality of meaning, but has value in itself, although it runs the risk of not seeming much compared with the omnipotence that we require of the totality of meaning.

For what makes us lose our heads when confronted with the extremely partial character of the significance that we discover in our human enterprises, the way in which we are overwhelmed by the absurdity of so many senseless events is so charged with suffering and dashed hopes that it either requires meaning to betotal or rejects it as such. That is why Jesus Christ dead and risen, God as he is manifested in Jesus Christ, are most often only given a divine status if it is possible to attribute a totality of meaning to them. The good news is that in his day Jesus died the most absurd of deaths, that he died at the hands of those who wanted to be guarantors of a God who would be the totality of meaning, that in his lifetime he faced up to absurdity and nonsense, that he approached those men and women whose life was most meaningless or had been emptied of all meaning by the religious and civil society of his day, and that he faced up to all this not to eliminate the absurd and the senseless in a miraculous way, but to demonstrate to people that God himself was becoming their neighbour, that God was more God if he shared the absurd and senseless than if he took it away, and that the resurrection of Jesus Christ cannot be represented as a triumphal cataclysm which swallows up the absurd and the meaningless but must be represented through the possibility that the Spirit of God gives to men and women who believe in him of making him, like God, partners in this absurdity and nonsense. But is it not already almost a luxury to see things in this way and to be able, if I can put it that way, to be content with them? Is it not necesary already to have relieved to some degree the pressure with which absurdity and nonsense overwhelm us in order to be able to perceive this? Are we not often so imprisoned in them that no one can approach us, become our neighbour, join us? Who could want us to expect only one thing, hear only one voice, the one that will come in triumph to throw down the walls which imprison us and make us triumphant beings? What chance does God have of making himself understood, what possibility does the Spirit have of making us understand Jesus Christ if they have no other power, no other way of signifying, no other meaning to offer us than that attested by the life, death and resurrection of Jesus Christ? Is it not understandable that we are so quick to attribute to God, to Jesus Christ and to the Spirit another power than that, another meaning than that, not to mention making idols of them? Have we not plenty of reasons for preferring these idols and the powers that we give them?

God, omnipotent?

I said that we must not be in a hurry to move on from the question of meaning to the question of God's action; if we are, the risk is that we shall misunderstand all that is concealed by the need for meaning to be totalized in one being, one reality that we call God. But I cannot postpone that move any longer. For one of the essential advantages of the totalization of meaning in God is that it bases on God the totalization of all power, omnipotence. If God can give meaning to everything, he is Everything in meaning, so he can act on anything, he is Everything in power. Nothing escapes his power, whether in heaven or on earth, in the heights or in the depths, in the past or in the future, in our lives or in the lives of others. He can do everything. Someone exists who can do everything, whom nothing can resist. Of course we hope that he will put some of his omnipotence at our disposal. We hope that all the more since we believe that this God is good and that he loves us. But in the end, even if he does not do so, the essential benefit for us does not lie there but in the fact that there is someone who has omnipotence.

Certainly, in a cruel way and throughout life we have the experience that this omnipotence barely seems to exist. Here too the big question is Why, why? Why does he allow that to happen? As people keep on saying, 'If there were a God, he would not allow that to happen...' Fortunately (if one can use that word in connection with the ills of the world, of our ills), it is not too difficult to elaborate 'explanations' which take into account the existence of evil while leaving completely intact the omnipotence that we attribute to God. Explaining the problem in terms of sin is the simplest and most effective way. In addition to its simplicity it has the by no means negligible benefit that I have mentioned in connection with the rechannelling of hatred of God (this God who allows it all to happen without lifting a finger) by means of self-accusation. If the omnipotence of God cannot be exercised directly and without limit in our favour, which is God's desire, too, since God is good, the simple reason is that human sin gets in the way; we mess things up, we spoil creation and ourselves, we spoil God's goodness. However, God's goodness is so great that he wants to pardon our sin. But he cannot miraculously blot out all its effects, all the opaqueness, all the inertia, all the entropy that our sin introduces into the world, into ourselves and others. The goodness of God sometimes goes so far as to use all the negative features in and around us to test us. They are instruments of education which allow us to approach him and to approach the deepest truth of our being. The goodness of God turns evil to good, not by suppressing the evil but by making it serve the good: *Etiam peccata. Felix culpa.*

As I have already pointed out, in this book and even more in *When I say God*, such a way of looking at evil and at God's relationship to evil ultimately leads to an absurd conception of God and humanity. I have stressed the gravity of the equivocation involved in identifying the characteristics of contingency and finitude with sin, and thus identifying the effects of salvation with the abolition of finitude and contingency. I have no illusions about the possibility of explaining such defences, since they come up against the full force of something that I want particularly to stress here, namely, that of everything which leads towards our attributing to God a certain kind of omnipotence and making him Everything for power as we make him Everything for meaning.

But if God is not omnipotent, is he God? If God is not omnipotent, is there a God? Are there not a thousand and one prayers which address him as omnipotent? Does not the creed proclaim him as Father Omnipotent, Maker of heaven and earth? However, I believe, both here and in connection with the view of God as being the totality of meaning, that believers need to reflect on the way in which God has been manifested in Jesus Christ, on what the life, death and resurrection of Jesus Christ and the life in the Spirit inaugurated at Pentecost teach us about what the power of God is, is not, and cannot be. More questions need to be asked about the different meanings that certain expressions take on in different cultural and religious contexts, differences of meaning which can be so great as to be opposite to the original meaning.

When Christians of the first centuries took care to include the expression 'omnipotent God' in the confessions of their faith, what did they want it to say about their God? Twenty centuries later, we have difficulty in imagining the nature of the religious universe at the heart of which these Christian men and women had to articulate their faith. From the time when they left the narrower framework of the Jewish communities from which they originated, they found themselves in a world in which the divine flourished extravagantly: there were not only the various divinized gods or heroes of the Greek and Roman pantheons, but all the more or less divine authorities that the various systems of thought – and particularly forms of gnosticism – had installed between the apex of the divine hierarchy and the humble human condition. For example, the creation of the universe and human beings was too sordid a task to be attributed to the highest God; so what was needed was a being inferior to him but nevertheless sufficiently divine to be able to be the creator responsible for it, or even a plurality of beings of this kind, one or more demiurges. The tendency to set up hierarchies of intermediate beings between the transcendence of God and the humility of the human condition was so strong at the time that even Judaism itself gave way and introduced such hierarchies. Its very strict monotheism was less altered by that than one might suppose, since it was specifically in a concern to preserve the transcendence of the supreme divine principle that all these hierarchies were initiated and tasks were devolved on them which, while certainly being divine or quasi-divine, were considered too trivial for the most elevated mode of deity. It was equally the case that this process ended up in the multiplication of more or less divine authorities, each of which had its own power, a power which dominated one or other sector of the world and the life of human beings.

When believers affirm that their God is creator of heaven and earth, against such a religious background, they are not being content to repeat the faith of their original Judaism; they are adopting a militant and forthright position in relation to their religious environment. They are rejecting the existence of all these intermediate beings between God and humanity; they are rejecting the view that the creation of the world is the action of a demiurge and proclaiming that it is the action of God himself; they are proclaiming that the transcendence of their God is not affected by his taking the initiative in establishing the saving relationship which they confess him to have with humanity and with the universe. Thus their proclamation of God as 'omnipotent' is quite polemic and equally conditioned by their religious environment. Its main function is not to bear witness that their God is capable of any miracle and of unimaginable revolutions; at that time everyone had no difficulty, or hardly any difficulty, in believing in the gods and the various divine authorities. The main function of their proclamation is to bear witness that God is the only one to enjoy a divine power; it seeks to deny the power and the existence of any intermediary authorities and to say that the destiny of human beings is in no other hands than those of God and themselves. Over the first centuries of Christianity so many church fathers did not write so much and give so much oral teaching on the theme of providence primarily to argue that the destiny of human beings depended on the gods: everyone believed that at the time. They were concerned to deny that human destiny depended equally on those more or less divinized authorities – destiny, *fatum, moira,* good fortune, and so on – to which the Greeks and Romans paid at least as much attention as to their gods, if not more. To proclaim that God is omnipotent is first of all to deny the power accorded to *moira,* good fortune, and so on.

The creed that we recite as though it were a liturgical prayer is not a liturgical prayer; it is a collection of dogmatic formulae which, like all dogmatic formulae, are not so much produced to enunciate positive truths as to exclude those views which the believing community feels to be contrary to its faith. The dogmatic formulae do not say what the mystery of God is, nor do they define what God is; they exclude ways of formulating this mystery which seem to them irreconcilable with faith. When Charlemagne called for the recitation of the creed at the Sunday eucharist in Western Christendom, he met with lively resistance from the pastoral authorities: his obstinancy and his victory do less honour to the nature of a dogmatic formulation or a liturgical prayer than to the political use which can effectively be made of dogmatic affirmations, when they are conceived as being more the unifying slogan of a social group than as space opened by a celebrating community in order to confess its God.

If the powers who want to base their power on that of God have everything to gain from seeing the omnipotence of God in a certain way, think of the equally powerful advantage each of us would have in understanding this omnipotence of God as the omnipotence that we would like to see taking its place against everything in us and around us that bears witness to our own impotence in the face of life and destiny, for others and for ourselves! There is no need to stress the mechanism, which is as much collective as individual, that consists in projecting on a real or mythical figure a power which is inversely proportional to our weakness: the child does this with his father and mother, the poor do it with the rich, the ignorant with the learned. While it may be true that it is better to be rich, knowledgeable and healthy than poor, ignorant and sick, it is no less true that what the child projects on the adult, the poor on the rich, the ignorant on the learned says far less about what the adult, etc., in fact is than about what the child, etc., is. The projection primarily describes the one who makes it, and says much less about the one on whom it is projected. Besides, when the child becomes adult and discovers who he is, he is so often deceived that all that is left for him to do is in turn to project himself on to a mythical and marvellous child who expresses more surely the nature of the adult who attributes to the child what he was or what childhood is. As various criticisms of religion, ancient and modern, have shown *ad nauseam*, the attribution of omnipotence to a deity says more about the misery and impotence of human beings than about the nature of a God to whom this omnipotence was attributed.

So we get back to the question: if God is not omnipotent in this way, is he still God? If his omnipotence is not like that, is there even a God? The question is not abstract or Byzantine. It is raised by all the impotence and misery which cry out for the existence of such omnipotence and such an omnipotent God. Here again, as with a God who would be the totality of meaning, Christian men and women should ask about the very disconcerting way in which God has manifested himself in Jesus Christ. When we ask if God is omnipotent and how he is omnipotent, we should not scrutinize the omnipotence that our impotence projects on God: we shall find only our own features there. We should scrutinize the manifestation of

God in Jesus Christ and ask ourselves what kind of power is at work there. What is the life, death and resurrection of Jesus Christ? What is it that the action of the Spirit since Pentecost shows us about the power of God? What type of power is at work there?

It is here that the interpretation of Jesus Christ is open to serious equivocation, so serious that in *When I say God* it concealed from me the truth for which the resurrection of Jesus Christ opens up a space. Yes, God has raised up Jesus and made him Lord. This is a manifestation of power. But, as I have said at greater length in an earlier part of this book, in connection with death, that is no proof that God has the omnipotence that we attribute to him. The resurrection of Jesus Christ does not prove that God is more powerful than death, and that from now on the problem of death has been resolved. Its point is to show that God is as he has manifested himself in Jesus Christ, that God is alive today and that he will be as alive tomorrow as he was yesterday in manifesting himself in Jesus Christ, that the Spirit of God can introduce today among human beings the type of relationship to God and the type of relationship among human beings that Jesus inaugurated. That is the power which God has shown in Jesus Christ. As the life, death and resurrection of Jesus Christ have shown, and as the way in which the working of the Spirit since Pentecost has shown, the God of Jesus Christ does not display any other power than that; Jesus Christ did not use any other power than that, and the Spirit does not use any other power than that.

It is fascinating to see at what point we believers are not content with this. We seize hold of these divine works of power and make them the works of quite a different power: that which we have so many reasons, excusable though they may be, for attributing to God. The death of Jesus is a manifestation of the power of God, but not primarily a manifestation of the omnipotence of God over suffering, treason and death, as if this death of Jesus recapitulated in itself and therefore did away with all suffering, all treason, all death, past and to come. It is a manifestation of the power with which God seeks to show himself as he does in Jesus Chist, and not otherwise, not as he has been asked to, not as he has been required to. It is the manifestation of the power with which Jesus commits himself to this manifestation of God. The fact that his commitment went as far as death, death through treachery, failure, abandonment and infamy, is not for all that the canonization of suffering, failure, treason or even death. Yes, there is no greater sign of love for one's own (namely his Father and us) than to give one's life for them. But only *when there is no other solution*. That is the power which is shown in the love of Jesus Christ, the power of this way of loving.

And we passionately seize hold of this death to make it the sign of an omnipotence over suffering, failure and death. Just think of the excuses we have. That is why it was appropriate for Jesus to take so much care to reject any other power. The temptation of the wilderness continues. Satan had said to him, 'Throw yourself off the temple and you will not kill yourself because the angels will catch you.' We say, 'Die, and you will be raised, and death will be conquered.' Yes, the resurrection of Jesus Christ is a work of power. Yes, the outpouring of the Spirit at Pentecost is a work of power. I have said what kind of power. But how we hasten to lay hands on it in order to make this resurrection and this Pentecost tangible and manipulable proofs of the power that we want to give to God! When I was writing earlier about death, I already described everything that leads us to deform the resurrection of Jesus in order to make it the guarantee of the power that we want to have over life and death. I already pointed out in *When I say God* how the religious powers, in order to augment and guarantee their own power, seize hold of Jesus Christ risen and the realities in which the Spirit can make him present: eucharist, scripture, church. I already pointed out how such senseless powers seize control of Jesus Christ and human beings at the price of a radical dissent over the way in which Jesus Christ can be present to us. I would not want to withdraw a word of these lines that I wrote ten years ago. But in the end all that does not amount to much, given the forces which impel all of us to seize hold of the manifestations of power of God in the life, death and resurrection of Jesus and the outpouring of his Spirit, and to distort them, manhandle them, manipulate them, pervert them so as to make them conform to what should be the manifestation of the omnipotence that we have so many reasons to attribute to God. Yes, the temptation continues. 'Worship me,' said Satan, 'and the world is yours.' We are more subtle: 'Let us worship you as the omnipotent one we need and the world will be yours.' Think of the strength, the power that this man needed to resist this temptation. Think of the strength, the power that God has so that he can prevent our efforts from stifling such a different voice, such a different power that is his. But we cannot but tremble in seeing it swept away, so strong in us is the need for things to be different!

God is better, because he is other and because he is himself

We have considered God the totality of meaning, God whose meaning would totalize all meanings, would complete partial meanings and give meaning to the absurd. We have considered omnipotent God, whose power would complete all limited power and abolish all our helplessness. It would also be appropriate to mention God the All Good, whose goodness would abolish all our misfortune and whose mercy would blot out all our sins. I have already discussed him often here (not to go back to what I said in *When I Say God*) in relation to either death or guilt. At all events, the approach to take would be the same as that towards God who is the totality of meaning or God the omnipotent: beginning by noting everything in us that could impel us to raise this question in a totalizing way and then trying to note what God has shown of his goodness in Jesus Christ and in the life that the Spirit makes possible through him, discovering here again that the goodness of God is at the same time more and less than what we would like to assign to him. Less, because he is not the totality of goodness: the fact that all goodness comes from God does not prevent other goodnesses than his own from not being his own, just as the being of creatures is not reduced to the being of God, and is not the being of God, even if it proceeds from the being of God. Once again we must not fail to understand that creation sets up the creature in the difference, just as love's charity sets up its objects in the difference as well as in the similarity. If God is not the totality of goodness (even if he is all goodness), the goodness that he shows in Jesus Christ is in a certain sense less than that which we would desire to be his. But in another sense it is more than we would assign to him. It is about this more, because it is other, that I would prefer to ask questions here, because a crucial point arises here in connection with totalitarization, as crucial for the goodness of God or his power as for any of the attributes that we assign to him in a totalizing and totalitarian way.

I have described that part of us which projects itself in order to establish a certain kind of omnipotence of God, totality of meaning and so on. I commented right at the beginning of this last section, in connection with the love of charity and sexuality, that human beings attributed to God a concern to be Everything for love more for their own benefit than for God's. They do so in order to assure themselves that their infinite demand for love will be completely satisfied and that they will be definitively spared every loss, however partial, that human beings attribute to God in being Everything for love. Certainly from then on one has to sacrifice everything to him for the longer or shorter term, but burdensome though it may be, this sacrifice is a good investment if it assures one of being in contact with the one who is Everything. The words and actions of certain mystics can lend themselves to illustrating this mechanism – whatever may be the meaning that they had for the mystics themselves. It is worth the trouble of being nothing, nothing, nothing, of wanting to have nothing, nothing, nothing, if it is in order to find oneself one day possessing the heavens, the world and everything in it, the Virgin Mary and Christ himself. It is worth the trouble of having as an emblem what one considers to be the two greatest humiliations of Christ, namely the childhood and the agony ('of the Infant Jesus and the Holy Countenance') and to repeat indefinitely that one is the littlest and that one is following the way of the littlest, if that makes it possible to announce one's religious profession in the form of an invitation to marriage with the king himself, thus becoming a queen. But – and once again independently of what these words or actions may have consciously signified for those who performed them, for it is the use made of them that interests me here – while this mechanism sets up certain fascinating and fulfilling figures, these figures are never other than the reverse side of the needs which set them up. The more total the self-annihilation that one practises, the more total (and totalitarian) the counterpart that one sets up. The extremity to which the process is taken does not alter in any way its nature, except that this extremity reveals the extremity of the needs and forces which come to be accomplished in it.

There is no need to be amazed at the extremity of these forces or to blame them for being such, or men and women for being their playthings. I would not want to make the same mistake here as the one I made in *When I say God* about the desire for eternity and the need of the infinite. The desire for omnipotence and the omnipotence of desires is as constitutive a feature of the mechanisms of the human psyche as the desire for eternity and the need of the infinite. But here again, there are ways and ways. Omnipotence remains definitively one of the planes which circumscribe the space of human psyche, like the need for the infinite or the desire for eternity. However, it would seem that everything depends on these planes not being planes which define a space in which our different possible objects can be situated, but becoming objects which fill and close up this space. Far from setting up a real relationship with an object and providing a basis for the subject, these mechanisms, contrary to their claims, only succeed in preventing any real relationship with another object and preventing the subject from having any other basis than the supposed fulfilment of his or her omnipotence. In fact the other cannot be present as the other and as someone different. All that can be present is the other set up in the omnipotence, the all-goodness, the totality of meaning which our helplessness attributes to him or her. The other is neither other nor different; he or she is simply our inverted self, the inverted totality of our infirmity. The fulfilment of omnipotence is not life but death, or more exactly the unthinkable, indescribable overwhelming of the subject. This totality is only our own and that is why it is our death.

The other can only be the other, he can only possibly be our life and not our death if we do not make him our Everything. The same thing is true of God, the only difference – which is not only a vital but even often a disastrous difference – being that everything leads us to make God this Everything and thus reduce him to ourselves, and in consequence prevent him from being himself, being God, being other, being for us the life that he wants to be. That is why I find so dangerous the sermons, the apologetic and theologies which invite us to seek God and find him in the questions posed to us by the partial character of meaning, power, goodness that we experience, or in the questions posed to us by absurdity, suffering and evil. I much prefer preaching, theology and celebrations which try to express how God is manifested in Jesus Christ, how this manifestation makes present Another who is not Everything because he is not ourselves, and so makes it possible for us to be ourselves more fully and in a better way, not by fulfilling ourselves but by making Another present in us.

And what about the cry of our suffering? What about the unhappiness of our helplessness? What has that to do with this manifestation? Beyond a certain point, nothing. As St Vincent de Paul said, when people are hungry, we must not catechize them but give them food. But can one hope to make oneself heard above the din made by the voice in which there is no salvation? For there is no possible salvation in setting up this Everything which is ourselves. If there is salvation, it is possible only in the possibility of an encounter – which by definition will be partial – with another who is different because he is himself, and in the way in which we set ourselves up – which by definition will again be partial – as a result of this encounter. Perhaps it might even be important to avoid here the excessively personalist vocabulary of 'encounter' to allow room for the otherness which makes the other other, and to bring out the mystery of our own existence in a certain otherness in relation to the 'person', the identity, the façade that we display. Yes, our suffering, our unhappiness, our misfortune sometimes give us no respite. That is our greatest misfortune, since the impossibility of respite precipitates us into setting up this Everything which is our own and makes us think that salvation lies there, that that is our God.

A Christian who has meditated long on the *acta et passa Christi*, what Jesus did and suffered, who has also meditated long on what Jesus did not do and suffer, cannot fail here to remember how Jesus made close contact with the helplessness, the suffering, the ills of the men and women whom he met and how he brought them near to his God. Certainly he did miracles. Who did not in his day? Other miracle workers in the Jewish and Hellenistic world did more than he did. But, as people have noted since the beginning of Christianity, the small number of miracles that he did and their very nature show that their aim was not to suppress evil and suffering, human infirmity and helplessness, but to 'signify' that God was bringing himself close to human misfortune, suffering, infirmity, helplessness. That is the incredibe thing; that is what he had to show. Jesus did not have anything else to show. The demands made on him were those that are made on miracle workers, the omnipotent, the gods. And all he had to give was the kingdom that comes close to the poor, the lame, the blind, the lepers, the publicans, the prostitutes, the sinners. 'Are you he who should come, or should we look for another?' Yes, we must look for another if we are waiting for a miracle worker, an omnipotent figure, a God who is everything. Or at least – and it is unfortunate that Christianity has often wanted to triumph in this way – we must transform Jesus into what he was not, so that we need no longer wait for another, since the truth does not visibly conform to the fulfilment of what we desire of him. With the help of the Spirit, can we now and tomorrow, like other men and women who have partially succeeded, restore body and soul to this extraordinary proximity of Jesus to suffering, misery, helplessness? To this unrealizable combination of humility, privation, helplessness in the face of suffering and misfortune, and respect, concern, blessing for men and women caught in their own helplessness, imprisoned in their sin, overwhelmed by their sufferings? Is it possible, twenty centuries afterwards, with the help of the Spirit, in our own way to bring something of this to men and women when at the same time we are not bringing them what their misfortune makes them ask for? Is it possible to bring just a little relief, when this relief is given in such a different way? Is it possible to love effectively, when we bring so little of what is asked of us by those whom we love, and bring it in a completely different way?

It is precisely because the gift of God in Jesus Christ is of such a different order from what our wretchedness requires of him that none of these questions arising from our wretchedness, our suffering and our helplessness is invalidated as a result. The fact that these are not the questions to which God gives answers does not make them idle ones. They are only meaningless or treacherous to the degree that we think that they are the questions we must ask God, or more precisely the questions to which he can give answers. To raise the questions which are put to us by meaninglessness, suffering and evil is part of the greatness of being human. Certainly, human beings progress far more by the way in which they learn to ask questions than by the way in which they give answers. But is this not one of the greatnesses of the human condition? It is also one of its greatnesses to be able to resolve problems, eliminate certain evils, sufferings, deficiences in power; to be able to overcome certain forces, to be able individually and collectively to establish fragments of truth, happiness, justice. But the radical questions remain. For some decades the best of the modern Western world seems to have joined forces with some perceptions from the Near East and the Far East in suggesting that the specific character of man consists more in his allowing himself to be invaded and troubled by these questions than in claiming to give an answer to them and to solve them.

The same is true of the questions of philosophers. I have never been very fond of Pascal's maxim which led more or less implicitly to scorn for the God of the philosophers in the name of the God of Abraham, Isaac and Jacob. My lack of enthusiasm used to derive from the fact that I thought them, if not identical, at least related. I no longer think that this is the case, but I do not think that their difference authorizes us to disqualify one in the name of the other. I have taught, listened to and read enough philosophy to know that what I have written in the preceding pages raises enormous philosophical questions. Given what I have said, what can be the meaning of a God who is not the totality of meaning, who is not omnipotent? What does it mean that God is Being and the source of being without being all Being, Goodness and the source of all goodness without being all Goodness? I am not saying that this does or does not make sense philosophically. I am not saying that these questions are meaningless or absurd on the grounds that they are not (as it seems to me) the essential questions that faith is led to raise, or more exactly the questions raised for us by the manifestation of God in Jesus Christ. It is for philosophers to raise them if they are their concern. Faith makes no claim to give answers, any more than it is authorized to dismiss the questions on the grounds that they are not its concern. One of the consequences of the fact that God is not Everything – as logical as it is difficult to accept – is that faith does not have an answer to everything or power over everything. Other questions than those of faith are legitimate, and other needs than those of faith make their claims. If God is not Everything, faith is not Everything for man. One might venture to say that human beings have something other to do than have faith, even when they do have it. So faith cannot have any totalizing and totalitarian grip on their life, for the one, sufficient reason that God does not want to be Everything.

Practical Conclusion

That God is not Everything but that he is God is something which over the months and years has seemed to me to be good news about God and humanity. That is the note on which, after all these months, I want to end this book. For if such a way of looking at things involves fragmentation, reduces to fragments ideas and institutions of our faith and a number of our ideas of God, it seems to me that it also and above all reduces to fragments the fetters under which we are bowed down and allow us to stand upright – alive. I should also have been able to write these pages without much difficulty and finish the book. However, as I said, the detotalitarization proved full of obstacles, and these obstacles proved different from and more effective than those set up by forces which for some time I had already been able to describe in theoretical terms as exerting pressure towards totalitarization. Another interval of three months proved necessary between describing the difficulties of detotalitarization and describing the forces pressing in the opposite direction.

Three months. It took me that long to see the significance of the enormity of my reaction to the offer made to me of quite interesting full-time work which would have brought in 6500 francs a month for thirty-five hours a week. I told you my reaction, 'All the same, I don't want to clock in at the office every morning', and described how, as often happens in the life of the psyche, one only notes weeks or months afterwards the significance of the reaction or of such sudden and unthinking behaviour. Now that I am beginning to see what this remark involved, I am not surprised that it took three months for its implications to emerge. Indeed, I am amazed that three months were enough. It is true that the outline is still very summary, but its main features are precise enough now for me to be able to try to formulate them – indeed I have to.

Yes, it was a good way of ending this book to finish on the good news that God is God and that therefore he is not Everything. But if I could not succeed either in writing these lines or in accepting a job, the reason was that in actual fact, even if I was intellectually convinced that God is not Everything, even if in my way of living I had already found other objects of love and other centres of interest than God, something more profound continued to make me set him up as Everything, or more precisely (since I have already noted that human beings do this for their own benefit and not God's), something in me would continue to seek its own identity and status by setting up God as Everything in my life.

'I don't want to clock in at the office every morning for 6500 francs a month!' I know the job market and salary levels in France well enough to know that there was nothing dishonourable about such a salary: more than half French workers are paid less than this for more than thirty-five hours a week. Such pay would therefore be above average for France. Besides, it was far from being negligible in relation to my financial needs, which because of my situation were quite modest. Finally, it was my good fortune that the work in question was interesting and served a cause dear to me. Nor did I react by exclaiming to myself, 'All the same, I'm not going to earn that little', or, 'All the same, I'm not going to do uninteresting work.' No, what I said was, 'I'm not going to clock in at the office every morning'.

When I entered the Order thirty-five years ago (that was in 1949), the worker-priest movement was in full flood, though that did not prevent it from experiencing a number of difficulties even at that stage. Some Dominicans had been in the pioneer generation and with each new development new ones came to join the already existing teams or to found others. At that time it was a matter of clocking in at the factory rather than at the office. Clocking in was one of the symbols of belonging to the working class. 'Going to clock in' was a sign of the missionary and apostolic approach (that was still the terminology of the time) which impelled some of our number to want to join the working world. So clocking in was at that time a missionary and apostolic action directly linked to the God to whom we had devoted our lives and even directly linked – despite the reticence or the fury of some people – to the aim of the Dominican Order, namely the salvation of souls by preaching. Did I or did I not want to be a worker-priest at that time? At all events, I made friends with many of them and with their teams. When the question of giving me a job came up in 1956, the situation had changed a great deal. In 1954 Rome had suspended what the Vatican called the 'experience' of worker-priests, and they had been prohibited from remaining in the factories (thus being faced with the odious choice of either staying in their factories but ceasing to be priests or remaining priests but leaving work), though some of them – the minority – had managed to make a discreet compromise. So I was assigned to work in which one only had to 'clock in' in two ways. Both were familiar to me and were directly connected with the God to whom I had devoted my life: responding to the call of the great bell which summoned us to the offices where we celebrated him, and to that of the little bell which announced the time of theology courses and periods of work, theology and work which were directly dedicated to him.

Later, between 1965 and 1975, among Dominicans as among many other Orders and among the secular clergy, a group felt the need to do a 'secular' job. This time there was no question of an apostolic, missionary or evangelical aim. Rather, there was a conviction that professional work was a necessary stopping off place and even a place and way of life which were all the more essential for becoming a human being than sharing our most basic condition. So it was no longer a matter of going towards the working world to bring it the values of the gospel and at the same time allowing the values of the working world to penetrate the church; it was a matter of going to the working world (no matter what the work might be) to receive from it an indispensable complement of humanity.

This approach was not entirely lacking in missionary, apostolic, and evangelical intent (though this vocabulary is already beginning to date a little); sometimes that intent was even explicitly present, though not as it was among the worker-priests. It was no longer a matter of sharing the condition of the workers to learn how to preach the gospel to them or to bear witness by sharing the gospel with them; rather, it was primarily a matter of becoming oneself through professional work, becoming a human being worthy of the name, since this approach was a necessary prelude to hearing, understanding and sharing the gospel from a place within an essential dimension of the human condition. So working was not only a matter of wanting to become the real person that one would not be without it (a motivation to which those who disparage this tendency too easily reduce what inspires its adherents); working was a necessary prelude to the establishment of a real theological context, a status and a condition in life where one would be better placed to perceive and construct what could be the kingdom of God among human beings.

Although I had had considerable experience of Dominicans who thought in this way (at that time I was one of those involved in training them), I myself had never been very sensitive to this problem. Rightly or wrongly, I considered that the various tasks to which I devoted myself were as valuable and humanizing as professional work. Besides, they were very similar to the professional tasks of a certain number of university teachers or researchers who were my friends: teaching, with all the preparation that it involves, research, lectures, articles, books, congresses, meetings and so on. I even did my bit in the more onerous demands of the intellectual life, since I was involved for almost eight years with our very important library at Le Saulchoir, either as its head or in a subsidiary position. I was also involved in administrative tasks connected with intellectual matters, since I was part of the team which trained Dominicans and directed the faculties of theology and philosophy at Le Saulchoir: and it is common knowledge that this was a period overburdened with reform commissions, administrative commissions, control commissions and so on. I do not see how this kind of activity could have qualified me any less in human terms than the different professional activities of my various lay friends. I found it natural, constructive and sometimes harrassing to 'clock in' to all this, and did not feel the need to go elsewhere.

As for the more specifically religious activities – prayer, celebration, preaching – I was well enough aware of all the human enrichment and human happiness that these brought me (badly? too much? never mind!) to need to look for anything else in that respect. Before entering the Order I had 'secular' activities which enthused and enriched me. So I was not without points of comparison: what I did now had no cause to suffer in comparison with what I had done. 'Clocking in' at the offices, at celebrations or for sermons was just the same (to keep it modest, which I was not) as clocking in at the office, the ministry, the hospital, the factory, the theatre, the recital, the shop. So I had no complexes about things (except perhaps a superiority complex). I never argued against those who had the tendency I have just described, since I was not certain that they were wrong. But I never understood them very well and I was never tempted to join them – as I was tempted to join the worker-priests. I thought that on the whole I had the kind of work I needed to be able to consider myself and to be considered a whole human being.

The circumstances arising out of my condemnation meant that the various activities which did not make me envy those with a profession became finally impossible for me. I have remarked that in the long term, and since in any case I had no choice, I planned to profit from what this situation could offer. Rather than rot where I was for want of being able to put into practice what was essential to my life, why not use this situation to look elsewhere and in a different way for a way of living and a situation which would allow me to explore other ways of devoting myself to the 'God business'. Since I had also become aware how much a certain practice and theory of the religious life was too bound up with an excessive totalitarization of God, why not profit, also from this point of view, from circumstances which were killing the aims of the Dominican life for me and making meaningless the way in which I went about it? Why not try to explore other less totalitarian ways to God? Was I going to have to earn my living? And then? Was that not part of what one might call the epistemological and practical (in the sense of praxis) prelude to this new quest?

I have mentioned the inhibitions which prevented me from carrying out these ideas, which seemed to me to be as clear as they were noble. I said that while the explanations of the inhibitions which I gave myself were relevant, they did not remove them. It was then that the significance of my inner reaction, 'But I don't want to clock in at the office every day!' came home to me with brute force – even if it was some weeks later. If this was my reaction to this offer of work the limited but real advantages of which I knew (to tell the truth, they should have seemed substantial by comparison, since I had not found anything else apart from them), it arose quite simply from the fact that this new status was going to make me lose the exceptional status that I had in the eyes of others, and in my own eyes, by virtue of being a preacher, celebrant, theologian, a man defining himself socially and in his own eyes as dedicated to God's business. In the first part of this book I described the decomposition of which I had been the object. I said that it progressively found its way into the suffering caused by being deprived of these functions, like a wedge going into a log; it was a question about the way in which I had invested myself in these functions. Almost three years after writing this first part, after the twists and turns of my pilgrimage, after its deepening and its discoveries, I find myself brought back to these same questions, but in an even more constraining and embarrassing way.

At that time it was simply a matter of my conception of these functions: in addition, I had come quite naturally to raise questions, which generally went beyond my personal case, relating to the way in which these functions are conceived of and practised in the church community. This time, it was a matter of the most personal and most profound modes of my own commitment to these functions, or rather to this exceptional state. Certainly, I had succeeded in articulating theologically the way in which God is not Everything and does not want to be Everything because he is God and wants to be God for us. Certainly, I had come to articulate theologically the way in which the religious life is so often exploited and distorted by psychological and social forces which succeed in fulfilling themselves in the totalitarizing of God. But within me this detotalitarizing came up against a kind of rock, the rock on which it proved that I had built my personal and social identity: making me an exceptional being because I was devoted in an exceptional way to the 'God business'. It turned out that I was the beneficiary and the principal recipient of this process of consecration to God. It turned out that in spite of the measure of detotalitarization I had already been able to achieve, the order which I had given to my life had a totalizing and totalitarian function in the formation of my social and personal identity.

Such an observation does not have an infinite number of possible consequences. If I want to go further in the discovery of the good news which is that God is God and that therefore he is not Everything, if I want to go further into the mystery and be able to share it better, there is one thing I must do first, which is both epistemological and practical: I must break up the ordering of my life, break up that part of me which was being fulfilled in this totalitarization and which was protected by its totalitaranism. I must break this rock.

I am going to try. I do not know whether I shall succeed. I do not know whether I shall survive. I have no choice. I am well aware that other men and women, in other circumstances, could and should do otherwise. I am well aware, knowing some of them, that the radical quality of the solution to which I am drawn does not mean that their quest is less radical and less authentic because it does not lead to such radical solutions. There are other ways of living for the 'God business', of being as good a man or a woman as possible, than being forced to such fragmentation. I have said over and over again that it took the unforeseen combination of very diverse and chance elements for me to be personallly led to this point. But when after all that I have been through I keep coming up against such elementary and horrifying reflexes as, 'But I don't want to clock in at the office every day!', the situation is serious, and major action must be taken. I am going to break the ordering of my life. If I am not broken from top to bottom, what will come out of this? What will be born of this death, what life will this death produce and raise up? Will new energies emerge, all the more numerous and strong because of the number and strength of the energies which were mobilized in the setting up and maintenance of this strait-jacket?

If you take almost three years to write a book, you do not know in advance where it will lead you. One of the signs that the end is near is that one day you begin to look for titles, to sketch out conclusions. It is easy to guess that this present book has had several titles and that its present title only occurred to me very recently. As to the conclusion, I thought of several in succession, except for the only one which is worth while. If I am going to go further forward in the exploration of this good news that God is not Everything but that he is God, I must put down my pen, lay it on the table – probably for a long time – and break the order of my life.

I'm going to try.

Notes

1. That is why one priest is enough for a eucharistic celebration. Once the community has one priest to preside, other priests are unnecessary, and the fact that other members of the celebrating community are priests is not worth indicating: one could almost say then that the other priests are no longer priests or that at all events their capacity for being ministers is irrelevant. Hence my reluctance to stand as a priest alongside the president in concelebrations. That does not exclude the possibility that, for reasons not directly connected with the presbyteral ministry, it could be beneficial for a community to be able actually to see that a large number of priests have gathered together for a particular celebration (in a community, at a congress, on Maundy Thursday, and so on). But once the occasion becomes a habit, or even worse a system, both the eucharist and the ministers are falsified. It is wrong to say, 'Christ alone is priest, all are priests, some are priests'; what should be said is, 'Christ alone is priest, all are priests, some are ordained ministers.'

2. In fact, here I am being rather unfair about the benefits that academic theology still brings me and doubtless will always bring me (though its existence is, all in all, very recent). For example, exegetical study, the history of doctrine or the history of institutions, rites, behaviour, practices, and so on are enthralling when they are well done, and I always read them with profit. It would be a catastrophe for faith and the understanding of faith if such studies were to disappear, since they are indispensable for understanding faith, which is itself necessary – but not sufficient, far from it – for the present and future of the faith. My criticism of this kind of scientific theology is directed more at the monopoly that it claims to have over the whole of theology, often arrogantly ignoring the kind of understanding of the faith which emerges from the experience of faith among believers, men and women. Besides, this type of theology encourages a certain reluctance among theologians to involve their own faith and their own person in the practice of their theology: it is illegitimate for authors to claim to be theologians on the grounds that they are commenting on the theological writings of others, whether these are the writings of the authors of the New Testament, the documents of councils or popes, the works of Augustine, Thomas Aquinas, Bultmann or Rahner. This kind of commentary is a very important aid to theology, but it is only a prolegomenon and could not replace it, any more than the history of painting could replace painting. It is true that Roman Catholic theologians are sometimes very interested in restraining academic study, since while it is often difficult to think for oneself, it is always dangerous to do so. Finally, this kind of academic theology, which is necessarily directed more towards the past than towards the present or the future, encourages the already very marked tendency in Catholicism to confuse tradition with repetition of the past. From this point of view, while in some respects the biblical, patristic and liturgical 'renewals' have been extremely fruitful, in other respects they have

done us a bad turn in making us believe that it is enough to look to the past and to translate it or transpose it in order to construct the present and open up the future. For example, while the liturgical renewal owes some of its success to the eminent galaxy of palaeographers, archivists and historians who inspired it, it also owes some of its failure to these same people: when creating a liturgy it may be useful to have a perfect knowledge of the Leonine and Gelasian sacramentaries, but it is indispensable to know how to (and love to) make use of one's body and one's voice, know how to and love to make use of space and to pace out a service, to want the celebration and the word to give pleasure and happiness and above all to discover these things oneself. A perfect knowledge of the history of the sacraments in past centuries is one thing; to know how to help Christian men and women practise them in a way that one knows 'signifies' something, which is what one wants to do, is quite another. It is a shame that in Rome or in various organizations the former counts more than the latter. I shall come back to systematic theology, the planning and implementation of which pose another kind of problem.

3. If I speak here of the generation which preceded me, it is not in order to pass the blame on to others, but because this was the generation which, in the period between 1950 and 1968, when the decomposition began and then accelerated, supplied most of the superiors and those responsible for training, successfully inspired all the enterprises which ensured the vitality of the Order in France and could have given young people a taste to join it, or to stay with it once they had joined it.

4. I note in passing that this is the explanation of the success which these outdated symbolic forms continue to have in integralist circles, as do all the ancient forms of liturgy, theology, morality and so on. If it were a matter of rejecting as satanic all the transformations which these outdated forms have undergone and returning to the earlier state of things to which they were perfectly adapted, then in fact the *integral* preservation of and scrupulous respect for these forms would become the indispensable condition for survival. We know that all changes are frightening, and that the changes that we are experiencing are so profound as to seem particularly terrifying. We also know that regression to an earlier stage is a defence mechanism currently used by societies and individuals faced with the need for a mutation. So we must claim for individuals and groups the right to regression since, quite apart from the fact that this mechanism is sometimes useful or indispensable, people do not always have the personal or collective means of defending themselves in a more constructive way. So I would favour, for example, leaving Monsignor Lefebvre and his followers in peace, provided, of course, that they themselves allowed similar freedom to other groups of Christians whose conceptions differed from theirs, and that they did not seek to impose this form of regression – which is quite understandable and in no way dishonourable – as the apex of Christian maturity. Need I add that, in my view, the success of certain contemplative Orders stems from quite different reasons?

5. Even if it is far from being satisfactory in every respect, the best current theological view of the continuity and discontinuity between the different phases of revelation and the contingent historical forms of God with us is that of Ernst Käsemann. There is a searching study of his work, and particularly of the questions of the canon in the canon and the relationship between each historical form of Christianity and Jesus Christ in the knowledgable presentation of the

work of Käsemann by P.Gisel, *Vérité et Histoire, la théologie dans la modernité, Ernst Käsemann*, Paris 1977.

6. I think that this way of describing the resurrection as tipping Christ over into the transcendence of God will be criticized. I no longer find it very adequate. But when I remember that each time we recite the creed we say, 'He ascended into heaven, he is seated at the right hand of God', I ask myself what is so much more subtle about the expressions 'ascend into heaven' and 'be seated at the right hand of God' in comparison with the terms 'tip over' and 'divine transcendence'.

7. If, as historians now tend to think, Jesus of Nazareth was born in about 7 or 6 BC and died in AD 30, he would have been thirty-six or thirty-seven years old when he died, a relatively advanced age for his time, and one which was at any rate not reached by half the young people who passed the age of fifteen.

8. It is obvious that this phenomenon of aging happens in such a spectacular way above all in Western countries, and that a number of the previous considerations do not apply to the countries of the Third World, in the poorest of which life-expectation is very low. Be this as it may, the progress of medicine, hygiene and nutrition mean that the increase in longevity will soon have an effect throughout the planet. As I write these lines, in Vienna, under the aegis of the United Nations, a World Assembly on aging is being opened: the forecast is that in 2025, in less than half a century, when the population of the world will have tripled, the number of human beings aged more than sixty will have been multiplied fivefold. This phenomenon will be particularly noticeable in the developing countries, where the number of old people will be multiplied sevenfold, and fifteenfold in Mexico, Brazil and Nigeria.

9. It would perhaps be better to say specifically: *those women* whom they love rather than *those men* whom they love. The longevity of women is in fact greater than that of men in the majority of Western countries. In France this difference, which is not as great, is almost ten years. From sixty-five, the percentage of women increases as one considers the higher age groups: at eighty-five years of age, it reaches seventy-five per cent and goes on increasing. Extreme old age is an almost exclusively female problem.

10. In various Western countries, especially the United States and Great Britain, but also in France (particularly among the 'New Right'), there is a marked return to creationism. More than a century after Darwin, more than half a century after the beginnings of the amazing discoveries of molecular biology, people are trying to revive a conception of the creation of man which has nothing to do with the evolution of living matter. As a compensation for the misdeeds of evolutionary thought, significant sectors of public opinion in the United States have attempted to secure the teaching in schools of a kind of creationism which is akin to the strictest biblical fundamentalism. The complex of forces involved in these movements is very intricate. I think that the resistances provoked by the transformation of relationships between life and death that I have mentioned here play the same role for many people.

11. Several recent studies have shown the political and ecclesiastical background (or rather the ecclesiastical politics) behind the intellectual movement which from the middle of the nineteenth century promoted neo-Scholasticism and neo-Thomism. This movement is related to the one which sought to promote the strengthening of papal power up to the dogmatic proclamation of infallibility in 1870. The idea that there is a unique, definitive and perfect philosophy is the intellectual version of the idea that there is an absolute and infallible power: in

both cases it is a matter of setting oneself up above the contingency of historical forms. It must have crossed the minds of some of the supporters of the perennial philosophy that this was originally 'revealed'. Besides, the Thomists called St Thomas Aquinas *divus Thomas*, the divine Thomas. In fact, being divine remains, until the new order, the surest way of being eternal.

12. Hence the unpopularity of the scandalous parable of the workers signed on at the eleventh hour, who see themselves getting the same wages as those signed on at the first. Hence perhaps also the indication that Jesus Christ was concerned with something other than guaranteeing such a mastery. But if you try to make human beings believe this (*credere*) it will cost you dear. An attempt to achieve a similar mastery is involved when there is a prohibition against 'artificial' intervention in the processes of fertilization or death. Once it was accepted that human beings can intervene, with all the unknown factors proper to the exercise of their freedom as contingent beings, in the biological processes operative in fertility or death, it would be necessary to give up the claim that birth and death are events directly and personally dependent on God himself; it would thus be necessary to renounce the omnipotence and the control that this transference over God allows the human being to imagine to be his own. When I saw that this was one of the motive forces behind the resistance on the part of official Catholic doctrine to those methods of contraception that it describes as artificial, I understood that it would not be enough for that to change, as like others (including bishops!) I had long believed, and it would not be enough to wait for a new pope less agonized by questions of sexuality or less concerned to assert his authority by controlling the sexual life of believers (as powers of all kinds have always sought to do). More would be necessary than that, and the official authorities of the church would not be the only forces to oppose it.

13. To be more accurate, the church fathers had very different ways of denying the existence of sexuality before original sin. Some are very subtle but not very clear about it. For example, St Augustine did not deny that there was sexuality in Paradise. But this sexuality would have been a faculty exclusively devoted to reproduction, entirely subject to the will, which would use it only for the needs of reproduction. Above all it would have been free of any *libido*, which is actually a malady resulting from sin. Equally, original sin is not transmitted by the multiplication of the species by reproduction but through sexual pleasure, a proof of their intrinsic realationship. This reduction of 'paradisal' sexuality to the simple function of reproduction and identification of the *libido* with sin amounts to a denial of the existence of human sexuality before the Fall. As for St Gregory of Nyssa, himself also a saint and doctor of the church, he was even more radical. God gave man (the male) sexual organs and only created the woman with a view to what would happen to human beings after the fall of Adam. Otherwise, 'an immortal nature has no need of a feminine sex' (*Quaest. in Genesim*, c.3,q.37, PG 80,135). J.E.Kerns, *The Theology of Marriage. The Historical Development of Christian Attitudes toward Sex and Sanctity in Marriage*, New York 1964, is a practical anthology of this kind of text and others which take quite a different line.

14. It is well worth reading Pierre de Locht, *Les Couples et l'Église, Chronique d'un témoin*, Paris 1979. Having been involved in the work of these commissions almost from the beginning, the author has first-hand documentation: the second half of his book describes and analyses in detail works devoted to contraception at the periphery of the Council. Obviously his discretion has led him to omit

some proper names, but it is to be hoped that he will provide historians with more specific detail.

15. The text of these two reports, which were meant to be confidential, filtered through rapidly. In France, it was released through Jean-Marie Paupert, *Contrôle des naissances et Théologie, Le dossier de Rome*, Paris 1967. The personal career of Jean-Marie Paupert in relation to the church indicates that he may now regret having published these texts. This regret does not change the authenticity and the interest of the texts in question in any way.

16. For the enormous imbalance between the wishes expressed by the priests in numerous countries and relayed by their bishops, and the final result of the synod, for the capitulation of bishops in face of pressure from the Holy See and the disappointment of numerous local churches, see René Laurentin, *Réorientation de l'Église après le troisième synode*, Paris 1972.